# FIRST LANGUAGE LESSONS
FOR THE WELL-TRAINED MIND

LEVEL 4

This book is to be used in conjunction with the
First Language Lessons
for the Well-Trained Mind, Level 4
Student Workbook
ISBN 978-1-933339-33-7.
Available at www.peacehillpress.com
or wherever books are sold.

© 2008 Peace Hill Press

www.peacehillpress.com

Publisher's Cataloging-In-Publication Data
(Prepared by The Donohue Group, Inc.)

Wise, Jessie.
   First language lessons for the well-trained mind. Level 4 / by Jessie Wise and Sara Buffington.

      p. : ill. ; cm.

   Includes index.
   ISBN: 978-1-933339-34-4
1. English language--Grammar--Study and teaching (Primary)   2. English language--Composition and exercises--Study and teaching (Primary)   3. Language arts (Primary)   I. Buffington, Sara.   II. Title.

LB1528 .W573 2007
372.61   2007924667

FIRST LANGUAGE LESSONS
FOR THE WELL-TRAINED MIND

LEVEL 4

by Jessie Wise and Sara Buffington

Peace Hill Press
www.peacehillpress.com

TABLE OF CONTENTS

Contents

Contents

OPTIONAL END UNITS

WRITING LETTERS LESSONS

DICTIONARY SKILLS

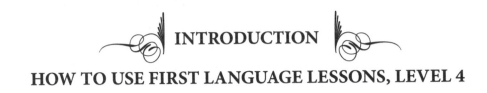

INTRODUCTION

HOW TO USE FIRST LANGUAGE LESSONS, LEVEL 4

The Four-Strand Approach

This series uses four different strands to teach grammar and punctuation rules, proper usage, and writing skills.

Strand 1: Memory Work

Memorizing Poetry

Memorizing poetry stores beautiful language in the student's mind. Poetry is the easiest kind of material to memorize because of its rhythm and rhyme. When a student memorizes a poem, it gives him confidence that he can memorize anything—material from history, science, and other subjects. Memorizing is an active exercise; it trains the student's attention span. There is a good memorization technique in the first poetry lesson of this book.

Memorizing Rules and Definitions

The technique for memorizing rules and definitions is practiced in the scripted lessons. A summary of the rules, definitions, and lists to be memorized is on page 545.

A note for students who have not used previous levels of First Language Lessons: Most of the definitions and memorized lists of parts of speech were introduced in earlier levels of this series. All of that material is reviewed in this book. However, you may wish to do extra review of these rules and lists. You may find it helpful to purchase the audio companion to *Levels 1 and 2* (a CD containing both chanted and sung versions of definitions and lists to be memorized) from Peace Hill Press at www.peacehillpress.com.

Strand 2: Copywork and Dictation

Copywork engages both the visual and motor memory of the student. It gives the student models of properly constructed sentences.

Dictation teaches the student to picture a sentence in his mind before putting it down on paper and also trains him to hold complete sentences in his memory as he writes. Dictation prepares the student for original writing, since it allows the young writer to practice mechanics without also struggling to produce original content.

This book uses dictation within the lessons, but most lessons also end with an optional dictation exercise if the student needs extra practice. If you are already using a writing program which includes dictation, you should probably not use the optional dictation unless the student needs drill in a particular skill.

Follow this procedure when giving dictation:

1. After you read a sentence, ask the student to visualize the beginning capital letter and the end punctuation mark.

2. Repeat the sentence once more.

3. Have the student repeat what you just said.

4. Have him write what he has just said, if it is accurate. If it is not accurate, repeat steps 2 and 3.

When giving dictation, provide the student with all necessary spelling help. If the student begins to write a word or punctuation mark incorrectly, gently stop him and give him the correct spelling or format. You should never allow a student to write dictation incorrectly.

Strand 3: Summary Exercises (Narration)

A student summarizes when he tells you in his own words about a passage that he has read. Summary exercises help the student to listen with attention, to grasp the main point of a work, to think through a sequence of events, and to reproduce the events in his own words in proper, logical order.

Strand 4: Grammar

A student studies grammar to learn how language works. This book teaches traditional grammar. Traditional grammar is not only acceptable; it is expected in the educated world.

This book practices sentence diagramming. A diagram is essentially a picture of a sentence; it shows visually how all of the sentence parts operate. As the student becomes more proficient in diagramming, he can use it as a tool to correct poorly constructed sentences in his own writing.

Oral usage exercises are included at the end of some lessons. These are optional. You don't have to confine these exercises to the student using the book. Practice them as a family at any time of the day you wish! For more exercises in oral usage, a good resource is *Oral Language Exercises* by William A. Kappele (A Beka Book Publications, 1982).

Using the Lessons

The lessons are scripted for your convenience, but neither you nor the student has to stick to the exact wording provided.

Instructor: Suggested wording for the instructor is in traditional print.

Student: *Suggested answers for the student are in italics.*

Workbook: Selected text from the Student Workbook is in a sans-serif typeface.

Answer Key: Answers to workbook exercises are also in a sans-serif typeface.

Notes to the instructor are in smaller, traditional print, between two lines.

Length of Lessons

This book is designed to be completed in one school year. If you do the lessons in the main part of the book but skip the end units, do two or three lessons each week for the school year (36 weeks). If you decide to include the end units as well, plan on three lessons per week. See the sample schedules on page 552.

The lessons that follow are of varying length; some contain more drill than others, depending on the difficulty of the topic. If a student does not need all of the repetition in any given lesson, you should feel free to skip it and move on.

Many of the lessons should be divided into two or even three days' worth of work. A student doing fourth-grade-level work will probably need to spend about thirty minutes on a lesson. If the lesson time exceeds thirty minutes, stop and pick up with the remainder of the lesson the following day.

The Use of Inclusive Pronouns

A note from Jessie Wise: I studied advanced traditional grammar in the 1950s as part of my training in teaching certification. I learned that the pronouns "he" and "him" were generic pronouns, used to refer to both men and women. Although I understand why some users would prefer to see an alternate use of "he" and "she," I find this style of writing awkward; my early training shapes my usage! So I have used "he" and "him" to refer to the student throughout. If you prefer, simply change these pronouns to "she" and "her."

The Student's Workbook

All of the lesson numbers in the teacher's book match the lesson numbers in the student's workbook (ISBN 978-1-933339-33-7, Peace Hill Press, 2008). The student needs a pencil for each workbook lesson. The student should keep a bookmark in his workbook to easily find his place at the start of the lesson.

The workbook pages are perforated and three-hole punched so you can file them in a binder if you wish. If the student writes letters for the optional end-unit lessons, you may wish to photocopy them before you mail them so you can file the letters as well.

Optional Follow-Ups

At the end of many lessons, there is an optional follow-up activity to reinforce the content of the lesson. You may choose to complete these or to skip them, depending on the student's level of mastery.

Optional End Units

The main part of this book consists of eighty-five lessons in grammar and writing. If you wish, you may choose to complete any or all of the three optional sections at the end of the book: contractions, writing letters, and dictionary skills. Suggested schedules for completing this book are on page 543. If you do the lessons on dictionary skills, it will be helpful for the student to have his own dictionary and thesaurus. We recommend *Merriam-Webster's Elementary Dictionary* (Merriam-Webster, 2000) and *Roget's Children's Thesaurus* (Scott Foresman, 2000).

LESSON 1

New: The Parts of This Book

In this book all of the lesson numbers in the teacher's book match the lesson numbers in the student's workbook. You will use Lesson 1 (page 1) in the Student Workbook.

Instructor: In this lesson, I am going to use my book to show you the parts of a book. The title of the book is printed on the front cover. It is the full name of the book. Read the whole title to me.

Student [reading the cover]: First Language Lessons for the Well-Trained Mind, Level 4.

Instructor: In **Exercise 1** of your workbook, copy the title.

Instructor: Look again at the cover of my book. Under the title, you will find the names of the authors, the people who wrote this book. Read the authors' names to me.

Student [reading the cover]: Jessie Wise and Sara Buffington.

Instructor: In **Exercise 2** of your workbook, copy the authors' names.

Instructor: The contents of every book printed in the United States are protected by federal copyright law. ("Federal" means that the law was passed by the U.S. government, not by an individual state.) Typically, the author of a book or the company that publishes the book holds the copyright to that book. A copyright is the legal right to publish and sell the contents of a book. No one else can copy this book and sell it for profit for themselves. There is a special symbol for the word copyright. It is the letter **c** with a circle around it. Following the symbol, you will see the year the book was first published and the company that published the book.

Turn to the back of the first page in the instructor's book; this shows the copyright information. Let the student search to see if he can find the copyright symbol, the year the book was published, and the copyright holder (Peace Hill Press). He will copy "© 2008 Peace Hill Press" in **Exercise 3** of his workbook.

Instructor: Copy the copyright information onto the lines of **Exercise 3** in your workbook. To make the copyright symbol, draw a small **c** and then put a circle around it.

Answer Key: © 2008 Peace Hill Press

Instructor: What kind of information do you think is in this book? To find out, we need to look at the table of contents. The table of contents tells you what will be in each lesson. The titles of the lessons are written in the order they appear in the book. Turn to the table of contents on page v. Find Lesson 6. What is Lesson 6 about?

Student: *Personal pronouns*

Instructor: Now look at the number across from Lesson 6. This is the page number on which you will find that lesson. On which page is Lesson 6 located?

Student: *Page 28*

Instructor: Now turn to page 28. Does Lesson 6 start on that page?

Student: *Yes*

Instructor: The table of contents is always printed near the beginning of a book. You can also find out more information about what is in a book by looking at the index. The index is always printed near the end of a book. The information in the index is not listed in the order in which it appears. Instead, it is listed in **ABC** (alphabetical) order.

Show the student the index and point out that the entries are organized alphabetically by letter. Find the index entries for *adverbs, prepositions,* and *quotations.* Tell him that the numbers next to each entry show the page or pages on which these topics are found. The student should look up at least one page for each topic.

Optional Dictation Exercise

If your student is not doing dictation in another subject, dictate the sentences to him, one at a time. If he is struggling, you may also decide to have the student write only one sentence. Instructions for giving dictation are on page 2 of the introduction under "Strand 2: Copywork and Dictation."

Dictation: Most books have the title and the author printed on the cover. A book may have more than one author.

Optional Follow-Up

Ask the student to pick five of his favorite books that you have on hand. Ask him to find the year that each book was published. Which of the five books was published first?

LESSON 2

New: Nouns

Instructor: A noun is the name of a person, place, thing, or idea. A boy is a person. The word *boy* is a noun. A cousin is a person. The word *cousin* is a noun. A mechanic is also a person. The word *mechanic* is a noun. Repeat after me: A noun is the name of a person.

Student: *A noun is the name of a person.*

Instructor: A noun is also the name of a place. A restaurant is a place. The word *restaurant* is a noun. A town is a place. The word *town* is a noun. A state is a place. The word *state* is a noun. Repeat after me: A noun is the name of a place.

Student: *A noun is the name of a place.*

Instructor: A noun is also the name of a thing. A plate is a thing. The word *plate* is a noun. A chimpanzee is a living thing. The word *chimpanzee* is a noun. A car is a thing. The word *car* is a noun. Repeat after me: A noun is the name of a thing.

Student: *A noun is the name of a thing.*

Instructor: A noun is also the name of an idea. An idea is something that you cannot see or touch. An idea can be an event—like a party, an adventure, or a game. An idea can be a feeling—like joy, fright, hunger, or relief. Ideas can also be periods of time—like a second, a minute, an hour, or a day. There are other ideas that you can think about but cannot see: beauty, health, thoughts, and mischief. You can name ideas, but you can't see them. Let's add *idea* to the definition of a noun. A noun is the name of a person, place, thing, or idea. Let's say that together.

TOGETHER: A noun is the name of a person, place, thing, or idea.

Instructor: Answer these questions with a noun that is a person. What do you call a person who paints pictures for a living?

Student: *An artist [or a painter]*

Instructor: *Artist* [or *painter*] is a noun. What do you call a person who writes books or stories?

Student: *An author [or a writer]*

Instructor: *Author* [or *writer*] is a noun. Answer these questions with a noun that is a place. What do you call a place where you can jump in and swim?

Student: *A pool [or a lake or the ocean]*

Instructor: *Pool* [or *lake* or *ocean*] is a noun. What do you call the thing in a kitchen that bakes cookies?

Student: *The oven [or stove]*

Instructor: *Oven* [or *stove*] is a noun.

Instructor: The names of ideas are also nouns. Although you can name ideas, you cannot see or touch them. *Thirst* is an idea. You can think about it in your mind. In **Exercise 1** of your workbook, read aloud to me three ideas.

Workbook: year

accident

surprise

Instructor: In your workbook read aloud each sentence in **Exercise 2**. When you get to the blank, write in the correct noun from **Exercise 1** that names an idea and makes sense in the sentence.

Answer Key: Having a day off with no school was a **surprise**.

I did not mean to drop my plate; it was an **accident**.

There are 365 days in a **year**.

Instructor: A noun is the name of a person, place, thing, or idea. Say that with me.

Together: A noun is the name of a person, place, thing, or idea.

Optional Dictation Exercise

Dictation: You can name ideas, but you cannot see or touch them. An idea can be an event or a feeling.

LESSON 3

New: **Forming Plural Nouns**
Review: Nouns

Because this lesson reviews previously learned concepts, it is longer than the previous lessons. Remember that you should adjust the length and repetition of each lesson to suit the student. If there is too much repetition of a concept, skip it and move on as soon as you feel that the student has mastered the material.

Also remember that many lessons may take more than a single day to complete. After the student has worked for half an hour, you can halt the lesson and continue on with it on the next day.

Instructor: Let's review the definition of a noun. A noun is the name of a person, place, thing, or idea. Say that with me.

TOGETHER: A noun is the name of a person, place, thing, or idea.

Instructor: In your workbook, read the list of nouns in **Exercise 1**.

Instructor: Read through the list again, and decide if the noun is a person, place, thing, or idea, and draw a line connecting the noun to PERSON, PLACE, THING, or IDEA.

Answer Key:

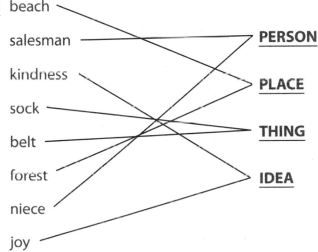

Instructor: Some nouns name one, single thing. These are called singular nouns. *Pencil* is a singular noun, because it names one, single pencil. Other nouns name more than one thing. These are called plural nouns. *Pencils* is a plural noun. You could have two, twenty, or two million pencils!

Instructor: Usually, add **s** to a noun to form the plural. Say this with me three times.

TOGETHER (three times): Usually, add **s** to a noun to form the plural.

Instructor: In **Exercise 2** of your workbook, you will see a list of singular nouns. Read the rule. Then I want you to add an **s** to the end of each word to make it plural.

Answer Key: Rule: Usually, add **s** to a noun to form the plural.

Singular Noun	Plural Noun
river	rivers
pillow	pillows
frog	frogs
table	tables
bracelet	bracelets

Instructor: Look again at the singular words in the list in **Exercise 2**. Tell me the final letter in each word as I point to it.

Student: *r, w, g, e, t*

In the following dialogue, letters and letter pairs that are printed in bold should be spelled aloud.

Instructor: None of these nouns in **Exercise 2** end in **s**, **sh**, **ch**, **x**, or **z**. If a noun ends in **s**, **sh**, **ch**, **x**, or **z**, we form the plural differently. Instead of a plain **s**, we add **es**. Add **es** to nouns ending in **s**, **sh**, **ch**, **x**, or **z**. Say this with me three times.

TOGETHER (three times): Add **es** to nouns ending in **s**, **sh**, **ch**, **x**, or **z**.

Point to the letters in the column in **Exercise 3** as you say them.

Workbook: Rule: Add **es** to nouns ending in **s**, **sh**, **ch**, **x**, or **z.**

s

sh

ch

x

z

Instructor: In **Exercise 4** of your workbook, you will see a list of singular nouns. Read the rule. Then I want you to add **es** to the end of each word to make it plural.

Answer Key: Rule: Add **es** to nouns ending in **s**, **sh**, **ch**, **x**, or **z**.

Singular Noun	Plural Noun
guess	guesses
dish	dishes
patch	patches
tax	taxes
buzz	buzzes

Instructor: Now you will practice how to form plurals of nouns that end in **y**. If a noun ends in **y** after a consonant, change the **y** to **i** and add **es**. Let's say this together three times.

TOGETHER (three times): If a noun ends in **y** after a consonant, change the **y** to **i** and add **es**.

Instructor: In your workbook, look at the chart in **Exercise 5**. Read the rule. Then copy the singular noun into the blank. After you have copied each noun, change the word to make it plural. Erase the **y**, change it to **i**, and add **es**.

You may wish to talk the student through the formation of each plural noun. You may use the questions in italics to prompt the student.

What is the last letter?

Is the letter before the **y** *a consonant?*

What do you change the **y** *to?*

Then what do you add after the **i**?

Answer Key: Rule: If a noun ends in **y** after a consonant, change the **y** to **i** and add **es**.

Singular Noun	Change to a Plural Noun
country	countries
party	parties
city	cities
hobby	hobbies

Instructor: This rule only works for nouns that end in a consonant and then a **y**. If a noun ends in **y** after a vowel, just add **s**. Say that with me three times.

TOGETHER (three times): If a noun ends in **y** after a vowel, just add **s**.

Instructor: In your workbook, look at the chart in **Exercise 6**. Read the rule. Then add **s** to the end of each word to make it plural.

You may wish to talk the student through the formation of each plural noun. You may use the questions in italics to prompt the student.

What is the last letter?

Is the letter before the **y** *a vowel?*

Then what do you add after the **y**?

Answer Key: Rule: If a noun ends in **y** after a vowel, just add **s**.

Singular Noun	Plural Noun
day	days
cowboy	cowboys
valley	valleys
guy	guys

Instructor: Do you remember our first rule? Usually, add **s** to a noun to form the plural. Look in your workbook at **Exercise 7**. All these words end in **f** or **fe**. Add **s** to the end of each word to make it plural.

Answer Key: Rule: Usually, add **s** to a noun to form the plural.

Singular Noun	Plural Noun
chief	chiefs
roof	roofs
cliff	cliffs
giraffe	giraffes

Instructor: These words you just looked at form their plurals the usual way: by adding **s**. However, there are some words that end in **f** or **fe** that form their plurals differently. You must change the **f** or **fe** to **v** and add **es**.

Instructor: In your workbook, look at the chart in **Exercise 8**. Read the statement. Then copy the singular noun into the blank. After you have copied each noun, change the word to make it plural. Erase the **f** or **fe**, and change it to **v** and add **es**. The first one has been done for you.

Answer Key: Rule: Some words that end in **f** or **fe** form their plurals differently. You must change the **f** or **fe** to **v** and add **es**.

Singular Noun	Change to a Plural Noun
leaf	leaves
shelf	shelves
knife	knives
loaf	loaves

Instructor: Now you will practice how to form plurals of nouns that end in **o**. If a noun ends in **o** after a vowel, just add **s**.

Instructor: In your workbook, look at the chart in **Exercise 9**. Read the rule. Then add **s** to the end of each word to make it plural.

Answer Key: Rule: If a noun ends in **o** after a vowel, just add **s**.

Singular Noun	Plural Noun
patio	patios
radio	radios
video	videos
zoo	zoos
igloo	igloos

Instructor: If a noun ends in **o** after a consonant, you form the plural by adding **es**. In your workbook, look at the chart in **Exercise 10**. Read the statement. Add **es** to the end of each word to make it plural.

Answer Key: If a noun ends in **o** after a consonant, form the plural by adding **es**.

Singular Noun	Plural Noun
potato	potatoes
tomato	tomatoes
volcano	volcanoes
echo	echoes

Instructor: There are some Italian musical words that end in **o** after a consonant. These words don't follow the pattern you just saw in **Exercise 10**. To form the plural of these words, you just add **s**. Read this statement at the beginning of **Exercise 11**. Then add an **s** at the end of each singular noun to make it plural.

Answer Key: Rule: To form the plural of these Italian words, just add **s**.

Singular Noun	Plural Noun
piano	pianos
solo	solos
soprano	sopranos
alto	altos

Instructor: Now let's look at some common English words that don't follow any pattern at all when forming their plurals. We call these words "irregular plurals" because they don't form their plurals the regular ways. In **Exercise 12** of your workbook, read the statement. Then read aloud the list of singular nouns and their irregular plural forms.

Workbook: Rule: Irregular plurals don't form their plurals the regular ways.

Singular Noun	Irregular Plural Noun
child	children
foot	feet
tooth	teeth
man	men
woman	women
mouse	mice
goose	geese
deer	deer
fish	fish

Optional Dictation Exercise

After the student writes each sentence, have him circle the noun that appears in both singular and plural form. Have him write "S" over the singular form and "P" over the plural form.

Dictation:

                                 S   P

I dropped the sugar dish from the set of blue dishes.

                          S   P

I made one guess and he made three guesses.

LESSON 4

New: Common and Proper Nouns
Review: Forming Plural Nouns
Learn to Proofread: Make Lowercase and Capitalize

Instructor: In the last lesson you learned about singular and plural nouns. In **Exercise 1** of your workbook, read aloud each rule and then in the blank write the plural form that follows this rule.

Answer Key: Rule: Usually, add **s** to form the plural.

Singular Noun	Plural Noun
cat	cats

Rule: Add **es** to nouns ending in **s**, **sh**, **ch**, **x**, or **z**.

Singular Noun	Plural Noun
patch	patches

Rule: If a noun ends in **y** after a consonant, change the **y** to **i** and add **es**.

Singular Noun	Plural Noun
city	cities

Rule: If a noun ends in **y** after a vowel, just add **s**.

Singular Noun	Plural Noun
day	days

Rule: Usually, add **s** to a noun to form the plural of words that end in **f** or **fe**.

Singular Noun	Plural Noun
cliff	cliffs

Rule: Some words that end in **f** or **fe** form their plurals differently. You must change the **f** or **fe** to **v** and add **es**.

Singular Noun	Plural Noun
leaf	leaves

Rule: If a noun ends in **o** after a vowel, just add **s**.

Singular Noun	Plural Noun
radio	radios

Rule: If a noun ends in **o** after a consonant, form the plural by adding **es**.

Singular Noun	Plural Noun
potato	potatoes

Rule: Irregular plurals don't form their plurals the regular ways.

Singular Noun	Plural Noun
mouse	mice

As you go through the following dialogue, have the student fill in the blanks in **Exercise 2** of his workbook.

Instructor: You know that a noun is the name of a person, place, thing, or idea. The first part of that definition is "a noun is the name of a person." You are a person. Are you a student or a teacher? In **Exercise 2** write your answer to **Sentence 1**, and then read the sentence aloud to me.

Student: *I am a student.*

Instructor: *Student* and *teacher* are naming words that are common to many persons, so we call them common nouns. The words *boy, girl, aunt, uncle, cousin, friend, veterinarian,* and *composer* are also common nouns. What is your name?

Student: *My name is ____ .*

Instructor: You are not just any student. You are ____ [use student's proper name]. In **Sentence 2** of **Exercise 2**, write your name. This is your own special, "proper" name. Proper names are the same as proper nouns. Proper nouns all begin with capital letters. What are the names of your mother and father? If you have brothers or sisters, what are their names?

Student: *My mother's name is ____ . My father's name is ____ . My brother's name is ____ .*

In **Exercise 2**, choose two of the sentences below to use for dictation. As necessary, remind the student to use an apostrophe-**s** and to capitalize the proper name.

My mother's name is [first name of mother].
My father's name is [first name of father].
My sister's name is [first name of sister].
My brother's name is [first name of brother].
My friend's name is [first name of friend].

Instructor: A noun is also the name of a place. The words *state, street, mountain,* and *supermarket* are words that are common to many places. These are all common nouns. What is the name of the state [or province] in which you live?

Student: *I live in _____ .*

Instructor: This is not just any state [or province]. This is the proper name for the special place where you live. Write the name of your state [or province] in **Exercise 3** of your workbook. Remember, proper nouns begin with a capital letter.

Instructor: A noun is also the name of a thing. Some living things that are common nouns are *dog, cat, ferret,* and *iguana.* What is the name of your pet?

If the student does not have a pet, ask the student to name the pet of a friend or relative.

Student: *The name of my pet is _____ .*

Instructor: This pet is not just any dog [cat, fish, bird]. This is the special, "proper" name of the pet. *[Name of pet]* is a proper noun. Complete the sentence in **Exercise 4**.

Student: *The proper name of the pet is_____ .*

Instructor: A noun is also the name of an idea. *Day* is an idea. It is a period of time. There are certain days, holidays, which begin with a capital letter. Holidays are special days. Read the list of holidays in **Exercise 5** and circle your favorite one. Then copy it in the sentence below.

The origin of the word *holiday* is "holy day." A holy day was a church celebration day, on which no one went to work.

Workbook: Thanksgiving

Christmas

Hanukkah

Easter

Valentine's Day

My favorite holiday is _____ .

Instructor: Put down your workbook and stand up. I am going to read you a story with common and proper nouns in it. When I say a common noun, a word common to many persons, places, things, or ideas, I want you to squat down, but be ready to stand up quickly. If the noun is a proper noun, the special proper name of a person, place, thing, or idea, I want you to jump up and reach for the sky, pretending you are the tall capital letter that begins every proper noun.

Read the story very slowly. Pause when you get to **an underlined** noun and say it emphatically. Do not ask the student to identify any nouns that are not **underlined**. (Remember that the common nouns in the following passage are not capitalized, but the proper nouns are.)

One day a **boy** named **Paco Garza** was walking through **Saguaro National Park**. There were many kinds of **birds** and **lizards** and **animals** in the **park**, and **Paco** found himself longing for a **pet** of his own. As he walked along **South Cactus Forest Drive**, he spotted a **lizard** sitting very still on a **rock**. Suddenly the **lizard** started doing something very curious—he began to do push-ups! "I must have that **lizard** as a **pet**," thought **Paco**. "I will take him **home** and name him **Benito**. He can live in my **terrarium**." **Paco** lunged for the **lizard**, but the **lizard** skittered away down the **street**. Soon **Paco** was chasing **Benito** down **East Old Spanish Trail**. "He's heading toward the **city**. I must catch him before he reaches central **Tucson**!" thought **Paco**. They passed his science **teacher**. **Mr. Pablo Santos** was walking his **dog**, **Hugo**. **Mr. Santos** called after his **student**, "**Paco**, you are chasing a collared **lizard**! You'll never catch him!" At that, **Benito** stood up straight and started to run on his hind **legs**. Now he was even faster than before. At last, a tired and sweaty **Paco** admitted defeat. "He was too fast for me. I suppose an energetic **lizard** like **Benito** would never be happy cramped up in a **terrarium** anyway!"

Over the course of this book, the student will memorize capitalization rules. Here is the complete list, for your reference:

1. *Capitalize the proper names of persons, places, things, and animals.*

2. *Capitalize holidays.*

3. *Capitalize the names of deities.*

4. *Capitalize the days of the week and the months of the year, but not the seasons.*

5. *Capitalize the first, last, and other important words in titles of books, magazines, newspapers, stories, poems, and songs.*

6. *Capitalize the word* I.

7. *Capitalize the first word in every line of traditional poetry.*

8. *Capitalize the first word of every sentence.*

9. *Capitalize the first word in a direct quotation.*

Instructor: Now you will memorize two capitalization rules. Think of these rules when you are writing. Here is the first rule: Capitalize the proper names of persons, places, things, and animals. Say this for me three times.

Student (three times): Capitalize the proper names of persons, places, things, and animals.

Instructor: Here is the next rule: Capitalize holidays. Say that three times.
Student (three times): Capitalize holidays.

Instructor: Now let's say both rules together three times.

TOGETHER (three times):
1. Capitalize the proper names of persons, places, things, and animals.
2. Capitalize holidays.

Instructor: Now read these two capitalization rules in **Exercise 6** of your workbook.

Learn to Proofread: lc and caps

The purpose of teaching proofreaders' marks at this level is to help the student search for and correct mistakes in his writing. We have followed the general style of proofreaders' marks found in *The Chicago Manual of Style*, 15th edition (University of Chicago Press, 2003).

Instructor: When you **proofread** your writing, you read it over and fix the mistakes. Over the course of this book you will learn how to mark mistakes with special symbols or abbreviations called **proofreaders' marks**. Look in your workbook at **Exercise 7**. This is the first proofreaders' mark. The abbreviation "lc" stands for "lowercase." Remember, there are two kinds of letters: capital letters (also called uppercase) and small letters (also called lowercase). If you see a word that is capitalized when it shouldn't be, draw a slanting line through it. Then, write the proofreaders' mark lc in the margin beside the incorrect sentence. Look at the sample sentence in **Exercise 7**. Read that aloud.

Answer Key: You are chasing a Lizard. lc

Instructor: *Lizard* should not begin with a capital letter—it a common noun, a name common to many lizards. Let's learn another proofreaders' mark. Look at **Exercise 8**. "Caps" stands for "capital letters." If you see a word that should be capitalized but it is not, underline the lowercase letter or letters that should be capitalized with three small lines. Then write caps in the margin beside the incorrect sentence. Look at the sample sentence in **Exercise 8**.

Workbook: The boy was named <u>p</u>aco.   (caps)

Instructor: *Paco* should be capitalized because that is the boy's special, proper name. Now read the sentence in **Exercise 9**. Use your proofreaders' marks to show the errors in capitalization. Then copy the sentence **correctly** on the lines below.

Answer Key: I will take him /Home and name him <u>b</u>enito.   (lc) (caps)

I will take him home and name him Benito.

Optional Dictation Exercise

Dictation: Paco chased Benito down the street. He tried to catch him before he got to the city of Tucson.

Optional Follow-Up

   In the story, Paco saw the collared lizard doing push-ups on a rock. Have the student look up "lizards" in an encyclopedia or the internet and find out why lizards do push-ups. (Answer: Male lizards do push-ups and other kinds of displays to impress females or intimidate other males.)

LESSON 5

New: Proper Nouns

You will need a calendar for this lesson.

Instructor: In the last lesson you learned about common and proper nouns. A common noun is a name common to many persons, places, things, or ideas. *Scientist, city,* and *holiday* are all common nouns. A proper noun is a special, "proper" name for a person, place, thing, or idea. *Albert Einstein, Detroit,* and *Labor Day* are all proper nouns. Proper nouns always begin with a capital letter.

Instructor: The names of deities are proper nouns. "Deities" is another name for "gods and goddesses." Follow along while I read the list of deities in **Exercise 1** of your workbook.

Workbook: God

Jehovah

Allah

Zeus (the king of the gods in Greek mythology)

Osiris (pronounced oh-SIGH-rus; he is the Egyptian god of the underworld)

Thor (the Norse god of thunder, weather, and crops)

This capitalization rule is drawn from the 15th edition of *The Chicago Manual of Style* (University of Chicago Press, 2003). According to item 8.98, "Names of deities, whether in monotheistic or polytheistic religions, are capitalized."

Instructor: The days of the week are capitalized. Read aloud the days of week in the left-hand column of **Exercise 2**.

Workbook: Sunday

Monday

Tuesday

Wednesday

Thursday

Friday

Saturday

Instructor: The days of the week are named for pagan gods and goddesses. Follow along while I read aloud the right-hand column in **Exercise 2** of your workbook. Look at the spelling of the name of the god or goddess, and see if you can figure out which day of the week was named for him or her. Then draw a line from the name of the day to the origin of that day's name.

Answer Key:

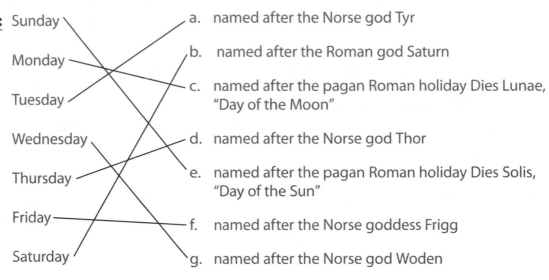

Sunday

Monday

Tuesday

Wednesday

Thursday

Friday

Saturday

a. named after the Norse god Tyr

b. named after the Roman god Saturn

c. named after the pagan Roman holiday Dies Lunae, "Day of the Moon"

d. named after the Norse god Thor

e. named after the pagan Roman holiday Dies Solis, "Day of the Sun"

f. named after the Norse goddess Frigg

g. named after the Norse god Woden

Instructor: The months of the year are also capitalized. Read aloud the months of the year in **Exercise 3**.

Workbook: January

February

March

April

May

June

July

August

September

October

November

December

Instructor: The months of the year are named for Latin words, Roman gods and goddess, and famous Roman men. Follow along while I read aloud the right-hand column in **Exercise 3** of your workbook. See if you can figure out the correct origin for the name of each month. Then draw a line from the name of the month to the origin of that month's name.

There is disagreement among scholars as to the origin of some of the names of the months. We have chosen accepted, simple origins suitable for this age group.

Answer Key:

January

February

March

April

May

June

July

August

September

October

November

December

a. from the Latin word *novem,* meaning "nine." This was the ninth month of the early Roman calendar.

b. named for Julius Caesar (assassinated in 44 BC). This is the month in which he was born.

c. from the Latin word *aperire,* meaning "to open." This is the month in which buds begin to open.

d. named after the Roman god of beginnings and endings, Janus. Janus has two faces, one in front and the other at the back of his head.

e. named for the first of the Roman emperors, Augustus.

f. from the Latin word *octo,* meaning "eight." This was the eighth month of the early Roman calendar.

g. named for Juno, queen of the gods and protector of women.

h. from the Latin word *decem,* meaning "ten." This was the tenth month of the early Roman calendar.

i. from the Latin word *septem,* meaning "seven." This was the seventh month in the early Roman calendar.

j. named for Maiesta, the Roman goddess of honor and reverence.

k. named for the Roman god of war, Mars.

l. named after Februalia, a time period when the Romans made sacrifices for sins.

Show the student a calendar and help him find today's date. The following instructions teach the student to write a date like this: January 5, 2009. If you live in a place where a date is written differently, modify the instructions to teach your student to correctly write a date in your country.

Instructor: Now write today's date in **Exercise 4** of your workbook. First you write the name of the month. Remember to capitalize it. Then you write the number of the day. Put a comma after the day. Then write the year.

Instructor: The names of the seasons, *spring, summer, fall,* and *winter,* are not capitalized. In **Exercise 5** of your workbook, underline the name of the season after you have read the poem aloud. Two of the poems have two seasons.

Tell the student that a *lea* (pronounced "lee") is a grassland pasture. In this poem, a child is pretending that he and his friends are pirates aboard their ship, even though they are really in a meadow.

Answer Key: From "A Pirate's Story" by Robert Louis Stevenson
Three of us afloat in the meadow by the swing,
Three of us abroad in the basket on the lea.
Winds are in the air, they are blowing in the <u>spring</u>,
And waves are on the meadow like the waves there are at sea.

From "Autumn Fires" by Robert Louis Stevenson
Sing a song of seasons!
Something bright in all!
Flowers in the <u>summer</u>,
Fires in the <u>fall</u>!

From "Bed in Summer" by Robert Louis Stevenson
In <u>winter</u> I get up at night
And dress by yellow candlelight.
In <u>summer</u> quite the other way,
I have to go to bed by day.

Instructor: The first, last, and other important words in the titles of books, magazines, and newspapers are capitalized. Read aloud the titles in **Exercise 6** and circle the capital letters in each title.

Answer Key: **Books**
(T)he (T)ale of (P)eter (R)abbit
(T)he (T)rumpet of the (S)wan

Magazines
(J)ack and (J)ill
(N)ational (G)eographic (K)ids (M)agazine

Newspapers
(N)ew (Y)ork (T)imes
(C)hicago (T)ribune

Instructor: When you see the titles of books, magazines, and newspapers in print, these titles are printed in italic letters (they are italicized). Notice the titles in **Exercise 6**. Each title is italicized. But when you handwrite the titles of books, magazines, and newspapers, you underline the titles. Using your best handwriting, copy one title of a book, a magazine, and a newspaper from **Exercise 6**. Make sure you underline the entire title.

Instructor: Did you notice that not every word in a title is capitalized? You only capitalize the first, last, and other important words. Small, unimportant words like *and*, *the*, and *of* are not capitalized unless the word comes first in the title.

This is a list of unimportant words:

✓ Articles (*a, an, the*)

✓ Conjunctions (*and, but, or*)

✓ Prepositions that are four letters or less (such as *at, by, for, from, in, into, like, near, of, off, on, over, past, to, up, upon, with*). There are varying opinions about this. *The Chicago Manual of Style* goes so far as to say all prepositions, regardless of length, should not be capitalized unless the word is stressed in the title (e.g., *A River Runs Through It*).

Instructor: Titles of stories, poems, and songs are also capitalized. These titles are put in quotation marks, rather than being italicized or underlined. Read aloud the titles in **Exercise 7** and circle the capital letters in each title.

Answer Key: **Stories**
"(T)he (R)ansom of (R)ed (C)hief" (by O. Henry)
"(T)he (G)olden (T)ouch" (by Nathaniel Hawthorne)

Poems
"(I)f" (by Rudyard Kipling)
"(B)ed in (S)ummer" (by Robert Louis Stevenson)

Songs

"Three Blind Mice"
"This Land Is Your Land"

Instructor: Just like the titles of books, magazines, and newspapers, you only capitalize the first, last, and other important words. Small, unimportant words like *of* and *an* are not capitalized unless the word comes first in the title. Using your best handwriting, copy one title of a story, a poem, and a song from **Exercise 7**. Make sure you put quotation marks around the title.

Instructor: Now you will memorize three more capitalization rules. You learned two rules last lesson. Capitalize the proper names of persons, places, things, and animals. Capitalize holidays. Here is the third rule: Capitalize the names of deities. Say this from memory for me three times.

Student (three times): Capitalize the names of deities.

Instructor: Here is the next rule: Capitalize the days of the week, the months of the year, but not the seasons. Say that three times.

Student (three times): Capitalize the days of the week, the months of the year, but not the seasons.

Instructor: You practiced one more rule this lesson: Capitalize the first, last, and other important words in titles of books, magazines, newspapers, stories, poems, and songs. Now say the first half of that with me five times: "Capitalize the first, last, and other important words in titles…"

TOGETHER (five times): Capitalize the first, last, and other important words in titles…

Instructor: Now let's say the second half of the rule five times: "…of books, magazines, newspapers, stories, poems, and songs."

TOGETHER (five times): …of books, magazines, newspapers, stories, poems, and songs.

Instructor: Let's say the whole rule together three times.

TOGETHER (three times): Capitalize the first, last, and other important words in titles of books, magazines, newspapers, stories, poems, and songs.

Instructor: Now can you say that alone?

Student: *Capitalize the first, last, and other important words in titles of books, magazines, newspapers, stories, poems, and songs.*

Instructor: In **Exercise 8**, you will see the capitalization rules you have learned so far in this book. Read aloud these rules to me.

Workbook: <u>Capitalization Rules</u>

1. Capitalize the proper names of persons, places, things, and animals.

2. Capitalize holidays.

3. Capitalize the names of deities.

4. Capitalize the days of the week and the months of the year, but not the seasons.

5. Capitalize the first, last, and other important words in titles of books, magazines, newspapers, stories, poems, and songs.

Optional Dictation Exercise

Dictate the titles the student copied in Exercises 6 and 7 of this lesson. Check for proper underlining, quotation marks, and capital letters.

Optional Follow-Up

Check out *A Child's Garden of Verses* by Robert Louis Stevenson from the library and read more poetry by him. Tell the student to notice capital letters in the titles of the poems.

LESSON 6

New: Personal Pronouns

If the student completed *First Language Lessons, Level 3*, he has already memorized the list of personal pronouns, and this part of the lesson will be a review. Ask the student to name the pronouns. If he can say the list without prompting (*I, me, my, mine; you, your, yours; he, she, him, her, it; his, hers, its; we, us, our, ours; they, them, their, theirs*), skip the pronoun list chanting in the beginning of the lesson.

Students who have not used previous levels of *First Language Lessons* may need to chant the list of personal pronouns three times each morning until the chant is memorized.

Instructor: Today we are going to talk about pronouns. Do you know the definition of a pronoun? Say it for me.

Student: *A pronoun is a word used in the place of a noun.*

If the student does not know the definition of a pronoun, say it with him three times, and then have him say it alone.

Instructor: We are going to practice memorizing personal pronouns. Personal pronouns take the place of nouns that are persons. *I, me, my, mine; you, your, yours.* Say this for me three times.

Student (three times): *I, me, my, mine; you, your, yours.*

Instructor: *He, she, him, her, it; his, hers, its.* Say this for me three times.

Student (three times): *He, she, him, her, it; his, hers, its.*

Instructor: Let's say these pronouns together three times from the beginning.

TOGETHER (three times): I, me, my, mine; you, your, yours; he, she, him, her, it; his, hers, its.

Instructor: Now we are going to practice more pronouns: *We, us, our, ours; they, them, their, theirs.* Say this for me three times.

Student (three times): *We, us, our, ours; they, them, their, theirs.*

Instructor: Let's say the whole list together three times from the beginning.

TOGETHER (three times):   I, me, my, mine
You, your, yours
He, she, him, her, it
His, hers, its
We, us, our, ours
They, them, their, theirs

Instructor: Now read these same pronouns in **Exercise 1** of your workbook.

Workbook: Personal Pronouns

I, me, my, mine

You, your, yours

He, she, him, her, it

His, hers, its

We, us, our, ours

They, them, their, theirs

Instructor: A pronoun is a word that takes the place of a noun. "[Student's name] went down the steps." Say that sentence back to me, except use the pronoun *I* instead of your name.

Student: *I went down the steps.*

Instructor: "Please give [student's name] a raincoat." Repeat that sentence, except use the pronoun *me* instead of your name.

Student: *Please give **me** a raincoat.*

Instructor: "[Student's name]'s umbrella is in the hall." Repeat that sentence, except use the pronoun *my* instead of your name.

Student: ***My** umbrella is in the hall.*

Instructor: "The yellow rain boots are [student's name]'s." Repeat that sentence, except use the pronoun *mine* instead of your name.

Student: *The yellow rain boots are **mine**.*

Instructor: "Will [instructor's name] give the dog a bath?" Repeat that sentence, except use the pronoun *you* instead of my name.

Student: *Will **you** give the dog a bath?*

Instructor: "Don't use [instructor's name]**'s** shampoo." Repeat that sentence, except use the pronoun *your* instead of my name.

Student: *Don't use **your** shampoo.*

Instructor: "The striped towel is [instructor's name]**'s.**" Repeat that sentence, except use the pronoun *yours* instead of my name.

Student: *The striped towel is **yours.***

Instructor: In your workbook, read each sentence in **Exercise 2**. In the blank at the end of each sentence, write the pronoun that can be used instead of the underlined noun or nouns. You may look at the list of pronouns in **Exercise 1** to help you.

If the student needs a hint, point to the line in the list in **Exercise 1** that contains the correct pronoun. Also help him with the pronunciation of the proper names. Most of these sentences are from history, but a few are just for fun!

Answer Key: William Frederick Cody, a famous frontiersman, shot more than four thousand buffalo in a year. William Frederick Cody became known as Buffalo Bill. [He]

In order for a family to have enough food for the wagon journey across the United States, the family had to take a thousand pounds of food in the wagon with the family. [them]

During David Livingstone's explorations in Africa, a lion attacked David Livingstone. He survived the attack! [him]

European explorers wanted all of Africa's wealth—its ivory, gold, silver, limestone, and fertile fields—to be the European explorers'. [theirs]

The Soviet Union launched the Soviet Union's first satellite, *Sputnik*, in October of 1957. [its]

You and I were born on the same day. [We]

President Franklin Delano Roosevelt created the Works Progress Administration to provide out-of-work Americans with jobs. The Works Progress Administration hired men to build roads and bridges. [It]

Many Argentinians were devoted to Eva Perón because she did so much to help the poor. The admiration of the people was Eva Perón's. [hers]

We know it sounds disgusting, but my sister's and my favorite lunch is peanut butter and pickle sandwiches. [our]

Leif Ericsson and Leif Ericsson's men explored North America. [his]

Some rich miners in Australia sprinkled gold dust on the miners' Christmas dinners! [their]

In 1957, the governor of Arkansas told Arkansas soldiers not to let Elizabeth Eckford into school because she was black. So the president sent federal troops to escort Elizabeth Eckford safely inside the school. [her]

The three-headed purple alien chased you and me through the amusement park until he found the funnel cake stand. [us]

Yes, the entire collection of ten thousand paper-chained gum wrappers is my friend's and mine. [ours]

Though many Allied troops died in the fight, the Allied troops captured the beaches at Normandy, France, on June 6, 1944. [they]

Instructor: Let's learn a capitalization rule about a pronoun. Read the rule in **Exercise 3** of your workbook.

Workbook: Rule: Capitalize the word *I*.

Instructor: Say that for me three times.
Student (three times): Capitalize the word I.

Optional Dictation Exercise
   After the student takes the dictation, have him circle all the personal pronouns.

Dictation/Answer Key: We reviewed her robot and his computer program and awarded them first place for their project.
May I ask you to give me my prize ribbons?

LESSON 7

New: Demonstrative Pronouns (this, that, these, those)
Review: Personal Pronouns

Instructor: In this lesson you are going to learn about four special pronouns: *this*, *that*, *these*, and *those*. *This*, *that*, *these*, and *those* are pronouns when they take the place of a noun. Imagine that you are looking at a big pile of crayons on the table. Some belong to you and some do not. You are pointing to some of the crayons. Read aloud the sentences in **Exercise 1** of your workbook and point to the imaginary crayons as you read.

Workbook: Look at the crayons.

This is mine.

That is not mine.

These are green.

Those are blue.

Instructor: In these sentences, *this*, *that*, *these*, and *those* are pronouns that take the place of the noun *crayon* or *crayons*. Do you know what the word *demonstrate* means? It means to point out or show clearly. The pronouns *this*, *that*, *these*, and *those* point out, or demonstrate, which crayon or crayons you are talking about. This special kind of pronoun is called a **demonstrative pronoun**, because it demonstrates or points out something.

If the student is not already doing so, have him sit in a chair. You should also be in a room with a door and a doorway.

Instructor: I want you to point to your chair and read the first sentence in **Exercise 2**.

Workbook: **This** is my chair.

Instructor: Now point to the door as you read the next sentence.

Workbook: **That** is the door.

Instructor: Use the pronoun *this* when you are pointing out something that is close to you. Use the pronoun *that* when you are pointing out something that is farther away. Point to your hands as you read the first sentence in **Exercise 3**.

Workbook: **These** are my hands.

Instructor: Now point to my hands as you read the next sentence.

Workbook: **Those** are your hands.

Instructor: Use the pronoun *these* when you are pointing out something that is close to you. Use the pronoun *those* when you are pointing out something that is farther away. Look around the room and find one object that is soft, one object that is brown, **two** objects that are breakable, and **two** objects that are big. Write these objects in the blanks in **Exercise 4** of your workbook.

Workbook: The _____ is soft.

The _____ is brown.

The _____ and the _____ are breakable.

The _____ and the _____ are big.

Instructor: Now copy the sentences in **Exercise 5**. After each demonstrative pronoun (*this, that, these,* or *those*), write the noun or nouns that you used in the sentences above. This will remind you that the demonstrative pronoun takes the place of the noun or nouns in the sentence.

Workbook: This _____ is soft.

That _____ is brown.

These _____ and _____ are breakable.

Those _____ and _____ are big.

Instructor: Let's review the personal pronouns you learned last lesson. Read aloud the list in **Exercise 6** of your workbook.

Workbook: Personal Pronouns

I, me, my, mine

You, your, yours

He, she, him, her, it

His, hers, its

We, us, our, ours

They, them, their, theirs

Instructor: A pronoun is a word that takes the place of a noun. There is a special name for the noun that is replaced. It is called the antecedent (pronounced "an-tuh-SEE-dent"). *Ante* is a Latin prefix that means "before." *Cedent* comes from a Latin word meaning "to go." So *antecedent* literally means "to go before." Usually, the antecedent noun **goes before** its pronoun. Read the sentences in **Exercise 7**. The pronoun is in bold. The antecedent is circled. Put your pencil on each bolded pronoun and draw an arrow from it back to the circled antecedent. Remember, the antecedent is the noun the pronoun replaces.

Answer Key:

antecedent
(Sally) went to the store. **She** bought eggs, milk, and apples.

antecedent
Before the (cat) pounced, **it** crept silently through the long grass.

antecedent
Do you see the ham (sandwich)? **That** is my lunch.

Instructor: If a pronoun replaces more than one person, place, thing, or idea, it can have more than one antecedent noun. Read the sentences in **Exercise 8** out loud. In each sentence, put your finger on the arrow that points from the pronoun back to the antecedents, and trace it backwards.

Workbook:

antecedent   antecedent
(Jill) and (I) enjoy stargazing, so **we** purchased a telescope for our camping trip.

antecedent   antecedent
The (campers) and the (counselors) set up **their** tents for the night.

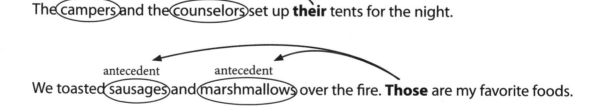

antecedent   antecedent
We toasted (sausages) and (marshmallows) over the fire. **Those** are my favorite foods.

Instructor: Read the sentences in **Exercise 9**. The pronouns are in bold type. Find the antecedent for each pronoun and circle it. Then draw an arrow from each pronoun back to its antecedent.

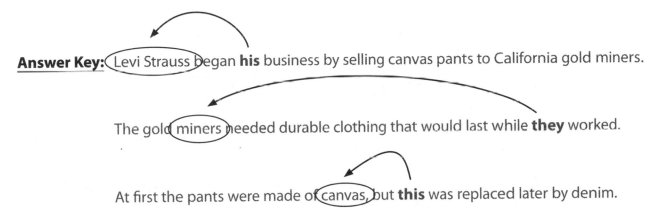

Answer Key: Levi Strauss began **his** business by selling canvas pants to California gold miners.

The gold miners needed durable clothing that would last while **they** worked.

At first the pants were made of canvas, but **this** was replaced later by denim.

Optional Dictation Exercise

The following selection is from *The Secret Garden* by Frances Hodgson Burnett. Tell the student that a young girl named Mary has discovered a secret, deserted garden. She comes across a large patch of tiny green shoots, and she hopes that these are the shoots from flower bulbs that spread and multiply like snowdrop flower bulbs.

Tell the student that you will pause whenever you come to a comma. Also, warn him that "snow-drops" is one word.

After the student takes the dictation, ask if he can find the demonstrative pronoun. If he cannot locate it, tell him that it is right at the beginning of the sentence. Then have him circle the demonstrative pronoun (*these*).

Dictation: These had been left to themselves for ten years and perhaps they had spread, like the snowdrops, into thousands.

LESSON 8

Introduction to Poem Memorization: "Afternoon on a Hill"

Follow this general procedure for all poem memorization:

1. *Read the poem to the student and make sure the student understands the meaning of all vocabulary words.*

2. *Read the title, the author, and the poem aloud to the student three times in a row. Or the student may read the poem aloud three times in a row.*

3. *Repeat this triple reading twice more during the day. Remember to read slowly and use expression that you wish your student to copy.*

4. *After the first day, read the poem aloud three times in a row, once daily. (You may wish to read the poem into a tape recorder three times in a row, and then have the student replay the tape.)*

5. *On the second day, and every day thereafter, ask the student to try to say specific parts of the poem along with you (or the tape recorder).*

6. *When he can say the entire poem with you, encourage him to repeat it to himself in a mirror and then recite it to real people. Remind him to stand up straight with his feet together and his hands still, speak clearly, and look at his audience.*

Instructor: In **Lesson 8** of your workbook, you will find a poem about a person who spends the afternoon relaxing on a hill. Follow along in your workbook as I read the poem.

Workbook:

"Afternoon on a Hill"
by Edna St. Vincent Millay

I will be the gladdest thing

Under the sun!

I will touch a hundred flowers

And not pick one.

I will look at cliffs and clouds

With quiet eyes,

Watch the wind bow down the grass,

And the grass rise.

And when the lights begin to show

Up from the town,

I will mark which must be mine,

And then start down!

Discuss the poem with the student. Ask him if he has any questions about the meaning of the poem. He may be confused by the last stanza; when the poet says, "I will mark which must be mine," she is looking at the light from her own house. After you have discussed the poem's meaning, read the poem to the student three times in a row (or he may read it). Repeat this triple reading twice more during the day. After each reading, the student should check a box in his workbook.

Instructor: Look at the poem "Afternoon on a Hill" again. Do you see how each line begins with a capital letter? Look at the rule in your workbook; it tells you that when you write poetry, you should capitalize the first word in every line of traditional poetry. Say this with me three times.

TOGETHER (three times): Capitalize the first word in every line of traditional poetry.

LESSON 9

Review: Forming Plural Nouns
Review: Common and Proper Nouns
Review: Personal and Demonstrative Pronouns

Read "Afternoon on a Hill" (Lesson 8) three times to the student. Then ask the student to try to say parts of the first stanza along with you (or the tape recorder).

Instructor: Let's begin this lesson by saying the definition of a noun together two times.

TOGETHER (two times): A noun is the name of a person, place, thing, or idea.

Exercises 1-4 review the rules for forming plurals of most nouns. The formation of irregular plurals is generally covered in spelling programs.

Instructor: Some nouns name one, single thing. These are called singular nouns. Other nouns name more than one thing. These are called plural nouns. Usually, add **s** to a noun to form the plural. Repeat that rule for me.

Student: *Usually, add **s** to a noun to form the plural.*

Instructor: Now read the rule again in **Exercise 1** of your workbook, and follow that rule to form the plural of *door*.

Answer Key:

Singular Noun	Plural Noun
door	doors

Instructor: In **Exercise 2** read the next rule with me **three** times: Add **es** to nouns ending in **s**, **sh**, **ch**, **x**, or **z**.

TOGETHER (three times): Add **es** to nouns ending in **s**, **sh**, **ch**, **x**, or **z**.

Instructor: Now read the rule again, and follow that rule to form the plural of *watch*.

Answer Key: Singular Noun   Plural Noun
watch   watches

Instructor: Now repeat the next rule: If a noun ends in **y** after a consonant, change the **y** to **i** and add **es**.

Student: *If a noun ends in **y** after a consonant, change the **y** to **i** and add **es**.*

Instructor: Now read the rule again in **Exercise 3** of your workbook, and follow that rule to form the plural of *lady*.

Answer Key: Singular Noun   Plural Noun
lady   ladies

Instructor: Now repeat the next rule: If a noun ends in **y** after a vowel, just add **s**.

Student: *If a noun ends in **y** after a vowel, just add **s**.*

Instructor: Now read the rule again in **Exercise 4** of your workbook, and follow that rule to form the plural of *toy*.

Answer Key: Singular Noun   Plural Noun
toy   toys

Instructor: Read the list of irregular plurals in **Exercise 5** of your workbook. First, say the singular word and then say its irregular plural.

Workbook:

Singular Noun	Irregular Plural Noun
child	children
foot	feet
tooth	teeth
man	men
woman	women
mouse	mice
goose	geese
deer	deer
fish	fish

Instructor: Now I am going to use a singular noun in a sentence. Then I will start another sentence, and you will finish the sentence by telling me the plural of that singular noun. If you need help, you may look at the list you just read in **Exercise 5**.

Instructor: One **woman** was spreading icing on the cake. She was making a cake for the other two _____.

Student: *Women*

Instructor: One **deer** was eating Mother's rose bush while the azaleas were nibbled by many other _____.

Student: *Deer*

Instructor: Each **child** put on a pair of roller skates. Soon the rink was filled with lots of _____.

Student: *Children*

Instructor: A **man** with a hard hat was directing the other _____.

Student: *Men*

Instructor: A large grey **goose** swam across the lake, leading the flock of _____.

Student: *Geese*

Instructor: Nouns that are common to many persons, places, things, or animals are called common nouns. Nouns that name specific, or particular, persons, places, things, or animals are called proper nouns. Proper nouns all begin with a capital letter. Let's review the capitalization rules you have learned so far.

Instructor: Repeat after me: Capitalize the proper names of persons, places, things, and animals.

Student: *Capitalize the proper names of persons, places, things, and animals.*

Instructor: Capitalize holidays.

Student: *Capitalize holidays.*

Instructor: Capitalize the names of deities.

Student: *Capitalize the names of deities.*

Instructor: Capitalize the days of the week and the months of the year, but not the seasons.

Student: *Capitalize the days of the week and the months of the year, but not the seasons.*

Instructor: Let's break the next rule into two parts. Capitalize the first, last, and all important words in titles…

Student: *Capitalize the first, last, and all important words in titles…*

Instructor: …of books, magazines, newspapers, stories, poems, and songs.

Student: *…of books, magazines, newspapers, stories, poems, and songs.*

Instructor: Now let's say that whole rule together two times.

TOGETHER (two times): Capitalize the first, last, and other important words in titles of books, magazines, newspapers, stories, poems, and songs.

Instructor: Repeat after me. Capitalize the word *I*.
Student: *Capitalize the word I.*

Instructor: Capitalize the first word in every line of traditional poetry.
Student: *Capitalize the first word in every line of traditional poetry.*

Instructor: All of these capitalization rules are printed in **Exercise 6** of your workbook. Read them aloud to me.

Instructor: When you encounter mistakes in your writing, you can mark them with special symbols or abbreviations called proofreaders' marks. Look at **Exercise 7** in your workbook. If you see a word that should be capitalized but is not, underline the lowercase letter or letters that should be capitalized with three small lines. Then write (caps) in the margin. Finally, rewrite the proper noun with correct capitalization on a line below the sentence. You may look at the capitalization rules in **Exercise 6** if you need to.

Answer Key: "In god we trust" is written on united states coins.   (caps)

God
United States

I read in the los angeles times that a panda bear named su lin was   (caps)

born at the zoo in san diego on a tuesday in the summer.   (caps)

<u>Los Angeles Times</u> (remind the student that the names of newspapers are in italics, and that we indicate this in handwriting by underlining)
Su Lin
San Diego
Tuesday

The song that kathleen sings on saint patrick's day, march 17,   (caps)

is "the wearing of the green."   (caps)

41

> Kathleen
> Saint Patrick's Day
> March
> "The Wearing of the Green"

Instructor: Do you remember the definition of a pronoun? Say it with me.

TOGETHER: A pronoun is a word used in place of a noun.

Instructor: Let's chant the list of personal pronouns together.

TOGETHER: I, me, my, mine
You, your, yours
He, she, him, her, it
His, hers, its
We, us, our, ours
They, them, their, theirs

Instructor: You have also learned about demonstrative pronouns: *this*, *that*, *these*, and *those*. These pronouns demonstrate, or point out, something. Read the sentences in **Exercise 8** of your workbook. When you say the demonstrative pronoun (printed in bold), physically point to the part of the body to which the pronoun refers.

Workbook: **This** is my elbow.

That is your elbow.

These are my knees.

Those are your knees.

LESSON 10

New: Action Verbs
New: Singular and Plural Verbs

Read "Afternoon on a Hill" (Lesson 8) three times to the student. Then ask the student to try to say parts of the first and second stanzas along with you (or the tape recorder).

Remember that you should break long lessons into half-hour segments and complete them over several days!

Instructor: In this lesson you are going to learn about a part of speech called a verb. A verb can do several different things in a sentence. Let's learn the definition of a verb. Repeat after me: A verb is a word that does an action ...

Student: *A verb is a word that does an action ...*

Instructor: Shows a state of being ...

Student: *Shows a state of being ...*

Instructor: Links two words together ...

Student: *Links two words together ...*

Instructor: Or helps another verb.

Student: *Or helps another verb.*

Instructor: I will say the whole definition to you three times.

Instructor (three times): A verb is a word that does an action, shows a state of being, links two words together, or helps another verb.

Instructor: Now I will say that definition three more times. Say as much of it with me as you can.

Together (three times): A verb is a word that does an action, shows a state of being, links two words together, or helps another verb.

Instructor: We will look at the first part of the definition: "A verb is a word that does an action." I will say a sentence, and I want you to do the action. "[Student's name] sings."

Student: *[sings]*

Instructor: *Sings* is an action verb.

Read the following sentences to the student. He should do each action and tell you the action verb (printed in bold). For example, if you say, "[Student's name] whistles," the student should whistle and then say, "*Whistles* is an action verb."

[Student's name] **opens** a door.

[Student's name] **walks** to his room and back.

[Student's name] **sits** in a chair.

[Student's name] **holds** a pencil.

[Student's name] **writes** his name on a piece of paper.

Instructor: In **Exercise 1** of your workbook, you will see this rule written down for you. Read it out loud to me once. Then, circle the action verb in each of the sentences that follow.

If the student has trouble finding the verb, ask him, "Is there a word in the sentence that you can act out?"

Answer Key:
1. The brothers (raced) each other.

2. Nadia (scattered) corn for the chickens.

3. They (captured) moths in an insect net.

4. The caterpillar (nibbled) a hole in its cocoon.

5. The cheetah (lunges) at its prey.

6. The speed skater (whizzes) over the ice.

7. Dad (vacuumed) the floor.

8. The baby (scooted) across the carpet.

Instructor: I am going to teach you a big word that has a simple definition. The word is *conjugate*. Let's say that together in syllables: con-ju-gate. To conjugate means to learn the various forms of a verb. When you are conjugating, you always start with the basic verb. Some examples are "to play," "to sing," "to run," and "to walk." The word *to* plus the basic form of a verb is called the *infinitive*. Let's say that word together in syllables: in-fin-i-tive. Read the words and definitions in **Exercise 2** of your workbook.

Workbook: con-ju-gate

conjugate

To learn the various forms of the verb

in-fin-i-tive

infinitive

to plus the basic form of the verb (example: "to play")

Instructor: The basic form of the verb changes slightly depending on the person (I, you, he, or they) who is doing the action. Read the sentences in **Exercise 3**. The verbs are underlined.

Workbook: I <u>play</u>.

You <u>play</u>.

He <u>plays</u>.

Instructor: Did you notice that the verb changed slightly in the last sentence? Listen carefully as I slowly say, "The form of the verb changes slightly depending on the person who does the verb." There are three kinds of persons: first person, second person, and third person. Here is a helpful way to learn which person is which. Imagine that you walk into an empty room. You say, "**I** am the **first person** in the room." *(Tell student to point to himself.)* Then your friend walks into the room. You say to your friend. "**I** am the **first person** in the room. **You** are the **second person** in the room." *(Tell student to point to an imaginary person in front of him.)* Then a third person walks into the room. He is a stranger. You whisper to your friend, "**I** am the **first person** in the room. **You** are the **second person** in the room. **He** is the **third person** in the room." *(Tell the student to point to an imaginary person at his side.)* Look at the chart in **Exercise 4** of your workbook.

Workbook:

	Singular
First person	I
Second person	you
Third person	he, she, it

Instructor: Do you remember our story about the people in the room? Each person enters the room individually. One, single person entered the room at a time. *I, you,* and *he* are called singular persons because each is one, single person. But suppose more than one, single person enters the room at one time. Imagine that your **whole family as a group** enters the room first. All of you say together, "**We** are the **first persons** in the room." Then a neighboring family enters the room. Your family says, "**We** are the **first persons** in the room. **You** are the **second persons** in the room." Then a family whom you have never met enters the room. Your family says to the neighbors, "**We** are the **first persons** in the room. **You** are the **second persons** in the room. **They** are the **third persons** in the room." Each family has more than one person in it. These are plural persons because there is more than one person in each group. Look at the chart in **Exercise 5** of your workbook.

Workbook:

	Singular	Plural
First person	I	we
Second person	you	you
Third person	he, she, it	they

Instructor: Now let's conjugate the verb "to walk." When we conjugate, we learn the various forms of a verb, and how a verb changes slightly depending on the person doing the action. Find the chart in **Exercise 6** of your workbook. You **walk** at the present moment. Let's look at the verb *walk*. Read the chart with me.

Read each line across and include the title of each as you read. For example, "First person singular: I walk, First person plural: we walk, Second person singular: you walk," etc.

Workbook:

	Singular	Plural
First person	I walk	we walk
Second person	you walk	you walk
Third person	he, she, it walks	they walk

Instructor: Now trace the box in the chart where the form of the verb *walk* changed slightly.

Instructor: Put your finger on the box you just traced. When we conjugate the verb "to walk," it changes form in the third person singular (he, she, it). Now let's chant the words in bold—the conjugation of "to walk" in singular and plural forms. I will say it once alone, as you follow along in the chart. Then we'll chant it together three times.

Instructor alone, then Together three times:

> I walk
> you walk
> he, she, it walks
>
> we walk
> you walk
> they walk

Instructor: Now let's chant some more conjugated verbs. Look at the charts in **Exercise 7**. We'll say each conjugation three times.

Chant the words in bold, singular forms first and then the plural forms (as you did in **Exercise 6**).

Workbook:

	Singular	**Plural**
First person	I play	we play
Second person	you play	you play
Third person	he, she, it plays	they play

	Singular	**Plural**
First person	I sing	we sing
Second person	you sing	you sing
Third person	he, she, it sings	they sing

Instructor: You have already learned about singular and plural nouns. Plural nouns usually end in the letter **s**. This is the opposite of the way verbs form plurals. Look at the last chart in **Exercise 7**. Put your finger on the third person singular box, "he, she, it sings." One, single person sings. The verb *sings* is singular, and it ends in the letter **s**. Plural verbs usually do not end in the letter **s**. Put your finger on the third person plural box, "they sing." Several people sing. The verb *sing* is plural; it does not end in the letter **s**. Read each sentence in **Exercise 8**. First, find the verb and circle it. Then write an **S** over the verb if it is singular, and write a **P** over the verb if it is plural. Look at the subject in each sentence. Is it a singular subject doing the action? Or is it a plural subject doing the action? A singular verb will have a singular subject. A plural verb will have a plural subject.

Answer Key:

She (skips.) — S

They (skip.) — P

He (stretches) — S

They (stretch.) — P

It (slithers.) — S

They (slither) — P

He (dives.) — S

They (dive.) — P

It (kicks.) — S

They (kick.) — P

She (climbs) — S

They (climb.) — P

LESSON 11

New: Sentences and Fragments
New: Diagramming Subjects and Verbs
Learn to Proofread: Insert a Period

Read "Afternoon on a Hill" (Lesson 8) three times to the student. Then ask the student to try to say parts of the first, second, and third stanzas along with you (or the tape recorder).

Instructor: Today we are going to learn about sentences. I will say the definition of a sentence to you three times.

Instructor (three times): A sentence is a group of words that expresses a complete thought. All sentences begin with a capital letter and end with a punctuation mark.

Instructor: Now I will say the definition three more times. Say as much of it with me as you can.

TOGETHER (three times): A sentence is a group of words that expresses a complete thought. All sentences begin with a capital letter and end with a punctuation mark.

Instructor: Look at **Exercise 1** in your workbook. Read the rule out loud to me.

Instructor: Now read aloud each of the three sentences in **Exercise 2**. Notice that each sentence begins with a capital letter and ends with a punctuation mark. These three sentences all end with the punctuation mark called a period.

Workbook: Wombats dig.

We shout.

Simon Oliver grins.

Instructor: Every sentence has a verb. Every verb has a subject. To find the subject of a verb, find the verb and then ask "who" or "what." In the first sentence, what is the action verb?

Student: *Dig*

Instructor: *Dig* is the verb. Now let's find the subject. What digs?

Student: *Wombats*

49

Instructor: *Wombats* is the subject. Now look at the second sentence. What is the verb?

Student: *Shout*

Instructor: *Shout* is the verb. Now let's find the subject. Who shouts?

Student: *We*

Instructor: *We* is the subject. Look at the third sentence. What is the verb?

Student: *Grins*

Instructor: *Grins* is the verb. Now let's find the subject. Who grins? This proper noun is made up of two words.

Student: *Simon Oliver*

Instructor: *Simon Oliver* is the subject. Did you know you can draw pictures of how the words in a sentence work together? This is called "diagramming" the sentence. Look at **Exercise 3** in your workbook. When you diagram a sentence, you begin with a simple frame that looks like the one in your workbook:

Workbook:

Instructor: The verb is written to the right of the center line, and the subject is written to the left of that line. Look at the diagram of "Wombats dig." *Dig* is the verb, so it is written to the right of the center line. To find the subject of a verb, find the verb and then ask "who" or "what." What digs? Wombats. *Wombats* is the subject, so it is written to the left of that line.

Wombats	dig

Instructor: In your workbook, look at **Exercise 4**. Read aloud this sentence again.

Workbook: Simon Oliver grins.

Instructor: You are going to diagram this sentence on the empty frame in your workbook.

Instructor: You write the verb to the right of the center line. What is the verb in the sentence "Simon Oliver grins"?

Student: *Grins*

Instructor: Write *grins* on your diagram. Now find the subject. Who grins? This is a proper name that consists of two words.

Student: *Simon Oliver*

Instructor: The proper noun *Simon Oliver* should be capitalized in the diagram because it is capitalized in the sentence. Write *Simon Oliver* to the left of the center line. Both words go on the subject line.

Answer Key:

Simon Oliver	grins

Instructor: In your workbook, I want you to diagram the three sentences in **Exercise 5**. You will read each sentence. For Sentence 1, fill in the frame. For Sentence 2, trace the dotted frame before you fill it in. For Sentence 3, draw your own frame in the space provided. Remember to copy the words exactly as they appear in the sentences. If the word begins with a capital letter in the sentence, it should also be capitalized in the diagram. No punctuation marks go on the diagram.

Workbook: 1. Olga Mervish swims.

2. This floats.

3. Frogs croak.

Use the following dialogue to help the student fill in each diagram.

1. *Find the verb. Write the verb to the right of your center line.*

2. *Find the subject. Ask "who" or "what" before the verb. [Prompt the student with a specific question like "Who swims?" or "What floats?"]*

   Write the subject to the left of the center line on your frame.

Answer Key:

Olga Mervish	swims

This	floats

Frogs	croak

Instructor: In the sentences you just diagrammed, point to each subject. Tell me if the word is a common noun, proper noun, or a pronoun.

Remind the student that the demonstrative pronouns are *this*, *that*, *these*, and *those* (Lesson 7).

Student: Olga Mervish *is a proper noun*. This *is a pronoun*. Frogs *is a common noun*.

Instructor: You have been diagramming sentences. A sentence is a group of words that expresses a complete thought. Some groups of words are just pieces of sentences. These pieces of sentences are called fragments. Fragments do not make sense by themselves—you need to add words, like a subject or a verb, to make a sentence that expresses a complete thought. Look at the fragments in **Exercise 6** of your workbook. Tell me what is missing: a subject or a verb. Then add words to make that fragment a complete sentence. [This is an oral exercise.]

Answer Key:

Sample Answers

The mosquito.   The mosquito **buzzed in my ear**.
                                    (needs verb)

Rolled in the dirt.   **The puppy** rolled in the dirt.
                                    (needs subject)

Picked flowers.   **Glenda** picked flowers.
                                    (needs subject)

The poison dart frog.   The poison dart frog **ate insects.**
                                    (needs verb)

Instructor: A sentence is a group of words that expresses a complete thought. All sentences begin with a capital letter and end with a punctuation mark. We now come to our newest capitalization rule: Capitalize the first word of every sentence. Say that with me three times.

TOGETHER (three times): Capitalize the first word of every sentence.

Instructor: Now let's review all the capitalization rules you have learned so far. I will say each rule, and you repeat it after me.

Here are the rules, in order:

1.   *Capitalize the proper names of persons, places, things, and animals.*

2.   *Capitalize holidays.*

3.   *Capitalize the names of deities.*

4.   *Capitalize the days of the week and the months of the year, but not the seasons.*

5.   *Capitalize the first, last, and other important words in titles of books, magazines, newspapers, stories, poems, and songs.*

6.   *Capitalize the word* I.

7.   *Capitalize the first word in every line of traditional poetry.*

8.   *Capitalize the first word of every sentence.*

Learn to Proofread: Insert a Period ⊙

Instructor: You have already learned some special symbols or abbreviations called proofreaders' marks. Look in your workbook at **Exercise 7**. This is the proofreaders' mark you will learn today. It is a period in a circle. When you see this mark, you should insert a period. Look at the sample sentence in **Exercise 7**. Read that aloud. "Fan Kuan was a Chinese painter" is a sentence and should end with a period. Now let's review all the proofreaders' marks you have learned so far. Read the sentence in **Exercise 8**. Use your proofreaders' marks to show the errors in capitalization and punctuation. Then copy the sentence **correctly** on the lines below.

Answer Key: fan kuan, who was born in 990, painted landscapes of china⊙

Fan Kuan, who was born in 990, painted landscapes of China.

Optional Dictation Exercise

Dictation: Fan Kuan's most famous painting is of towering mountains and winding streams in the northern part of China.

LESSON 12

Summary Exercise: *Mr. Popper's Penguins*

Read "Afternoon on a Hill" (Lesson 8) three times to the student. Then ask the student to try to say parts of the poem along with you (or the tape recorder).

Instructor: Today I am going to read a selection aloud to you that is fiction. Fiction is a made-up story. I will read it only once. (If the student is a fluent reader, you may choose to have him read it aloud or silently). Then I want you to tell me in your own words what you remember.

This story is from *Mr. Popper's Penguins* by Richard and Florence Atwater. Mr. Popper is a poor housepainter who is also a huge fan of Admiral Drake, an Antarctic explorer. When Admiral Drake finds out how much Mr. Popper loves the Antarctic, he sends Mr. Popper a penguin. Then Mr. Popper gets a second penguin from an aquarium, and before long, ten baby penguins hatch out of their eggs. But penguins eat a lot—so Mr. Popper turns the penguins into a travelling group of entertainers so that he can afford to feed them.

Mr. Popper's Penguins

It was expensive to have huge cakes of ice brought up to their hotel rooms, to cool the penguins. The bills in the fine restaurants where the Poppers often took their meals were often dreadfully high. Fortunately, however, the penguins' food had stopped being an expense to them. On the road, they had to give up having tank cars of live fish shipped to them because it was so hard to get deliveries on time. So they went back to feeding the birds on canned shrimps.

This cost them absolutely nothing, for Mr. Popper had written a testimonial saying: "Popper's Performing Penguins thrive on Owens' Oceanic Shrimp."

This statement, with a picture of the twelve penguins, was printed in all the leading magazines, and the Owens' Oceanic Shrimp Company gave Mr. Popper an order that was good for free cans of shrimps at any grocery store anywhere in the country.

Several other companies, such as the Great Western Spinach Growers' Association and the Energetic Breakfast Oats Company, wanted him to recommend their product, too, and offered him large sums of cash. But the penguins simply refused to eat spinach or oats, and Mr. Popper was much too honest to say they would, even though he knew the money would come in handy.

The purpose of summary exercises is to help students learn to *condense*. Before a student can write well, he must be able to state clearly and succinctly the *main point* of his composition. So do not allow the student to give you a long and detailed summary that covers every element in the story. Instead, encourage him to summarize briefly; the summary should be a maximum of three sentences long. You can use one of the following questions:

1. *What are two things that you remember about the passage?*

2. *What was the most important thing that you learned in the passage?*

3. *What was the most interesting thing in the passage?*

If the student speaks in phrases, turn his phrases into complete sentences. The student should then repeat the complete sentence back to you.

As the student summarizes in his own words, you may write his sentences down as he speaks or record them onto a tape recorder to write down when he is finished. You have three options for writing the narration:

1. *Write down the student's narration for him on his workbook page.*

2. *Write down the student's narration for him on a separate piece of paper and have him copy some or all of the sentences onto his workbook page.*

3. *Write down the student's narration on a separate piece of paper and dictate it to him, as he writes it on his workbook page.*

Once you have written the student's narration, he should read it aloud back to you.

LESSON 13

New: Adjectives That Tell What Kind, Which One, and How Many
New: Diagramming Adjectives

Read "Afternoon on a Hill" (Lesson 8) three times to the student. Then ask the student to try to say the whole poem with you (or the tape recorder). The student should practice saying the whole poem to himself in a mirror.

Instructor: In Lesson 11 you learned about sentences. A sentence is a group of words that expresses a complete thought. All sentences begin with a capital letter and end with a punctuation mark. Say that definition with me three times.

TOGETHER (three times): A sentence is a group of words that expresses a complete thought. All sentences begin with a capital letter and end with a punctuation mark.

Instructor: You also diagrammed some sentences. Remember, a sentence diagram is a picture of how the words in a sentence work together. In your workbook, read the sentence in **Exercise 1**.

Workbook: Rain poured.

Instructor: Diagram this sentence by filling in the empty frame. First you find the verb. What is the verb in the sentence "Rain poured"?

Student: *Poured*

Instructor: *Poured* is the verb. Write the verb to the right of the center line on your diagram. Now let's find the subject. What poured?

Student: *Rain*

Instructor: *Rain* is the subject. Write the subject to the left of the center line on your diagram. Your diagram is now complete.

Answer Key:

Rain	poured

Instructor: In this lesson you will learn about the part of speech called an adjective. An adjective is a word that describes a noun or pronoun. I will say that definition to you three times.

Instructor (three times): An adjective is a word that describes a noun or pronoun.

Instructor: Now I will say the definition three more times. Say it with me.

TOGETHER (three times): An adjective is a word that describes a noun or pronoun.

Instructor: Adjectives provide you with more information about a noun or pronoun. Let's think about the noun *hamburger*. You don't know very much information about the hamburger. If you add an adjective before the noun, you can tell what kind of hamburger it is. In your workbook, read the list of adjectives and nouns in **Exercise 2.** Do you see how the adjectives describe each hamburger?

Workbook: **juicy** hamburger

   hot hamburger

   delicious hamburger

   spicy hamburger

   tender hamburger

   brown hamburger

Instructor: All of the adjectives you just read tell you what kind of hamburger it is. Adjectives can tell you several things about a noun. In your workbook, look with me at the list in **Exercise 3.** Adjectives tell what kind, which one, how many, and whose.

Workbook: Adjectives tell

   • what kind

   • which one

   • how many

   • whose

Instructor: Now I will say this as a chant three times. Look at the list again as I say it.

Instructor (three times): Adjectives tell what kind, which one, how many, and whose.

Instructor: Now say the chant with me three times without looking at the list.

Together (three times): Adjectives tell what kind, which one, how many, and whose.

Instructor: *Juicy* hamburger. *Hot* hamburger. *Delicious, spicy, tender,* and *brown* hamburger. All of these adjectives tell you what kind of hamburger it is. Other kinds of adjectives tell you which hamburger it is. Read aloud the list in **Exercise 4** of your workbook.

Workbook: **this** hamburger

that hamburger

these hamburgers

those hamburgers

Instructor: Which hamburger is it? It is *that* hamburger. The adjective *that* tells you which one. You may remember *this*, *that*, *these*, and *those* can also be demonstrative pronouns. But in **Exercise 4**, they come before the noun *hamburger* to tell you which hamburger you are talking about. In **Exercise 4**, these words are adjectives. There are more adjectives that can tell you which one. Read aloud the list in **Exercise 5** of your workbook.

Workbook: **first** hamburger

second hamburger

next hamburger

last hamburger

Instructor: Imagine that a waiter brings a tray of four hamburgers to your family's table. You point to the hamburger nearest you. Which hamburger is it? It is the *first* hamburger. The adjective *first* tells you which hamburger you are talking about. Adjectives can also tell you how many. Read aloud the list in **Exercise 6** of your workbook.

Workbook: **one** hamburger

two hamburgers

twenty-one hamburgers

Instructor: When adjectives tell you how many, they sometimes do not tell you an exact number. In your workbook, read the list of adjectives in **Exercise 7** that tell you how many but do not tell you an exact number.

Workbook: **many** hamburgers

several hamburgers

all hamburgers

both hamburgers

some hamburgers

another hamburger

each hamburger

more hamburgers

most hamburgers

other hamburgers

Instructor: You know that adjectives tell what kind, which one, how many, and whose. You will learn about adjectives that tell whose in the next lesson. Right now you will learn how to add adjectives to a sentence diagram. In the sentence you diagrammed at the beginning of the lesson ("Rain poured") the word *Rain* was the subject. It is a noun. Let's add an adjective that describes the noun *Rain*. Read the sentence in **Exercise 8**.

Workbook: Cold rain poured.

Instructor: The subject of the sentence is still *rain*. What poured? Rain poured. But now there is an adjective that tells us more about the rain. What kind of rain is it? *Cold* rain. The adjective is written on a slanted line under the word it describes. Look at this diagram. Point to the adjective.

Workbook: Cold rain poured.

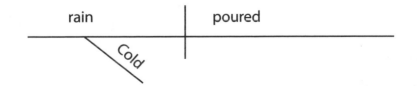

Instructor: Now in **Exercise 9** you will diagram sentences with adjectives in them. You read the sentence, and I will ask you questions to help you fill in the diagram. For Sentence 1, fill in the frame. For Sentence 2, trace the dotted frame before you fill it in. For Sentence 3, draw your own frame in the space provided. Remember to copy the words exactly as they appear in the sentence. If the word begins with a capital letter in the sentence, it should also be capitalized in the diagram.

Workbook:
1. Tiny bugs scattered.

2. That king ruled.

3. Two birds chirped.

Use the following dialogue to help the student fill in the diagrams.

1. *Find the verb. Write the verb to the right of your center line.*

2. *Find the subject. Ask "who" or "what" before the verb. [Prompt the student with a specific question like "What scattered?" or "Who ruled?"] Write the subject to the left of the center line on your frame.*

3. *Now you have found the two most basic parts of the sentence. Go back and look again at the subject. Is there a word that describes the subject? This is an adjective that could tell what kind, which one, how many, or whose. Write the adjective on the slanted line below the subject it describes.*

Answer Key:

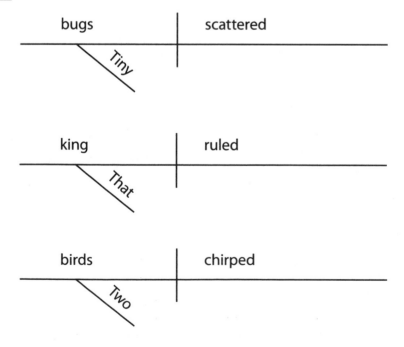

LESSON 14

New: Adjectives That Tell Whose (Possessive Nouns and Pronouns)
New: Articles

Read "Afternoon on a Hill" (Lesson 8) three times to the student. Then ask the student to say the poem along with you or the tape recorder. If the student is ready, he should recite the poem to real people today. If he is not, continue practicing daily until he is ready.

Instructor: In the last lesson you learned the definition of an adjective. An adjective is a word that describes a noun or pronoun. Say that with me three times.

TOGETHER (three times): An adjective is a word that describes a noun or pronoun.

Instructor: Adjectives tell what kind, which one, how many, and whose. Say that with me three times.

TOGETHER (three times): Adjectives tell what kind, which one, how many, and whose.

Instructor: Adjectives tell what kind. What color is your hair?
Student: [Answers will vary.]

Instructor: [Color of hair] is an adjective that tells what kind of hair. Rub your head. How would you describe the way your hair feels: thin, thick, soft, silky, tangled, clean, or greasy?
Student: [Answers will vary.]

Instructor: [Adjective the student chose] is an adjective that tells what kind of hair. Adjectives can also tell which one. In your workbook, read the list in **Exercise 1**.

Workbook: **this** squid

that squid

these squid

those squid

Instructor: Repeat after me: *This, that, these,* and *those* are adjectives that tell which one.
Student: This, that, these, *and* those *are adjectives that tell which one.*

Instructor: There are other adjectives that can tell you which one. In your workbook, read aloud the list in **Exercise 2**.

Workbook: **first** groundhog

sixth groundhog

next groundhog

final groundhog

Instructor: Adjectives like *first*, *sixth*, *next*, and *final* tell you which one. Adjectives can also tell you how many. Sometimes these adjectives tell you an exact number like "one mango," and sometimes they tell you a general amount like "several mangoes." Answer this question with a number. How many toes do you have?

Student: *Ten*

Instructor: Ten toes. *Ten* is an adjective that tells how many toes. Could you count how many hairs are on your head? Well, maybe you could, but it would take a very long time. If I asked you how many hairs are on your head, you could just say "I have many hairs on my head." *Many* is an adjective that tells how many hairs, even if it doesn't tell you the exact number. In **Exercise 3** of your workbook, read the list of adjectives that tell you how many but do not tell you an exact number.

Workbook: **several** dominoes

all dominoes

both dominoes

some dominoes

another domino

each domino

more dominoes

most dominoes

other dominoes

Instructor: You have now read adjectives that tell what kind, which one, and how many. Now let's learn about adjectives that tell whose. In **Exercise 4** of your workbook, read the sentence aloud.

Workbook: It is the **boy's** shirt.

Instructor: Whose shirt is it? The boy's. *Boy's* is an adjective that tells whose. Look at the word *boy's* in the sentence. Do you see the apostrophe that comes before the letter **s**? The punctuation mark called an apostrophe changes the way a word acts in the sentence. The word *boy* (without the apostrophe and the **s**) is a noun that names a person. But when you add an apostrophe and the letter **s** to *boy*, the new word, *boy's*, tells you whose shirt it is. The apostrophe-**s** turns the noun into an adjective that tells whose!

Instructor: In your workbook, look at the chart in **Exercise 5**. First you will read a singular noun. Then, you will write that word in the blank and add an apostrophe-**s** to it. The noun will turn into an adjective that tells whose.

Answer Key: Adjectives tell whose.

Noun	Adjective That Tells Whose		
eagle	the	**eagle's**	talons
car	the	**car's**	engine
Kim		**Kim's**	sweater

Instructor: Now you know how an apostrophe-**s** can turn a singular noun into an adjective. You can turn plural nouns into adjectives, too. Remember, plural nouns name more than one thing. In **Exercise 6** of your workbook, read the sentence aloud.

Workbook: The **girls'** boots are muddy.

Instructor: Whose boots are they? The girls'. *Girls'* is an adjective that tells whose. Look at the word *girls'* in the sentence. Do you see the apostrophe? This time the apostrophe comes at the end of the word. It is not followed by the letter **s**. That is because the plural noun *girls* already ends in an **s**. You don't need to add another one. If you did, it would sound funny: *girls's*. The *girls's* boots. That doesn't sound right! In order to change a plural noun that already ends in **s** into an adjective that tells whose, all you need to do is add that powerful punctuation mark called an apostrophe.

Instructor: Look at the chart in **Exercise 7** of your workbook. First you will read a plural noun. Then you will write that word in the blank and add an apostrophe to it. The plural noun will turn into an adjective that tells whose.

Answer Key: Adjectives tell whose.

Noun	Adjective That Tells Whose		
horses	the	**horses'**	manes
ants	the	**ants'**	tunnels
Calders	the	**Calders'**	books

Instructor: When a plural noun ends in **s**, as many plurals do, you add an apostrophe to turn the plural noun into an adjective that tells whose. But there are some plurals that do not end in **s**. These nouns don't follow any rules to form their plurals. We call these "irregular plurals" because they don't form their plurals the regular ways. In **Exercise 8** of your workbook, read this list of singular nouns and their irregular plural forms to me.

Workbook:

Singular Noun	Plural Noun
child	children
foot	feet
tooth	teeth
man	men
woman	women
mouse	mice
goose	geese
deer	deer
sheep	sheep
fish	fish

Instructor: These irregular plurals also don't follow the rules when it comes to turning them into adjectives that tell whose. Normally, you would just add an apostrophe to a plural noun to turn it into an adjective. But with irregular plurals (because they don't already end in **s**), you need to add an apostrophe and the letter **s**. Read **Exercise 9** to me. The adjectives in bold print all tell whose.

Workbook: three **children's** lollipops

many **sheep's** wool

both **geese's** dinner

Instructor: Now let's talk about another kind of adjective that tells whose. Do you remember the personal pronouns? Say them with me.

TOGETHER: I, me, my, mine
You, your, yours
He, she, him, her, it
His, hers, its
We, us, our, ours
They, them, their, theirs

Instructor: Some of these pronouns are called possessive pronouns. Possessive pronouns act like adjectives that tell whose. Look at the list of personal pronouns in **Exercise 10**. I will slowly say the possessive pronouns. Find and circle each possessive pronoun as I say it. The possessive pronouns are *my, mine, your, yours, his, her, hers, its, our, ours, their,* and *theirs.*

Answer Key: Personal Pronouns

I, me, my, mine

You, your, yours

He, she, him, her, it

His, hers, its

We, us, our, ours

They, them, their, theirs

Instructor: Read the sentences in **Exercise 10** of your workbook. The possessive pronouns that act like adjectives that tell whose are in bold print.

After the student reads each sentence, ask him to identify the possessive noun by answering a "whose" question. For example, the student reads, "My foot hurts." You ask, "Whose foot?" The student answers, "**My** foot." The personal pronouns have three groups: possessive pronouns (listed above), subject pronouns (*I, you, he, she, it, we, they*), and object pronouns (*me, you, him, her, it, us, them*). The student will learn about subject and object pronouns in later lessons.

Workbook: **My** foot hurts.   *(Whose foot?)*

Your kettle is whistling.   *(Whose kettle?)*

His tie is crooked.   *(Whose tie?)*

Her poodle yipped.   *(Whose poodle?)*

Our marshmallows toasted.   *(Whose marshmallows?)*

Their clothes were drenched.   *(Whose clothes?)*

Instructor: There are three special, little adjectives that we have not talked about yet. These adjectives are called articles. The articles are *a, an, the.* Here is a little poem to help you learn them. Follow along in **Exercise 11** while I read the poem.

If the student already knows this poem from an earlier level of *First Language Lessons*, you need only read it once and have the student repeat it after you from memory. If this is the first time the student is learning about articles, read the poem to the student three times in a row at three different times during the day. Have the student join you when he is able. Review this poem on subsequent days if necessary.

Workbook: Articles are little words,

You need know only three.

The articles that describe nouns

are **a, an, the**.

Instructor: You use the article *a* before a word that begins with a consonant sound. A pig. A towel. A bath. You use the article *an* before a word that begins with a vowel sound. An octopus. An egg. An iguana. An avalanche. An umbrella. Read the sentences in **Exercise 12**, and circle the articles. Some of the sentences have more than one article. Remember, articles act like adjectives—they describe nouns.

If the student asks, the article *the* is pronounced "thuh" before a word that begins with a consonant sound. It is pronounced "thee" before a word that begins with a vowel sound or if you are trying to emphasize a word ("It is **the** car to buy.").

The following sentences are adapted from *Heidi* by Johanna Spyri.

Answer Key: Heidi is a happy little girl.

Heidi's grandfather was an old man.

Heidi picked many flowers and filled an apron with them.

She looked about till she found a shed where the goats were kept.

You are the next of kin to the child.

The child is to remain with you.

Instructor: Now in **Exercise 13** you will review diagramming sentences with adjectives in them. You read the sentence, and I will ask you questions to help you fill in the diagram. For Sentence 1, fill in the frame. For Sentence 2, trace the dotted frame before you fill it in. For Sentence 3, draw your own frame in the space provided. Remember to copy the words exactly as they appear in the sentence. If the word begins with a capital letter in the sentence, it should also be capitalized in the diagram.

Workbook:
1. Cindy's face brightened.
2. Her mother smiled.
3. The rain stopped.

Use the following dialogue to help the student fill in the diagrams.

1. *Find the verb. Write the verb to the right of your center line.*

2. *Find the subject. Ask "who" or "what" before the verb. [Prompt the student with a specific question like "What brightened?" or "Who smiled?"] Write the subject to the left of the center line on your frame.*

3. *Now you have found the two most basic parts of the sentence. Go back and look again at the subject. Is there a word that describes the subject? This is an adjective that could tell what kind, which one, how many, or whose. Also look for the articles (a, an, the), because they act like adjectives. Write the adjective on the slanted line below the subject it describes.*

Answer Key:

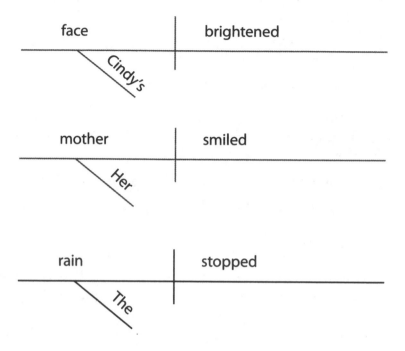

───────────────────────────────

Optional Dictation Exercise

The following sentences are adapted from E. Nesbit's *The Railway Children*. After the student takes the dictation, have him circle the possessive pronoun that acts like an adjective that tells whose.

Dictation: He said that (his) eyes were red because he had a cold.

Mother read (her) poetry and Peter felt better.

LESSON 15

Review: Adjectives
Learn to Proofread: Insert an Apostrophe

Instructor: Let's review the definition of an adjective. An adjective is a word that describes a noun or pronoun. Say that definition with me.

TOGETHER: An adjective is a word that describes a noun or pronoun.

Instructor: Adjectives tell what kind, which one, how many, and whose. Say that with me two times.

TOGETHER (two times): Adjectives tell what kind, which one, how many, and whose.

Instructor: In **Exercise 1** of your workbook, follow along as I read you some adjectives that tell what kind. I want you to use each adjective I say to describe any noun you wish. For example, if I say "crunchy," you might say "crunchy carrot."

Workbook: red

chubby

scratchy

sticky

quiet

friendly

fluffy

relaxing

Instructor: In **Exercise 2**, follow along as I read you some adjectives that tell which one. I want you to use each adjective I say to describe any noun you wish. For example, if I say "this," you might say "this flamingo."

Workbook: this

that

these

those

first

seventh

next

last

Instructor: In **Exercise 3**, follow along as I read you some adjectives that tell how many. I want you to use each adjective I say to describe any noun you wish. For example, if I say "forty-six," you might say "forty-six lima beans."

Workbook: twelve

two

eighty-seven

most

several

another

all

Instructor: In **Exercise 4**, follow along as I read you some adjectives that tell whose. I want you to use each adjective I say to describe any noun you wish. For example, if I say "girl's," you might say "girl's socks." Look carefully at the end of each word so you will know if the word is singular or plural.

Answer Key:

puppy's	(singular)
singer's	(singular)
elephant's	(singular)
Mom's	(singular)
Larry's	(singular)
beetles'	(plural)
warriors'	(plural)
nurses'	(plural)

Instructor: Do you remember the three special, little words called articles? Articles act like adjectives—they describe nouns. We memorized a poem about articles. Say it with me if you can.

TOGETHER: Articles are little words,
You need know only three.
The articles that describe nouns
are **a**, **an**, **the**.

Instructor: Again, what are the three articles?
Student: *A, an, the*

Instructor: Follow along as I read you the poem in **Exercise 5**. Then I want you to circle the articles.

Answer Key:

"(The) Arrow and (the) Song"
by Henry Wadsworth Longfellow

I shot (an) arrow into (the) air,

It fell to earth, I knew not where;

For, so swiftly it flew, (the) sight

Could not follow it in its flight.

I breathed (a) song into (the) air,

It fell to earth, I knew not where;

For who has sight so keen and strong,

That it can follow (the) flight of song?

Long, long afterward, in (an) oak

I found (the) arrow, still unbroke;

And (the) song, from beginning to end,

I found again in (the) heart of (a) friend.

Instructor: In **Exercise 6** there is a sentence with only a subject and a verb. Read the sentence and look at the diagram.

Workbook: Dragonflies zoom.

Dragonflies	zoom

Instructor: You have already learned how to add adjectives to a sentence diagram. You diagram adjectives by writing them on a slanted line under the word they describe. Read the next sentence and look at its diagram.

Workbook: The glittering dragonflies zoom.

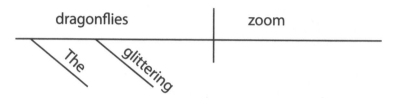

Instructor: I will point out words on the diagram as I explain. There are two adjectives in this sentence that describe the noun *dragonflies*. There is an article that acts like an adjective: *The*. The dragonflies. There is also an adjective that tells what kind. What kind of dragonflies zoom? Glittering dragonflies. *The* is written before *glittering* on the diagram because *The* comes before *glittering* in the sentence.

Now in **Exercise 8**, you will diagram sentences with **three** adjectives in them. You read each sentence, and I will ask you questions to help you fill in the diagram. For Sentence 1, fill in the frame. For Sentence 2, trace the dotted frame before you fill it in. For Sentence 3, draw your own frame in the space provided. Remember to copy the words exactly as they appear in the sentence. If the word begins with a capital letter in the sentence, it should also be capitalized in the diagram.

1. Trevor's quick, shiny goldfish hid.

2. The last golden sunflower bloomed.

3. Several fuzzy, warm chicks peeped.

Use the following dialogue to help the student fill in the diagrams.

1. *What is the verb? Write the verb to the right of your center line.*

2. *Find the subject. Ask "who" or "what" before the verb. [Prompt the student with a specific question like "What hid?" or "What bloomed?"] Write the subject to the left of the center line on your frame.*

3. *Now you have found the two most basic parts of the sentence. Go back and look again at the simple subject. Are there any words that describe the subject that come before the verb? These adjectives can tell what kind, which one, how many, or whose. Also look for the articles (a, an, the), because they act like adjectives. Write each adjective on a slanted line below the subject it describes.*

Answer Key:

Trevor's quick, shiny goldfish hid.

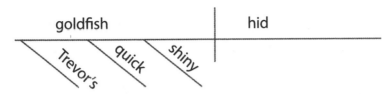

The last golden sunflower bloomed.

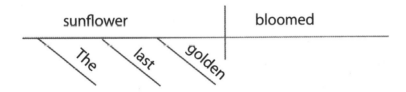

Several fuzzy, warm chicks peeped.

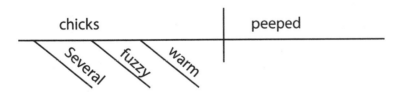

Learn to Proofread: Insert an Apostrophe ⋎

Instructor: You have already learned some special symbols or abbreviations called proofreaders' marks. Look in your workbook at **Exercise 9**. This is the proofreaders' mark you will learn today. It is an apostrophe with an arrowhead underneath it. When you see this mark, you should insert an apostrophe. Look at the sample sentence in **Exercise 9**. Read that aloud.

Workbook: The books⋎ first line is "A column of smoke rose thin and straight from the cabins⋎ chimney."

Instructor: This sentence is missing two apostrophes. *Book's* is an adjective that tells whose first line. *Cabin's* is an adjective that tells whose chimney. Now let's review all the proofreaders' marks you have learned. Read the sentence in **Exercise 10**. Use your proofreaders' marks to show the errors in capitalization and punctuation. Then copy the sentence **correctly** on the lines below.

Answer Key: this is the First Line from marjorie kinnan rawlingss Novel,　　(caps)　(lc)

the yearling.

This is the first line from Marjorie Kinnan Rawlings's novel, The Yearling.

Optional Dictation Exercise

The following sentence is from C. S. Lewis's *The Lion, the Witch, and the Wardrobe*. Tell the student you will pause when you get to a comma. Once the student has taken the dictation, have him find and circle the adjectives.

Dictation: There was crisp, dry snow under his feet and more snow lying on the branches of the trees.

LESSON 16

Poem Memorization: "Ozymandias"

Instructor: In **Lesson 16** of your workbook, you will find a poem called "Ozymandias." It is about an ancient king named Ozymandias who tried to make his kingdom so great and powerful that it would last forever. Follow along in your workbook as I read the poem—and then tell me whether the king was successful or not.

"Ozymandias"
by Percy Bysshe Shelley

I met a traveller from an antique land

Who said: "Two vast and trunkless legs of stone

Stand in the desert. Near them, on the sand,

Half sunk, a shattered visage lies, whose frown,

And wrinkled lip, and sneer of cold command,

Tell that its sculptor well those passions read

Which yet survive, stamped on these lifeless things,

The hand that mocked them, and the heart that fed:

And on the pedestal these words appear:

'My name is Ozymandias, king of kings:

Look on my works, ye Mighty, and despair!'

Nothing beside remains. Round the decay

Of that colossal wreck, boundless and bare

The lone and level sands stretch far away."

Read the poem to the student three times in a row. Repeat this triple reading twice more during the day. Have the student check the boxes in his workbook when this is done.

LESSON 17

New: Adverbs That Tell How and When
New: Diagramming Adverbs

Read "Ozymandias" (Lesson 16) three times to the student. Then ask the student to try to say parts of the poem along with you (or the tape recorder).

Instructor: Let's review the definition of an adjective. Say this with me two times: An adjective is a word that describes a noun or pronoun.

TOGETHER (two times): An adjective is a word that describes a noun or pronoun.

Instructor: In this lesson you will learn another part of speech that describes words: an adverb. An adverb is a word that describes a verb, an adjective, or another adverb. I will say that definition to you three times.

Instructor (three times): An adverb is a word that describes a verb, an adjective, or another adverb.

Instructor: Now I will say that definition three more times. Say it with me.

TOGETHER (three times): An adverb is a word that describes a verb, an adjective, or another adverb.

Instructor: We will talk about adverbs that describe adjectives and other adverbs later in this book. In this lesson we will focus on adverbs that describe verbs. In your workbook, put your finger on **Exercise 1**. Follow along as I read. Adverbs tell how, when, where, how often, and to what extent.

Workbook: Adverbs tell

- how

- when

- where

- how often

- to what extent

Instructor: Say that with me three times. Adverbs tell how, when, where, how often, and to what extent.

TOGETHER (three times): Adverbs tell how, when, where, how often, and to what extent.

Instructor: Adverbs tell how. How do you talk? In **Exercise 2**, read each of the sentences to me. The adverb that tells how is in bold print.

Workbook: I talk **softly**.

I talk **rapidly**.

I talk **slowly**.

I talk **loudly**.

I talk **excitedly**.

Instructor: We are going to practice identifying adverbs that tell how. Look at **Exercise 3**. I will ask you a "how" question and you will read the three choices. Choose your favorite adverb and say the answer to the question in a complete sentence. Then write your adverb of choice in the blank.

Instructor: How do you sleep?

Workbook: deeply

restlessly

quietly

Student: *I sleep [adverb of choice].*

Instructor: *[Adverb of choice]* is an adverb that tells how you sleep.

Instructor: When eating, how do you chew?

Workbook: noisily

daintily

thoroughly

Student: *I chew [adverb of choice].*

Instructor: *[Adverb of choice]* is an adverb that tells how you chew.

Instructor: Adverbs also tell when. When do you study? In **Exercise 4**, read each of the sentences to me. The adverb that tells when is in bold print.

Workbook: I study **today**.

I study **early**.

I study **late**.

I study **now**.

Instructor: Look at **Exercise 5**. We are going to practice identifying adverbs that tell when. I will ask you a "when" question and you will read the three choices. Choose your favorite adverb and answer the question in a complete sentence. Then write your adverb of choice in the blank.

Instructor: When will you play?

Workbook: momentarily

soon

tomorrow

Student: *I will play [adverb of choice].*

Instructor: *[Adverb of choice]* is an adverb that tells when you will play.

Instructor: When did you help?

Workbook: already

before

yesterday

Student: *I helped [adverb of choice].*

Instructor: *[Adverb of choice]* is an adverb that tells when you helped.

Instructor: In **Exercise 6**, read the first sentence and look at its diagram.

Workbook: Peacocks strut.

Peacocks	strut

Instructor: In this lesson you will learn how to add adverbs to a sentence diagram. In the sentence "Peacocks strut," the word *Peacocks* is the subject. The verb is *strut*. Let's add an adverb that tells how the peacocks strut. Read the new sentence and look at its diagram.

Workbook: Peacocks strut proudly.

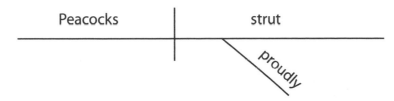

Instructor: *Proudly* is an adverb that tells how the peacocks strut. You write an adverb on a slanted line under the verb it describes.

Instructor: Now find **Exercise 7** in your workbook. Read the first sentence and look at its diagram.

Workbook: Bakers awake.

Bakers | awake

Instructor: In this sentence, the word *Bakers* is the subject. The word *awake* is the verb. Let's add an adverb that tells when Bakers awake. Read the new sentence and look at its diagram.

Workbook: Bakers awake early.

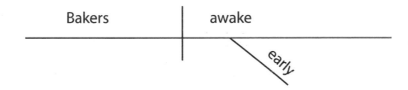

Instructor: *Early* is an adverb that tells when bakers awake. You write an adverb on a slanted line under the verb it describes.

Instructor: Now in **Exercise 8** you will diagram sentences with adverbs in them. You read the sentence, and I will ask you questions to help you fill in the diagram. For Sentence 1, fill in the frame. For Sentence 2, trace the dotted frame before you fill it in. For Sentences 3 and 4, draw your own frames in the spaces provided. Remember to copy the words exactly as they appear in the sentence. If the word begins with a capital letter in the sentence, it should also be capitalized in the diagram.

Use the following dialogue to help the student fill in the diagrams.

1. *Find the verb. Write the verb to the right of your center line.*

2. Find the subject. Ask "who" or "what" before the verb. [Prompt the student with a specific question like "Who flipped?" or "What works?"] Write the subject to the left of the center line on your frame.

3. Now you have found the two most basic parts of the sentence. Go back and look again at the verb. Is there a word that describes the verb? This is an adverb that tells how or when. Write the adverb on the slanted line below the verb it describes.

Answer Key: 1. Shannon Miller flipped flawlessly.

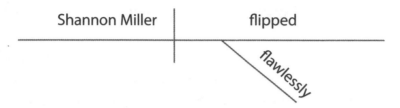

2. Ants work diligently.

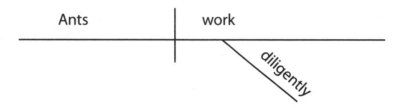

3. He arrived promptly.

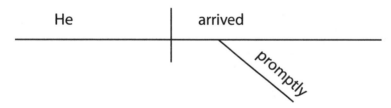

4. Fall begins today.

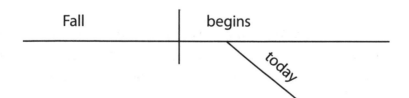

LESSON 18

New: Adverbs That Tell Where and How Often

Read "Ozymandias" (Lesson 16) three times to the student. Then ask the student to try to say parts of the poem along with you (or the tape recorder).

Instructor: An adverb is a word that describes a verb, an adjective, or another adverb. Adverbs tell how, when, where, how often, and to what extent. I will say that to you again. An adverb is a word that describes a verb, an adjective, or another adverb. Adverbs tell how, when, where, how often, and to what extent. Now I will say that three more times. Say it with me.

TOGETHER (three times): An adverb is a word that describes a verb, an adjective, or another adverb. Adverbs tell how, when, where, how often, and to what extent.

Instructor: Adverbs tell where. Where do you shop? In **Exercise 1** of your workbook, read each of the sentences to me. The adverb that tells where is in bold print.

Workbook: I shop **nearby**.

I shop **downtown**.

I shop **anywhere**.

I shop **indoors**.

I shop **there**.

Instructor: We are going to practice identifying adverbs that tell where. Look at **Exercise 2**. I will ask you a "where" question and you will read the three choices. Choose your favorite adverb and answer the question in a complete sentence. Then write your adverb of choice in the blank.

Instructor: Where do you dig?

Workbook: underground

nowhere

upstream

Student: *I dig [adverb of choice].*

Instructor: *[Adverb of choice]* is an adverb that tells where you dig.

Instructor: Where do you whistle?

If the student asks, the following words are not used as nouns in this sentence because they describe the verb *whistle*. They answer the question "whistle where?" The words would be nouns if they acted as a subject: "Outside is my favorite place."

Workbook: inside

outside

everywhere

Student: *I whistle [adverb of choice].*

Instructor: *[Adverb of choice]* is an adverb that tells where you whistle.

Instructor: Adverbs tell how often. How often do you make plans ahead of time? In **Exercise 3** of your workbook, read each of the sentences to me. The adverb that tells how often is in bold print.

Workbook: I plan **daily**.

I plan **monthly**.

I plan **rarely**.

I plan **yearly**.

Instructor: We are going to practice identifying adverbs that tell how often. Look at **Exercise 4**. I will ask you a "how often" question and you will read the three choices. Choose your favorite adverb and answer the question in a complete sentence. Then write your adverb of choice in the blank.

Instructor: How often do you shiver?

Workbook: sometimes

frequently

often

Student: *I shiver [adverb of choice].*

Instructor: *[Adverb of choice]* is an adverb that tells how often you shiver.

Instructor: How often do you mumble?

Workbook: habitually

rarely

occasionally

Student: *I mumble [adverb of choice].*

Instructor: *[Adverb of choice]* is an adverb that tells how often you mumble.

Instructor: In **Exercise 5**, read the first sentence and look at its diagram.

Workbook: Sacagawea journeyed.

Sacagawea	journeyed

Sacagawea is the Native American woman who traveled with Lewis and Clark as a guide and translator. With her help, Lewis and Clark were able to explore much of the newly purchased Louisiana Territory.

Instructor: In the sentence "Sacagawea journeyed," *Sacagawea* is the subject. The word *journeyed* is the verb. Let's add an adverb that tells where Sacagawea journeyed. Read the new sentence and look at its diagram.

Workbook: Sacagawea journeyed westward.

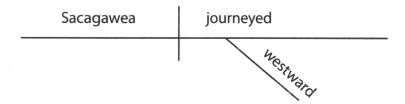

Instructor: *Westward* is an adverb that tells where Sacagawea journeyed. You write an adverb on a slanted line under the verb it describes. Read the next simple sentence and look at its diagram.

Workbook: Bison graze.

Bison	graze

Instructor: The word *Bison* is the subject. The word *graze* is the verb. Let's add an adverb that tells how often bison graze. Read the new sentence and look at its diagram.

Workbook: Bison graze daily.

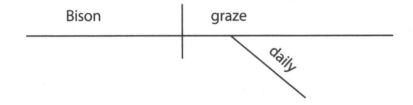

Instructor: *Daily* is an adverb that tells how often. You write an adverb on a slanted line under the verb it describes.

Instructor: The adverbs you have practiced so far have come after the verb in the sentence. Sometimes adverbs come before the verb, but they are diagrammed in the same way. In **Exercise 6**, read each of the sentences to me. Each sentence contains an adverb that tells how often. In these sentences, the adverbs come before the verbs.

Workbook: I **always** breathe.

She **never** teases.

Joey **seldom** rushes.

Instructor: In **Exercise 7** you will diagram sentences with adverbs in them. You read the sentence, and I will ask you questions to help you fill in the diagram. For Sentence 1, fill in the frame. For Sentence 2, trace the dotted frame before you fill it in. For Sentences 3 and 4, draw your own frames in the spaces provided. Remember to copy the words exactly as they appear in the sentence. If the word begins with a capital letter in the sentence, it should also be capitalized in the diagram.

Use the following dialogue to help the student fill in the diagrams.

1.   *Find the verb. Write the verb to the right of your center line.*

2.   *Find the subject. Ask "who" or "what" before the verb. [Prompt the student with a specific question like "What drives?" or "Who travels?"] Write the subject to the left of the center line on your frame.*

3.   *Now you have found the two most basic parts of the sentence. Go back and look again at the verb. Is there a word that describes the verb? This is an adverb that tells where or how often. Write the adverb on the slanted line below the verb it describes.*

Answer Key: 1.   Racers drive forward.

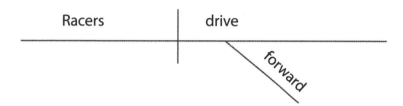

2.   Jamal often travels.

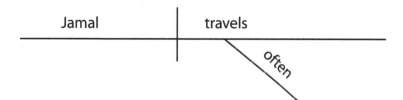

3.   Stella rarely frowns.

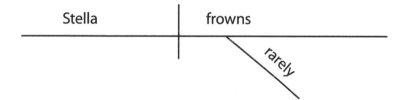

4.   Myra reads nightly.

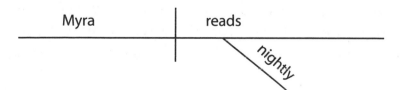

LESSON 19

New: Adverbs That Tell to What Extent

Read "Ozymandias" (Lesson 16) three times to the student. Then ask the student to try to say parts of the poem along with you (or the tape recorder).

Instructor: An adverb is a word that describes a verb, an adjective, or another adverb. Say that with me two times.

TOGETHER (two times): An adverb is a word that describes a verb, an adjective, or another adverb.

Instructor: Up until this point, we have focused on adverbs that describe verbs. These adverbs tell how, when, where, and how often. In this lesson, you will see how adverbs can also describe adjectives and other adverbs, too. They don't tell how, when, where, or how often. They tell you something else called "to what extent."

Instructor: Let's say this three times together: Adverbs tell how, when, where, how often, and to what extent.

TOGETHER (three times): Adverbs tell how, when, where, how often, and to what extent.

Instructor: Look at **Exercise 1**. Let's do a quick review. You read the first sentence, and I will ask you a question to help you find the adverb in that sentence.

Workbook: I sigh wearily.

Instructor: How do you sigh?
Student: *Wearily*

Instructor: *Wearily* is an adverb that tells how you sigh. Read the next sentence.

Workbook: I sigh again.

Instructor: When do you sigh?
Student: *Again*

Instructor: *Again* is an adverb that tells when you sigh. Read the third sentence.

86

Workbook: I sigh anywhere.

Instructor: Where do you sigh?
Student: *Anywhere*

Instructor: *Anywhere* is an adverb that tells where you sigh. Read the fourth sentence.

Workbook: I sigh frequently.

Instructor: How often do you sigh?
Student: *Frequently*

Instructor: *Frequently* is an adverb that tells how often you sigh.

Instructor: Remember, up until this lesson, we have focused on adverbs that describe verbs. These adverbs tell how, when, where, and how often. But adverbs can describe more than just verbs: they can describe adjectives and other adverbs, too. These new adverbs don't tell how, when, where, or how often. They tell you something called "to what extent." Although there are many adverbs like these, we are going to focus on eight extremely common adverbs. In fact, I just used one of those adverbs: *extremely*! Read aloud the list of adverbs in **Exercise 2**.

Workbook: too

very

really

quite

so

extremely

rather

slightly

Instructor: These adverbs can describe adjectives, like the adjective *timid*. Read the list in **Exercise 3** to see what I mean.

Workbook: **too** timid

very timid

really timid

> **quite** timid
>
> **so** timid
>
> **extremely** timid
>
> **rather** timid
>
> **slightly** timid

Instructor: All these adverbs tell "to what extent" a person is timid. She is timid. To what extent is she timid? She is *too* timid. Or she is *very* timid, or *really* timid, or *quite* timid, or *so* timid, or *extremely* timid, or only *rather* timid or *slightly* timid. Read the sentence in **Exercise 4**.

Workbook: Extremely chubby bulldogs drool.

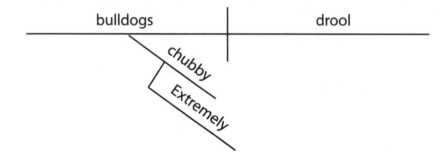

Instructor: What is the action verb?
Student: *Drool*

Instructor: What is the subject? What drools?
Student: *Bulldogs*

Instructor: This sentence has an adjective that describes the subject *bulldogs*. What is the adjective? What kind of bulldogs?
Student: *Chubby*

Instructor: What is the adverb that describes the adjective *chubby*? To what extent are the bulldogs chubby?
Student: *Extremely*

Instructor: Look at the diagram of the sentence "Extremely chubby bulldogs drool."

Instructor: I will point out words on the diagram as I explain. *Bulldogs* is the subject. *Drool* is the action verb. What kind of bulldogs? Chubby bulldogs. The adjective *chubby* describes the subject. There is a word in this sentence that describes the adjective *chubby*. The adverb *Extremely* tells us to what extent the bulldogs are chubby. Because *Extremely* describes *chubby*, it is written on the slanted line beneath the adjective.

Instructor: In **Exercise 5** you will diagram sentences with adverbs that describe adjectives. You read the sentence, and I will ask you questions to help you fill in the diagram. For Sentence 1, fill in the frame. For Sentence 2, trace the dotted frame before you fill it in. For Sentences 3 and 4, draw your own frames in the spaces provided. Remember to copy the words exactly as they appear in the sentence. If the word begins with a capital letter in the sentence, it should also be capitalized in the diagram.

Use this dialogue to help the student fill in the diagrams.

1. *Find the verb. Write the verb to the right of your center line.*

2. *Find the subject. Ask "who" or "what" before the verb. [Prompt the student with a specific question like "What gathered?" or "What flashed?"] Write the subject to the left of the center line on your frame.*

3. *Now you have found the two most basic parts of the sentence. Go back and look again at the simple subject. Are there any words that describe the subject that come before the verb? These adjectives can tell what kind, which one, how many, or whose. Also look for the articles* (a, an, the), *because they act like adjectives. Write each adjective on a slanted line below the subject it describes.*

4. *Look again at the adjective. Is there an adverb such as* too, very, really, quite, so, extremely, rather, *or* slightly? *These adverbs tell to what extent. Write the adverb on the slanted line beneath the adjective it describes.*

Answer Key: 1. Rather dark clouds gathered.

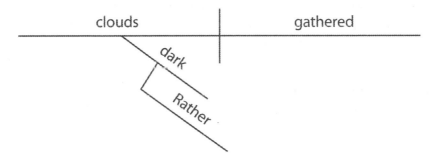

2. Really bright lightning flashed.

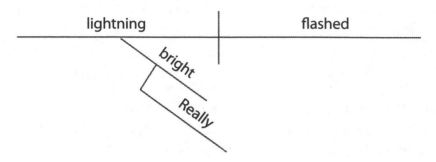

3. Very strong winds howled.

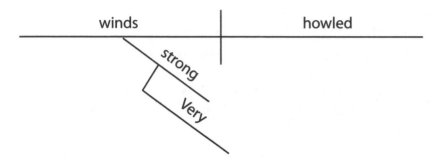

4. Too many hailstones fell.

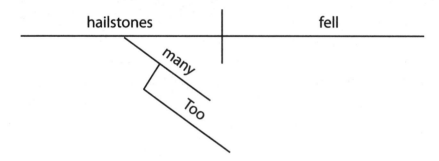

Instructor: In **Exercise 6** read the list of adverbs again.

Workbook: too

very

really

quite

so

extremely

rather

slightly

Instructor: You have seen that these adverbs can describe adjectives. They can also describe other adverbs, like the adverb *slowly*. Read the list in **Exercise 7** to see what I mean.

Workbook: **too** slowly

very slowly

really slowly

quite slowly

so slowly

extremely slowly

rather slowly

slightly slowly

Instructor: All of these adverbs tell to what extent. He drives slowly. To what extent does he drive slowly? He drives *too* slowly. Or he drives *very* slowly, or *really* slowly, or *quite* slowly, or *so* slowly, or *extremely* slowly, or only *rather* slowly or *slightly* slowly. Now read the sentence in **Exercise 8**. This sentence has two adverbs. One adverb describes a verb; the other adverb describes another adverb.

Workbook: We travel rather often.

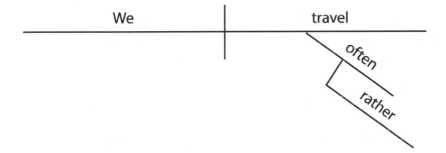

Instructor: What is the verb?
Student: *Travel*

Instructor: Find the subject. Who travels?
Student: *We*

Instructor: There is an adverb that tells how often. How often do we travel?
Student: *Often*

Instructor: Now there is another adverb that describes the adverb *often*. To what extent do we travel often?
Student: *Rather*

Instructor: Look at the diagram of the sentence "We travel rather often."

Instructor: I will point out words on the diagram as I explain. *We* is the subject. *Travel* is the verb. How often do we travel? Often. *Often* is an adverb that tells how often we travel, so it is written on a slanted line beneath the verb. There is a word in this sentence that describes the adverb *often*. The adverb *rather* tells us to what extent we travel often. Because *rather* describes *often*, *rather* is written on the slanted line beneath the adverb *often*.

Instructor: In **Exercise 9** you will diagram sentences with adverbs that describe other adverbs. You read each sentence, and I will ask you questions to help you fill in the diagram. For Sentence 1, fill in the frame. For Sentence 2, trace the dotted frame before you fill it in. For Sentences 3 and 4, draw your own frames in the spaces provided.

Use this dialogue to help the student fill in the diagrams.

1. *What is the verb? Write the verb to the right of your center line.*

2. *Find the subject. Ask "who" or "what" before the verb. [Prompt the student with a specific question like "What looms?" or "What climbs?"] Write the subject to the left of the center line on your frame.*

3. *Now you have found the two most basic parts of the sentence. Go back and look again at the verb. Is there a word that describes the verb? This is an adverb that could tell how, when, where, or how often. Write the adverb on the slanted line below the verb it describes.*

4. *Look again at the adverb. Is there another adverb in the sentence, such as* too, very, really, quite, so, extremely, rather *or* slightly *that describes the first adverb? These adverbs tell to what extent. Write one of these adverbs (*too, very, really, quite, so, extremely, rather, *or* slightly*) on the slanted line beneath the adverb it describes.*

Answer Key: 1.   Mountains loom very high.

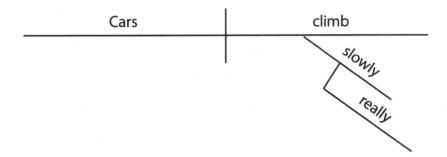

2.   Cars climb really slowly.

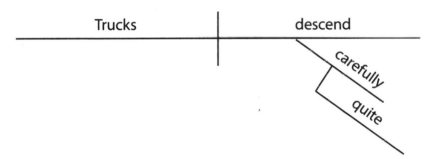

3.   Trucks descend quite carefully.

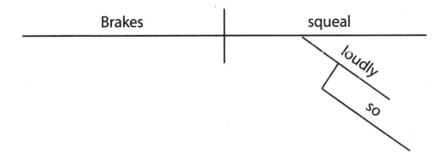

4.   Brakes squeal so loudly.

LESSON 20

Review: Adjectives
Review: Adverbs

Read "Ozymandias" (Lesson 16) three times to the student. Then ask the student to try to say parts of the poem along with you (or the tape recorder).

Whenever the student is able to recite the entire poem without difficulty, you can eliminate these practice readings.

Instructor: Let's review the definition of an adjective. An adjective is a word that describes a noun or pronoun. Say that with me once.

TOGETHER: An adjective is a word that describes a noun or pronoun.

Instructor: Adjectives tell what kind, which one, how many, and whose. Say that with me once.

TOGETHER: Adjectives tell what kind, which one, how many, and whose.

Instructor: Adjectives tell what kind. In **Exercise 1** of your workbook, read the first sentence.

Workbook: Curious meerkats burrow.

Instructor: What is the adjective in the sentence? What kind of meerkats burrow?
Student: *Curious*

Instructor: Adjectives tell which one. Read the next sentence.

Workbook: That meerkat listens.

Instructor: What is the adjective in the sentence? Which one of the meerkats listens?
Student: *That*

Instructor: Adjectives tell how many. Read the next sentence.

Workbook: Five meerkats forage.

Instructor: What is the adjective in the sentence? How many meerkats forage?

Student: *Five*

Instructor: Adjectives can tell whose. Read the next sentence.

Workbook: Meerkats' tunnels connect.

Instructor: What is the adjective in this sentence? Whose tunnels connect?

Student: *Meerkats'*

Instructor: Do you remember the three special, little words called articles? Articles act like adjectives—they describe nouns. What are these three articles?

Student: *A, an, the*

If the student cannot remember the articles, repeat the poem from Lesson 14.

Instructor: In your workbook, read the sentences in **Exercise 2** and circle the articles.

Answer Key: (A) meerkat eats beetles, spiders, and scorpions.

(The) sentinel meerkat alerts (the) others when it sees (an) approaching predator.

Instructor: Let's review the definition of an adverb. An adverb is a word that describes a verb, an adjective, or another adverb. Adverbs tell how, when, where, how often, and to what extent. I will say that to you again. An adverb is a word that describes a verb, an adjective, or another adverb. Adverbs tell how, when, where, how often, and to what extent. Now I will say that three more times. Say it with me.

TOGETHER (three times): An adverb is a word that describes a verb, an adjective, or another adverb. Adverbs tell how, when, where, how often, and to what extent.

Instructor: Adverbs tell how. In **Exercises 3**, **4**, **5**, and **6** in your workbook, I will ask you a "how," "when," "where," or "how often" question and you will read the four choices. Choose your favorite adverb and answer the question in a complete sentence. Then write your adverb of choice in the blank.

Instructor: How do you shower?

Workbook: fast

          slowly

          energetically

          carefully

Student: *I shower [adverb of choice].*

Instructor: *[Adverb of choice]* is an adverb that tells how you shower. Adverbs tell when. Look at **Exercise 4**. When do you rush?

Workbook: tonight

          now

          early

          immediately

Student: *I rush [adverb of choice].*

Instructor: *[Adverb of choice]* is an adverb that tells when you rush. Adverbs tell where. Look at **Exercise 5**. Where do you search for missing items?

Workbook: everywhere

          outside

          inside

          here

Student: *I search [adverb of choice].*

Instructor: *[Adverb of choice]* is an adverb that tells where you search. Adverbs tell how often. Look at **Exercise 6**. How often do you snatch things away from somebody else?

Workbook: sometimes

          rarely

          often

          infrequently

Student: *I snatch [adverb of choice].*

Instructor: *[Adverb of choice]* is an adverb that tells how often you snatch. Adverbs also tell to what extent. These adverbs can describe adjectives or other adverbs. We learned eight of these adverbs: *too, very, really, quite, so, extremely, rather,* and *slightly*. Circle these adverbs in the sentences in **Exercise 7**.

Answer Key: (Very) hungry jackals prowl.

(Extremely) tricky animals escape.

They sing (rather) sweetly.

(Really) brave airmen parachute.

Paige practices (so) carefully.

(Slightly) nervous actors fumble.

You snore (too) loudly.

I sleep (quite) soundly.

Instructor: Let's diagram a sentence with adjectives and adverbs in it. Read the sentence in **Exercise 8** of your workbook. I will ask you questions to help you fill in the frame beneath the sentence

Workbook: Very graceful dancers twirl around.

Instructor: What is the action verb in the sentence?
Student: *Twirl*

Instructor: Write *twirl* to the right of the center line on your diagram. Now find the subject. Who twirls?
Student: *Dancers*

Instructor: *Dancers* is the subject. Write *dancers* to the left of the center line on your diagram. You have now found the two most basic parts of the sentence. Look again at the subject *dancers*. Is there an adjective that describes dancers? What kind of dancers twirl?
Student: *Graceful*

Instructor: *Graceful* is an adjective that tells what kind of dancers. Write *graceful* on the slanted line directly below the subject. Look at the sentence, specifically the adjective *graceful*. Is there an adverb such as *too, very, really, quite, so, extremely, rather,* or *slightly*? These adverbs tell to what extent.
Student: *Very*

Instructor: *Very* is an adverb that tells to what extent the dancers were graceful. Write the adverb *Very* on the slanted line beneath *graceful*, the adjective it describes. Capitalize *Very* because the word is capitalized in the sentence.

Instructor: Now look again at the verb in the sentence. Is there an adverb that describes the verb *twirl*? This is an adverb that could tell how, when, where, or how often. Where do the dancers twirl?

Student: *Around*

Instructor: Write the adverb *around* on the slanted line beneath the verb *twirl*.

Answer Key:

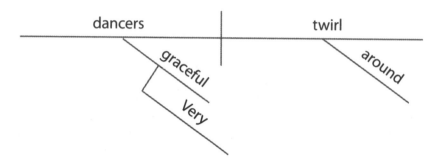

Instructor: In **Exercise 9** you will diagram two sentences with adjectives and adverbs in them. You read each sentence, and I will ask you questions as you fill in each diagram. For Sentence 1, trace the dotted frame before you fill it in. For Sentence 2, draw your own frame in the space provided. Remember to copy the words exactly as they appear in the sentence. If the word begins with a capital letter in the sentence, it should also be capitalized in the diagram.

Use the following dialogue to help the student fill in the diagram.

1. *Find the verb. Write the verb to the right of your center line.*

2. *Find the subject. Ask "who" or "what" before the verb. [Prompt the student with a specific question like "What scampers?" or "Who bathes?"] Write the subject to the left of the center line on your frame.*

3. *Now you have found the two most basic parts of the sentence. Go back and look again at the subject. Are there any words that describe the subject? These adjectives can tell what kind, which one, how many, or whose. Also look for the articles (a, an, the), because they act like adjectives. Write each adjective on a slanted line below the subject it describes.*

4. *Look at the adjective. Is there an adverb such as* too, very, really, quite, so, extremely, rather, or slightly? *These adverbs tell to what extent. Write the adverb on the slanted line beneath the adjective it describes.*

5. *Go back and look again at the verb. Is there a word that describes the verb? This is an adverb that could tell how, when, where, or how often. Write the adverb on the slanted line below the verb it describes.*

Answer Key: 1.   Rather inquisitive squirrels scamper eagerly.

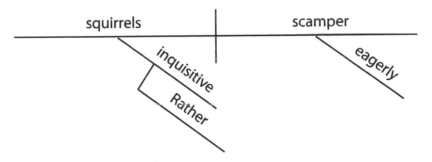

2.   Slightly dirty children bathe daily.

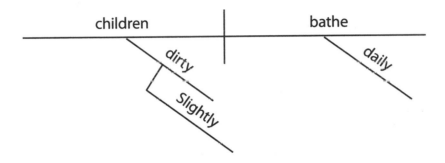

Instructor: Let's diagram another sentence together. Read the sentence in **Exercise 10** of your workbook. I will ask you questions to help you fill in the frame beneath the sentence.

Workbook: Hibernating woodchucks sleep so deeply.

Instructor: What is the action verb in the sentence?
Student: *Sleep*

Instructor: Write *sleep* to the right of the center line on your diagram. Now find the subject. What sleeps?
Student: *Woodchucks*

Instructor: *Woodchucks* is the subject. Write *woodchucks* to the left of the center line on your diagram. You have now found the two most basic parts of the sentence. Look again at the subject *woodchucks*. Is there an adjective that describes woodchucks? What kind of woodchucks sleep?
Student: *Hibernating*

Instructor: *Hibernating* is an adjective that tells what kind of woodchucks. Write *Hibernating* on the slanted line directly below the subject. Capitalize *Hibernating* because the word is capitalized in the sentence.

Instructor: Look at the verb *sleep* again. Is there an adverb that describes the verb *sleep*? This is an adverb that could tell how, when, where, or how often. How do the woodchucks sleep?

Student: *Deeply*

Instructor: *Deeply* is an adverb that tells how. Write the adverb *deeply* on the slanted line directly beneath the verb *sleep*. Look again at the adverb *deeply* in the sentence. Is there another adverb such as *too, very, really, quite, so, extremely, rather,* or *slightly* that describes the verb? These adverbs tell to what extent.

Student: *So*

Instructor: *So* is an adverb that tells to what extent the woodchucks sleep deeply. Write the adverb *so* on the slanted line beneath *deeply*, the adverb it describes.

Answer Key: Hibernating woodchucks sleep so deeply.

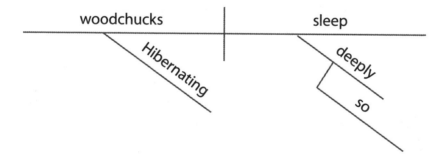

Instructor: In **Exercise 11** you will diagram two sentences with adjectives and adverbs in them. You read each sentence, and I will ask you questions as you fill in each diagram. For Sentence 1, trace the dotted frame before you fill it in. For Sentence 2, draw your own frame in the space provided. Remember to copy the words exactly as they appear in the sentence. If the word begins with a capital letter in the sentence, it should also be capitalized in the diagram.

Use the following dialogue to help the student fill in the diagram.

1. *Find the verb. Write the verb to the right of your center line.*

2. *Find the subject. Ask "who" or "what" before the verb. [Prompt the student with a specific question like "What growls?" or "What shines?"] Write the subject to the left of the center line on your frame.*

3. *Now you have found the two most basic parts of the sentence. Go back and look again at the subject. Are there any words that describe the subject? These adjectives can tell what kind, which one, how many, or whose. Also look for the articles (a, an, the), because they act like adjectives. Write each adjective on a slanted line below the subject it describes.*

4. *Go back and look again at the verb. Is there a word that describes the verb? This is an adverb that could tell how, when, where, or how often. Write the adverb on the slanted line below the verb it describes.*

5. *Look at the adverb. Is there an adverb such as* too, very, really, quite, so, extremely, rather, *or* slightly *that describes the first adverb? These adverbs tell to what extent. Write the adverb on the slanted line beneath the adverb it describes.*

Answer Key: 1. Gigantic bears growl quite hungrily.

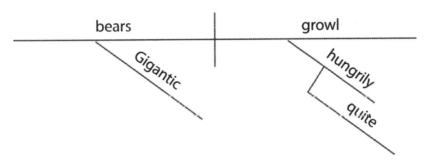

2. Brilliant stars shine extremely brightly.

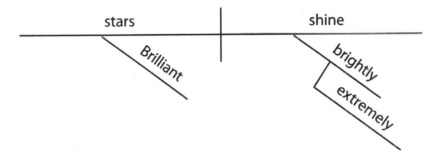

LESSON 21

Review: Nouns, Pronouns, Verbs, Adjectives, and Adverbs

You will need two index cards for this lesson.

Read "Ozymandias" (Lesson 16) three times to the student. Then ask the student to try to say parts of the poem along with you (or the tape recorder).

Be sure to adapt the lesson to your student's attention span. Many students will need two or more days to complete a lesson of this length.

Instructor: A noun is the name of a person, place, thing, or idea. Say that definition with me.

TOGETHER: A noun is the name of a person, place, thing, or idea.

Instructor: There are two types of nouns: common and proper. A common noun is a name common to many persons, places, or things. The words *airplane*, *river*, and *game* are all common nouns. A proper noun is a special, "proper" name for a person, place, or thing. *Alaska Airlines*, *Yellow River*, and *Sorry* are all proper nouns. Proper nouns always begin with a capital letter.

Write "common noun" on one index card and "proper noun" on the other (or have the student do this). Alternately, you can skip the cards entirely and have the student stand for a proper noun and squat low for a common noun, or the student can just tell you if the noun is common or proper. The capitalized nouns that follow are proper nouns; the others are common nouns.

Instructor: I am going to read you some nouns. If the noun is a common noun, hold up the "common noun" card. If the noun is a proper noun, hold up the "proper noun" card.

Instructor: Arctic Ocean
tiger
Texas
city
country

mechanic
President Harry Truman
Alabama
park
rose
Grand Canyon National Park
ship

Instructor: Nouns can be either singular or plural. The word *book* is a singular noun because you have only one, single book. The word *books* is a plural noun because you have two or more books. In **Exercise 1** of your workbook, read aloud each rule and then in the blank write the plural form that follows this rule.

This is the last time the formation of plurals will be reviewed in this book. Forming plurals should be covered in more depth in your spelling program.

Answer Key: Rule: Usually add s to form the plural.

Singular Noun	Plural Noun
car	cars

Rule: Add **es** to nouns ending in **s**, **sh**, **ch**, **x**, or **z**.

Singular Noun	Plural Noun
beach	beaches

Rule: If a noun ends in **y** after a consonant, change the **y** to **i** and add **es**.

Singular Noun	Plural Noun
berry	berries

Rule: If a noun ends in **y** after a vowel, just add **s**.

Singular Noun	Plural Noun
key	keys

Rule: Usually, add **s** to a noun to form the plural of words that end in **f** or **fe**.

Singular Noun	Plural Noun
cuff	cuffs

Rule: Some words that end in **f** or **fe** form their plurals differently. You must change the **f** or **fe** to **v** and add **es**.

Singular Noun	Plural Noun
loaf	loaves

Rule: If a noun ends in **o** after a vowel, just add **s**.

Singular Noun	Plural Noun
stereo	stereos

Rule: If a noun ends in **o** after a consonant, you form the plural by adding **es**.

Singular Noun	Plural Noun
tomato	tomatoes

Rule: Irregular plurals don't form their plurals the regular ways.

Singular Noun	Plural Noun
deer	deer

Instructor: Let's review the capitalization rules we have learned so far. They are printed in **Exercise 2** of your workbook. I will say each rule, and you will repeat it after me.

Workbook:
1. Capitalize the proper names of persons, places, things, and animals.

2. Capitalize holidays.

3. Capitalize the names of deities.

4. Capitalize the days of the week and the months of the year, but not the seasons.

5. Capitalize the first, last, and other important words in titles of books, magazines, newspapers, stories, poems, and songs.

6. Capitalize the word *I*.

7. Capitalize the first word in every line of traditional poetry.

8. Capitalize the first word of every sentence.

Instructor: Now let's read the list of rules together twice.

Instructor: In **Exercise 3** of your workbook you will see a paragraph about Abraham Lincoln. None of the words are capitalized, but some should be. Mark each incorrect lowercase letter by drawing a triple line beneath it and writing caps in the margin. You may look at the capitalization rules if you have any questions.

Answer Key: abraham lincoln was born on february 12, 1809, in kentucky. he is honored (caps)

on presidents' day. his picture is on the penny. "in god we trust" is the (caps)

motto printed on this coin. the lincoln memorial is in washington, d. c. (caps)

i am going to see it on thursday. i read all about lincoln in the *smithsonian* (caps)

magazine. (caps)

Instructor: Now look at **Exercise 4** in your workbook. You already know the definition of a pronoun. A pronoun is a word used in the place of a noun. Say that with me.

TOGETHER: A pronoun is a word used in the place of a noun.

Instructor: Now we are going to practice the list of personal pronouns. Read them together with me.

TOGETHER: I, me, my, mine

You, your, yours

He, she, him, her, it

His, hers, its

We, us, our, ours

They, them, their, theirs

If the student already knows the list of pronouns, have him say them alone from memory once. If he needs to review, say the list with him three times.

The following oral exercise helps the student understand the relationship between a noun and the pronoun that replaces it.

Instructor: Look at **Exercise 5** in your workbook. Each sentence contains a pronoun. After you read each sentence, substitute a noun or a noun and a pronoun for which the underlined pronoun could stand.

Workbook: Storms frighten <u>him</u>.
Student: *Storms frighten [any boy's name, the boy].*

Workbook: <u>We</u> watched thunderstorms brewing in the distance.

Student: *[Any person] and [student's name or I] watched thunderstorms brewing in the distance.*

Workbook: <u>They</u> rumble and flash in a scary way.

Student: *[Thunderstorms] rumble and flash in a scary way.*

Workbook: Would <u>you</u> be frightened of thunderstorms?

Student: *Would [Instructor's name] be frightened of thunderstorms?*

Instructor: In addition to personal pronouns, you also learned demonstrative pronouns: *this, that, these,* and *those.* These pronouns demonstrate, or point out, something. Look at **Exercise 6** in your workbook. Read the first sentence.

Workbook: <u>This</u> tastes like raspberries.

Instructor: Now let's think of a noun for which the underlined pronoun could stand. What could taste like raspberries? Choose one: the popsicle, the lollipop, or the bubble gum.

Student: *[The popsicle, The lollipop, or The bubblegum.]*

Instructor: The pronoun *This* stands for the noun *[popsicle, lollipop,* or *bubblegum].* The *[popsicle, lollipop, bubblegum]* tastes like raspberries. *This* tastes like raspberries. Now read the rest of the sentences in **Exercise 6**. After you read each sentence, substitute a noun for which the underlined pronoun could stand.

Workbook: <u>That</u> is huge!

Student: *[The skyscraper, The shark, The watermelon, etc.] is huge!*

Workbook: <u>These</u> are noisy.

Student: *[The monkeys, The children, The parakeets, etc.] are noisy.*

Workbook: <u>Those</u> are covered with dust.

Student: *[The books, The tables, The maps, etc.] are covered with dust.*

Instructor: Let's review what you know about pronouns. A pronoun is a word that takes the place of a noun. There is a special name for the noun that is replaced. It is called the antecedent (pronounced "an-tuh-SEE-dent"). *Ante* is a Latin prefix that means "before." *Cedent* comes from a Latin word meaning "to go." So *antecedent* literally means "to go before." Usually, the antecedent noun **goes before** its pronoun. Read the sentence in **Exercise 7**. The pronoun is in dark print. The antecedent is circled. An arrow starts at the pronoun and points back to its antecedent. Remember, the antecedent is the noun the pronoun replaces.

Workbook:

antecedent

Before the (volcano) erupted, **it** released hot gases into the air.

Instructor: If a pronoun replaces more than one person, place, thing, or idea, it can have more than one antecedent noun. Read the sentence in **Exercise 8**.

Workbook: antecedent antecedent

(Randy) and (I) both like puzzles, so **we** worked together to complete a puzzle that had five hundred pieces.

Instructor: Read each sentence in **Exercise 9**. The pronoun is in bold. Find the antecedent and circle it. Then draw an arrow from the pronoun to its antecedent, the noun the pronoun replaces.

Answer Key:

A soldier (termite) defends **its** nest by biting enemies with **its** strong jaws.

(Termites) may look like white ants, but **they** are not really ants at all.

(Termites) may look small and harmless, but **these** are destructive pests that can devour your house from the inside out.

Instructor: Now let's practice the definition of a verb. A verb is a word that does an action, shows a state of being, links two words together, or helps another verb. Say this with me three times.

Together (three times): A verb is a word that does an action, shows a state of being, links two words together, or helps another verb.

Instructor: In **Exercise 10** read each **action verb.** After you read the verb, I want you to do the action and then use the word in a sentence. For example, if you read the action verb *wiggle,* you would wiggle all around and say "I wiggle."

Workbook: stretch

tiptoe

whisper

sing

hide

spin

chuckle

relax

Instructor: Now let's review what you know about adjectives. An adjective is a word that describes a noun or pronoun. Adjectives tell what kind, which one, how many, and whose. Say that with me.

Together: An adjective is a word that describes a noun or pronoun. Adjectives tell what kind, which one, how many, and whose.

Instructor: Look at **Exercise 11** in your workbook. I am going to read you some adjectives that tell **what kind**. I want you to use each adjective I say to describe any noun you wish. For example, if I say "slimy," you might say "slimy toad."

Workbook: strong

noisy

dark

delicate

weak

dry

Instructor: Look at **Exercise 12** in your workbook. I am going to read you some adjectives that tell **which one**. I want you to use each adjective I say to describe any noun you wish. For example, if I say "that," you might say "that aircraft carrier."

Workbook: this

that

these

those

third

next

last

Instructor: Look at **Exercise 13** in your workbook. I am going to read you some adjectives that tell **how many**. I want you to use each adjective I say to describe any noun you wish. For example, if I say "seventeen," you might say "seventeen wasps."

Workbook: ninety-nine

forty-two

three

each

several

more

some

Instructor: Look at **Exercise 14** in your workbook. I am going to read you some adjectives that tell **whose**. I want you to use each adjective I say to describe any noun you wish. For example, if I say "Greg's," you might say "Greg's marshmallow." Follow along with your eyes as I read. The adjective that tells whose is in bold print.

Answer Key:	Possible Answers
the **sun's**	the sun's rays
the **fisherman's**	the fisherman's boat
the **gardener's**	the gardener's hoe
all the **games'**	all the games' pieces
some **cities'**	some cities' traffic
the **deer's**	the deer's antlers
the **mice's**	the mice's holes

Instructor: Now let's talk about adverbs. An adverb is a word that describes a verb, an adjective, or another adverb. Adverbs can tell how, when, where, how often, and to what extent. Say that with me.

TOGETHER: An adverb is a word that describes a verb, an adjective, or another adverb. Adverbs can tell how, when, where, how often, and to what extent.

Instructor: Read the sentence at the beginning of **Exercise 15** in your workbook.

Workbook: I laugh quietly.

Instructor: *Laugh* is the action I am doing—it is the verb in the sentence. *Quietly* is an adverb that tells how I laugh. Read each column of adverbs in **Exercise 15** of your workbook. Begin by reading the title of the column, for example, "How: wildly, quickly," etc.

Workbook:

How	When	Where	How Often
wildly	tonight	outdoors	hourly
quickly	today	here	daily
loudly	now	there	nightly
happily	again	underwater	occasionally
gleefully	immediately	everywhere	sporadically
nervously	afterward	anywhere	often
silently	suddenly	inside	regularly

Instructor: Now read the sentences below the columns. Choose two adverbs from each column to tell how, when, where, and how often I laugh.

Answer Key: **How** do I laugh?   Possible Answers

       I laugh _____ .   gleefully

       I laugh _____ .   silently

When do I laugh?

       I laugh _____ .   immediately

       I laugh _____ .   tonight

Where do I laugh?

    I laugh _____ .   underwater

    I laugh _____ .   here

How often do I laugh?

    I laugh _____ .   occasionally

    I laugh _____ .   daily

Instructor: Adverbs tell how, when, where, and how often. Adverbs also tell to what extent. These adverbs can describe adjectives or other adverbs. We learned eight of these adverbs: *too, very, really, quite, so, extremely, rather,* and *slightly.* Circle these adverbs in the sentences in **Exercise 16**.

Answer Key: (Very) clever squirrels steal birdseed.

(Extremely) smart squirrels bury nuts in flower beds.

These squirrels hide food (so) carefully.

(Really) fat squirrels store lots of food.

Pesky squirrels enter houses (quite) sneakily.

When the exterminator arrives, these squirrels exit (rather) quickly.

(Slightly) aggravated homeowners are relieved.

LESSON 22

Summary Exercise: *Mark Twain*

Read "Ozymandias (Lesson 16) three times to the student. Then ask the student to try to say parts of the poem along with you (or the tape recorder).

Instructor: Today I am going to read a selection aloud to you from a biography. Do you remember what a biography is? (Give the student time to tell you if he knows.) A biography is the true written history of a person's life. I will read you a short portion of a biography of Mark Twain. Samuel Clemens was his **real** name. Mark Twain was his **pen name**. A pen name is a name a person uses when he writes for publication. The selection is about the time in Samuel Clemens's life when he and his brother Orion decided to go west.

I will read the selection only once. (If the student is a fluent reader, you may choose to have him read it aloud or silently.) Then I want you to tell me in your own words what you remember.

This excerpt is from the book *Mark Twain and the Queens of the Mississippi* by Cheryl Harness.

Mark Twain

As he rode the westbound stage, Sam was delighted to see "the swift phantom of the desert": a Pony Express rider pounding away with the U. S. mail and news of the war back East. Orion began his government job and Sam took up silver mining and news reporting in the Nevada Territory. Sam had a way of telling more than just the facts, though, which led to his writing funny stories such as "The Celebrated Jumping Frog of Calaveras County" for newspapers in San Francisco, Sacramento, and Virginia City in the Nevada Territory.

The most famous humorist of the day had a pen name: Artemus Ward. So Sam tried out a few for himself: "Josh," "Rambler," and "Thomas Jefferson Snodgrass." On February 2, 1863, Sam signed a story "Mark Twain," a river term meaning two fathoms (twelve feet) deep. The name stuck.

For guidance in teaching summary exercises, see Lesson 12.

LESSON 23

New: Helping Verbs
New: Present, Past, and Future Tense

Read "Ozymandias" (Lesson 16) three times to the student. Then ask the student to try to say the whole poem with you (or the tape recorder). The student should practice saying the whole poem to himself in a mirror.

Instructor: A verb is a part of speech that can do several different things in a sentence. Let's practice the definition of a verb. A verb is a word that does an action, shows a state of being, links two words together, or helps another verb. Say this with me three times.

TOGETHER (three times): A verb is a word that does an action, shows a state of being, links two words together, or helps another verb.

Instructor: You already know about verbs that do actions. In **Exercise 1** of your workbook there is a list of verbs. I want you to read each verb, do the action, and then use the verb in a sentence. For example, if you read the action verb *giggle*, you would giggle as you say the sentence "I giggle."

Workbook: nod

frown

exhale

sit

growl

plod

dance

sway

Instructor: A verb is a word that does an action, shows a state of being, links two words together, or helps another verb. You already know about action verbs, and you will learn about verbs that show state of being and link two words together

113

in a later lesson. In this lesson we are going to talk about the last part of that definition: a verb can help another verb. Listen to this sentence: The pandas were munching bamboo. The pandas were doing something active. What were they doing? Answer me in a complete sentence starting with "They were …"

Student: *They were munching bamboo.*

Instructor: But if I just said "They munching bamboo," that wouldn't sound right! *Munching* needs **another** verb to help it. The verb *were* is helping the verb *munching*. Working together, the verbs make sense in the sentence. The verb *were* is called a helping verb because it helps the main verb, *munching*. In order to recognize a helping verb, you need to know all of them. Read the list in **Exercise 2** of your workbook one time. Then we will practice chanting them together without your looking at them.

After the student has read through the list in his workbook, say the helping verbs chant and demonstrate the claps. If the student remembers the chant from the previous levels and can say the helping verbs by himself, move onto **Exercise 3**.

Instructor: Am [clap]
Is [clap]
Are, was, were. [clap]
Be [clap]
Being [clap]
Been. [clap] [clap]

Instructor: Listen as I say the rest of the helping verbs in a chant.
Have, has, had [clap]
Do, does, did [clap]
Shall, will, should, would, may, might, must [clap, clap]
Can, could!

Instructor: Now let's say the entire chant together three times. Clap along with me.

TOGETHER (three times):
Am [clap]
Is [clap]
Are, was, were. [clap]
Be [clap]
Being [clap]
Been. [clap] [clap]
Have, has, had [clap]
Do, does, did [clap]

Shall, will, should, would, may, might, must [clap, clap]
Can, could!

If the student did not memorize the list of helping verbs in the previous levels of *First Language Lessons* (or if he can't remember the helping verbs), practice the chant with him daily until he learns it.

Instructor: Read the sentence in **Exercise 3** and look at its diagram.

Workbook: I am writing.

I	am writing

Instructor: Do you see that two words are on the verb line? The helping verb *am* helps the action verb *writing* to make this sentence sound right. "I writing" sounds funny, doesn't it? You need the helping verb for the sentence to make sense. Since the two verbs work together, they are both written on the verb line.

Instructor: In **Exercise 4** you will diagram four sentences with helping verbs and action verbs. Remember, these verbs work together so they are **both** written on the verb line. You read the sentence, and I will ask you questions as you fill in the diagram. For Sentence 1, fill in the frame. For Sentence 2, trace the dotted frame before you fill it in. For Sentences 3 and 4, draw your own frames in the spaces provided. Remember to copy the words exactly as they appear in the sentence. If the words begin with a capital letter in the sentence, they should also be capitalized in the diagram.

Use the following dialogue to help the student fill in each diagram.

1. *Find the verb. There are two verbs in this sentence. What is the helping verb? Look in* **Exercise 2** *of your workbook if you need help remembering the list of helping verbs. What is the action verb? You write both these verbs on your verb line.*

2. *Find the subject. Ask "who" or "what" before the verb. [Prompt the student with a specific question like "What were crawling?" or "What are digging?"] Write the subject to the left of the center line on your frame.*

Answer Key: 1. Spiders were crawling.

Spiders	were crawling

2. Ants are digging.

Ants	are digging

3. Birds can fly.

Birds	can fly

4. Frogs may hibernate.

Frogs	may hibernate

Instructor: Earlier in this book you learned the word *conjugate* (Lesson 10). To conjugate means to learn the various forms of a verb. When you are conjugating, you always start with the basic verb. Some examples are "to play," "to sing," "to run," and "to walk." The word *to* plus the basic form of a verb is called the *infinitive*. Read the words and definitions in **Exercise 5** of your workbook.

Workbook: **conjugate**   To learn the various forms of the verb

infinitive   *to* plus the basic form of the verb (example: "to work")

Instructor: The basic form of the verb changes slightly depending on the person (I, you, he, or they) who is doing the action. Read the sentences in **Exercise 6**. The verbs are underlined.

Workbook: I <u>work</u>.

You <u>work</u>.

He <u>works</u>.

Instructor: Did you notice that the verb changed slightly in the last sentence? Listen carefully as I slowly say, "The form of the verb changes slightly depending on the person who does the verb." There are three kinds of persons: first person, second person, and third person. In Lesson 10, the following story helped us learn which person was which. Imagine that you walk into an empty room. You say, "**I** am the **first person** in the room." *(Tell student to point to himself.)* Then your friend walks into the room. You say to your friend, "**I** am the **first person**

in the room. **You** are the **second person** in the room." *(Tell student to point to an imaginary person in front of him.)* Then a third person walks into the room. He is a stranger. You whisper to your friend, "**I** am the **first person** in the room. **You** are the **second person** in the room. **He** is the **third person** in the room." *(Tell the student to point to an imaginary person at his side.)* Look at the chart in **Exercise 7** of your workbook.

Workbook:	Singular
First person	**I**
Second person	**you**
Third person	**he, she, it**

Instructor: Do you remember our story about the people in the room? Each person enters the room individually. One, single person entered the room at a time. *I, you,* and *he* are called singular persons because each is one, single person. But suppose more than one, single person enters the room at one time. Imagine that your **whole family as a group** enters the room first. All of you say together, "**We** are the **first persons** in the room." Then a neighboring family enters the room. Your family says, "**We** are the **first persons** in the room. **You** are the **second persons** in the room." Then a family you have never met enters the room. Your family says to the neighbors, "**We** are the **first persons** in the room. **You** are the **second persons** in the room. **They** are the **third persons** in the room." Each family has more than one person in it. These are plural persons because there is more than one person in each group. Look at the chart in **Exercise 8** of your workbook.

Workbook:	Singular	Plural
First person	**I**	**we**
Second person	**you**	**you**
Third person	**he, she, it**	**they**

Instructor: Now let's conjugate the verb "to work." When we conjugate, we learn the various forms of a verb, and how a verb changes slightly depending on the person doing the action. Find the chart in **Exercise 9** of your workbook. You **work** at the present moment. Let's look at the verb *work*. Read the chart with me.

Read each line across and include the title of each as you read. For example, "First person singular: I work, First person plural: we work, Second person singular: you work," etc.

Workbook:

	Singular	Plural
First person	**I work**	**we work**
Second person	**you work**	**you work**
Third person	**he, she, it works**	**they work**

Instructor: Now trace the box where the form of the verb *work* changed slightly.

Instructor: Put your finger on the box you just traced. When we conjugate the verb "to work," it changes form in the third person singular (he, she, it). Now let's chant the words in bold—the conjugation of the verb "to work" in both singular and plural forms. I will say it once alone, as you follow along in **Exercise 9**. Then we'll chant it together three times.

Instructor alone, then **TOGETHER** three times:

I work

you work

he, she, it works

we work

you work

they work

Instructor: A verb can show present time, past time, or future time. In grammar, we call the time a verb is showing its *tense*. *Tense* means "time." In the sentence "Today you work," the verb tense, or time, is present. You are working today, right now, in the present. We just conjugated the present tense of the verb "to work." I work today. You work today. He, she, it works today. We work today. You work today. They work today.

Instructor: A verb can also show past time, or past tense. Listen to this sentence: "Yesterday you worked." The verb tense, or time, is past. You worked yesterday, in the past. Now let's conjugate the past tense of the verb "to work." Look at the chart in **Exercise 10**. We'll chant the words in bold three times.

Chant the words in bold, first the singular form. Then chant the plural form.

Workbook:

	Singular	Plural
First person	**I worked**	**we worked**
Second person	**you worked**	**you worked**
Third person	**he, she, it worked**	**they worked**

Instructor: A verb can also show future time, or future tense. Listen to this sentence: "I will work tomorrow." The verb tense, or time, is future. You will work tomorrow, in the future. To show future time, the main verb *work* needs a helping verb. Helping verbs help main verbs by showing tense. In order for a verb to be in the future tense, it needs the helping verb *shall* or *will* in front of it. Now let's conjugate the future tense of the verb "to work." Look at the first chart in **Exercise 11**. We will say the singular forms first and then the plural forms. We'll say these three times.

	Singular	Plural
First person	**I will work**	**we will work**
Second person	**you will work**	**you will work**
Third person	**he, she, it will work**	**they will work**

Instructor: We just conjugated the future tense of "to work." We added the helping verb *will* to the main verb *work* to show the tense. We could have added the verb *shall* instead of *will*—*shall* also tells us the verb is in the future tense. Let's chant the second chart in **Exercise 11**, saying the singular forms first. We will say this chart only once.

	Singular	Plural
First person	**I shall work**	**we shall work**
Second person	**you shall work**	**you shall work**
Third person	**he, she, it shall work**	**they shall work**

Instructor: Read the sentences in **Exercise 12**. Underline the verb and the helping verb, if there is one. Then tell whether the verb is present tense, past tense, or future tense.

Answer Key:

I <u>took</u> the last cookie from the cookie jar.	Past tense
I <u>tutor</u> my little sister in spelling.	Present tense
Dominic <u>selects</u> five books in the library.	Present tense
I <u>shall panic</u> during an earthquake.	Future tense
The mailman <u>delivered</u> Grandma's letter to me.	Past tense
Adrian <u>will scour</u> the burned kettle.	Future tense
The cat <u>chased</u> the moth around the porch.	Past tense
The cockroaches <u>scattered</u> in the light.	Past tense
Daddy <u>tickles</u> the baby's toes.	Present tense
The magician <u>will vanish</u> at the end of his trick.	Future tense
They <u>wave</u> at the marching band in the parade.	Present tense
The dolphin <u>will propel</u> his body out of the water.	Future tense

LESSON 24

New: Direct Objects
New: Subject and Object Pronouns
Review: Helping Verbs

Read "Ozymandias" (Lesson 16) three times to the student. Then ask the student to say the poem along with you or the tape recorder. If the student is ready, he should recite the poem to real people today. If he is not, continue practicing daily until he is ready.

Instructor: A verb is a part of speech that can do several different things in a sentence. Let's practice the definition of a verb. A verb is a word that does an action, shows a state of being, links two words together, or helps another verb. Say this with me.

TOGETHER: A verb is a word that does an action, shows a state of being, links two words together, or helps another verb.

Instructor: You already know that action verbs are verbs you can do or act out, like *clap*, *dance*, and *write*. In the last lesson you learned about verbs that can help other verbs. Let's review these. Listen to this sentence: Huskies were pulling the sled. What were they doing? Answer me in a complete sentence starting with "They were …"

Student: *They were pulling the sled.*

Instructor: But if I just said "They pulling the sled," that wouldn't sound right! *Pulling* needs **another** verb to help it. The verb *were* is helping the verb *pulling*. Working together, the verbs make sense in the sentence. The verb *were* is called a helping verb because it helps the main verb, *pulling*. In order to recognize a helping verb, you need to know all of them. Read the list in **Exercise 1** of your workbook one time. Then we will practice chanting them together without your looking at them.

If the student remembers the chant from the previous levels and can say the helping verbs by himself, move on to **Exercise 2**.

TOGETHER (three times): Am [clap]
Is [clap]
Are, was, were. [clap]

        Be [clap]
        Being [clap]
        Been. [clap] [clap]
        Have, has, had [clap]
        Do, does, did [clap]
        Shall, will, should, would, may, might, must [clap, clap]
        Can, could!

Instructor: Read the sentence in **Exercise 2** and look at its diagram.

Workbook: You are sprinting.

You	are sprinting

Instructor: Do you see that two words are on the verb line? The helping verb *are* helps the action verb *sprinting* to make this sentence sound right. "You sprinting" sounds funny, doesn't it? You need the helping verb *are* for the sentence to make sense. Since the two verbs work together, they are both written on the verb line.

Instructor: Let's review the definition of a sentence. A sentence is a group of words that expresses a complete thought. All sentences begin with a capital letter and end with a punctuation mark. Say that with me three times.

TOGETHER (three times): A sentence is a group of words that expresses a complete thought. All sentences begin with a capital letter and end with a punctuation mark.

Instructor: Read the sentence in **Exercise 3** of your workbook.

Workbook: Annie Sullivan taught.

Instructor: Every sentence has a verb and a subject. What is the action verb in the sentence?
Student: *Taught*

Instructor: *Taught* is the verb. Now let's find the subject. Who taught?
Student: *Annie Sullivan*

Instructor: *Annie Sullivan* taught. Remember, *taught* is the action verb. Sometimes there is a noun that follows the verb that receives the action of the verb. I will show you what I mean. Read the sentence in **Exercise 4** of your workbook.

Workbook: Annie Sullivan taught Helen Keller.

Instructor: *Annie Sullivan* is the subject. *Taught* is the verb. Whom did Annie Sullivan teach? Helen Keller. *Helen Keller* receives the action of the verb. The proper noun *Helen Keller* is called the direct object. To find the direct object, ask "whom" or "what" after the verb. Now you will try to find the direct object in a sentence. Direct objects receive the action of the verb. You will read each sentence in **Exercise 5**, and I will ask you a question that will help you find the direct object.

Workbook: Louis Armstrong played the trumpet.

Instructor: Played what? Answer me with one word.
Student: *Trumpet*

Instructor: *Trumpet* is the direct object. It receives the action of the verb *played*. Read the next sentence.

Workbook: Earle Dickson invented Band-Aids.

Instructor: Invented what?
Student: *Band-Aids*

Instructor: *Band-Aids* is the direct object. It receives the action of the verb *invented*. Read the next sentence.

Workbook: Edward Lear wrote poems.

Instructor: Wrote what?
Student: *Poems*

Instructor: *Poems* is the direct object. It receives the action of the verb *wrote*. Read the next sentence.

Workbook: We are visiting Grandmother.

Instructor: Are visiting whom?
Student: *Grandmother*

Instructor: *Grandmother* is the direct object. It receives the action of the verbs *are visiting*. In **Exercise 6**, read the sentence and look at its diagram.

Workbook: Scott boiled eggs.

Scott	boiled	eggs

Instructor: Boiled what? Eggs. The direct object *eggs* is written next to the verb. It is divided from the verb by a short line that does not go through the main horizontal line. Now you will diagram four sentences with direct objects in **Exercise 7** of your workbook. You read each sentence, and I will ask you questions as you fill in the diagram. For Sentence 1, fill in the frame. For Sentence 2, trace the dotted frame before you fill it in. For Sentences 3 and 4, draw your own frames in the spaces provided. Remember to copy the words exactly as they appear in the sentence. If the words begin with a capital letter in the sentence, they should also be capitalized in the diagram.

Use the following dialogue to help the student fill in each diagram.

1.   *Find the verb. Write the verb to the right of your center line.*

2.   *Find the subject. Ask "who" or "what" before the verb. [Prompt the student with a specific question like "What digs?" or "What eats?"] Write the subject to the left of the center line on your frame.*

3.   *Is there a direct object that receives the action of the verb? I will ask you a question that will help you find the direct object.*

     Sentence 1: Dig what?

     Sentence 2: Eat what?

     Sentence 3: Washed what?

     Sentence 4: Helped whom?

     Write the direct object to the right of the verb on your diagram. The direct object is separated from the verb by a short, straight line.

Answer Key: 1.   Puppies dig holes.

Puppies	dig	holes

2. Robins eat worms.

Robins	eat	worms

3. Tanya washed clothes.

Tanya	washed	clothes

4. We helped Jake.

We	helped	Jake

Instructor: Now we are going to review the list of personal pronouns. They are printed in **Exercise 8** of your workbook. Glance at the list, and then say them with me from memory.

TOGETHER: I, me, my, mine
You, your, yours
He, she, him, her, it
His, hers, its
We, us, our, ours
They, them, their, theirs

Instructor: Some of these pronouns are called subject pronouns, because they are the pronouns that are used as subjects of sentences. Read the list of subject pronouns in **Exercise 9** of your workbook. Then read the sentences that have subject pronouns as their subjects.

Workbook: Subject Pronouns

I

he

she

we

they

I startled the deer.

She grabbed the apple.

He dunked the doughnut.

We delivered presents.

They dodged the ball.

Instructor: There are other pronouns that are called object pronouns, because they are the pronouns used as objects in sentences. Remember a direct object receives the action of the verb. Read the list of object pronouns in **Exercise 10** of your workbook. Then read the sentences that have object pronouns as their direct objects.

Workbook: <u>Object Pronouns</u>

me

him

her

us

them

Mom measured **me**.

Alex helped **her**.

Estella observed **him**.

Uncle greeted **us**.

Auntie hugged **them**.

Instructor: Look at **Exercise 11** in your workbook. There are five sentences; each sentence has two pronouns in it. I want you to circle each pronoun and write "S" over it if it is a subject pronoun used as the subject of the sentence. If the pronoun is an object pronoun, used as the direct object in the sentence, write "O" over it.

Workbook:

Subject Pronouns (Write **S**)	Object Pronouns (Write **O**)
I	me
he	him
she	her
we	us
they	them

Answer Key:

S   O
(I) caught (him.)

S   O
(She) fed (us.)

S   O
(They) fought (them.)

S   O
(He) answered (me.)

S   O
(We) saved (her.)

LESSON 25

New: Indirect Objects
Review: Direct Objects
Review: Subject and Object Pronouns

Review "Afternoon on a Hill" (Lesson 8) and "Ozymandias" (Lesson 16) today. If the student has trouble remembering the poems, have him practice them daily until he is confident.

This lesson introduces indirect objects. Many grammar programs do not cover indirect objects in fourth grade, but it seems logical to us to introduce direct and indirect objects at the same time. However, indirect objects are trickier to find than direct objects. We do not expect mastery of this concept at this level. Understanding will come with practice.

Instructor: Let's review the definition of a sentence. A sentence is a group of words that expresses a complete thought. All sentences begin with a capital letter and end with a punctuation mark. Say that with me.

Together: A sentence is a group of words that expresses a complete thought. All sentences begin with a capital letter and end with a punctuation mark.

Instructor: Read the sentence in **Exercise 1** of your workbook.

Workbook: Pythons swallow lizards.

Instructor: Every sentence has a verb and a subject. What is the action verb in the sentence?
Student: *Swallow*

Instructor: *Swallow* is the verb. Now let's find the subject. What swallows?
Student: *Pythons*

Instructor: Pythons swallow. Remember, *swallow* is the action verb. Sometimes there is a noun or pronoun that follows the verb that receives the action of the verb. This noun or pronoun is called the direct object. To find the direct object, ask "whom" or "what" after the verb. Pythons swallow lizards. Swallow what?
Student: *Lizards*

Instructor: *Lizards* is the direct object. It receives the action of the verb *swallow*. Let's find more direct objects in sentences. You will read each sentence in **Exercise 2**, and I will ask you a question that will help you find the direct object.

Workbook: The baker frosted the cake.

Instructor: Frosted what? Answer me with one word.
Student: *Cake*

Instructor: *Cake* is the direct object. It receives the action of the verb *frosted*. Read the next sentence.

Workbook: The explorers had discovered it.

Instructor: Had discovered what?
Student: *It*

Instructor: *It* is the direct object. It receives the action of the verbs *had discovered*. In **Exercise 3**, read the sentence and look at its diagram.

Workbook: Jessica cooked dinner.

Jessica	cooked	dinner

Instructor: Cooked what? Dinner. The direct object *dinner* is written next to the verb. It is divided from the verb by a short line that does not go through the main horizontal line. Let's add a word to the sentence to give us more information. Read the new sentence in **Exercise 4**.

Workbook: Jessica cooked Mother dinner.

Instructor: This sentence still has the same direct object. Cooked what? Dinner. (She certainly didn't cook her mother!) This sentence also has something called an indirect object. An indirect object is a noun or pronoun that is **between** the action verb and the direct object of a sentence. It answers the question "to whom" or "for whom" the action is done, but the words *to* or *for* are usually not in the sentence. *To* or *for* are just understood.

Instructor: Look at the sentence again. Jessica cooked Mother dinner. Cooked dinner for whom? Mother. *Mother* is the indirect object. Read the sentences in **Exercise 5** of your workbook. I will ask you questions to help you identify the direct object and the indirect object in each sentence. Read the first sentence.

Workbook: Advertisers send us catalogs.

Instructor: Let's find the direct object. Send what?
Student: *Catalogs*

Instructor: *Catalogs* is the direct object. Now let's find the indirect object. Send catalogs to whom?
Student: *Us*

Instructor: *Us* is the indirect object. Read the next sentence.

Workbook: The dealer sold Terrence a car.

Instructor: Let's find the direct object. Sold what?
Student: *Car*

Instructor: *Car* is the direct object. (He certainly didn't sell *Terrence*!) Now let's find the indirect object. Sold a car to whom?
Student: *Terrence*

Instructor: *Terrence* is the indirect object. Read the next sentence.

Workbook: The farmer built the cows a barn.

Instructor: Let's find the direct object. Built what?
Student: *Barn*

Instructor: *Barn* is the direct object. (The farmer didn't build the *cows*!) Now let's find the indirect object. Built a barn for whom?
Student: *Cows*

Instructor: *Cows* is the indirect object. Read the next sentence.

Workbook: Wiley painted Bud a picture.

Instructor: Let's find the direct object. Painted what?
Student: *Picture*

Instructor: *Picture* is the direct object. (Wiley didn't paint his friend *Bud*!) Now let's find the indirect object. Painted a picture for whom?

Student: *Bud*

Instructor: *Bud* is the indirect object. Read the sentence in **Exercise 6** and look at its diagram.

Workbook: Sophie baked them lasagna.

Instructor: Let's find the direct object. Baked what? Lasagna. (Sophie didn't bake *them*!) The direct object *lasagna* is written next to the verb. It is divided from the verb by a short line that does not go through the main horizontal line. Let's find the indirect object. Baked lasagna for whom? *Them.* The indirect object *them* is written underneath the verb, on the little horizontal line. When diagramming indirect objects, **nothing is written on the slanted line.**

Instructor: Now you will diagram four sentences with direct objects and indirect objects in **Exercise 7** of your workbook. You read the sentence, and I will ask you questions as you fill in the diagram. For Sentence 1, fill in the frame. For Sentence 2, trace the dotted frame before you fill it in. For Sentences 3 and 4, draw your own frames in the spaces provided. Remember to copy the words exactly as they appear in the sentence. If the words begin with a capital letter in the sentence, they should also be capitalized in the diagram.

Use the following dialogue to help the student fill in each diagram.

1. *Find the verb. Write the verb to the right of your center line.*

2. *Find the subject. Ask "who" or "what" before the verb. [Prompt the student with a specific question like "Who brings?" or "Who writes?"] Write the subject to the left of the center line on your frame.*

3. *Is there a direct object that receives the action of the verb? I will ask you a question that will help you find the direct object.*

   Sentence 1: Brings what?

   Sentence 2: Write what?

   Sentence 3: Gave what?

   Sentence 4: Toss what?

> *Write the direct object to the right of the verb on your diagram. The direct object is separated from the verb by a short, straight line.*

4. *Is there an indirect object between the verb and the direct object? I will ask you a question that will help you find the indirect object.*

> *Sentence 1: Brings soup for whom?*
>
> *Sentence 2: Write letters to whom?*
>
> *Sentence 3: Gave presents to whom?*
>
> *Sentence 4: Toss birdseed to whom?*

Answer Key: 1. Mother brings them soup.

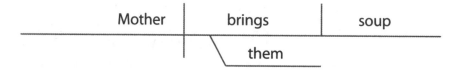

2. I write Marie letters.

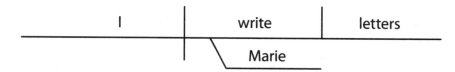

3. Grandma gave me presents.

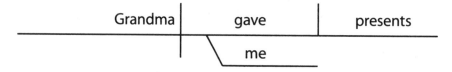

4. Visitors toss pigeons birdseed.

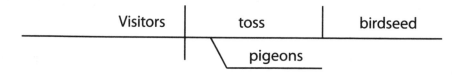

Instructor: In the last lesson you learned the difference between subject pronouns and object pronouns. Subject pronouns are the pronouns that are used as subjects of sentences. Object pronouns are the pronouns used as objects in sentences. Read the lists of subject pronouns and object pronouns in **Exercise 8** of your workbook.

Workbook: | Subject Pronouns | Object Pronouns

Subject Pronouns

I

he

she

we

they

Object Pronouns

me

him

her

us

them

Instructor: Object pronouns are the pronouns used as objects, like direct objects and indirect objects. Look at **Exercise 9** in your workbook. There are five sentences; four of the sentences have two pronouns in them, and the other has only one pronoun. I want you to circle each pronoun and write "S" over it if it is a subject pronoun used as the subject of the sentence. If the pronoun is an object pronoun used as the direct or indirect object in the sentence, write "O" over it.

Answer Key:

S   O
(She) gave (me) a list.

S   O
(I) bought (us) apples.

S   O
(They) sold (him) pears.

S
(He) peeled the pear.

S   O
(We) fed (them) fruit.

LESSON 26

Review: Direct and Indirect Objects
Review: Subjects, Verbs, Adjectives, Adverbs

Review "Afternoon on a Hill" (Lesson 8) and "Ozymandias" (Lesson 16) today. If the student has trouble remembering the poems, have him practice them daily until he is confident.

Instructor: Let's review the definition of a sentence. A sentence is a group of words that expresses a complete thought. All sentences begin with a capital letter and end with a punctuation mark. Say that with me.

Together: A sentence is a group of words that expresses a complete thought. All sentences begin with a capital letter and end with a punctuation mark.

Instructor: Read the sentence in **Exercise 1** of your workbook.

The sentences in **Exercises 1** and **2** are adapted from *A Pocket for Corduroy* by Don Freeman.

Workbook: The manager gave Lisa a bear.

Instructor: Every sentence has a verb and a subject. What is the action verb in the sentence?
Student: *Gave*

Instructor: *Gave* is the verb. Now let's find the subject. Who gave? Answer me with one word.
Student: *Manager*

Instructor: The manager gave. Remember, *gave* is the action verb. Sometimes there is a noun or pronoun that follows the verb that receives the action of the verb. This noun or pronoun is called the direct object. To find the direct object, ask "whom" or "what" after the verb. Gave what? Answer me with one word.
Student: *Bear*

Instructor: *Bear* is the direct object. (The manager didn't give Lisa to somebody!) *Bear* receives the action of the verb *gave*. This sentence also has something called an indirect object. An indirect object is a noun or pronoun that is **between**

the action verb and the direct object of a sentence. It answers the question "to whom" or "for whom" the action is done, but the words *to* or *for* are usually not in the sentence. *To* or *for* are just understood. The manager gave Lisa a bear. Gave a bear to whom?

Student: *Lisa*

Instructor: *Lisa* is the indirect object. Read the sentence in **Exercise 2** and look at its diagram.

Workbook: Lisa sewed the bear a pocket.

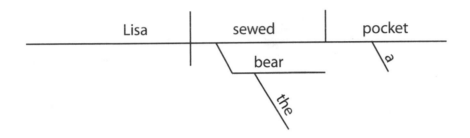

Instructor: *Sewed* is the action verb. Who sewed? Lisa. *Lisa* is the subject. Let's find the direct object. Sewed what? *A pocket*. The direct object *pocket* is written next to the verb. It is divided from the verb by a short line that does not go through the main horizontal line. The direct object *pocket* has an article that acts like an adjective. The article *a* is written in a slanted line below the noun it describes. Let's find the indirect object. Sewed a pocket for whom? *The bear*. The indirect object *bear* is written underneath the verb, on the little horizontal line. When diagramming indirect objects, **nothing is written on the slanted line**. The indirect object *bear* has an article that acts like an adjective. The article *the* is written on a slanted line below the noun it describes.

Instructor: Now we will diagram a little sentence, and we will add words to make it bigger and bigger. Read the first sentence in **Exercise 3** of your workbook.

Workbook: Ships used sails.

Ships | used | sails

Instructor: Find the verb. *Used* is the verb. Now find the subject. What used? *Ships* used. Used what? Sails. *Sails* receives the action of the verb *used*. The noun *sails* is the direct object. Look at the diagram of this sentence.

Instructor: The direct object is written to the right of the verb. The direct object is separated from the verb by a short, straight line. Let's add to this sentence an adjective that describes *Ships*. Read the new sentence and look at its diagram.

Workbook: Early ships used sails.

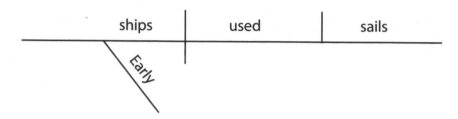

Instructor: The adjective *Early* is written on a slanted line beneath the subject *ships* because *Early* describes *ships*. Adjectives describe nouns. There is another noun besides *ships* in this sentence: *sails*. Let's add an adjective that describes the noun *sails*. This adjective will tell what kind of sails they were. Read the next sentence and look at its diagram.

Workbook: Early ships used huge sails.

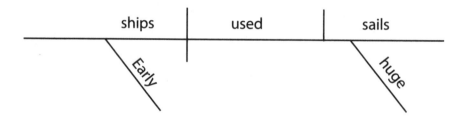

Instructor: The adjective *huge* is written on a slanted line beneath the word it describes, *sails*. Let's add another word to the sentence: an adverb. Remember, adverbs can describe verbs. This adverb comes before the verb. Read the next sentence and look at its diagram.

Workbook: Early ships often used huge sails.

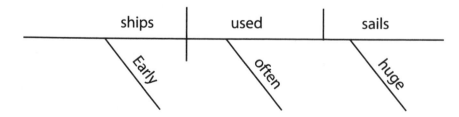

Instructor: How often did early ships use huge sails? Often. The adverb *often* is written on a slanted line below the verb because it describes the verb *used*.

Instructor: Let's add one final word to our sentence. This is an adverb that describes another adverb. Read the last sentence in **Exercise 4** and look at its diagram.

Workbook: Early ships quite often used huge sails.

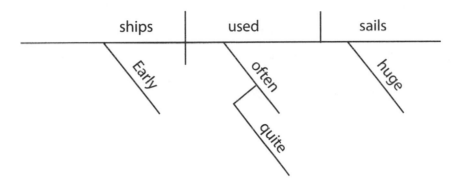

Instructor: Look at the adverb *often*. Is there an adverb that tells to what extent the ships often used sails? *Quite* often. The adverb *quite* is written on the slanted line beneath the adverb it describes.

Instructor: Now in **Exercises 4**, **5**, **6**, and **7** of your workbook, you will diagram four new groups of sentences: one about sailors, one about Robert Fulton, one about tugboats, and one about passenger ships. You read each sentence. As you work through each group of sentences, the parts of the diagram that you have filled in will be already printed on the next diagram. You will only have to add new words as you answer my questions. I will cover the diagrams below where you are working so you don't see the answers.

Group 1 (Exercise 4 in the Student Workbook)

Sailors fought pirates	(Ask questions 1, 2, and 3)
Many sailors fought pirates.	(Ask question 4)
Many sailors fought wicked pirates.	(Ask question 5)
Many sailors bravely fought wicked pirates.	(Ask question 6)
Many sailors very bravely fought wicked pirates.	(Ask question 7)

Group 2 (Exercise 5 in the Student Workbook)

Robert Fulton built ships.	(Ask questions 1, 2, and 3)
Clever Robert Fulton built ships.	(Ask question 4)
Clever Robert Fulton built steam ships.	(Ask question 5)
Clever Robert Fulton built steam ships carefully.	(Ask question 6)
Clever Robert Fulton built steam ships extremely carefully.	(Ask question 7)

Group 3 (Exercise 6 in the Student Workbook)

Tugboats push boats.	(Ask questions 1, 2, and 3)
Powerful tugboats push boats.	(Ask question 4)
Powerful tugboats push large boats.	(Ask question 5)
Powerful tugboats push large boats slowly.	(Ask question 6)
Powerful tugboats push large boats rather slowly.	(Ask question 7)

Group 4 (Exercise 7 in the Student Workbook)

Ships entertain guests.	(Ask questions 1, 2, and 3)
Passenger ships entertain guests.	(Ask question 4)
Passenger ships entertain their guests.	(Ask question 5)
Passenger ships entertain their guests well.	(Ask question 6)
Passenger ships entertain their guests really well.	(Ask question 7)

Use the following dialogue to help the student fill in each diagram. After the student reads a sentence in each sentence group (about sailors or Robert Fulton or tugboats or passenger ships), you will prompt him with the question(s) in italics listed across from that sentence (for example, "Ask questions 1, 2, and 3").

1. *Find the verb. Write the verb to the right of the center line on your frame.*

2. *Find the subject. Ask "who" or "what" before the verb. [Prompt the student with a specific question like "Who fought?" or "Who built?" or "What pushed?" or "What entertains?"] Write the subject to the left of the center line on your frame.*

3. *Is there a direct object that receives the action of the verb? I will ask you a question that will help you find the direct object.*

    Sentence Group 1: Fought whom?

    Sentence Group 2: Built what?

    Sentence Group 3: Push what?

    Sentence Group 4: Entertain whom?

    Write the direct object to the right of the verb on your diagram. The direct object is separated from the verb by a short, straight line.

4. *Go back and look again at the subject. Are there any words that describe the subject? These adjectives can tell what kind, which one, how many, or whose. Also look for the articles (a, an, the), because they act like adjectives. Write each adjective on a slanted line below the subject it describes.*

5. Look again at the direct object. Are there any words that describe the direct object? These adjectives can tell what kind, which one, how many, or whose. Also look for the articles (a, an, the), because they act like adjectives. Write each adjective on a slanted line below the direct object it describes.

6. Look at the verb. Is there a word that describes the verb? This is an adverb that could tell how, when, where, or how often. This adverb can come before or after the verb (or even at the end of the sentence). Write the adverb on the slanted line below the verb it describes.

7. Look at the adverb. Is there an adverb such as too, very, really, quite, so, extremely, rather, or slightly that describes the first adverb? These adverbs tell to what extent. Write the adverb on the slanted line beneath the adverb it describes.

Answer Key for Exercises 4–7:

Many sailors very bravely fought wicked pirates.

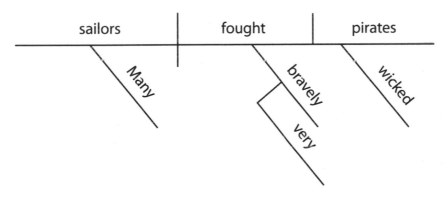

Clever Robert Fulton built steam ships extremely carefully.

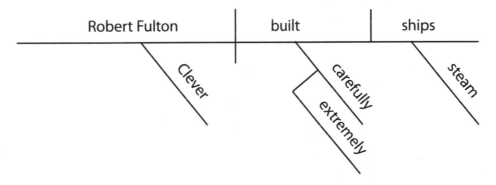

Powerful tugboats push large boats rather slowly.

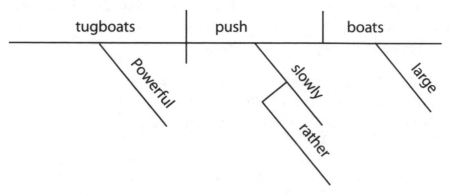

Passenger ships entertain their guests really well.

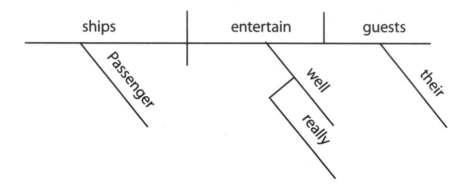

LESSON 27

Poem Memorization: "How Doth…"

Instructor: In **Lesson 27** of your workbook, you will find a poem about a crocodile. Follow along as I read the poem to you.

"How Doth…"
by Lewis Carroll

How doth the little crocodile

Improve his shining tail,

And pour the waters of the Nile

On every golden scale!

How cheerfully he seems to grin,

How neatly spreads his claws,

And welcomes little fishes in

With gently smiling jaws!

Read the poem to the student three times in a row. Repeat this triple reading twice more during the day. Have the student check the boxes in his workbook when this is done.

141

LESSON 28

New: Simple Versus Complete Subjects and Predicates
Review: Subjects, Verbs, Adjectives, Adverbs, and Direct Objects

---

Read "How Doth…" (Lesson 27) three times to the student. Then ask the student to try to say parts of the poem along with you (or the tape recorder).

Instructor: Two lessons ago you diagrammed some long sentences with subjects, verbs, direct objects, adjectives, and adverbs. Read the long sentence in **Exercise 1** of your workbook and look at its diagram.

Workbook: Many people quite often wear various hats.

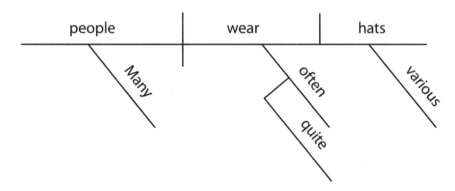

Instructor: Every sentence has a subject and a verb. On a diagram, the subject and the verb are separated by a straight line that runs down the center of the frame.

Point to the line that divides *people* and *wear* on the diagram.

Instructor: To the left of this center line, you will find all the words that tell you more about the subject, *people*. The subject of the sentence is simply the word *people*, so it is called the simple subject. But when you add other words that tell you more about *people* you get a longer, more complete description of the subject. *Many* tells us more about *people*. *Many people* is the complete subject. The simple subject is always written on the subject line (*people*).

> On the diagram in the workbook, point to the horizontal subject line and the simple subject, *people.*

Instructor: The complete subject is the simple subject and all the words that hang off the simple subject (*Many people*). The complete subject includes all the words to the left of the straight line that runs down the center of the frame.

> On the diagram in the workbook, point to the different words in the complete subject. Show the student that all these words are printed to the left of the straight, center line.

Instructor: Now read the sentence in **Exercise 2** of your workbook. Then look at its diagram.

Workbook: Russian farmers so gladly choose fur hats.

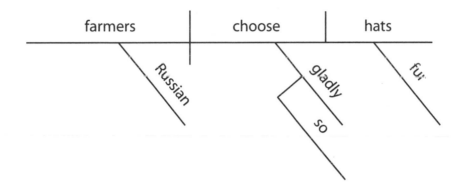

Instructor: On a diagram, the subject and the verb are separated by a straight line that runs down the center of the frame. Look at the word to the left of the center line. What is the simple subject of the sentence? The simple subject is always written on the subject line.

Student: *Farmers*

Instructor: But when you add other words that tell you more about the subject, *farmers*, you get a longer, more complete description of the subject. On a diagram, the complete subject includes all the words to the left of the straight line that runs down the center of the frame. What is the complete subject of the sentence?

Student: *Russian farmers*

Instructor: Look again at the diagram of the sentence about farmers. The words to the right of the center, straight line are the verb and other words that tell us what is said about the subject. The verb in this sentence is simply the word *choose*. But more is said about the farmers than just "farmers choose." We know that they "so gladly choose fur hats." All these words tell us what is said about the subject, *farmers*. These words together are called the complete predicate. The word predicate comes from the Latin word *praedicare* meaning "to proclaim." The predicate of a sentence is what is said or proclaimed about the subject.

Since the "simple predicate" of a sentence is the verb, we are not requiring the student to learn two terms for the same word at this time.

Point to each word or line on the diagram that is printed in bold in the following instructor script.

Instructor: Let's look closely at the words in the complete predicate.

- *Choose* is the verb. The verb is always written on the **verb line**.
- *Gladly* tells us more about the verb *choose*. It is an adverb that tells us how farmers choose.
- *So* tells us more about the adverb *gladly*. It is an adverb that tells us to what extent the farmers choose gladly.
- *Hats* is the direct object. It tells us what the farmers choose.
- *Fur* is an adjective that also belongs in the complete predicate, because it tells us what kind of hats the farmers choose.

The complete predicate is the verb and all the words attached to the verb line (*so gladly choose fur hats*). The complete predicate includes all the words to the right of the straight line that runs down the center of the frame.

Instructor: Read again the sentence in **Exercise 1** and look at its diagram.

Workbook: Many people quite often wear various hats.

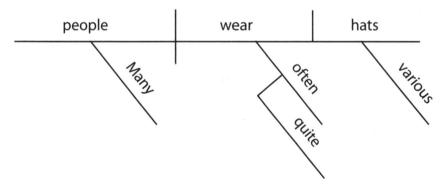

Instructor: What is the verb in the sentence?
Student: *Wear*

Instructor: The complete predicate is the verb and all the words attached to the verb line. It includes all the words to the right of the straight line that runs down the center of the frame. What is the complete predicate of the sentence?

Student: *Quite often wear various hats [It is okay if the student says the words in a different order.]*

Instructor: Now in **Exercises 3**, **4**, and **5**, I will help you diagram three groups of sentences: one about students selecting books, one about parents reading poetry, and one about students writing sentences. You will read each sentence. As you work through each group of sentences, the parts of the diagram that you have filled in will be already printed on the next diagram. You will only have to add new words as you answer my questions. Remember to copy the words exactly as they appear in the sentence. I will cover the filled-in diagrams that are below where you are working so you don't see the answers.

Group 1 (Exercise 3 in the Student Workbook)

Students select books.   (Ask questions 1, 2, and 3)

Students select interesting books.   (Ask question 4)

Many students select interesting books.   (Ask question 5)

Many students select interesting books quickly.   (Ask question 6)

Many students select interesting books really quickly.   (Ask question 7)

Group 2 (Exercise 4 in the Student Workbook)

Parents read poetry.   (Ask questions 1, 2, and 3)

Some parents read poetry.   (Ask question 4)

Some parents read lovely poetry.   (Ask question 5)

Some parents faithfully read lovely poetry.   (Ask question 6)

Some parents very faithfully read lovely poetry.   (Ask question 7)

Group 3 (Exercise 5 in the Student Workbook)

Students write sentences.   (Ask questions 1, 2, and 3)

Neat students write sentences.   (Ask question 4)

Neat students write long sentences.   (Ask question 5)

Neat students write long sentences carefully.   (Ask question 6)

Neat students write long sentences extremely carefully.   (Ask question 7)

Use the following dialogue to help the student fill in each diagram. After the student reads each sentence in the sentence group (about books or poetry or writing sentences), you will prompt him with the question(s) in italics listed across from that sentence (for example, *Ask questions 1, 2, and 3*).

1. *Find the verb. Write the verb to the right of the center line on your frame.*

2. *Find the subject. Ask "who" or "what" before the verb. [Prompt the student with a specific question like "Who selects?" or "Who reads?"] Write the subject to the left of the center line on your frame.*

3. *Is there a direct object that receives the action of the verb? I will ask you a question that will help you find the direct object.*

   Sentence Group 1: Select what?

   Sentence Group 2: Read what?

   Sentence Group 3: Write what?

   Write the direct object to the right of the verb on your diagram. The direct object is separated from the verb by a short, straight line.

4. *Go back and look again at the subject. Are there any words that describe the subject? These adjectives can tell what kind, which one, how many, or whose. Also look for the articles (a, an, the), because they act like adjectives. Write each adjective on the slanted line below the subject it describes.*

5. *Look again at the direct object. Are there any words that describe the direct object? These adjectives can tell what kind, which one, how many, or whose. Also look for the articles (a, an, the), because they act like adjectives. Write each adjective on the slanted line below the direct object it describes.*

6. *Is there a word that describes the verb? This is an adverb that could tell how, when, where, or how often. This adverb can come before or after the verb (or even at the end of the sentence). Write the adverb on the slanted line below the verb it describes.*

7. *Look at the adverb. Is there an adverb such as* too, very, really, quite, so, extremely, rather, or slightly *that describes the first adverb? These adverbs tell to what extent. Write the adverb on the slanted line beneath the adverb it describes.*

Answer Key for Exercises 3–5:

Many students select interesting books really quickly.

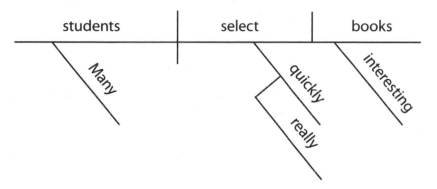

Some parents very faithfully read lovely poetry.

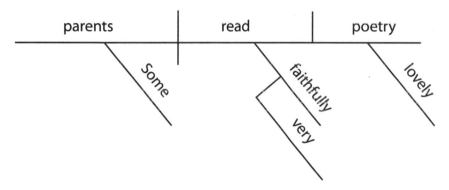

Neat students write long sentences extremely carefully.

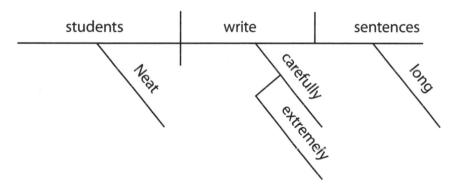

Use the following dialogue to help the student practice identifying the simple subject, complete subject, verb, and complete predicate in the sentences he just diagrammed. You will need to go through the entire dialogue below for each of the three sentences: first for the selecting books sentence, second for the reading poetry sentence, and third for the writing sentences sentence.

Instructor: Look again at the last completed diagram in **Exercise [3, 4, 5]**. [*Instructor reads sentence*]. On a diagram, the subject and the verb are separated by a straight line that runs down the center of the frame. Point to the word on the subject line [*students, parents, students*]. What is the simple subject of the sentence? The simple subject is always written on the subject line.

Student: [*students; parents; students*]

Instructor: But when you add other words that tell you more about the subject [*students; parents; students*], you get a longer, more complete description of the subject. On a diagram, the complete subject includes all the words to the left of the straight line that runs down the center of the frame. What is the complete subject of the sentence?

Student: [*Many students; Some parents; Neat students*]

Instructor: Look again at the same diagram. The words to the right of the center, straight line are in the complete predicate. What is the verb?

Student: [*select; read; write*]

Instructor: The verb tells us what the subject does. The verb answers the question "What does the subject do?" But there are other words that tell us more completely what is said about the subject. All of these words together are called the complete predicate. The complete predicate is written to the right of the straight line that runs down the center of the frame. What is the complete predicate of the sentence?

Student: [*select interesting books really quickly; very faithfully read lovely poetry; write long sentences extremely carefully*]

LESSON 29

New: State of Being Verbs
New: Conjugating the Verb "To Be"
Review: Action and Helping Verbs

Read "How Doth…" (Lesson 27) three times to the student. Then ask the student to try to say parts of the poem along with you (or the tape recorder).

Instructor: You already know the definition of a verb. A verb is a word that does an action, shows a state of being, links two words together, or helps another verb. Say that with me three times.

Together (three times): A verb is a word that does an action, shows a state of being, links two words together, or helps another verb.

Instructor: You have been reading and diagramming sentences that contain action verbs. In your workbook, read the sentences in **Exercise 1** and circle the action verb in each sentence.

Answer Key: 1.   The submarine (surfaced)

2.   Neil (proofread) his sentence.

3.   The water (evaporates)

Instructor: You have also learned about helping verbs. These verbs help other verbs. In order to recognize a helping verb, you need to know all of them. I will say a chant of the helping verbs to you. Then we will say it together two times.

Instructor: Am [clap]
Is [clap]
Are, was, were. [clap]
Be [clap]
Being [clap]
Been. [clap] [clap]
Have, has, had [clap]
Do, does, did [clap]

> Shall, will, should, would, may, might, must [clap, clap]
> Can, could!

Instructor: Now let's say the entire chant together two times.

TOGETHER (two times): [Say chant above.]

Instructor: Read the sentence in **Exercise 2** and look at its diagram. This sentence has a helping verb and an action verb in it.

Workbook: Salt is dissolving.

Salt	is dissolving

Instructor: Do you see that two words are on the verb line? The helping verb *is* helps the action verb *dissolving* to make this sentence sound right. "Salt dissolving" sounds funny, doesn't it? You don't know when the salt is dissolving. Is it dissolving in the present? Was it dissolving in the past? Will it be dissolving in the future? You need a helping verb to show time in order to make the other verb in the sentence sound right. "Salt is dissolving." Since the two verbs work together, they are both written on the verb line of a diagram.

Instructor: In this lesson you are going to learn about another kind of verb: a state of being verb. Some verbs are words that you can do, like the action verbs *scamper*, *scold*, *strike*, and *type*. Some verbs help other verbs make sentences sounds right. But the verbs in some sentences show that you just are! You can do an action verb, but a state of being verb just shows that you exist. Here are the state of being verbs: *am, is, are, was, were, be, being, been.*

Instructor: Now say the state of being verbs with me.

TOGETHER: Am [clap]
Is [clap]
Are, was, were. [clap]
Be [clap]
Being [clap]
Been. [clap] [clap]

Instructor: Does this chant sound familiar? It should. The verbs that show state of being are from the first part of the helping verb chant. The verbs in this list can either help another verb **or** they can stand alone in a sentence to show that someone or something exists. When these verbs come before another verb in the sentence, they are helping verbs. When they are all alone, they are state of being verbs. Look at **Exercise 3** in your workbook. I am going to read you a question and you will read the answer. Each answer you read contains a state of being verb printed in bold.

Workbook: Are you in this room?
I **am**.

Is your brother in the room?
He **is**.

Is your mother with you?
She **is**.

Is your cup on the table?
It **is**.

Who is in the house?
We **are**.

Who is near you?
You **are**.

Who is outside?
They **are**.

Who was in the yard yesterday?
You **were**.

Who else was in the yard?
She **was**.

Instructor: You just read some really short sentences with the state of being verbs *am*, *is*, *are*, *was*, and *were*. *Am*, *is*, *are*, *was*, and *were* are state of being verbs that can just be by themselves in a sentence. But the state of being verbs *be*, *being*, and *been* almost always need another verb to help them. Often, they don't make sense if they stand alone. You would never say "I be." But if you add the helping verb *will*, you get a sentence that makes sense: "I will be." In **Exercise 4**, follow along while I read each question. Then you read each answer. In each answer, the state of being verb is in bold print, but the helping verb is not.

Workbook: Will you be home tonight?
I will **be**.

Will Jody be there, too?
She might **be**.

> Has your family been here before?
> They have **been**.

Instructor: Now go back and read each answer again. Underline the state of being verb in bold print, and then circle the helping verb that helps it.

Answer Key: I (will) **be**.

She (might) **be**.

They (have) **been**.

Instructor: Let's say the state of being verbs together one more time.

TOGETHER: Am [clap]
Is [clap]
Are, was, were. [clap]
Be [clap]
Being [clap]
Been. [clap] [clap]

Instructor: In **Exercise 5** you will diagram three sentences with state of being verbs. These sentences are not long and complicated like the sentences you have been diagramming in the past few lessons. They are simple and short, so you can clearly see how a sentence with a state of being verb is diagrammed. You read the sentence, and I will ask you questions as you fill in the diagram. For Sentence 1, fill in the frame. For Sentence 2, trace the dotted frame before you fill it in. For Sentence 3, draw your own frame in the space provided. Remember to copy the words exactly as they appear in the sentence. If the words begin with a capital letter in the sentence, they should also be capitalized in the diagram.

Use the following dialogue to help the student fill in the diagrams for the sentences in **Exercise 5** of the student's workbook.

1. *What is the state of being verb? This verb tells us that something just exists. Write the verb to the right of your center line.*

2. *Find the subject. Ask "who" or "what" before the verb. [Prompt the student with a specific question like "Who is?" or "Who are?"] Write the subject to the left of the center line on your frame.*

3. *Is there a word that describes the verb? This is an adverb that could tell how, when, where, or how often. This adverb can come before or after the verb (or even at the end of the sentence). Write the adverb on the slanted line below the verb it describes.*

Answer Key: 1. She is here.

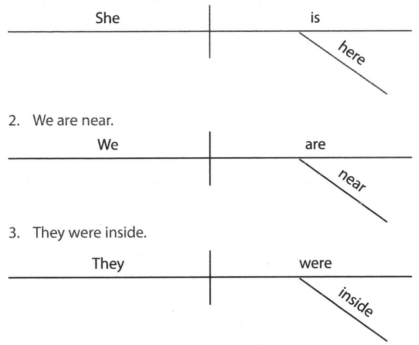

2. We are near.

3. They were inside.

Instructor: Earlier in this book you learned the word *conjugate* (Lessons 10 and 23). To conjugate means to learn the various forms of a verb. When you are conjugating, you always start with the basic verb. Some examples are "to jump," "to listen," "to read," and "to enjoy." The word *to* plus the basic form of a verb is called the *infinitive*.

Instructor: The basic form of the verb changes slightly depending on the person (I, you, he, or they) who is doing the action. There are three kinds of persons: first person, second person, and third person. *I, you,* and *he* are called singular persons because each is one, single person. *We, you,* and *they* are plural persons because there is more than one person in each group. Look at the chart in **Exercise 6** of your workbook.

Workbook:

	Singular	Plural
First person	**I**	**we**
Second person	**you**	**you**
Third person	**he, she, it**	**they**

Instructor: Now let's conjugate the verb "to be." When we conjugate, we learn the various forms of a verb, and how a verb changes slightly depending on the person doing the action. We will conjugate "to be" in the present tense, or time. Read the chart in **Exercise 7** with me.

Read each line across and include the title of each as you read. For example, "First person singular: I am, First person plural: we are, Second person singular: you are," etc. Then read the chart **again**, this time **down the columns** as a chant. Read just the words in bold: "I am, you are, he, she, it is, we are, you are, they are."

Workbook: Infinitive: to be

Present Tense

	Singular	Plural
First person	**I am**	**we are**
Second person	**you are**	**you are**
Third person	**he, she, it is**	**they are**

Instructor: "To be" is considered an irregular verb because the forms of the verb do not follow the regular pattern. If they did, you would conjugate "to be" like this: "I be, you be, he, she, it bees…" That's not right! "To be" is an irregular verb in the present tense. "To be" is also irregular in the past tense. Read the chart in **Exercise 8** with me.

Chant the words in bold, starting with the singular forms and then chanting the plural forms.

Workbook: Infinitive: to be

Past Tense

	Singular	Plural
First person	**I was**	**we were**
Second person	**you were**	**you were**
Third person	**he, she, it was**	**they were**

Instructor: "To be" is considered an irregular verb in the past tense because the forms of the verb do not follow the regular pattern. If they did, you would conjugate "to be" like this: "I beed, you beed, he, she, it beed…" That's not how it goes! "To be" is an irregular verb in the past tense. Read the sentences in **Exercise 9** and write the correct form of the verb "to be" in the blank. Look at the charts in **Exercises 7** and **8** if you need help.

Answer Key: Choose the correct form of "to be" in the **present tense**.

1. It **is** a perfect day for playing baseball.

2. We **are** excited to play against this excellent team.

3. You **are** the pitcher.

4. They **are** in the outfield.

5. He **is** the best shortstop in the league.

6. I **am** the first one to hit a home run!

7. We told the opposing team, "You **are** really good!"

Choose the correct form of "to be" in the **past tense**.

1. They **were** league champions last year.

2. She **was** their coach.

3. We **were** dedicated to playing our best.

4. I **was** ready for the final inning.

5. You **were** faithful in cheering for our victory!

6. The opposing team said, "You **were** a tough team to play!"

Optional Dictation Exercise

Before giving the dictation, tell the student that *cello* is an Italian word. Even though it sounds like it begins with c-h, it is spelled c-e-l-l-o. (Other Italian words in which the **c** is pronounced like c-h are *fettuccine*, the pasta, and *bocce*, the lawn-bowling game.) After the student has written the sentences, have him underline the state of being verbs.

Dictation: The guitar and the banjo <u>are</u> both in the music room.

The violin and the cello <u>are</u> still in their cases.

LESSON 30

New: Linking Verbs
New: Predicate Nominatives
New: Conjugating the Verb "To Do"
Review: Action Verbs, Helping Verbs, and State of Being Verbs

---

Read "How Doth…" (Lesson 27) three times to the student. Then ask the student to try to say the whole poem with you (or the tape recorder). The student should practice saying the whole poem to himself in a mirror.

Instructor: A verb is a word that does an action, shows a state of being, links two words together, or helps another verb. Say that definition with me two times.

TOGETHER (two times): A verb is a word that does an action, shows a state of being, links two words together, or helps another verb.

Instructor: Action verbs show action. In your workbook, read the sentences in **Exercise 1** and circle the action verb in each sentence.

Answer Key: 1. The giant squid (squirts) its ink.

2. The paint (splattered) on her new white dress.

3. The pleasant aroma of buttered popcorn (drifted) down the hall.

Instructor: Verbs that help other verbs are called helping verbs. Let's say the helping verb chant together.

Instructor: Am [clap]
Is [clap]
Are, was, were. [clap]
Be [clap]
Being [clap]
Been. [clap] [clap]
Have, has, had [clap]
Do, does, did [clap]
Shall, will, should, would, may, might, must [clap, clap]
Can, could!

Instructor: In **Exercise 2** read the sentence. This sentence has a helping verb and an action verb in it. Write "H.V." over the helping verb and "A.V." over the action verb in the sentence.

                        H.V. A.V.

Answer Key: An eel might shock you.

Instructor: Now look at the diagram. Do you see that two words are on the verb line? The helping verb *might* helps the action verb *shock* to make this sentence sound right. "An eel shock you" sounds funny, doesn't it? You need the helping verb for the sentence to make sense. Since the two verbs work together, they are both written together on the verb line in the diagram.

Workbook:

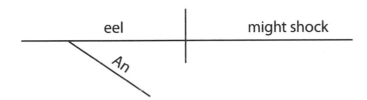

Instructor: In the last lesson you learned about state of being verbs. Let's say the chant of state of being verbs together twice.

TOGETHER (two times):
    Am [clap]
    Is [clap]
    Are, was, were. [clap]
    Be [clap]
    Being [clap]
    Been. [clap] [clap]

Instructor: State of being verbs just show that you exist. In the last lesson we read some questions and answers together. Let's do that again. Look at **Exercise 3** in your workbook and follow along as I read each question. Then you will read the answer. Each answer contains a state of being verb printed in bold.

Workbook: Are you in your room?
I **am**.

Is your sister at home?
She **is**.

Was she at the post office?
She **was**.

Is your birthday package here yet?
It **is**.

Who is in the house now?
You **are**.

Who is here now?
We **are**.

Is your mother in the house too?
She **is**.

Are your friends here?
They **are**.

Who was just in the hall?
You **were**.

Is the big present here?
It **is**.

Are you in suspense?
I **am**!

Instructor: I just used the state of being verbs *am, is, are, was,* and *were*. These verbs can stand alone in a sentence, but the state of being verbs *be, being,* and *been* almost always need another verb to help them. In **Exercise 4**, follow along while I read each question. Then you read each answer. The state of being verb in each answer is in bold print, but the helping verb is not.

Workbook: Will you be at the party?
I will **be**.

Should your older brother be here, too?
He should **be**.

Who has been in the kitchen baking the cake?
She has **been**.

Instructor: Now go back and read each answer again. Underline the state of being verb in bold print, and then circle the helping verb that helps it.

Answer Key: I ⟨will⟩ **be**.

He ⟨should⟩ **be**.

She ⟨has⟩ **been**.

Instructor: There is one type of verb that we haven't talked about yet: a verb that links two words together. These verbs are easy to recognize because they are the same verbs as the state of being verbs: *am, is, are, was, were, be, being, been.* These verbs can do one of several different things in a sentence. Read **Exercise 5** to me.

Workbook: The verbs **am, is, are, was, were, be, being, been** can

- help another verb

- show a state of being

- link two words together

Instructor: Verbs that link two words together are called linking verbs. Do you know how to link hands with someone else? Let's link hands. We are joining hands. Now we are connected together. Do you know what we call the parts of a chain that are joined together? We call the parts of a chain "links." A link is something that connects or joins things. Linking verbs can link or connect words together in a sentence. In **Exercise 6**, read the sentence with a linking verb in it. The linking verb is followed by a noun.

Workbook: Armadillos **are** mammals.

Instructor: *Are* is the linking verb in the sentence. The linking verb *are* links the subject *Armadillos* with a noun that renames the subject (*renames* means "gives the subject another name"). What are armadillos? Armadillos are mammals. In **Exercise 7**, read the sentence to me.

Workbook: I **am** Frances.

Instructor: What is the linking verb in this sentence? *Am* is the linking verb. It connects the subject *I* with a proper noun, *Frances*, that renames the subject. *Frances* tells who the subject is. In this sentence, who is *I*? *Frances*. In **Exercise 8,** read the sentence to me.

Workbook: They **were** dentists.

Instructor: What is the linking verb in this sentence? *Were* is the linking verb. It connects the subject *They* with a noun, *dentists*, that renames the subject. Who were they? They were dentists. *Dentists* is in the complete predicate of the sentence. Remember, the complete predicate includes all the words that tell us what is said about the subject. *Dentists* is a noun. A noun or pronoun in the complete predicate that renames the subject is called a predicate nominative. The word *nominative* may sound strange, but you know a similar word. Have you ever heard the word *nominate*? If you nominate a person for president, you name the person you would like to be president. *Nominate* means "name." So a predicate nominative is a noun or pronoun in the complete predicate that *renames* the subject. Remember, *renames* means "gives the subject another name." In **Exercise 9**, look at a diagram of the sentence "They were dentists."

Workbook:

```
_____They_____|_____were_____dentists_____
                      |
```

Instructor: *Dentists* renames the subject *They*. It is written to the right of the verb on the diagram because it follows the verb in the sentence. Because the noun *dentists* is in the complete predicate of the sentence, it is a predicate nominative. I will say that again: predicate nominative. *Predicate* tells you where the word is in the sentence. *Nominative* tells you that it *renames* the subject.

In order to keep the student's eyes focused on what you are explaining, physically point out the words and lines on the student's diagram as they appear in the Instructor's script.

Instructor: Look again at the diagram of "They were dentists." Do you see the slanted line that separates the linking verb *were* from the predicate nominative? That slanted line points back toward the subject to remind you that *dentists* is a predicate nominative that renames the subject *They*. Imagine that the slanted line is an arrow that points back to the subject. Look at the diagram with the arrow.

Workbook:

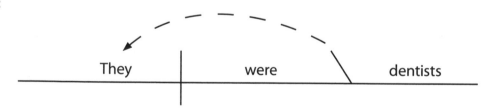

Instructor: The arrow isn't really printed on a normal diagram; you will just see the slanted line. But it is helpful to imagine that an arrow is there. Look at the diagrams in **Exercise 10**. Earlier in the lesson, you read these sentences. In the first diagram, put your pencil on the slanted line next to the predicate nominative *mammals*. Start drawing an arrow that points back to the subject, *Armadillos*. This reminds you that *mammals* is a predicate nominative that renames the subject *Armadillos*.

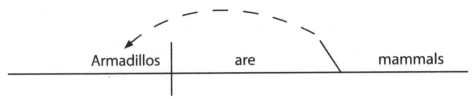

Instructor: Now look at the next diagram. Draw an arrow from the predicate nominative *Frances* back to the subject *I*. This reminds you that *Frances* is a predicate nominative that renames the subject *I*.

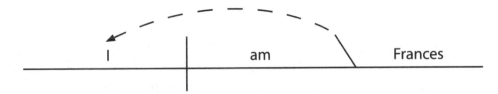

Instructor: In **Exercise 11**, we will look at another sentence with a linking verb and a predicate nominative. Read the sentence about raptors to me.

Workbook: Raptors were carnivores.

Instructor: What is the linking verb in the sentence?
Student: *Were*

Instructor: What is the subject of the sentence?
Student: *Raptors*

Instructor: This sentence contains a predicate nominative. This noun is in the complete predicate of the sentence, and it renames the subject. What is the predicate nominative?
Student: *Carnivores*

Instructor: *Carnivores* is the predicate nominative. A carnivore is an animal that only eats meat. Look at the diagram of the sentence "Raptors were carnivores."

Instructor: The word *carnivores* is a noun that renames the subject *Raptors*. It is the predicate nominative. The predicate nominative *carnivores* is separated from the linking verb by a slanted line. That slanted line points back toward the subject to remind you that a predicate nominative renames the subject.

Instructor: In this lesson you have been reading sentences with nouns that follow linking verbs. These nouns rename the subject; they are called predicate nominatives. But, remember, a noun can follow an action verb, too. These nouns are direct objects, and you practiced them in Lessons 24, 25, 26, and 28. Direct objects can only follow action verbs—they cannot follow linking verbs. Let's review that. Read the first sentence in **Exercise 12** to me. This sentence does not contain a linking verb. It contains an action verb and a direct object.

Workbook: Juliet mashed a banana.

Instructor: The action verb *mashed* is followed by the direct object *banana*. *Banana* receives the action of the verb *mashed*. What did Juliet mash? A banana. Now we will compare the direct object sentence with a sentence that has a linking verb in it. The linking verb is also followed by a noun. Read the next sentence about Juliet.

Workbook: Juliet is a chef.

Instructor: There is no action in the sentence. Juliet is not doing anything. What is the linking verb? *Is* is the linking verb. It links the subject *Juliet* with a noun in the complete predicate that renames the subject. What is Juliet? Juliet is a chef. *Chef* is the predicate nominative because it renames the subject. Predicate nominatives can only follow linking verbs—they cannot follow action verbs.

Instructor: Remember, direct objects can only follow action verbs. They can't follow linking verbs! And predicate nominatives can't follow action verbs. They can only follow linking verbs! Read aloud the sentences in **Exercise 12** again.

Instructor: Is *mashed* an action verb or a linking verb?
Student: *Action verb*

Instructor: Is *banana* a direct object or a predicate nominative? Remember, predicate nominatives can't follow action verbs!
Student: *Direct object*

Instructor: *Banana* is a direct object because *mashed* is an action verb. *Chef* is a predicate nominative because *is* is a linking verb. Now read the first sentence in **Exercise 13**, and write the predicate nominative *chef* in the blank. This is where the direct object *banana* used to be. What does the new sentence say?

Student:	*Juliet mashed a chef.*

Instructor: That doesn't make sense, does it? Put a large X over the word *chef* to show that it is wrong. Now read the second sentence in **Exercise 13**, and write the direct object *banana* in the blank. This is where the predicate nominative *chef* used to be. What does the new sentence say?

Student: *Juliet is a banana.*

Instructor: Put a large X over the word *banana* to show that it is wrong. So you see, a direct object can't follow a linking verb—and a predicate nominative can't follow an action verb!

Instructor: In this lesson we will conjugate another verb. Remember, to conjugate means to learn the various forms of a verb. When you are conjugating, you always start with the basic verb, for example, "to stand," "to swing," or "to think." The word *to* plus the basic form of a verb is called the *infinitive.*

Instructor: The basic form of the verb changes slightly depending on the person (I, you, he, or they) who is doing the action. There are three kinds of persons: first person, second person, and third person. *I, you,* and *he* are called singular persons because each is one, single person. *We, you,* and *they* are plural persons because there is more than one person in each group.

Instructor: Now let's conjugate the verb "to do." When we conjugate, we learn the various forms of a verb, and how a verb changes slightly depending on the person doing the action. We will conjugate "to do" in the present tense. Read the chart in **Exercise 14** with me.

Read each line across and include the title of each as you read. For example, "First person singular: I do, First person plural: we do, Second person singular: you do," etc. Then read the chart **again**, this time **down the columns** as a chant. Read just the words in bold: "I do, you do, he, she, it does," etc.

Workbook: Infinitive: to do

Present Tense

	Singular	Plural
First person	**I do**	**we do**
Second person	**you do**	**you do**
Third person	**he, she, it does**	**they do**

Instructor: "To do" is a regular verb in the present tense, but it is an **irregular** verb in the past tense. Read the chart in **Exercise 15** with me.

Chant the words in bold.

Workbook: Infinitive: to do

Past Tense

	Singular	Plural
First person	**I did**	**we did**
Second person	**you did**	**you did**
Third person	**he, she, it did**	**they did**

Instructor: "To do" is considered an irregular verb in the past tense because the forms of the verb do not follow the regular pattern. If they did, you would just add **ed** to the end of the present form. It would sound like this: "I doed, you doed, he, she, it doed…" That sounds ridiculous! "To do" is an irregular verb in the past tense. Read the sentences in **Exercise 16** and write the correct form of the verb "to do" in the blank. The verb "to do" is most often used as a helping verb. Look at the charts in **Exercises 14** and **15** if you need help.

Answer Key: Choose the correct form of "to do" in the **present tense**.

1. Mother said to us, "You **do** eat a lot of cookies!"

2. She **does** make the best gingersnaps.

3. You **do** the mixing.

4. We **do** help our mother with the cleanup.

5. We give cookies to the neighbors, and they **do** enjoy them!

6. I **do** like to bake cookies.

Choose the correct form of "to do" in the **past tense**.

1. We **did** most of the baking.

2. It **did** occupy us for the afternoon.

LESSON 31

Review: Linking Verbs
Review: Predicate Nominatives
Review: Subject and Object Pronouns

Read "How Doth…" (Lesson 27) three times to the student. Then ask the student to say the poem along with you or the tape recorder. If the student is ready, he should recite the poem to real people today. If he is not, continue practicing daily until he is ready.

Instructor: Let's begin by saying the definition of a verb. A verb is a word that does an action, shows a state of being, links two words together, or helps another verb. Say that with me.

TOGETHER: A verb is a word that does an action, shows a state of being, links two words together, or helps another verb.

Instructor: Verbs that link two words together are called linking verbs. Linking verbs can link or connect words together in a sentence. Let's say the chant of the linking verbs.

TOGETHER: Am [clap]
Is [clap]
Are, was, were. [clap]
Be [clap]
Being [clap]
Been. [clap] [clap]

Instructor: Linking verbs can link the subject with a noun or pronoun in the complete predicate that renames the subject. In **Exercise 1** of your workbook, read the sentence to me. The linking verb is in bold print.

Workbook: Jimmy Carter **was** president.

Jimmy Carter	was \ president

165

Instructor: Look at a diagram of the sentence you just read.

Instructor: The noun *president* is written to the right of the slanted line on the diagram. Remember, the slanted line points back to the subject that is renamed. *President* renames who *Jimmy Carter* was. *President* is in the complete predicate. Remember, the complete predicate includes the verb and all the words that follow the verb in the sentence. The complete predicate tells us what is said about the subject. So, a noun or pronoun in the complete predicate of the sentence that renames the subject is called a predicate nominative. The word *nominative* is similar to the word *nominate*. Do you remember that the word *nominate* means "name"? If you nominate a person for president, you name the person you would like to be president. So a predicate nominative is a noun or pronoun in the complete predicate that renames the subject.

Instructor: In **Exercise 2,** I will help you diagram two sentences with linking verbs that link the subject to a predicate nominative. You read each sentence, and I will ask you questions as you fill in the diagram. For Sentence 1, trace the dotted frame before you fill it in. For Sentence 2, draw your own frame in the space provided. Remember to copy the words exactly as they appear in the sentence. If the words begin with a capital letter in the sentence, they should also be capitalized in the diagram.

Use the following dialogue to help the student complete the diagrams in **Exercise 2**.

1. *What is the linking verb? This verb links the subject to a word in the complete predicate. Write the verb to the right of your center line.*

2. *Find the subject. Ask "who" or "what" before the verb. [Prompt the student with a specific question like "What is?" or "What are?"] Write the subject to the left of the center line on your frame.*

3. *This sentence contains a predicate nominative. This noun is in the complete predicate of the sentence, but it renames the subject. What is the predicate nominative in this sentence? Because the predicate nominative follows the verb in the sentence, it is written to the right of the verb on the diagram. Write the predicate nominative to the right of the slanted line on your diagram. That slanted line points back toward the subject to remind you that a predicate nominative renames the subject.*

Answer Key:

| Water | is | liquid |

166

```
   Leeches        |        are      \   parasites
_____|_____
                  |
```

Instructor: Now read the sentence in **Exercise 3** and look at its diagram.

Workbook: The two sisters were best friends.

```
   sisters        |        were     \   friends
_____|_____
  \       \       |                  \
   The     two                        best
```

Instructor: What is the linking verb in the sentence?
Student: *Were*

Instructor: Now we will find the subject. Answer me with one word. Who were?
Student: *Sisters*

Instructor: The sentence contains a predicate nominative. The noun is in the complete predicate, but it renames the subject *sisters*. Answer me with one word. What were the sisters?
Student: *Friends*

Instructor: Because the predicate nominative *friends* follows the verb in the sentence, it is written to the right of the verb on the diagram. The slanted line before the predicate nominative points back toward the subject to remind you that *friends* renames the subject *sisters*.

Instructor: Look again at the subject of the sentence, *sisters*. What are the adjectives that describe sisters? (Hint: One is an article and the other tells how many sisters.)
Student: *The* and *two*

Instructor: *The* and *two* are written on slanted lines below the subject they describe. Look again at the predicate nominative *friends*. What adjective tells you what kind of friends?
Student: *Best*

Instructor: *Best* is written on a slanted line below the noun it describes. In **Exercise 4**, I will help you diagram two sentences with linking verbs that link the subject to a predicate nominative. You read each sentence, and I will ask you questions as you fill in the diagram. For Sentence 1, fill in the frame. For Sentence 2, trace the dotted frame before you fill it in.

Use the following dialogue to help the student complete the two diagrams in **Exercise 4**.

1. *What is the linking verb? This verb links the subject to a word in the complete predicate. Write the verb to the right of your center line.*

2. *Find the subject. Ask "who" or "what" before the verb. [Prompt the student with a specific question like "What is?" or "What are?"] Write the subject to the left of the center line on your frame.*

3. *This sentence contains a predicate nominative. This noun is in the complete predicate of the sentence, but it renames the subject. What is the predicate nominative in this sentence? Because the predicate nominative follows the verb in the sentence, it is written to the right of the verb on the diagram. Write the predicate nominative to the right of the slanted line on your diagram. That slanted line points back toward the subject to remind you that a predicate nominative renames the subject.*

4. *Go back and look again at the subject. Are there any words that describe the subject that come before the verb in the sentence? This adjective is in the complete subject. An adjective can tell what kind, which one, how many, or whose. Also look for an article (a, an, the), because it acts like an adjective. Write each adjective on a slanted line below the subject it describes.*

5. *Look at the predicate nominative again. Are there any words that describe this noun? These adjectives can tell what kind, which one, how many, or whose. Also look for articles (a, an, the), because they act like adjectives. Write each adjective on a slanted line below the predicate nominative it describes.*

Answer Key: 1. My dog is a beagle.

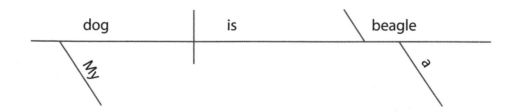

2. Fudge popsicles are tasty treats.

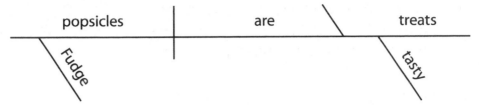

Instructor: In Lesson 24 you learned the difference between subject pronouns and object pronouns. Subject pronouns are the pronouns that are used as subjects of sentences. Object pronouns are the pronouns used as objects in sentences. Read the lists of subject pronouns and object pronouns in **Exercise 5** of your workbook.

Workbook:

Subject Pronouns	Object Pronouns
I	me
he	him
she	her
we	us
they	them

Instructor: Subject pronouns are typically used as subjects. When you **rename** the subject, you also use a subject pronoun, even though it is in the predicate. A noun or pronoun in the predicate that renames the subject is called a **predicate nominative**. Look at **Exercise 6** in your workbook. I want you to circle each pronoun and write "S" over the subject pronoun in the predicate. This is your predicate nominative.

Answer Key:

1. It is (I).

2. This is (he).

3. That is (she).

4. It is (we).

5. Those are (they).

LESSON 32

New: Predicate Adjectives
Review: Linking Verbs
Review: Predicate Nominatives

Instructor: Let's begin by saying the definition of a verb. A verb is a word that does an action, shows a state of being, links two words together, or helps another verb. Say that with me.

TOGETHER: A verb is a word that does an action, shows a state of being, links two words together, or helps another verb.

Instructor: Verbs that link two words together are called linking verbs. Linking verbs can link or connect words together in a sentence. Let's say the chant of the linking verbs.

TOGETHER: Am [clap]
Is [clap]
Are, was, were. [clap]
Be [clap]
Being [clap]
Been. [clap] [clap]

Instructor: Linking verbs can link the subject with a noun or pronoun in the complete predicate that renames the subject. In **Exercise 1**, read the sentence and look at its diagram.

Tell the student that arachnids have eight jointed legs and two main body parts.

Workbook: Spiders are arachnids.

| Spiders | are \ arachnids |

Instructor: *Are* is a linking verb. It connects the subject *Spiders* with a pronoun that renames the subject. *Arachnids* renames the subject. What are spiders? *Arachnids*. *Arachnids* is in the complete predicate of the sentence. Remember, the complete predicate includes the verb and all the words that follow it in the sentence. The complete predicate tells us what is said about the subject. A noun or pronoun in the complete predicate that renames the subject is called a predicate nominative. *Arachnids* renames the subject *Spiders* and is written to the right of the verb on the diagram because it follows the verb in the sentence.

In order to keep the student's eyes focused on what you are explaining, physically point out the words and lines on the student's diagram as you mention them in the explanation below.

Instructor: Look again at the diagram. Do you see the slanted line that separates the linking verb *are* from the predicate nominative? That slanted line points back toward the subject to remind you that *arachnids* is a predicate nominative that renames the subject *Spiders*. Now I will help you diagram a sentence with a predicate nominative in **Exercise 2**. Draw a frame like the one in **Exercise 1** of your workbook.

Tell the student that *decapod* means "ten-legged."

Use the following dialogue to help the student complete the diagram in **Exercise 2**.

1. *What is the linking verb? This verb links the subject to a word in the complete predicate. Write the verb to the right of your center line.*

2. *Find the subject. Ask "who" or "what" before the verb. [Prompt the student with a specific question, "What are?"] Write the subject to the left of the center line on your frame.*

3. *This sentence contains a predicate nominative. This noun is in the complete predicate of the sentence, but it renames the subject. What is the predicate nominative in this sentence? Because the predicate nominative follows the verb in the sentence, it is written to the right of the verb on the diagram. Write the predicate nominative to the right of the slanted line on your diagram. That slanted line points back toward the subject to remind you that a predicate nominative renames the subject.*

Answer Key:

Lobsters	are	\ . decapods

Instructor: You have learned that linking verbs can link the subject with a noun or pronoun that renames the subject. But linking verbs can also link the subject with an adjective in the complete predicate. Look at **Exercise 3**. I will read you a noun and a linking verb and let you complete the sentence by writing in an adjective that describes the subject. The linking verb in bold print will link, or connect, the subject noun with the adjective you choose. Follow along as I read and point to the parts of the sentences in **Exercise 3**.

Workbook: The pepper **is** _____.

Instructor: Can you tell me what color a pepper is? (This is the kind of pepper that grows in the garden, not the kind of pepper that you put on your food!)

Student: *The pepper is green [or red or yellow].*

Instructor: The linking verb *is* connects *pepper* with its color! Can you tell me something about sweaters that describes the way they feel?

Workbook: Sweaters **are** _____.

Student: *Sweaters are [soft, warm, scratchy].*

Instructor: The linking verb *are* connects or links the word *sweaters* with the word *[the word the student chose].* Now finish this sentence:

Workbook: The marshmallow **was** _____.

Student: *The marshmallow was [gooey, squishy, fluffy].*

Instructor: The linking verb *was* connects or links the word *marshmallow* with the word that describes the marshmallow: *[the word the student chose].*

Instructor: In **Exercise 4**, read the sentence about germs. This sentence contains a linking verb.

Tell the student that if something is microscopic, you can only see it with a microscope.

Workbook: Germs are microscopic.

Germs	are \ microscopic

Instructor: The linking verb *are* links the subject of the sentence, *Germs*, with the adjective *microscopic*. The adjective *microscopic* describes the subject *Germs*. Because *microscopic* follows the linking verb *are*, it is located in the complete predicate. Remember, the complete predicate includes all the words that tell us what is said about the subject. Adjectives that describe the subject but are found in the complete predicate are called predicate adjectives. Look at the diagram of the sentence.

Instructor: *Microscopic* is an adjective that describes the subject *Germs*. It is written to the right of the verb on the diagram because it follows the verb in the sentence. Because the adjective is in the complete predicate of the sentence, it is a predicate adjective.

In order to keep the student's eyes focused on what you are explaining, physically point out the words and lines on the student's diagram as you mention them in the explanation below.

Instructor: Do you see the slanted line that separates the linking verb *are* from the predicate adjective? That slanted line points back toward the subject to remind you that *microscopic* is an adjective that describes the subject *Germs*. As you can see, predicate adjectives are diagrammed the same way that predicate nominatives are diagrammed, because they both refer back to the subject.

Instructor: In **Exercise 5**, I will help you diagram some sentences with linking verbs that link the subject to a predicate adjective. You read each sentence, and I will ask you questions as you fill in the diagram. For Sentence 1, fill in the frame. For Sentence 2, trace the dotted frame before you fill it in. For Sentences 3 and 4, draw your own frames in the spaces provided.

Tell the student that pikas are a small relative of the rabbit. They have round ears but no tail! The American pika lives in rocky mountain areas in the West. It makes its home in rock piles and slides. Pikas line their burrows with vegetation when they hibernate. They are found in North America, and they line their burrows with hay to provide insulation when they hibernate.

Use the following dialogue to help the student complete the four diagrams.

1. *What is the linking verb? This verb links the subject to a word in the complete predicate. Write the verb to the right of your center line.*

2. *Find the subject. Ask "who" or "what" before the verb. [Prompt the student with a specific question like "What are?"] Write the subject to the left of the center line on your frame.*

3. *This sentence contains a predicate adjective. This adjective is in the complete predicate of the sentence, but it describes the subject. A predicate adjective can tell what kind, which one, how many, or whose. Can you find an adjective in the complete predicate that describes the subject? Because the predicate adjective follows the verb in the sentence, it is written to the right of the verb on the diagram. Write the predicate adjective to the right of the slanted line on your diagram. That slanted line points back toward the subject to remind you that a predicate adjective describes the subject.*

Answer Key: 1. Pikas are brown.

| Pikas | are | \ brown |

2. They are shy.

| They | are | \ shy |

3. Pikas are active.

| Pikas | are | \ active |

4. Pikas are territorial.

| Pikas | are | \ territorial |

LESSON 33

Summary Exercise: *Cowboys*

Instructor: Today I am going to read a selection aloud to you from a history book called *Cowboys* by David H. Murdoch. What makes a book a *history* book? (*Give the student time to tell you if he knows.*) History is a *true account* of past events. I am going to read you a selection about real cowboys. I will read the selection only once. (*If the student is a fluent reader, you may choose to have* him *read it aloud or silently*). Then I want you to tell me in your own words what you remember.

The original Stetson hats were often called ten-gallon hats. Differing opinions about the origin of the term "ten-gallon" may be read on Wikipedia under the topic "Ten gallon hats."

Cowboys

A cowboy's hat was his trademark. Styles might vary—from sombreros to Stetsons—but the functions were the same. In blazing sun, the high crown kept the head cool while the broad brim shaded the eyes and neck. In rain and snow the hat was a mini-umbrella; it also protected against thorns and low-hanging branches. Made of high quality felt, it was meant to take years of wear. This was fortunate because a cowboy used his versatile hat as an alternative to a quirt (whip), to carry water (as shown in the famous Stetson label), to fan fires (or put them out), and occasionally even as a pillow.

For guidance in teaching summary exercises, see Lesson 12.

LESSON 34

Review: Common and Proper Nouns
Review: Pronouns
Review: Capitalization Rules

This is a long lesson. Remember that you should spend about half an hour per day on grammar; lessons can stretch over two or three days (or more!).

Review "Afternoon on a Hill" (Lesson 8) today. If the student has trouble remembering the poem, have him practice it daily until he is confident.

Instructor: Say the definition of a noun with me.

Together: A noun is the name of a person, place, thing, or idea.

Instructor: Nouns can be either common or proper. A common noun is a name common to many persons, places, or things. A proper noun is a special, "proper" name for a person, place, or thing. Proper nouns always begin with a capital letter. The word *student* is a common noun, but *[student's name]* is a proper noun. I am going to say a common noun to you, and I want you answer my question with a proper noun (a special, "proper" name for a common noun).

Instructor: *Woman* is a common noun. What is the special, "proper" name of a woman that you know?

Student: *[Acceptable answers include Mommy, Aunt _____, Ms. _____.]*

Instructor: *Country* is a common noun. What is the special, "proper" name of the country in which you live?

Student: *[Name of country.]*

Instructor: Now I am going to read you some nouns, and I want you identify if the noun is common or proper.

Have the student stand for a proper noun and squat low for a common noun, or the student can just tell you if the noun is common or proper.

Instructor: river
    Cairo
    state
    Iraq
    Big Horn Mountains
    city
    Michigan
    Colorado River
    man
    country
    Egypt
    mountains
    Daniel Defoe

Instructor: This brings us to our first capitalization rule: Capitalize the proper names of persons, places, things, and animals. Say that for me.

Student: *Capitalize the proper names of persons, places, things, and animals.*

Instructor: The names of holidays are also proper nouns. Repeat the next rule after me: Capitalize holidays.

Student: *Capitalize holidays.*

Instructor: Write the name of your favorite holiday in **Exercise 1** of your workbook. Remember, all proper nouns begin with a capital letter.

Instructor: We also capitalize the names of deities. Did you know the planets in our solar system, except for Earth, are named for gods in Greek and Roman mythology?

Rewrite the name of the Greek or Roman god with correct capitalization in **Exercise 2**, and, just for fun, see if you can match it to the correct description of who the god was. Draw a line to connect the god with his or her description.

Answer Key:

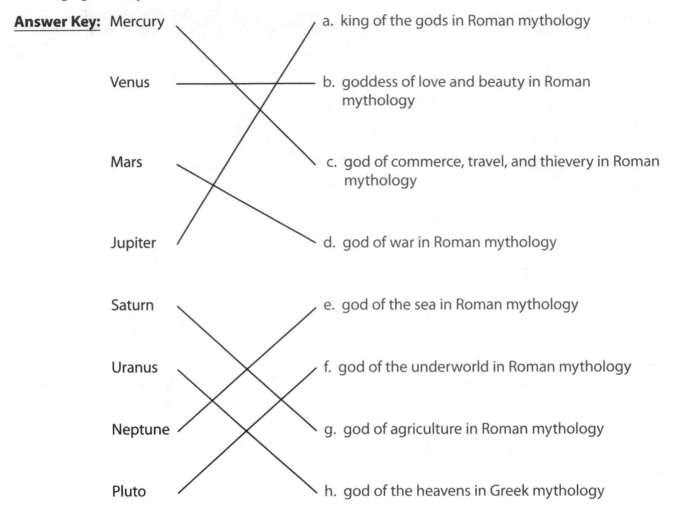

Mercury
Venus
Mars
Jupiter

Saturn
Uranus
Neptune
Pluto

a. king of the gods in Roman mythology

b. goddess of love and beauty in Roman mythology

c. god of commerce, travel, and thievery in Roman mythology

d. god of war in Roman mythology

e. god of the sea in Roman mythology

f. god of the underworld in Roman mythology

g. god of agriculture in Roman mythology

h. god of the heavens in Greek mythology

Instructor: You just practiced the third capitalization rule. Repeat after me: Capitalize the names of deities.

Student: *Capitalize the names of deities.*

Instructor: Repeat the fourth capitalization rule after me: Capitalize the days of the week and the months of the year, but not the seasons.

Student: *Capitalize the days of the week and the months of the year, but not the seasons.*

Instructor: The days of the week and the months of the year are proper nouns. They each begin with a capital letter. In **Exercise 3**, read aloud the names of the months and days to me. Read the months first, then the days. Circle the capital letter at the beginning of each month and day.

Workbook:

Months of the Year	Days of the Week
January	Monday
February	Tuesday
March	Wednesday
April	Thursday
May	Friday
June	Saturday
July	Sunday
August	
September	
October	
November	
December	

Instructor: The seasons are all common nouns. They do not begin with a capital letter. Read the list of seasons in **Exercise 4** of your workbook. Circle the first letter of each season name.

Workbook:

Seasons
spring
summer
fall
winter

Instructor: The first, last, and other important words in the titles of books, magazines, and newspapers are capitalized. In **Exercise 5** there is a list of unimportant words. Read them aloud to me.

Workbook: This is a list of unimportant words:

Articles (*a, an, the*)

Conjunctions (*and, but, or*)

Prepositions that are four letters or less (such as *at, by, for, from, in, into, like, near, of, off, on, over, past, to, up, upon, with*)

Instructor: In **Exercise 6**, notice that none of the words in these titles are capitalized. Rewrite the titles using correct capitalization. Then underline the entire title.

Answer Key:

Book

The cricket in times square   The Cricket in Times Square

Magazine

highlights   Highlights

Newspaper

wall street journal   Wall Street Journal

Instructor: Titles of stories, poems, and songs are also capitalized. They follow the same rules as books, magazines, and newspapers: capitalize the first, last, and other important words. These titles are put in quotation marks, rather than being italicized or underlined. Read aloud the titles in **Exercise 7**. Rewrite the titles with correct capitalization. Be sure to put these titles of stories, poems, and songs in quotation marks.

Answer Key:

Story

"the crow and the pitcher"   "The Crow and the Pitcher"

Poem

"the first snowfall"   "The First Snowfall"

Song

"i've been working on the railroad"   "I've Been Working on the Railroad"

Instructor: We have just practiced the fifth capitalization rule: Capitalize the first, last, and other important words in titles of books, magazines, newspapers, stories, poems, and songs. Say that with me two times.

Together (two times): Capitalize the first, last, and other important words in titles of books, magazines, newspapers, stories, poems, and songs.

Instructor: Let's review pronouns. Repeat after me: A pronoun is a word used in the place of a noun.

Student: *A pronoun is a word used in the place of a noun.*

Instructor: Now we are going to practice the list of personal pronouns.
<u>Personal Pronouns</u>
I, me, my, mine
You, your, yours
He, she, him, her, it
His, hers, its
We, us, our, ours
They, them, their, theirs

If the student already knows the list of pronouns, have him say them alone from memory once. If he needs to review, say the list with him three times.

Instructor: One of those pronouns is always capitalized, no matter where it is in the sentence. What pronoun is always capitalized? (Hint: It is the pronoun you most often use to refer to yourself.)

Student: *I*

Instructor: Repeat the sixth capitalization rule after me: Capitalize the word *I*.

Student: *Capitalize the word I.*

Instructor: The personal pronouns that tell whose act like adjectives. These pronouns are called possessive pronouns: *my, mine, your, yours, his, her, hers, its, our, ours, their,* and *theirs*. Read the sentences in **Exercise 8** of your workbook. The possessive pronouns that act like adjectives that tell whose are in bold print. Some of these adjectives are in the subject. Others are predicate adjectives. But all of them describe nouns. Draw an arrow from each possessive pronoun to the noun that it modifies.

If the student has difficulty finding the noun that the possessive pronoun modifies, ask, "[Possessive pronoun] what?"

Answer Key:	Question to ask student:
My ears wiggle.	My what?
Those bracelets are **mine**.	What are mine?
Your speech was inspiring.	Your what?
The last cookie is **yours**.	What is yours?
His eyes twinkled.	His what?

The sneakiest hamster is **hers**.　　What is hers?

Our car is green.　　Our what?

The casseroles were **ours**.　　What were ours?

The trophy was **theirs**.　　What was theirs?

Instructor: The personal pronouns can be divided into three groups: possessive pronouns (we just reviewed those), subject pronouns, and object pronouns. Let's review the difference between subject pronouns and object pronouns. Subject pronouns are the pronouns that are typically used as subjects of sentences. Object pronouns are the pronouns used as objects in sentences. Read the lists of subject pronouns and object pronouns in **Exercise 9** of your workbook.

Workbook:

Subject Pronouns	Object Pronouns
I	me
he	him
she	her
we	us
they	them

Instructor: Subject pronouns are typically used as subjects. You also use a subject pronoun for a predicate nominative, since it **renames** the subject. Object pronouns are the pronouns used as objects, like direct objects and indirect objects. Look at **Exercise 10** in your workbook. Read each sentence and circle the subject or object pronoun in it. Write "S" over it if it is a subject pronoun used as the subject or predicate nominative. If the pronoun is an object pronoun used as the direct or indirect object in the sentence, write "O" over it.

Answer Key:

S　　　　O
(She) handed (me) a flower.

　　　S
It is (I.)

S　　　O
(I) loaned (him) my suitcase.

S　　　　O
(They) cooked (us) spaghetti for dinner.

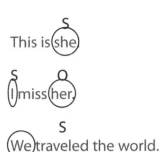

Instructor: In addition to personal pronouns, you have also learned about demonstrative pronouns: *this, that, these,* and *those.* These pronouns demonstrate, or point out, something. Look at **Exercise 11** in your workbook. Read the first sentence.

Workbook: This is your favorite subject.

Instructor: Now let's think of a noun for which the underlined pronoun could stand. What is your favorite subject?

Student: *[History, math, grammar, etc.]*

Instructor: The pronoun *This* stands for the noun *[history, math, or grammar]. [History, math, or grammar]* is your favorite subject. **This** is your favorite subject. Now read the rest of the sentences in **Exercise 11**. After you read each sentence, substitute a noun for which the underlined pronoun could stand.

Workbook: That is delicious!

Student: *[The cupcake, spaghetti, etc.] is delicious!*

Workbook: These are brown.

Student: *[The dogs, the potatoes, the shoes, etc.] are brown.*

Workbook: Those are so tiny!

Student: *[The bugs, the babies, the earrings, etc.] are so tiny!*

Instructor: A pronoun is a word that takes the place of a noun. There is a special name for the noun that is replaced. It is called the antecedent. *Antecedent* means "to go before." Usually, the antecedent noun **goes before** its pronoun. Read the sentence in **Exercise 12**. The pronoun is in bold. The antecedent is circled. There is an arrow that starts at the pronoun and points back to its antecedent. Remember, the antecedent is the noun the pronoun replaces.

183

Workbook: When (Scotty) raised a caterpillar, **he** put leaves and water in the jar.

antecedent

Instructor: If a pronoun replaces more than one person, place, thing, or idea, it can have more than one antecedent noun. Read the sentences in **Exercise 13**.

antecedent   antecedent

Workbook: When (Madison) and (I) made a terrarium, **we** collected moss.

Instructor: Read the sentences in **Exercise 14**. The pronoun is in bold. Find the antecedent and circle it. Then draw an arrow from the pronoun to its antecedent, the noun the pronoun replaces.

Answer Key: A buzzing (housefly) beats **its** wings twenty thousand times per minute!

Male (crickets) rub **their** wings together to attract female crickets.

When the queen (bee) lays eggs, **her** workers provide food for **her**.

Instructor: Earlier in the lesson you capitalized the title of a poem, "The First Snowfall." Read one verse from that poem now in **Exercise 15** of your workbook.

Tell the student that the *gloaming* is the time when the sun is setting.

Workbook:

The First Snowfall

by James Russell Lowell

The snow had begun in the gloaming,

And busily all the night

Had been heaping field and highway

With a silence deep and white.

Instructor: Repeat the seventh capitalization rule after me: Capitalize the first word in every line of traditional poetry.

Student: *Capitalize the first word in every line of traditional poetry.*

Instructor: Reread the poem to yourself and circle the capital letter in the first word in every line of the poem.

Instructor: There is one last capitalization rule that you have learned. Repeat after me: Capitalize the first word in every sentence.

Student: *Capitalize the first word in every sentence.*

LESSON 35

New: Four Types of Sentences
New: Conjugating the Verb "To Go"

Review "Ozymandias" (Lesson 16) today. If the student has trouble remembering the poem, have him practice it daily until he is confident.

Instructor: Let's review the definition of a sentence. A sentence is a group of words that expresses a complete thought. All sentences begin with a capital letter and end with a punctuation mark.

Instructor: Now I will say the definition three times. Say as much of it with me as you can.

TOGETHER (three times): A sentence is a group of words that expresses a complete thought. All sentences begin with a capital letter and end with a punctuation mark.

Instructor: There are four different types of sentences: statements, commands, questions, and exclamations. A statement gives information. "Alaska is a state" is a statement. It gives information. Statements always end with a period. Read the four statements in **Exercise 1** of your workbook.

Workbook: Many Alaskan villages are isolated.

Some villages have airstrips.

Fishing is an important industry.

Dogsleds are common.

Instructor: The second type of sentence is a command. A command gives an order or makes a request. In your workbook, read each of the command sentences in **Exercise 2**.

Workbook: Meet me at the lake.

Bring your fishing pole with you.

Make sure your boat is ready.

Don't be late!

Instructor: Now look again at the command sentences. A command sentence ends with either a period or an exclamation point. Point to the punctuation mark at the end of each command sentence you just read, and tell me what it is.

Instructor: The third type of sentence is a question. A question asks something. A question always ends with a question mark. Let's pretend we are planning a trip to northern Alaska. In **Exercise 3**, read the questions that we might ask the tour guide so we can prepare for our trip.

Workbook: What kind of coats do we need?

Are special snow boots necessary?

Will the charter plane land on a frozen lake?

Can we try ice fishing?

Instructor: The fourth type of sentence is an exclamation. An exclamation shows sudden or strong feeling. An exclamation always ends with an exclamation point. Read the sentences in **Exercise 4**. Remember to read exclamation sentences with lots of expression because they show strong feeling!

Workbook: A blizzard is coming!

I can't see three feet in front of me!

I need to get inside quickly!

I feel frozen!

Instructor: In this lesson we will conjugate another verb. Remember, to conjugate means to learn the various forms of a verb. When you are conjugating, you always start with the basic verb, for example, "to swim," "to explore," or "to hike." The word *to* plus the basic form of a verb is called the *infinitive*.

Instructor: The basic form of the verb changes slightly depending on the person (I, you, he, or they) who is doing the action. There are three kinds of persons: first person, second person, and third person. *I, you,* and *he* are called singular persons because each is one, single person. *We, you,* and *they* are plural persons because there is more than one person in each group.

Instructor: Now let's conjugate the verb "to go." When we conjugate, we learn the various forms of a verb, and how a verb changes slightly depending on the person doing the action. We will conjugate "to go" in the present tense. Read the chart in **Exercise 5** with me.

Read each line across and include the title of each as you read. For example, "First person singular: I go, First person plural: we go, Second person singular: you go," etc. Then read the chart **again**, this time **down the columns** as a chant. Read just the words in bold: "I go, you go, he, she, it goes," etc.

Workbook: Infinitive: to go

Present Tense

	Singular	Plural
First person	**I go**	**we go**
Second person	**you go**	**you go**
Third person	**he, she, it goes**	**they go**

Instructor: "To go" is a regular verb in the present tense, but it is an **irregular** verb in the past tense. Read the chart in **Exercise 6** with me.

Chant the words in bold.

Workbook: Infinitive: to go

Past Tense

	Singular	Plural
First person	**I went**	**we went**
Second person	**you went**	**you went**
Third person	**he, she, it went**	**they went**

Instructor: "To go" is considered an irregular verb in the past tense because the forms of the verb do not follow the regular pattern. If they did, you would just add **ed** to the end of the present form. It would sound like this: "I goed, you goed, he, she, it goed…" That sounds strange, doesn't it? "To go" is an irregular verb in the past tense. Read the sentences in **Exercise 7** and write the correct form of the verb "to go" in the blank. Look at the charts in **Exercises 5** and **6** if you need help.

Answer Key: Choose the correct form of "to go" in the **present tense**.

1. I **go** to Mount McKinley.

2. Father **goes** with me.

3. You **go** and tour Alaska's coastline by boat.

Choose the correct form of "to go" in the **past tense**.

1. We **went** to Alaska to see the salmon run.

2. The salmon **went** upstream to fertilize eggs.

LESSON 36

New: Commands (with Diagramming)
Review: Statements

Review "Ozymandias" (Lesson 16) again today. If the student has trouble remembering the poem, have him practice it daily until he is confident.

Instructor: In your workbook, look at **Exercise 1**. Read the two short statement sentences to me.

Workbook: Marge travels.

Pilots fly.

Instructor: In Lesson 11, you learned that every sentence has a subject and a verb. In the first sentence, what is the verb?

Student: *Travels*

Instructor: *Travels* is the verb in the sentence. Now find the subject. Who travels?

Student: *Marge*

Instructor: *Marge* is the subject of the sentence. Now look at the second sentence. What is the verb?

Student: *Fly*

Instructor: *Fly* is the verb in the sentence. Now find the subject. Who flies?

Student: *Pilots*

Instructor: *Pilots* is the subject of the sentence. It is easy to find the subject and the verb in these statement sentences because they are only two words long. One word is the subject; the other word is the verb. It is easy to diagram these statement sentences. They are just like the sentences you have been diagramming so far in this book. What do you do if a sentence has only one word in it? Some command sentences contain only one word. Read the sentence in **Exercise 2**. This is what the mother commands her toddler to do when he is standing on the chair.

190

Workbook: Sit.

Instructor: This command is a complete sentence, although it only consists of one word. It has a subject, but the subject is not written because it is understood to be the word *you*. The mother is telling the toddler to sit. She does not give a command by saying "You sit"; she simply says "Sit." Look at the diagram of the short command sentence "Sit."

Remind the student that he is not to put punctuation on the diagram.

(you)	Sit

Instructor: Notice that the word *you* is written inside parentheses. This shows us that although the word *you* is not actually written in the sentence, it is still understood to be the subject. Read the command sentences in **Exercise 3**. Although these sentences do not have a subject that is written, the subject is understood to be *you*.

Workbook: Listen.

Paddle faster!

Instructor: Now we will diagram the first sentence, "Listen," onto the empty frame in **Exercise 4** of your workbook.

Instructor: What is the verb in the sentence?
Student: *Listen*

Instructor: *Listen* is the verb in the sentence. Write the word *Listen* on the verb line. Remember to capitalize *Listen* because it is capitalized in the sentence. Now find the subject. What one word tells us who is commanded to look? Remember, this word is not written in the command sentence, but it is understood to be the subject.
Student: *You*

Instructor: *You* is the subject. Write the word *you* on the subject line. Because the subject *you* is not written in the sentence but is just understood, you should put *you* in parentheses. Now your diagram is complete.

(you)	Listen

Instructor: Now we will diagram the sentence "Paddle faster!" onto the empty frame in **Exercise 5** of your workbook.

Instructor: What is the verb in the sentence?
Student: *Paddle*

Instructor: *Paddle* is the verb in the sentence. Write the word *Paddle* on the verb line. Remember to capitalize *Paddle* because it is capitalized in the sentence. Now find the subject. What one word tells us who is commanded to paddle? Remember, this word is not written in the command sentence, but it is understood to be the subject.
Student: *You*

Instructor: *You* is the subject. Write the word *you* on the subject line. Because the subject *you* is not written in the sentence but is just understood, you should put *you* in parentheses.

Instructor: Look again at the verb *Paddle*. Is there a word that describes the verb? This is an adverb that could tell how, when, where, or how often you should paddle.
Student: *Faster*

Instructor: *Faster* is an adverb that tells how you are commanded to paddle. Write *faster* on the slanted line beneath the word *Paddle*.

Point to the diagrams in **Exercises 2**, **4**, and **5** as you explain the following.

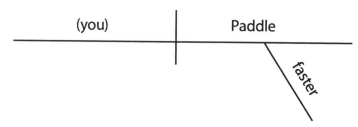

Instructor: Read the sentences in **Exercise 6** and look at their diagrams. The first sentence is a statement; the second sentence is a command.

Workbook: Reid measured carefully.

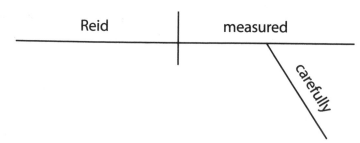

Workbook: Measure carefully.

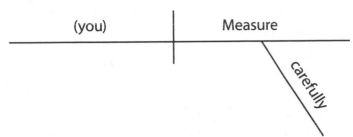

Instructor: In the statement sentence "Reid measured carefully," the subject *Reid* is written in the sentence. You would just copy his name onto the subject line of the diagram. In the command sentence "Measure carefully," the subject is not in the sentence, but it is understood to be the word *you*. That is why you put the word *you* in parentheses on the diagram. Now in **Exercises 7** through **10** you will diagram some pairs of statement sentences and command sentences. Remember, the subject of a command sentence is always the word *you*. You read each sentence. I will ask you questions as you fill in the diagram. Remember to copy the words exactly as they appear in the sentence. If the words begin with a capital letter in the sentence, they should also be capitalized in the diagram.

Use the following dialogue to help the student fill in each diagram in **Exercises 8** through **10**. After the student reads a sentence, you will prompt him with the questions in italics listed across from that sentence (for example, Ask questions 1a, 2a, and 7).

1a. *What is the verb? Write the verb to the right of your center line.*

1b. *What is the linking verb? This verb links the subject to a word in the complete predicate. Write the verb to the right of your center line.*

2a. *Find the subject. Ask "who" or "what" before the verb. [Prompt the student with a specific question like "Who packs?" or "Who picks?"] Write the subject to the left of the center line on your frame.*

2b. *Find the subject. Ask "who" or "what" before the verb. [Prompt the student with a specific question like "Who should pack?" or "Who should pick?" or "Who should be?"] In a command sentence, the subject is understood to be the word* you. *Write the subject to the left of the center line on your frame. Remember to put* you *in parentheses.*

3. *This sentence contains a predicate adjective. This adjective is in the complete predicate of the sentence, but it describes the subject. A predicate adjective can tell what kind, which one, how many, or whose. Can you find an adjective in the complete predicate that*

describes the subject? Because the predicate adjective follows the verb in the sentence, it is written to the right of the verb on the diagram. Write the predicate adjective to the right of the slanted line on your diagram. That slanted line points back toward the subject to remind you that a predicate adjective describes the subject.

4. Is there a direct object that receives the action of the verb? I will ask you a question that will help you find the direct object.

Exercise 8: *Picks what?*

Exercise 10: *Drops what?*

Write the direct object to the right of the verb on your diagram. The direct object is separated from the verb by a short, straight line.

5. Go back and look again at the simple subject. Are there any words in the complete subject that describe the simple subject? These adjectives can tell what kind, which one, how many, or whose. Also look for the articles (a, an, the), because they act like adjectives. Write each adjective on a slanted line below the subject it describes.

6. Look again at the direct object. Are there any words that describe the direct object? These adjectives can tell what kind, which one, how many, or whose. Also look for the articles (a, an, the), because they act like adjectives. Write each adjective on a slanted line below the direct object it describes.

7. Look again at the verb. Is there a word that describes the verb? This is an adverb that could tell how, when, where, or how often. Write the adverb on the slanted line below the verb it describes.

Answer Key: Exercise 7

Father packs carefully.   (Ask questions 1a, 2a, and 7)

Pack carefully.   (Ask questions 1a, 2b, and 7)

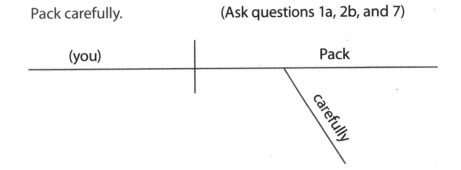

Exercise 8

Jamila picks ripe berries.   (Ask questions 1a, 2a, 4, and 6)

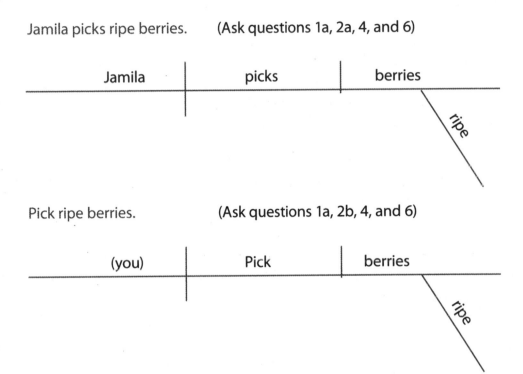

Pick ripe berries.   (Ask questions 1a, 2b, 4, and 6)

Exercise 9

Larry is ready.   (Ask questions 1b, 2a, and 3)

Be ready.   (Ask questions 1b, 2b, and 3)

Exercise 10

Nikki drops the ball.   (Ask questions 1a, 2a, 4, and 6)

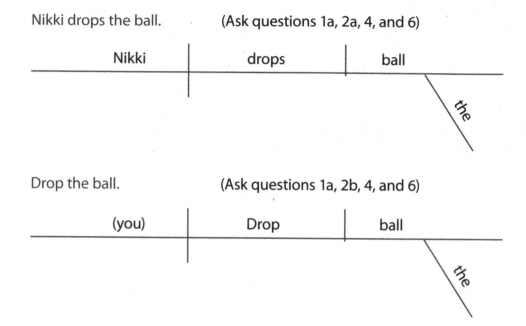

Drop the ball.   (Ask questions 1a, 2b, 4, and 6)

LESSON 37

New: Questions (with Diagramming)
Learn to Proofread: Insert a Question Mark

Review "Afternoon on a Hill" (Lesson 8) and "Ozymandias" (Lesson 16) today. If the student has trouble remembering the poems, have him practice them daily until he is confident.

Instructor: You already know that every sentence has two parts: a subject and a verb. Today you will learn that in some sentences, the subject is not at the beginning of the sentence; it is in the middle! Read the question sentence in **Exercise 1** of your workbook.

Workbook: Are acorns falling?

Instructor: In order to find the subject of a question sentence, it is helpful to rearrange the words in the question so that it becomes a statement. In **Exercise 2**, read the question sentence again, and then read the statement sentence beneath it.

Workbook: Are acorns falling?

Acorns are falling.

Instructor: Each of these sentences has a helping verb and an action verb. What are the two verbs that work together in these sentences?

Student: *Are falling*

Instructor: *Are falling* are the two verbs in both the question and the statement sentences. Now find the subject. What are falling?

Student: *Acorns*

Instructor: *Acorns* is the subject of both the question and the statement sentences. In **Exercise 3**, read another question sentence.

197

Workbook: Can trees transpire?

Instructor: Just as we perspire, or sweat, to cool ourselves, trees transpire. They release water through their leaves. As the water evaporates off the leaf, it cools the tree. Let's rearrange the words in the question sentence so that we have a statement sentence. In **Exercise 4**, read the question sentence again, and then read the statement sentence beneath it.

Workbook: Can trees transpire?

                  Trees can transpire.

Instructor: Each of these sentences has a helping verb and an action verb. What are the two verbs that work together in these sentences?

Student: *Can transpire*

Instructor: *Can transpire* are the two verbs in both the question and the statement sentences. Now find the subject. What can transpire?

Student: *Trees*

Instructor: *Trees* is the subject of both the question and the statement sentences. In **Exercise 5**, we will practice rearranging more question sentences so that they become statement sentences. Read each question, and then say it as a statement. I will help you if you need it. (Answers are on page 199.)

Instructor: To diagram a question sentence, you must first turn it into a statement. In **Exercise 6** write each question as a statement, and then fill in the diagram for each question. Remember to copy the words exactly as they appear in the question sentence. If the words begin with a capital letter in the question sentence, they should also be capitalized in the diagram. Remember, punctuation marks are not put on diagrams.

Use the following dialogue to help the student fill in the diagrams.

1. *Before you diagram a question sentence, you need to rearrange the words to make a statement sentence. What is the statement? [The student may need to write down the statement on the long line after each question in his workbook.]*

2. *Find the verb. There are two verbs in this sentence. What is the helping verb? What is the action verb? You write both these verbs on your verb line.*

3. *Now find the subject. Ask "who" or "what" before the verb. [Prompt the student with a specific question like "What will drop?" or "Who may look?"] Write the subject to the left of the center line on your frame.*

Answer Key: 1. Will acorns drop?   (Acorns will drop.)

acorns	Will drop

2. May I look?   (I may look.)

I	May look

3. Could squirrels fly?   (Squirrels could fly.)

squirrels	Could fly

4. Do squirrels scamper?   (Squirrels do scamper.)

squirrels	Do scamper

5. Does he hide?   (He does hide.)

he	Does hide

Learn to Proofread: Insert a Question Mark

Instructor: Today you will learn another proofreaders' mark. Look in your workbook at **Exercise 7**. This is the proofreaders' mark you will learn today. It is a question mark with an arrowhead below it. When you see this mark, you should insert a question mark. Look at the sample sentence in **Exercise 7**. Read that aloud.

Workbook: What are the names of the Supreme Court Justices

Instructor: "What are the names of the Supreme Court Justices" is a question sentence and should end with a question mark. Now let's review all the proofreaders' marks you have learned. Read the sentences in **Exercise 8**. Use your proofreaders' marks to show the errors in capitalization and punctuation. Justices, Supreme Court, and Chief Justice are all proper nouns and begin with capital letters.

Workbook:

Proofreader's Mark	Meaning
(lc)	make lowercase
(caps)	capitalize
⊙	insert period
' ∧	insert apostrophe
? ∧	insert question mark

Answer Key:

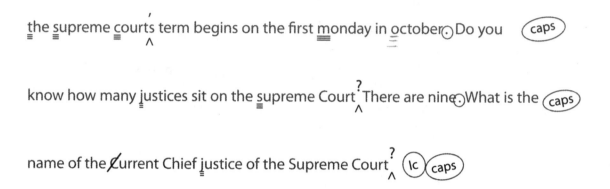

the supreme courts term begins on the first monday in october. Do you (caps)

know how many justices sit on the supreme Court? There are nine. What is the (caps)

name of the current Chief justice of the Supreme Court? (lc)(caps)

The student can find out more information about the Supreme Court by visiting its website, www.supremecourtus.gov.

LESSON 38

New: Interrogative Pronouns
Review: Pronouns

Review "How Doth…" (Lesson 27) again today. If the student has trouble remembering the poem, have him practice it daily until he is confident.

Instructor: Let's say the definition of a pronoun together.

TOGETHER: A pronoun is a word used in the place of a noun.

Instructor: Now we are going to practice the list of personal pronouns.
Personal Pronouns
I, me, my, mine
You, your, yours
He, she, him, her, it
His, hers, its
We, us, our, ours
They, them, their, theirs

If the student already knows the list of pronouns, have him say them alone from memory once. If he needs to review, say the list with him three times.

Instructor: In addition to personal pronouns, you also learned demonstrative pronouns: *this, that, these,* and *those.* These pronouns demonstrate, or point out, something. Look at **Exercise 1** in your workbook. Read the first sentence.

Workbook: <u>This</u> is my favorite day of the week.

Instructor: Now let's think of a noun for which the underlined pronoun could stand. What is your favorite day of the week?

Student: *[Friday, Saturday, Sunday, etc.]*

Instructor: The pronoun *This* stands for the noun [Friday, Saturday, or Sunday]. [Friday, Saturday, or Sunday] is your favorite day of the week. **This** is your favorite day of the week. Now read the rest of the sentences in **Exercise 1**. After you read each sentence, tell me a noun for which the underlined pronoun could stand.

Workbook: <u>That</u> is very delicate.

Student: *[The flower, teacup, etc.] is very delicate.*

Workbook: <u>These</u> are shiny.

Student: *[The cars, The mirrors, The coins, etc.] are shiny.*

Workbook: <u>Those</u> will bite me!

Student: *[The flies, The gerbils, The mosquitoes, etc.] will bite me!*

Instructor: A pronoun is a word that takes the place of a noun. There is a special name for the noun that is replaced. It is called the antecedent. Usually, the antecedent noun goes before its pronoun. Read the sentence in **Exercise 2**. The pronoun is in bold. The antecedent is circled. There is an arrow that starts at the pronoun and points back to its antecedent. Remember, the antecedent is the noun the pronoun replaces.

antecedent

Workbook: When (Ray) collects shells, **he** puts them in a glass case.

Instructor: If a pronoun replaces more than one person, place, thing, or idea, it can have more than one antecedent noun. Read the sentences in **Exercise 3**.

antecedent

Workbook: (Ray) and (I) combed **our** favorite beach for shells.

Instructor: Read the sentences in **Exercise 4**. The pronoun is in bold. Find the antecedent and circle it. Then draw an arrow from the pronoun to its antecedent, the noun the pronoun replaces.

Answer Key:

(Sue) said, "That life preserver is **mine**."

The (children's) life preservers kept **them** safe.

(Dad) and (Mom) said, "The beach is **ours** today."

Instructor: Let's review the difference between subject pronouns and object pronouns. Subject pronouns are the pronouns that are typically used as subjects of sentences. Object pronouns are the pronouns used as objects in sentences. Read the lists of subject pronouns and object pronouns in **Exercise 5** of your workbook.

Workbook:

Subject Pronouns	Object Pronouns
I	me
he	him
she	her
we	us
they	them

Instructor: Subject pronouns are typically used as subjects. You also use a subject pronoun for a predicate nominative, since it renames the subjects. Object pronouns are the pronouns used as objects, like direct objects and indirect objects. Look at **Exercise 6** in your workbook. Read each sentence and circle the subject or object pronoun in it. Write "S" over it if it is a subject pronoun used as the subject or predicate nominative. If the pronoun is an object pronoun used as the direct or indirect object in the sentence, write "O" over it.

Answer Key:

(We) went to a beach with lots of children. — S

A lifeguard watched (us.) — O

He watched (me) swim. — O

(I) met a new friend. — S

My brother helped (her) build a sandcastle. — O

(She) showed (him) a sand crab. — S O

(They) played until the sun was too hot. — S

Instructor: Now we are going to learn a new kind of pronoun that we use when we ask questions. Read the list of these question pronouns in **Exercise 7**.

Workbook: Interrogative Pronouns (Used in Questions)

who

whom

which

what

Instructor: These question pronouns have a special name. They are called interrogative pronouns. *Interrogative* is a big word, but you may know a similar word: *interrogate*. When there is a crime, police interrogate the suspect. They ask the suspect a lot of questions. "Who ran away?" "Whom did you drive?" "Which is your car?" "What were you carrying?" The word *interrogative* means "asking a question." So, interrogative pronouns are pronouns you use when you are asking a question. They always come at or near the beginning of a sentence. Read the sentences in **Exercise 8** and circle the interrogative pronouns.

Whose is sometimes considered an interrogative pronoun, but we are not including it in our list because it functions as an adjective in a sentence (e.g., "Whose book is that?"). *Whose* is an interrogative adjective. *What* and *which* can also be interrogative adjectives (e.g., "What time is dinner?" or "Which postcard did you receive?"). Interrogative adjectives will be taught in a later grade. This lesson focuses on interrogative pronouns—words used in the place of a noun. Interrogative pronouns are simply introduced at this level.

Answer Key: (Who) is the leader?

(Whom) will you ask?

(Which) was the faster runner?

(What) is your favorite food?

(Who) disturbed the sleeping dog?

(Whom) will you believe?

(Which) is the older twin?

(What) were you singing?

Instructor: Now we will diagram some question sentences. Look at **Exercise 9** in your workbook. Read the first sentence. Here is a question the police asked the suspect.

Workbook: Who ran away?

Instructor: The suspect answered the question, and the police inspector repeated his answer. "Tina ran away." Look at the diagram of "Tina ran away."

Workbook: Tina ran away.

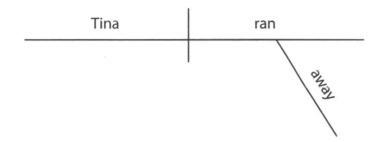

Instructor: What is the verb in the sentence?
Student: *Ran*

Instructor: What is the subject? Who ran?
Student: *Tina*

Instructor: This sentence contains an adverb that tells where. Where did Tina run?
Student: *Away*

Instructor: *Away* is an adverb. It is written on the line beneath the verb it describes. Now look again at the first sentence in **Exercise 9**, "Who ran away?" How would you diagram that particular sentence? The first thing you do is rewrite the question as a statement. This is very easy, because the words are already in the correct order. Read the two sentences above the empty frame.

Workbook: Who ran away?

Who ran away.

Instructor: You diagram "Who ran away?" the same way as "Tina ran away." I will ask you questions to complete the diagram. What is the verb?
Student: *Ran*

Instructor: Write *ran* on the verb line. What is the subject? Who ran? (Hint: The answer is in the question I just asked you.)
Student: *Who*

Instructor: The interrogative pronoun *Who* is the subject. Write *Who* on the subject line. What is the adverb that tells where Who ran?

Student: Away

Instructor: Write *away* on the slanted line beneath the verb it describes.

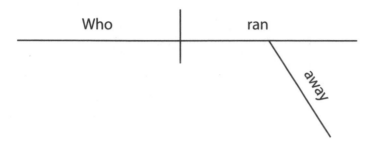

Instructor: Look at **Exercise 10** in your workbook. Read the first sentence. Here is the next question the police asked the suspect.

Workbook: Whom did you drive?

Instructor: The suspect answered the question, and the police inspector repeated his answer. "You did drive Alex." Look at the diagram of "You did drive Alex."

Workbook: You did drive Alex.

You	did drive	Alex

Instructor: What are the two verbs in the sentence?
Student: Did drive

Instructor: What is the subject? Who did drive?
Student: You

Instructor: This sentence contains a direct object that receives the action of the verb. Did drive whom?
Student: Alex

Instructor: *Alex* is the direct object. It is written to the right of the verb. Now look again at the first sentence in **Exercise 10**, "Whom did you drive?" In order to diagram that question sentence, you first rewrite the question as a statement. Read the two sentences above the empty frame.

Workbook: Whom did you drive?

You did drive whom.

Instructor: "Whom did you drive?" is diagrammed the same way as "You did drive Alex." I will ask you questions to complete the diagram. What are the verbs?

Student: *Did drive*

Instructor: Write *did drive* on the verb line. What is the subject? Who did drive?

Student: *You*

Instructor: *You* is the subject. Write *you* on the subject line. Do not capitalize it, because *you* is not capitalized in the question sentence. This sentence contains a direct object that receives the action of the verb. Did drive whom? (Hint: The answer is in the question I just asked you.)

Student: *Whom*

Instructor: Write *Whom* to the right of verb. Remember to capitalize *Whom*, because it is capitalized in the question sentence.

you	did drive	Whom

Instructor: You have now diagrammed two question sentences, one beginning with *Who* and the other with *Whom*. *Who* and *whom* are subject and object pronouns. *Who* is used as a subject or a predicate nominative, since it renames the subjects. *Whom* is used as an object, like a direct object.

Instructor: Look at **Exercise 11** in your workbook. Read each question sentence, and then rewrite the question as a statement. In each of your rewritten statements, circle the interrogative pronoun. Write "S" over the interrogative pronoun if it is used as a subject and write "DO" if it is used as a direct object.

Answer Key: Whom did you visit?

Statement: You did visit (whom). [DO]

Who is winning?

Statement: (Who) is winning. [S]

LESSON 39

New: Conjugating the Verb "To Have"
Review: Four Types of Sentences

Review "Afternoon on a Hill" (Lesson 8), "Ozymandias" (Lesson 16), and "How Doth…" (Lesson 27) today. If the student has trouble remembering a poem, have him practice it daily until he is confident.

Instructor: Let's begin this lesson by conjugating another verb. Remember, to conjugate means to learn the various forms of a verb. When you are conjugating, you always start with the basic verb, for example, "to pick," "to rake," or "to gather." The word *to* plus the basic form of a verb is called the infinitive.

Instructor: The basic form of the verb changes slightly depending on the person (I, you, he, or they) who is doing the action. There are three kinds of persons: first person, second person, and third person. *I, you,* and *he* are called singular persons because each is one, single person. *We, you,* and *they* are plural persons because there is more than one person in each group. [This was covered in Lessons 10 and 23.]

Instructor: Now let's conjugate the verb "to have." When we conjugate, we learn the various forms of a verb, and how a verb changes slightly depending on the person doing the action. We will conjugate "to have" in the present tense. Read the chart in **Exercise 1** with me.

Read each line across and include the title of each as you read. For example, "First person singular: I have, First person plural: we have, Second person singular: you have," etc. Then read the chart again, this time down the columns as a chant. Read just the words in bold: "I have, you have, he, she, it has," etc.

208

Workbook: Infinitive: to have

Present Tense

	Singular	Plural
First person	**I have**	**we have**
Second person	**you have**	**you have**
Third person	**he, she, it has**	**they have**

Instructor: "To have" is an irregular verb in the present tense, because its third person singular form doesn't follow the regular pattern. If it did, you would just add **s** to *have*: "he, she, it haves." That is not right! The verb "to have" is also irregular in the past tense. Read the chart in **Exercise 2** with me.

Chant the words in bold.

Workbook: Infinitive: to have

Past Tense

	Singular	Plural
First person	**I had**	**we had**
Second person	**you had**	**you had**
Third person	**he, she, it had**	**they had**

Instructor: "To have" is considered an irregular verb in the past tense because the forms of the verb do not follow the regular pattern. If they did, you would just add **ed** to the end of the present form. It would sound like this: "I haved, you haved, he, she, it haved…" That sounds odd, doesn't it? "To have" is an irregular verb in the past tense. Read the sentences in **Exercise 3** and write the correct form of the verb "to have" in the blank. Look at the charts in **Exercises 1** and **2** if you need help.

Answer Key: Choose the correct form of "to have" in the **present tense**.

1. **Have** you ever eaten a cranberry?

2. A cranberry **has** a tart flavor.

3. We **have** cranberry sauce every Thanksgiving dinner.

Choose the correct form of "to have" in the **past tense**.

1. They **had** to flood the cranberry bog to harvest the cranberries.

2. You **had** to see it!

Instructor: Now you are going to review how to diagram the four types of sentences. Let's begin by saying the definition of a sentence. A sentence is a group of words that expresses a complete thought. All sentences begin with a capital letter and end with a punctuation mark. Say that with me.

TOGETHER: A sentence is a group of words that expresses a complete thought. All sentences begin with a capital letter and end with a punctuation mark.

Instructor: There are four different types of sentences: statements, commands, questions, and exclamations. A statement gives information. In **Exercise 4** of your workbook, read the statement sentence.

Workbook: A cranberry is an edible red berry.

Instructor: This is a statement: "A cranberry is an edible red berry." It gives information. Statements always end with a period. Let's diagram the sentence onto the empty frame in **Exercise 4** of your workbook. I will help you by asking questions and giving commands!

Instructor: What is the linking verb?
Student: *Is*

Instructor: *Is* is your verb. Write the verb on the verb line. Now find the subject. What is?
Student: *Cranberry*

Instructor: *Cranberry* is the subject. Write the subject to the left of the center line on your frame.

Instructor: This sentence contains a predicate nominative. What noun in the predicate renames the subject *cranberry*?
Student: *Berry*

Instructor: *Berry* is the predicate nominative. Write the predicate nominative to the right of the verb on your diagram. The predicate nominative is separated from the verb by a slanted line that points back to the subject.

Instructor: Look at the subject, *cranberry,* again. What is the article used to describe *cranberry?*

Student: *A*

Instructor: Write *A* on the slanted line beneath the subject it describes. Now look again at the predicate nominative *berry.* What are the three words that describe *berry?*

Student: *An, edible, red*

Instructor: Write these adjectives below *berry,* the noun they describe. Write them in the order in which they appear in the sentence. Now your diagram is complete.

Instructor: The second type of sentence is a command. A command gives an order or makes a request. It ends with either a period or an exclamation point. In **Exercise 5**, read the command sentence.

Workbook: Make the cranberry sauce.

Instructor: Now I will help you diagram this sentence onto the empty frame in **Exercise 5** of your workbook. What is the verb?

Student: *Make*

Instructor: *Make* is the verb. Write the word *Make* on the verb line. Remember to capitalize *Make* because it is capitalized in the sentence. Now find the subject. Remember, command sentences do have a subject, but the subject is not written in the sentence. It is understood to be the word *you.* Someone is telling you to make the cranberry sauce. She does not command you by saying "You make the cranberry sauce"; she simply says "Make the cranberry sauce." So, again, what is the subject of this command sentence? Who should make the cranberry sauce?

Student: *You*

Instructor: *You* is the subject. Write the word *you* on the subject line. Because the subject *you* is not written in the sentence but is just understood, put *you* in parentheses.

Instructor: Look again at the verb *Make.* Is there a direct object that receives the action of the verb? I will ask you a question that will help you find the direct object. Answer me with one word. Make what?

Student: *Sauce*

If the student answers "cranberry," ask him to read the command sentence again. Say "Now are you being asked to make a tiny cranberry? Or are you being asked to make a sauce? Sauce is the direct object."

Instructor: Write the direct object *sauce* to the right of the verb on your diagram. The direct object is separated from the verb by a short, straight line. Are there any words that describe the direct object *sauce?* There are two in this sentence.

Student: *The, cranberry*

Instructor: Write these adjectives below the direct object *sauce. The* is written on the first adjective line and *cranberry* is written on the second adjective line because that is the order in which they appear in the sentence. Your diagram is complete.

(you)	Make	sauce

the   cranberry

Instructor: The third type of sentence is a question. A question asks something. A question always ends with a question mark. In **Exercise 6,** read the question.

Workbook: Do you eat cranberries?

Instructor: Now I will help you diagram this sentence.

Instructor: In order to find the subject of a question sentence, it is helpful to rearrange the words in the question so that it becomes a statement. Read the question in **Exercise 6** again, and then write the statement beneath it.

Answer Key: Do you eat cranberries?

You do eat cranberries.

Instructor: Now diagram this sentence on the empty frame in **Exercise 6** of your workbook. There are two verbs in this sentence: a helping verb and an action verb. What are those verbs?

Student: *Do eat*

Instructor: Write both of these verbs on your verb line. Remember to capitalize *Do* on the diagram because it is capitalized in the sentence. What is the subject of the question "Do you eat cranberries?" Think of the statement "You do eat cranberries." Who eats cranberries?

Student: *You*

Instructor: Look again at *Do eat*. Is there a direct object that receives the action of the verb? I will ask you a question that will help you find the direct object. Do eat what?

Student: *Cranberries*

Instructor: Write the direct object *cranberries* to the right of the verb on your diagram. The direct object is separated from the verb by a short, straight line. Now your diagram is complete.

you	Do eat	cranberries

Remind the student that he is not to put punctuation on the diagram.

Instructor: The fourth type of sentence is an exclamation. An exclamation shows sudden or strong feeling. An exclamation always ends with an exclamation point. In **Exercise 7**, read the exclamation sentence. Read it with lots of expression because exclamations show strong feeling!

Workbook: Raw cranberries are tart!

Instructor: Diagramming an exclamation sentence is just like diagramming a statement. I will help you diagram the sentence "Raw cranberries are tart!" onto the empty frame in **Exercise 7**.

Instructor: What is the linking verb in this sentence?

Student: *Are*

Instructor: The verb *are* links the subject to a word in the complete predicate. Write the verb to the right of your center line. Now find the subject. Answer me with one word. What are?

Student: *Cranberries*

Instructor: Write the word *cranberries* on the subject line.

Instructor: This sentence contains a predicate adjective. This adjective is in the complete predicate of the sentence, but it describes the subject. What kind of cranberries are they?

Student: *Tart*

Instructor: Because the predicate adjective *tart* follows the verb in the sentence, it is written to the right of the verb on the diagram. Write the predicate adjective to the right of the slanted line on your diagram. That slanted line points back toward the subject to remind you that a predicate adjective describes the subject.

Instructor: Go back and look again at the subject. Are there any words in the complete subject that describe the simple subject? This adjective tells what kind of cranberries.

Student: *Raw*

Instructor: Write the adjective *Raw* on a slanted line below the subject it describes. Now your diagram is complete.

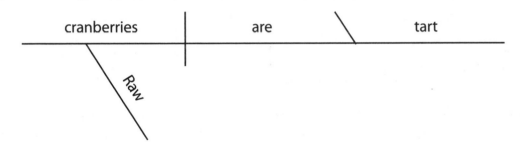

LESSON 40

Poem Memorization: "Learning to Read"

Instructor: In Lesson 40 of your workbook, you will find a poem about a freed slave who learned to read late in life. After the Civil War, teachers from the North ("Yankee teachers") came down to teach the former slaves how to read. The slaves' former masters had tried to keep them from reading, because reading would encourage them to be free people. The poet refers to "Rebs"—this is short for "Rebels," the nickname for the Southern fighters in the Civil War. The poem also mentions pot liquor fat, which is the liquid left after meat is boiled.

This poem is written in the dialect of the uneducated slave, Chloe.

"Learning to Read"
by Frances Ellen Watkins Harper

Very soon the Yankee teachers

Came down and set up school;

But, oh! How the Rebs did hate it, —

It was agin' their rule.

Our masters always tried to hide

Book learning from our eyes;

Knowledge didn't agree with slavery—

'Twould make us all too wise.

But some of us would try to steal

A little from the book,

And put the words together,

And learn by hook or crook.

I remember Uncle Caldwell,

Who took pot liquor fat

And greased the pages of his book,

And hid it in his hat.

And had his master ever seen

The leaves upon his head,

He'd had thought them greasy papers,

But nothing to be read.

And there was Mr. Turner's Ben,

Who heard the children spell,

And picked the words right up by heart,

And learned to read 'em well.

Well, the Northern folks kept sending

The Yankee teachers down;

And they stood right up and helped us,

Though the Rebs did sneer and frown.

And I longed to read my Bible,

For precious words it said;

But when I begun to learn it,

Folks just shook their heads,

And said there is no use trying,

Oh! Chloe, you're too late;

But as I was rising sixty,

I had no time to wait.

So I got a pair of glasses,

And straight to work I went,

And never stopped till I could read

The hymns and Testament.

Then I got a little cabin

A place to call my own —

And I felt as independent

As the queen upon her throne.

Discuss the meaning of the poem with the student. Then read the poem to the student three times in a row. Repeat this triple reading twice more during the day. Have the student check the boxes in his workbook when this is done.

LESSON 41

Review: Four Kinds of Verbs
Review: Direct and Indirect Objects
Review: Predicate Nominatives and Adjectives

Read "Learning to Read" (Lesson 40) three times to the student. Then ask the student to try to say parts of the first and second stanzas along with you (or the tape recorder).

Instructor: Let's begin by saying the definition of a verb. A verb is a word that does an action, shows a state of being, links two words together, or helps another verb. Say that with me two times.

TOGETHER (two times): A verb is a word that does an action, shows a state of being, links two words together, or helps another verb.

Instructor: Action verbs show action. *Hiss*, *squeeze*, and *rattle* are all action verbs a snake might do. Action verbs are sometimes followed by a direct object that receives the action of the verb. Now you will find the direct objects in a few sentences. Look at **Exercise 1** in your workbook. After you read each sentence, I will help you find the direct object by asking you "what" or "whom" after the verb.

Workbook: Burrowing snakes eat slugs.

Instructor: Eat what?
Student: *Slugs*

Instructor: *Slugs* is the direct object. It receives the action of the verb *eat*. Write "D.O." for direct object over the word *slugs*. Read the next sentence.

Workbook: Boa constrictors squeeze rodents.

Instructor: Squeeze what?
Student: *Rodents*

Instructor: *Rodents* is the direct object. It receives the action of the verb *squeeze*. Write "D.O." for direct object over the word *rodents*. Read the third sentence.

Workbook: The herpetologist studied venom.

Instructor: A herpetologist is a scientist who studies reptiles, including snakes. Studied what?

Student: *Venom*

Instructor: *Venom* is the direct object. It receives the action of the verb *studied*. Look at the diagram of "The herpetologist studied venom."

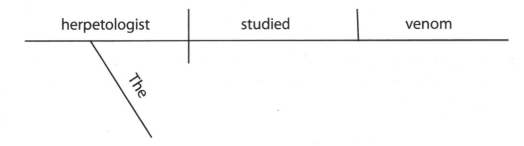

Instructor: The direct object *venom* is written next to the verb *studied*. It is divided from the verb by a short line. Read the sentence in **Exercise 2**.

Workbook: The herpetologist handed me a kingsnake.

Instructor: Let's find the direct object. Handed what?

Student: *Kingsnake*

Instructor: *Kingsnake* is the direct object. (The herpetologist didn't hand me to somebody!) *Kingsnake* receives the action of the verb *handed*. This sentence also has something called an indirect object. An indirect object is a noun or pronoun that is **between** the action verb and the direct object of a sentence. It answers the question "to whom" or "for whom" the action is done, but the words *to* or *for* are usually not in the sentence. *To* or *for* are just understood. The herpetologist handed me a kingsnake. Handed a kingsnake to whom?

Student: *Me*

Instructor: *Me* is the indirect object. Read the next sentence in **Exercise 2** and look at its diagram.

Workbook: I gave the kingsnake my attention.

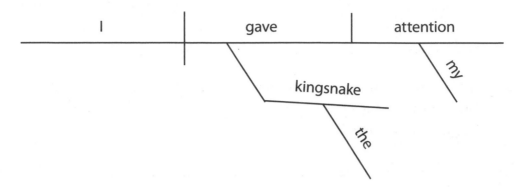

Instructor: *Gave* is the action verb. Who gave? I gave. *I* is the subject. Let's find the direct object. Gave what? My attention. *Attention* is an idea noun, and the direct object of the sentence. The direct object *attention* is written next to the verb. It is divided from the verb by a short line that does not go through the main horizontal line. The direct object *attention* has a possessive pronoun that acts like an adjective that tells whose. The possessive pronoun *my* is written in a slanted line below the idea noun it describes. Let's find the indirect object. Gave my attention to whom? *The kingsnake.* The indirect object *kingsnake* is written underneath the verb, on the little horizontal line. When diagramming indirect objects, **nothing is written on the slanted line**. The indirect object *kingsnake* has an article that acts like an adjective. The article *the* is written on a slanted line below the noun it describes.

Instructor: Let's talk about helping verbs. They help other verbs. Chant the first part of the list of helping verbs with me.

TOGETHER: Am [clap]
Is [clap]
Are, was, were. [clap]
Be [clap]
Being [clap]
Been. [clap] [clap]

Instructor: Now let's chant the rest of the helping verbs together.

TOGETHER: Have, has, had [clap]
Do, does, did [clap]
Shall, will, should, would, may, might, must [clap, clap]
Can, could!

Instructor: Read the sentences in **Exercise 3**. Circle the helping verbs. Each helping verb helps the action verb in the sentence.

Answer Key: Snakes(do)hibernate.

Snakes(can)shed their skin.

The copperhead(was)camouflaged in the dead leaves.

Instructor: Another type of verb, a state of being verb, just shows that you exist. Let's chant the state of being verbs together. This is the same chant as the first part of the helping verb chant.

Together: Am [clap]
Is [clap]
Are, was, were. [clap]
Be [clap]
Being [clap]
Been. [clap] [clap]

Instructor: In **Exercise 4**, read the sentences with state of being verbs. Circle the state of being verb in the sentence.

Answer Key: I(am.)

She(is)here.

They(are)there.

Instructor: State of being verbs don't show action or help other verbs—they just show that someone or something exists. There is one more type of verb: linking verbs. Linking verbs link, or join, two words together. These verbs are easy to recognize because they are the same verbs as the state of being verbs: *am, is, are, was, were, be, being, been.* These verbs can do three of the four things in your verb definition! Read aloud in **Exercise 5** of your workbook.

Workbook: The verbs **am, is, are, was, were, be, being, been** can

- help another verb

- show a state of being

- link two words together

Instructor: If you see the verb *am* in a sentence, you have to read the whole sentence to tell what kind of verb it is—a helping verb, state of being verb, or linking verb. Read aloud the first sentence in **Exercise 6**.

Workbook: I am practicing.

Instructor: *Am* is a helping verb in that sentence. *Am* helps the verb *practicing*. Write "H.V." for helping verb over *am*. Read the next sentence.

Workbook: I am at the zoo.

Instructor: The verb *am* just shows that someone exists. *Am* is a state of being verb in that sentence. Write "S.B.V." for state of being verb over *am*. Read the next sentence.

Workbook: I am excited.

Instructor: *Am* is a linking verb in that sentence. It links the subject *I* with the predicate adjective *excited*. Write "L.V." for linking verb over *am*. Let's use some linking verbs in sentences. I will read you a noun and a linking verb and let you complete the sentence by choosing a predicate adjective that describes the subject. Write the word in the blank in your workbook. The linking verb in bold print will link, or connect, the subject noun with the adjective you choose. Follow along as I read and point to the parts of the sentences in **Exercise 7**. The first sentence is about rattlesnakes. How would you describe a rattlesnake? Tell me your answer and write it in the blank.

Workbook: A rattlesnake is _____.
Student: *A rattlesnake is scaly [or brown, poisonous, or dangerous].*

If the student says, "A rattlesnake is a reptile" or "A rattlesnake is a snake," remind him that he is supposed to provide you with an adjective (a word that describes), not a noun (a word that renames).

Instructor: The linking verb *is* connects the subject *rattlesnake* with the adjective *[the word the student chose]*! Can you describe a garter snake? Tell me your answer and write it in the blank.

Workbook: The garter snake was _____.
Student: *The garter snake was [little, thin, common, harmless].*

Instructor: The linking verb *was* connects the subject *garter snake* with the adjective *[the word student chose]*.

Instructor: Let's say the chant of the linking verbs. I will do the chant first, and you will join me the second time through.

Instructor, then together:
>Am [clap]
>Is [clap]
>Are, was, were. [clap]
>Be [clap]
>Being [clap]
>Been. [clap] [clap]

Instructor: Read the sentence in **Exercise 8** and look its diagram. This sentence contains a linking verb. I will point out words on the diagram as I explain.

Workbook: Snakes are legless.

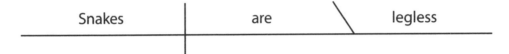

In order to keep the student's eyes focused on what you are explaining, physically point out the words and lines on the student's diagram as they appear in the following two paragraphs of the instructor's script.

Instructor: The linking verb *are* connects the subject of the sentence, *Snakes*, with the adjective *legless*. *Legless* is an adjective that describes the subject *Snakes*. It is written to the right of the verb on the diagram because it follows the verb in the sentence. Because the adjective is in the complete predicate of the sentence, it is a **predicate adjective.** On the diagram, draw an arrow from the predicate adjective *legless* that points back to the subject *Snakes*.

Instructor: Remember, the complete predicate is the verb and all the words attached to the verb line on a diagram. These words tell us what is said about the subject. Do you see the slanted line on the diagram that separates the linking verb *are* from the predicate adjective? That slanted line points back toward the subject to remind you that *legless* is an adjective that describes *Snakes*.

Instructor: Linking verbs can also link the subject with a noun or pronoun in the complete predicate that renames the subject. This noun or pronoun is called the predicate nominative. Read the sentence in **Exercise 9** to me and look at its diagram.

Workbook: Snakes are reptiles.

Snakes	are	reptiles

Instructor: *Are* is a linking verb. It connects the subject *Snakes* with a noun that renames the subject. *Reptiles* tells what the subject is. What are snakes? Reptiles. *Reptiles* is in the complete predicate of the sentence. A noun or pronoun in the complete predicate that renames the subject is called a **predicate nominative**. Even though *reptiles* renames the subject *Snakes*, it is written to the right of the verb on the diagram because it follows the verb in the sentence. On the diagram, draw an arrow from the predicate nominative *reptiles* that points back to the subject *Snakes*.

Optional Dictation Exercise

The sentences today are adapted from *The Last Snake in Ireland* by Sheila MacGill-Callahan, a fairy tale about what happened when Saint Patrick rang a snake call on his magic bell. Tell the student, "In your dictation you will hear the words 'Loch Ness.' 'Loch' is the Scottish word for lake. 'Ness' is the name of the lake."

After the dictation is completed, ask the student to write AV over the three action verbs, DO over the two direct objects, and PN over the predicate nominative.

Dictation:

                                      AV   AV

All the snakes, except one, crawled into the sea. Saint Patrick tricked

                                   DO   AV   DO

that biggest, oldest, and sneakiest snake and dumped him into a lake.

                        PN

He is the Loch Ness Monster.

LESSON 42

New: Prepositions

Read "Learning to Read" (Lesson 40) three times to the student. Then ask the student to try to say parts of the third and fourth stanzas along with you (or the tape recorder).

You will need a plate, two slices of bread, a slice of cheese, a lettuce leaf, a tomato slice, and mayonnaise or mustard for the student to make a sandwich. This exercise will make the lesson a memorable one for the student. It is worth the extra effort. If making a real sandwich is not possible, the student can assemble a "play sandwich" using cut-out pictures of the food.

This lesson assumes that the student memorized the list of prepositions in a previous level of *First Language Lessons*. If the student did not use that book, he will now start memorizing a long list of prepositions. The student will find a memorized list of prepositions invaluable when he analyzes sentences, because the object of a preposition is never the subject, direct object, or indirect object. The student will learn the definition of a preposition as well, but learning the definition is not enough. He should also memorize the list, since not all prepositions follow the definition exactly.

Instructor: This lesson is about the part of speech called a preposition. I will say the entire definition to you: A preposition is a word that shows the relationship of a noun or pronoun to another word in the sentence. Now repeat after me: A preposition is a word that shows the relationship …

Student: *A preposition is a word that shows the relationship …*

Instructor: … of a noun or pronoun to another word in the sentence.

Student: *… of a noun or pronoun to another word in the sentence.*

Instructor: Let's say the entire definition together three times.

TOGETHER (three times): A preposition is a word that shows the relationship of a noun or pronoun to another word in the sentence.

Lay out the plate, bread, cheese, lettuce, tomato, and the mayonnaise or mustard bottle in front of the student.

Instructor: You have worked so hard on the definition that I think you need to take a snack break. Let's make a preposition sandwich with two slices of bread, cheese, lettuce, tomato, and mayonnaise (or mustard). Read the directions printed in **Exercise 1** of your workbook. The prepositions are in bold print. Then follow the directions to make the sandwich.

Some prepositions in the following sentences are intentionally not in bold type. This exercise focuses on the prepositions that show a concrete relationship between the sandwich ingredients.

Workbook:
1. Put a slice of bread **on** the plate.

2. Spread mayonnaise (or mustard) **across** the slice of bread.

3. Now arrange a slice of cheese **over** the slice of bread.

4. Add lettuce. Do you see the cheese **under** the lettuce?

5. Now add a slice of tomato and another slice of bread. Do you notice the tomato is **beneath** the bread?

Instructor: You have made a preposition sandwich showing relationships between all the parts of this snack. You can eat this sandwich at the end of the lesson. Now read the first sentence in **Exercise 2**.

Workbook: The <u>bread</u> **on** the <u>plate</u> is made from flour.

Instructor: *On* is a preposition that shows the relationship between the noun *plate* and the noun *bread*. Which bread? The bread on the plate. Read the next sentence.

Workbook: I spread <u>mayonnaise</u> **across** the <u>bread</u>.

Instructor: *Across* is a preposition that shows the relationship between the mayonnaise and the bread. Where did you spread the mayonnaise? Across the bread. Read the next sentence.

Workbook: The <u>cheese slice</u> is **over** the <u>mayonnaise</u>.

Instructor: *Over* is a preposition that shows the relationship between the cheese slice and the mayonnaise. Where is the cheese slice? Over the mayonnaise. Read the next sentence.

Workbook: The <u>cheese</u> **under** the <u>lettuce</u> is American cheese.

Instructor: *Under* is a preposition that shows the relationship between the noun *lettuce* and the noun *cheese*. Which cheese? The cheese under the lettuce. Read the last sentence.

Workbook: The <u>tomato</u> is **beneath** the <u>bread</u>.

Instructor: *Beneath* is a preposition that shows the relationship between the noun *bread* and the noun *tomato*. Where is the tomato? Beneath the bread.

Instructor: A preposition is a word that shows the relationship of a noun or pronoun to another word in the sentence. In **Exercise 3** of your workbook, there is a list of common prepositions that you will begin to memorize. Let's read them together.

Workbook: <u>Prepositions</u>

Aboard, about, above, across.
After, against, along, among, around, at.

Before, behind, below, beneath.
Beside, between, beyond, by.

Down, during, except, for, from.
In, inside, into, like.

Near, of, off, on, over.
Past, since, through, throughout.

To, toward, under, underneath.
Until, up, upon.
With, within, without.

Once you have read through the list together, the student may check the box in his workbook. The student should practice the list every day until he has memorized the entire list. Focus on memorizing the first section today (*aboard* through *at*). Once the student can say the first section from memory, he may check it off in his workbook.

As you read the following instructions, point to the words in the example sentence ("The Greater Roadrunner …") to make the explanation clearer to the student. These words are italicized in the instructor's script. Do this for all of the example sentences in **Exercise 4**.

Instructor: In **Exercise 4**, read the first sentence to me.

Answer Key: 1.   The Greater Roadrunner (in) the Southwest mostly runs rather than flies.

Instructor: *In* is a preposition. Circle it. It shows the relationship between the noun *Southwest* and the noun *Greater Roadrunner*. Which Greater Roadrunner? The one in the Southwest. Read the second sentence to me, and then tell me the preposition. You may look at the list of prepositions.

Answer Key: 2.   He eats centipedes (under) rocks.

Student: *Under*

Instructor: *Under* is a preposition. Circle it. It shows the relationship between the noun *rocks* and the noun *centipedes*. Which centipedes? Answer me beginning with "The centipedes that are …"

Student: *The centipedes that are under rocks.*

Instructor: Read the third sentence to me, and then say the preposition as you circle it.

Answer Key: 3.   He turns his back (toward) the warm sun and fluffs his feathers.

Student: *Toward*

Instructor: *Toward* is a preposition. It shows the relationship between the noun *sun* and the noun *back*. Where does he turn his back? Answer me beginning with "He turns…"

Student: *He turns his back toward the sun.*

Instructor: Read the fourth sentence to me, and then say the preposition as you circle it.

Answer Key: 4.   The skin (around) his eyes is wrinkled.

Student: *Around*

Instructor: *Around* is a preposition. It shows the relationship between the noun *eyes* and the noun *skin*. Which skin is it? Answer me beginning with "It is the skin …"

Student: *It is the skin around his eyes.*

Instructor: Read the fifth sentence to me, and then say the preposition as you circle it.

Answer Key: 5. This bird grabs his prey (with) his sharp bill.

Student: *With*

Instructor: *With* is a preposition. It shows the relationship between the noun *bill* and the verb *grabs*. How does this bird grab his prey? Answer me beginning with "This bird grabs his prey…"

Student: *This bird grabs his prey with his sharp bill.*

Instructor: Now you will practice finding prepositions in sentences. Read each sentence in **Exercise 5** and circle its preposition. You may use the list in **Exercise 3** to help you.

Answer Key:
1. The pitcher threw the ball (to) the batter.
2. Airplanes land (at) airports.
3. Windshield wipers clear rain (from) car windows.
4. Clouds floated (across) the moon.
5. There were clouds (beyond) the mountains.
6. The doormat was (by) the door.
7. Buses operate (within) the city.
8. The boiling magma (inside) the volcano might explode!
9. Venice, Italy, has many canals (for) boats.
10. Mr. Brock took the pumpkins (into) the cellar.
11. Dorothy had a dream (during) the storm.
12. Children (throughout) the village enjoyed the fair.
13. We went (aboard) the plane.
14. The dog (without) the collar was lost.
15. Rita's story was the one (about) frightening gargoyles.
16. A sunset (like) fire blazed westward.
17. You have limped (since) your accident.
18. The weather (after) March is warmer.

19. The vine (against) the stone wall was English ivy.

20. The dusty rug (behind) the bed was rarely vacuumed.

21. The criminal (before) the judge pleaded guilty.

22. Boxes (of) tomatoes were shipped overseas.

23. Humpty Dumpty fell (off) the wall.

24. We will sleep (until) sunrise.

25. He gave a fierce cry and leapt (upon) the snarling tiger!

26. Friday traffic (through) the tunnel was heavy.

27. Our suitcases (beside) the car are ready to go!

28. The woodpecker (up) the pine tree is boring a cavity.

29. This rare purple flower only grows (between) these two mountains.

30. The cereal (above) the refrigerator is quite stale.

31. All the children (except) Ada have had colds.

32. The purple, scaly sea monster lurked (beneath) the water's surface.

33. The shiny flecks (among) the river rocks are gold dust!

34. I crept nervously (near) the snoring giant.

35. The women hiked (along) the Appalachian Trail.

36. The children nestled (under) the warm blankets.

37. The algae (on) the pond's surface are dark red.

38. The skiers zoomed (down) the slope.

39. There is a peanut butter cup buried (below) the ice cream.

40. The chess master studied his opponent (across) the table.

41. He trudged (over) the mountain, wondering if he would ever find the treasure.

LESSON 43

New: Prepositional Phrases and Objects of the Preposition

Read "Learning to Read" (Lesson 40) three times to the student. Then ask the student to try to say parts of the first through fourth stanzas along with you (or the tape recorder).

Instructor: You learned about prepositions in the last lesson. A preposition is a word that shows the relationship of a noun or pronoun to another word in the sentence. Let's say that definition together three times.

TOGETHER (three times): A preposition is a word that shows the relationship of a noun or pronoun to another word in the sentence.

If the student knows the list of prepositions in **Exercise 1**, have him review it by saying it once. If he does not yet have the whole list memorized, focus on the second section today (*before* through *by*), and review the first section. The student may check off his accomplishments in the workbook.

Workbook: Prepositions

Aboard, about, above, across.
After, against, along, among, around, at.

Before, behind, below, beneath.
Beside, between, beyond, by.

Down, during, except, for, from.
In, inside, into, like.

Near, of, off, on, over.
Past, since, through, throughout.

To, toward, under, underneath.
Until, up, upon.
With, within, without.

Instructor: Read the first sentence in **Exercise 2** to me.

Instructor: What is the preposition in the sentence?

Student: *Between*

Answer Key: 1. The lake (between) the mountains shimmered in the sunlight.

Instructor: Circle *between*. The lake between what? Between the mountains. "Between the mountains" is called a **prepositional phrase**. A prepositional phrase begins with a preposition and ends with a noun or pronoun. In fact, the word *preposition* is from a Latin word that means "placed before." A preposition is always **placed before** a noun or pronoun. To find the whole prepositional phrase, you typically ask "whom" or "what" after the preposition. Now read the second sentence to me.

Instructor: What is the preposition in the sentence?

Student: *Behind*

Answer Key: 2. The guard (behind) the gate barked the orders.

Instructor: Circle *behind*. To find the prepositional phrase, ask "whom" or "what" after the preposition. Behind what? Behind the gate. "Behind the gate" is the prepositional phrase. It begins with the preposition *behind* and ends with the noun *gate*. Read the third sentence.

Instructor: What is the preposition in the sentence?

Student: *Beneath*

Answer Key: 3. The rabbits made their home (beneath) the tree.

Instructor: Circle *beneath*. To find the prepositional phrase, ask "whom" or "what" after the preposition. Beneath what? Beneath the tree. "Beneath the tree" is the prepositional phrase. It begins with the preposition *beneath* and ends with the noun *tree*. Now you try. Read the fourth sentence to me.

Instructor: What is the preposition in the sentence?

Student: *After*

Answer Key: 4. We walked home (after) the fireworks.

Instructor: Circle *after*. To find the prepositional phrase, ask "whom" or "what" after the preposition. After what? Answer me beginning with "After..."

Student: *After the fireworks*

Instructor: "After the fireworks" is a prepositional phrase. It begins with the preposition *after* and ends with the noun *fireworks*. As you have seen, a prepositional phrase begins with a preposition and ends with a noun or pronoun. That noun or pronoun is called the **object of the preposition**. In the prepositional phrase "after the fireworks," the object of the preposition is the noun *fireworks*. Read the first sentence in **Exercise 3**.

Workbook: 1. She trimmed the hedges along the fence.

Instructor: What is the preposition in the sentence?
Student: *Along*

Instructor: Circle *along*. Now find the prepositional phrase. Along what?
Student: *Along the fence.*

Instructor: Underline it. The prepositional phrase "along the fence" begins with the preposition *along* and ends with the noun *fence*. The noun or pronoun that follows a preposition is called the object of the preposition. What is the object of the preposition in the prepositional phrase "along the fence"?
Student: *Fence*

Answer Key:
O.P.
1. She trimmed the hedges(along)the fence.

Instructor: Write "O.P." for "object of the preposition" over *fence*. Read the second sentence to me.

Workbook: 2. My brother sat beside me.

Instructor: What is the preposition in the sentence?
Student: *Beside*

Instructor: Circle *beside*. Now find the prepositional phrase. Beside whom?
Student: *Beside me.*

Instructor: Underline it. The prepositional phrase "beside" begins with the preposition *beside* and ends with the pronoun *me*. The noun or pronoun that follows a preposition is called the object of the preposition. What is the object of the preposition in the prepositional phrase "beside me"?
Student: *Me*

Answer Key:

O.P.

2. My brother sat (beside) me.

Instructor: Write "O.P." over *me*. The object of the preposition is just a single word—a noun or pronoun. A **prepositional phrase** contains the preposition, the object of the preposition, and any words that describe it. Read the fourth sentence to me.

Workbook: 3. The lighthouse beyond the rocky shore shines nightly.

Instructor: What is the preposition in the sentence?
Student: *Beyond*

Instructor: Circle *beyond*. Now find the prepositional phrase. Beyond what?
Student: *Beyond the rocky shore*

Instructor: Underline it. The prepositional phrase "beyond the rocky shore" begins with the preposition *beyond* and ends with the noun *shore*. The noun or pronoun that follows a preposition is called the object of the preposition. What is the object of the preposition in the prepositional phrase "beyond the rocky shore"?
Student: *Shore*

If necessary, explain to the student that "shore" is the noun which serves as the object of the preposition, while "rocky" is an adjective that describes *what kind* of shore it is.

Answer Key:

O.P.

3. The lighthouse (beyond) the rocky shore shines nightly.

Instructor: Write "O.P." over *shore*. I will ask you to read each of the sentences, numbers 4 through 8, in your workbook. Then I will ask you to circle the preposition, underline the prepositional phrase, and write "O.P." over the object of the preposition in that phrase.

Workbook: 4. The weary knight leaned against a tree.

Instructor: What is the preposition?
Student: *Against*

Instructor: What is the prepositional phrase?
Student: *Against a tree*

Instructor: What is the object of the preposition?
Student: *Tree*

Answer Key:

O.P.
4.   The weary knight leaned (against) a tree.

Workbook: 5.   The girl <u>at the park</u> shared her snack.

Instructor: What is the preposition?
Student: *At*

Instructor: What is the prepositional phrase?
Student: *At the park*

Instructor: What is the object of the preposition?
Student: *Park*

Answer Key:

O.P.
5.   The girl (at) the park shared her snack.

Workbook: 6.   I have always wanted a house by the sea.

Instructor: What is the preposition?
Student: *By*

Instructor: What is the prepositional phrase?
Student: *By the sea*

Instructor: What is the object of the preposition?
Student: *Sea*

Answer Key:

O.P.
6.   I have always wanted a house (by) the sea.

Workbook: 7.   We brush our teeth <u>before bed</u>.

Instructor: What is the preposition?
Student: *Before*

Instructor: What is the prepositional phrase?
Student: *Before bed*

Instructor: What is the object of the preposition?
Student: *Bed*

Answer Key:
                                       O.P.
    7.   We brush our teeth (before) bed.

Workbook: 8.   The windsurfer sailed <u>across the bay</u>.

Instructor: What is the preposition?
Student: *Across*

Instructor: What is the prepositional phrase?
Student: *Across the bay*

Instructor: What is the object of the preposition?
Student: *Bay*

Answer Key:
                                         O.P.
    8.   The windsurfer sailed (across) the bay.

Instructor: Read the sentences in **Exercise 4**.

Workbook: The tired wolf fell **behind**.

                I will go **inside**.

                The birds soared **above**.

Instructor: The words in bold are prepositions, right? Wrong! A preposition is always part of a prepositional phrase. A preposition is always followed by its object, the object of the preposition. So what is the function of the words *behind*, *inside*, and *above* in the sentences you just read? They are adverbs, of course! They tell where. The tired wolf fell behind. Fell where? Behind. I will go inside. Will go where? Inside. The birds soared above. Soared where? Above. Don't be fooled into thinking these words are always prepositions. They can sometimes be adverbs. Remember, a preposition is always part of a prepositional phrase. A preposition is always followed by its object, the object of the preposition. Now read the sentences in **Exercise 5**. In these sentences, the preposition is part of a prepositional phrase. The preposition is followed by its object.

Workbook: The tired wolf fell <u>**behind** the others</u>.

                I will go <u>**inside** the cave</u>.

                The birds soared <u>**above** the treetops</u>.

Optional Dictation Exercise

The following sentence is from *Mike Mulligan and His Steam Shovel* by Virginia Lee Burton. In this imaginative story for children, Mike Mulligan has a steam shovel named Mary Anne. After the student has written the dictation, have him circle the prepositions, write "O.P." over the objects of the preposition, and underline all the prepositional phrases.

Dictation: It was Mike Mulligan and Mary Anne who dug deep holes (for) the

O.P.   O.P.   O.P.

cellars (of) the tall skyscrapers (in) the big cities.

Oral Usage

This oral usage exercise trains the student to **not** say, "I always keep my pencil besides my book." *Beside* is a preposition meaning "next to." *Besides* is an infrequent preposition meaning "in addition to." Read each sentence; the student repeats it back to you.

1. I always keep my pencil beside my book.

2. James was sitting beside me.

3. Who is that beside you?

4. The oak log was laid beside the fireplace.

5. Joey was riding beside Jerry in the car.

LESSON 44

New: Prepositional Phrases That Describe Subjects

You will need nine index cards for the optional follow-up.

Read "Learning to Read" (Lesson 40) three times to the student. Then ask the student to try to say parts of the fifth and sixth stanzas along with you (or the tape recorder).

Instructor: A preposition is a word that shows the relationship of a noun or pronoun to another word in the sentence. Let's say that definition together three times.

TOGETHER (three times): A preposition is a word that shows the relationship of a noun or pronoun to another word in the sentence.

If the student knows the list of prepositions in **Exercise 1**, have him review it by saying it once. If he does not yet have the whole list memorized, focus on the third section today (*down* through *like*), and review the first two sections. The student may check off his accomplishments in the workbook.

Workbook: Prepositions

Aboard, about, above, across.
After, against, along, among, around, at.

Before, behind, below, beneath.
Beside, between, beyond, by.

Down, during, except, for, from.
In, inside, into, like.

Near, of, off, on, over.
Past, since, through, throughout.

To, toward, under, underneath.
Until, up, upon.
With, within, without.

Instructor: Read the first sentence in **Exercise 2** to me.

Workbook: 1.   The store down the block is open.

Instructor: What is the preposition in the sentence?
Student: *Down*

Instructor: Circle the preposition *down*. Down what? Down the block. Underline "down the block." "Down the block" is the prepositional phrase. A prepositional phrase begins with a preposition and ends with a noun or pronoun. That noun or pronoun is called the object of the preposition. In the prepositional phrase "down the block," the object of the preposition is the noun *block*.

Answer Key: O.P.
1.   The store (down) the block is open.

Instructor: Now you will find the preposition, object of the preposition, and prepositional phrase for yourself. I will ask you questions to help you. Read each of the sentences, numbers 2 through 8, in your workbook. Circle the preposition, write "O.P." over the object of the preposition, and underline the whole prepositional phrase.

Answer Key: O.P.
2.   Some people, (like) my cousin, can curl their tongues.

Instructor: What is the preposition?
Student: *Like*

Instructor: What is the object of the preposition?
Student: *Cousin*

Instructor: What is the prepositional phrase?
Student: *Like my cousin*

Answer Key: O.P.
3.   The blanket (for) my granddaughter is handmade.

Instructor: What is the preposition?
Student: *For*

Instructor: What is the object of the preposition?

Student: *Granddaughter*

Instructor: What is the prepositional phrase?
Student: *For my granddaughter*

Answer Key: O.P.
           4. The monkeys (from) Africa jabbered excitedly.

Instructor: What is the preposition?
Student: *From*

Instructor: What is the object of the preposition?
Student: *Africa*

Instructor: What is the prepositional phrase?
Student: *From Africa*

Answer Key: O.P.
           5. The noise (during) takeoff was deafening.

Instructor: What is the preposition?
Student: *During*

Instructor: What is the object of the preposition?
Student: *Takeoff*

Instructor: What is the prepositional phrase?
Student: *During takeoff*

Answer Key: O.P.
           6. The girl (in) the costume is my sister.

Instructor: What is the preposition?
Student: *In*

Instructor: What is the object of the preposition?
Student: *Costume*

Instructor: What is the prepositional phrase?
Student: *In the costume*

Answer Key:

O.P.

7.   That path (into) the forest was muddy.

Instructor: What is the preposition?
Student: *Into*

Instructor: What is the object of the preposition?
Student: *Forest*

Instructor: What is the prepositional phrase?
Student: *Into the forest*

Answer Key:

O.P.

8.   The jewel (inside) the locket is an emerald.

Instructor: What is the preposition?
Student: *Inside*

Instructor: What is the object of the preposition?
Student: *Locket*

Instructor: What is the prepositional phrase?
Student: *Inside the locket*

Instructor: Do you remember the definition of an adjective? An adjective is a word that describes a noun or pronoun. Adjectives tell what kind, which one, how many, and whose. Say that with me.

Together: An adjective is a word that describes a noun or pronoun. Adjectives tell what kind, which one, how many, and whose.

Instructor: Sometimes whole prepositional phrases act like adjectives. They describe nouns or pronouns. They tell what kind, which one, how many, and whose. When prepositional phrases act like adjectives, they are called adjective phrases. I will show you what I mean. Look at the first sentence in **Exercise 3**. This is the same as the first sentence you read in **Exercise 2**.

Instructor: What is the preposition?
Student: *Down*

Instructor: What is the object of the preposition?
Student: *Block*

Instructor: What is the prepositional phrase?
Student: *Down the block*

Instructor: Put a box around the prepositional phrase "down the block." Now let's find the subject and the verb in the sentence. The subject and the verb are never part of the prepositional phrase, so ignore all the words inside the box. Look for the subject and the verb in the rest of the sentence. What is the linking verb?
Student: *Is*

Instructor: What is the subject?
Student: *Store*

Instructor: Write "S" for subject over *store*. Now let's find the adjective phrase. Which store? Answer me with the prepositional phrase you have already put in the box.
Student: *Down the block*

Instructor: "Down the block" acts like an adjective because it tells which one. It describes the subject *store*. Which store is open? The one down the block. Draw an arrow starting with the adjective phrase "down the block" and pointing back to *store*, because this is the noun it describes. In this lesson, the adjective phrase will follow the noun or pronoun it describes. Let's practice finding the prepositional phrases that act like adjectives in Sentences 2-8 and putting boxes around them. Write "S" over the subject in each sentence. Then draw an arrow from the adjective phrase back to the subject, because this is the noun the adjective phrase is describing.

Answer Key:

                S

1. The store down the block is open.

Answer Key:

                S

2. Some people, like my cousin, can curl their tongues.

Instructor: What is the prepositional phrase? Put a box around it.
Student: *Like my cousin*

Instructor: What are the verbs? There is a helping verb and an action verb.
Student: *Can curl*

Instructor: What is the subject? Who can curl?
Student: *People*

Instructor: The prepositional phrase is an adjective phrase describing the subject. What kind of people?

Student: *Like my cousin*

Instructor: Draw an arrow from the adjective phrase back to the subject.

Answer Key:

3. The blanket for my granddaughter is handmade.

Instructor: What is the prepositional phrase? Put a box around it.

Student: *For my granddaughter*

Instructor: What is the linking verb?

Student: *Is*

Instructor: What is the subject? What is?

Student: *Blanket*

Instructor: The prepositional phrase is an adjective phrase describing the subject. Which blanket?

Student: *For my granddaughter*

Instructor: Draw an arrow from the adjective phrase back to the subject.

Answer Key:

4. The monkeys from Africa jabbered excitedly.

Instructor: What is the prepositional phrase? Put a box around it.

Student: *From Africa*

Instructor: What is the verb?

Student: *Jabbered*

Instructor: What is the subject? What jabbered?

Student: *Monkeys*

Instructor: The prepositional phrase is an adjective phrase describing the subject. Which monkeys?

Student: *From Africa*

Instructor: Draw an arrow from the adjective phrase back to the subject.

Answer Key:

S

5. The noise during takeoff was deafening.

Instructor: What is the prepositional phrase? Put a box around it.
Student: *During takeoff*

Instructor: What is the linking verb?
Student: *Was*

Instructor: What is the subject? What was?
Student: *Noise*

Instructor: The prepositional phrase is an adjective phrase describing the subject. Which noise?
Student: *During takeoff*

Instructor: Draw an arrow from the adjective phrase back to the subject.

Answer Key:

S

6. The girl in the costume is my sister.

Instructor: What is the prepositional phrase? Put a box around it.
Student: *In the costume*

Instructor: What is the linking verb?
Student: *Is*

Instructor: What is the subject? Who is?
Student: *Girl*

Instructor: The prepositional phrase is an adjective phrase describing the subject. Which girl?
Student: *In the costume*

Instructor: Draw an arrow from the adjective phrase back to the subject.

Answer Key:

S

7. The path into the forest was muddy.

Instructor: What is the prepositional phrase? Put a box around it.
Student: *Into the forest*

Instructor: What is the linking verb?
Student: *Was*

Instructor: What is the subject? What was?
Student: *Path*

Instructor: The prepositional phrase is an adjective phrase describing the subject. Which path?
Student: *Into the forest*

Instructor: Draw an arrow from the adjective phrase back to the subject.

Answer Key:

S

8.   The jewel inside the locket is an emerald.

Instructor: What is the prepositional phrase? Put a box around it.
Student: *Inside the locket*

Instructor: What is the linking verb?
Student: *Is*

Instructor: What is the subject? What is?
Student: *Jewel*

Instructor: The prepositional phrase is an adjective phrase describing the subject. Which jewel?
Student: *Inside the locket*

Instructor: Draw an arrow from the adjective phrase back to the subject.

Instructor: Read the sentence in **Exercise 4**, and look at its diagram.

Workbook: The store down the block is open.

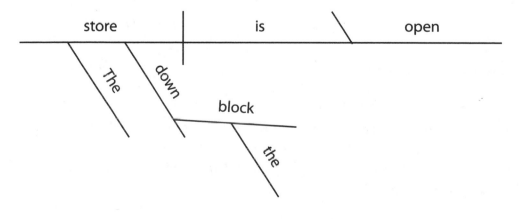

> Point to the words on the diagram as you read the explanation below. Pointing to each thing as you explain will make the material easier to understand.

Instructor: *Is* is the linking verb. *Store* is the subject. *Open* is the predicate adjective. There is an article that describes the subject *store*: *The*. It is written on a slanted line below the noun it describes. There is a prepositional phrase in the sentence: "down the block." The prepositional phrase is an adjective phrase describing the subject *store*. Which store? The one down the block. "Down the block" is an adjective phrase that describes *store*. The preposition *down* is written on the slanted line. The object of the preposition, *block*, is written on the flat line. *Down* is written on the slanted line that connects *block* to *store* because the preposition *down* shows the relationship between the noun *block* and the noun *store*. Which store? The store down the block. Look again at the object of the preposition, *block*. There is a word in the prepositional phrase that describes *block*; it is the article *the*. *The* is written on a slanted line beneath the word it describes.

Instructor: Now you will diagram some sentences with prepositional phrases in **Exercise 5** of your workbook. These prepositional phrases are adjective phrases that describe the subject. You read the sentence, and I will ask you questions that will help you identify the different parts of each sentence. Then you will fill in the diagram. For Sentences 1 and 2, fill in the frame. For Sentence 3, trace the dotted frame before you fill it in. Remember to copy the words exactly as they appear in the sentence. If the words begin with a capital letter in the sentence, they should also be capitalized in the diagram.

Use the following dialogue to help the student mark each sentence, and then fill in each diagram.

1. *This sentence has a prepositional phrase. First find the preposition; that's the beginning of the prepositional phrase. Then find the object of the preposition; that's the end of the phrase. Put a box around the entire prepositional phrase, and ignore the words inside the box as you find the other parts of the sentence.*

2. *What is the linking verb? This verb links the subject to a word in the complete predicate. Write the verb to the right of your center line.*

3. *Find the subject. Ask "who" or "what" before the verb. [Prompt the student with specific questions like "What was?" or "What is?"] Write the subject to the left of the center line on your frame.*

4. *This sentence contains a predicate adjective. This adjective is in the complete predicate of the sentence, but it describes the subject. A predicate adjective can tell what kind, which one, how many, or whose. Can you find an adjective in the complete predicate that*

describes the subject? Because the predicate adjective follows the verb in the sentence, it is written to the right of the verb on the diagram. Write the predicate adjective to the right of the slanted line on your diagram. That slanted line points back toward the subject to remind you that a predicate adjective describes the subject.

5. Go back and look again at the simple subject. Are there any single words in the complete subject that describe the simple subject? These adjectives can tell what kind, which one, how many, or whose. Also look for the articles (a, an, the), because they act like adjectives. Write each adjective on a slanted line below the subject it describes.

6. Look again at the prepositional phrase inside the box. This is an adjective phrase that describes the subject. An adjective phrase can tell what kind, which one, how many, or whose. Write the preposition on the slanted line below the subject, and write the object of the preposition on the flat line.

7. Are there any words in the prepositional phrase that describe the object of the preposition? These adjectives can tell what kind, which one, how many, or whose. Also look for the articles (a, an, the), because they act like adjectives. Write each adjective on a slanted line below the object of the preposition it describes. (Omit this question on Sentence 1.)

Answer Key: 1. The noise during takeoff was deafening.

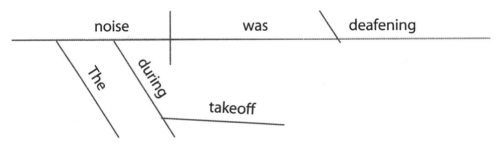

2. The blanket for my granddaughter is handmade.

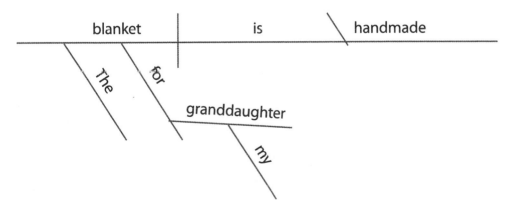

3.   The path into the forest was muddy.

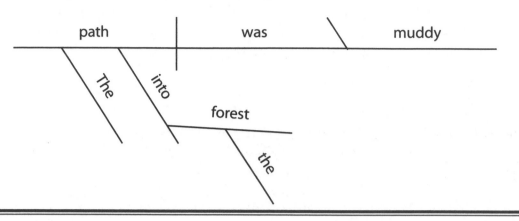

Optional Dictation Exercise

The following is the opening sentence of *Hans Brinker, or The Silver Skates* by Mary Mapes Dodge. Tell the student you will pause briefly when you get to the comma. After he has written the sentence, have him circle the prepositions and then underline the prepositional phrases.

Dictation: (On) a bright December morning long ago, two poorly clad children were kneeling (upon) the bank (of) a frozen canal (in) Holland.

Optional Follow-Up

Using nine index cards, write each of the prepositional phrases below (not the words in parentheses) on a card. The student tapes a prepositional phrase to an object (suggested objects are in the parentheses below) and places the object where the prepositional phrase indicates. For example, the student will tape "in a book" to a bookmark, and then put the bookmark in a book.

(bookmark) in a book

(shoe) under the table

(a picture or drawing) over the bed

(towel) beside the sink

(blocks) inside a container

(book) on the shelf

(flip flops) between my toes

(food item) near the refrigerator

(book bag) upon my shoulders

LESSON 45

New: Prepositional Phrases That Describe Direct Objects

Read "Learning to Read" (Lesson 40) three times to the student. Then ask the student to try to say parts of the seventh and eighth stanzas along with you (or the tape recorder).

Instructor: A preposition is a word that shows the relationship of a noun or pronoun to another word in the sentence. Let's say that definition together two times.

Together (two times): A preposition is a word that shows the relationship of a noun or pronoun to another word in the sentence.

If the student knows the list of prepositions in **Exercise 1**, have him review it by saying it once. If he does not yet have the whole list memorized, focus on the fourth section today (*near* through *throughout*), and review the first, second, and third sections. The student may check off his accomplishments in the workbook.

Workbook: Prepositions

Aboard, about, above, across.
After, against, along, among, around, at.

Before, behind, below, beneath.
Beside, between, beyond, by.

Down, during, except, for, from.
In, inside, into, like.

Near, of, off, on, over.
Past, since, through, throughout.

To, toward, under, underneath.
Until, up, upon.
With, within, without.

Instructor: Read the first sentence in **Exercise 2** to me.

Instructor: What is the preposition in the sentence?
Student: *With*

Instructor: Circle the preposition *with*. With what? With silver flecks. Underline "with silver flecks." "With silver flecks" is the prepositional phrase. A prepositional phrase begins with a preposition and ends with a noun or pronoun. That noun or pronoun is called the object of the preposition. In the prepositional phrase "with silver flecks," the object of the preposition is the noun *flecks*.

Answer Key:
O.P.
1. Olive gathered rocks (with) silver flecks.

Instructor: Now you will find the preposition, object of the preposition, and prepositional phrase for yourself. I will ask you questions to help you. Read each of the sentences, numbers 2 through 8, in your workbook. Circle the preposition, write "O.P." over the object of the preposition, and underline the whole prepositional phrase.

Answer Key:
O.P.
2. Olive started a collection (of) pretty rocks.

Instructor: What is the preposition?
Student: *Of*

Instructor: What is the object of the preposition?
Student: *Rocks*

Instructor: What is the prepositional phrase?
Student: *Of pretty rocks*

Answer Key:
O.P.
3. She polished the rocks (in) her collection.

Instructor: What is the preposition?
Student: *In*

Instructor: What is the object of the preposition?
Student: *Collection*

Instructor: What is the prepositional phrase?
Student: *In her collection*

Answer Key:
O.P.
4. Olive had read stories (about) precious metals.

Instructor: What is the preposition?
Student: *About*

Instructor: What is the object of the preposition?
Student: *Metals*

Instructor: What is the prepositional phrase?
Student: *About precious metals*

Answer Key: O.P.
    5. Olive dug the holes (near) the cliff.

Instructor: What is the preposition?
Student: *Near*

Instructor: What is the object of the preposition?
Student: *Cliff*

Instructor: What is the prepositional phrase?
Student: *Near the cliff*

Answer Key: O.P.
    6. She examined the silvery rock (from) the largest hole.

Instructor: What is the preposition?
Student: *From*

Instructor: What is the object of the preposition?
Student: *Hole*

Instructor: What is the prepositional phrase?
Student: *From the largest hole*

Answer Key: O.P.
    7. Olive followed the road (to) her yard.

Instructor: What is the preposition?
Student: *To*

Instructor: What is the object of the preposition?
Student: *Yard*

Instructor: What is the prepositional phrase?
Student: *To her yard*

Answer Key: O.P.
8. Hungry Olive ate bread(with)butter.

Instructor: What is the preposition?
Student: *With*

Instructor: What is the object of the preposition?
Student: *Butter*

Instructor: What is the prepositional phrase?
Student: *With butter*

Instructor: Let's review the definition of an adjective. An adjective is a word that describes a noun or pronoun. Adjectives tell what kind, which one, how many, and whose. Say that with me.

Together: An adjective is a word that describes a noun or pronoun. Adjectives tell what kind, which one, how many, and whose.

Instructor: Sometimes prepositional phrases act like adjectives. They describe nouns or pronouns. They tell what kind, which one, how many, and whose. When prepositional phrases act like adjectives, they are called adjective phrases. Look at the first sentence in **Exercise 3**.

Workbook: Olive gathered rocks with silver flecks.

Instructor: What is the preposition?
Student: *With*

Instructor: What is the object of the preposition?
Student: *Flecks*

Instructor: What is the prepositional phrase?
Student: *With silver flecks*

Instructor: Put a box around the prepositional phrase "with silver flecks." Now let's find the subject and the verb in the sentence. The subject and the verb are never part of the prepositional phrase, so ignore all the words inside the box. Look for the subject and the verb in the rest of the sentence. What is the action verb?

Student: *Gathered*

Instructor: What is the subject? Who gathered?
Student: *Olive*

Instructor: This sentence has a direct object that receives the action of the verb. Gathered what?
Student: *Rocks*

Instructor: Write "D.O." for direct object over *rocks*. Now let's find the adjective phrase. What kind of rocks? Answer me with the prepositional phrase you have already put in the box.
Student: *With silver flecks*

Instructor: "With silver flecks" acts like an adjective because it tells what kind. It describes the direct object *rocks*. What kind of rocks? Rocks with silver flecks. Draw an arrow starting at the adjective phrase "with silver flecks" and pointing back to *rocks*, because this is the noun it describes. The adjective phrase follows the noun or pronoun it describes. Let's practice finding the prepositional phrases that act like adjectives in Sentences 2-8 and putting boxes around them. Write "D.O." over the direct object in each sentence. Then draw an arrow from the adjective phrase back to the direct object, because this is the noun or pronoun the adjective phrase is describing.

Answer Key:
                   D.O.
1. Olive gathered rocks [with silver flecks].

Answer Key:
                   D.O.
2. Olive started a collection [of pretty rocks].

Instructor: What is the prepositional phrase? Put a box around it.
Student: *Of pretty rocks*

Instructor: What is the verb?
Student: *Started*

Instructor: What is the direct object? Started what? Write "D.O." over it.
Student: *Collection*

Instructor: The prepositional phrase is an adjective phrase describing the direct object. What kind of collection?

Student: *Of pretty rocks*

Instructor: Draw an arrow from the adjective phrase back to the direct object.

Answer Key:

D.O.

3. She polished the rocks in her collection.

Instructor: What is the prepositional phrase? Put a box around it.
Student: *In her collection*

Instructor: What is the verb?
Student: *Polished*

Instructor: What is the direct object? Polished what? Write "D.O." over it.
Student: *Rocks*

Instructor: The prepositional phrase is an adjective phrase describing the direct object. Which rocks?
Student: *In her collection*

Instructor: Draw an arrow from the adjective phrase back to the direct object.

Answer Key:

D.O.

4. Olive had read stories about precious metals.

Instructor: What is the prepositional phrase? Put a box around it.
Student: *About precious metals*

Instructor: What are the verbs? There is a helping verb and an action verb.
Student: *Had read*

Instructor: What is the direct object? Had read what? Write "D.O." over it.
Student: *Stories*

Instructor: The prepositional phrase is an adjective phrase describing the direct object. What kind of stories?
Student: *About precious metals*

Instructor: Draw an arrow from the adjective phrase back to the direct object.

Answer Key:

D.O.

5. Olive dug the holes near the cliff.

Instructor: What is the prepositional phrase? Put a box around it.
Student: *Near the cliff*

Instructor: What is the verb?
Student: *Dug*

Instructor: What is the direct object? Dug what? Write "D.O." over it.
Student: *Holes*

Instructor: The prepositional phrase is an adjective phrase describing the direct object. Which holes?
Student: *Near the cliff*

Instructor: Draw an arrow from the adjective phrase back to the direct object.

Answer Key:

6. She examined the silvery rock from the largest hole.

Instructor: What is the prepositional phrase? Put a box around it.
Student: *From the largest hole*

Instructor: What is the verb?
Student: *Examined*

Instructor: What is the direct object? Examined what? Write "D.O." over it.
Student: *Rock*

Instructor: The prepositional phrase is an adjective phrase describing the direct object. Which rock?
Student: *From the largest hole*

Instructor: Draw an arrow from the adjective phrase back to the direct object.

Answer Key:

7. Olive followed the road to her yard.

Instructor: What is the prepositional phrase? Put a box around it.
Student: *To her yard*

Instructor: What is the verb?
Student: *Followed*

Instructor: What is the direct object? Followed what? Write "D.O." over it.
Student: Road

Instructor: The prepositional phrase is an adjective phrase describing the direct object. Which road?
Student: To her yard

Instructor: Draw an arrow from the adjective phrase back to the direct object.

Answer Key:

D.O.
8. Hungry Olive ate bread with butter.

Instructor: What is the prepositional phrase? Put a box around it.
Student: With butter

Instructor: What is the verb?
Student: Ate

Instructor: What is the direct object? Ate what? Write "D.O." over it.
Student: Bread

Instructor: The prepositional phrase is an adjective phrase describing the direct object. What kind of bread?
Student: With butter

Instructor: Draw an arrow from the adjective phrase back to the direct object.

Instructor: Read the sentence in **Exercise 4**, and look at its diagram.

Workbook: Olive gathered rocks with silver flecks.

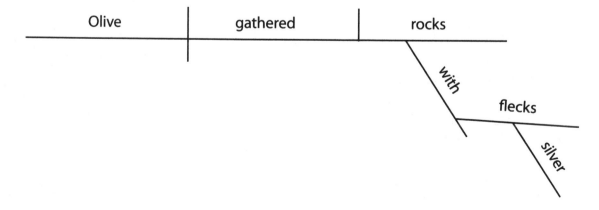

Point to the words on the diagram as you read the explanation below. Pointing to each thing as you explain will make the diagram easier to understand.

Instructor: *Gathered* is the action verb. *Olive* is the subject. *Rocks* is the direct object. There is a prepositional phrase in the sentence: "with silver flecks." The prepositional phrase is an adjective phrase describing the direct object *rocks*. What kind of rocks? The rocks with silver flecks. "With silver flecks" is an adjective phrase that describes *rocks*. The preposition *with* is written on the slanted line. The object of the preposition, *flecks*, is written on the flat line. *With* is written on the slanted line that connects *flecks* to *rocks* because the preposition *with* shows the relationship between the noun *flecks* and the noun *rocks*. What kind of rocks? Rocks with silver flecks. Look again at the object of the preposition, *flecks*. There is a word in the prepositional phrase that describes *flecks*; it is the adjective *silver*. What kind of flecks? Silver flecks. *Silver* is written on a slanted line beneath the word it describes.

Instructor: Now you will diagram some sentences with prepositional phrases in **Exercise 5** of your workbook. These prepositional phrases are adjective phrases that describe the direct object. You read the sentence, and I will ask you questions that will help you find the preposition phrases, and then fill in the diagram. Remember to copy the words exactly as they appear in the sentence. If the words begin with a capital letter in the sentence, they should also be capitalized in the diagram.

Use the following dialogue to help the student fill in each diagram.

1. *This sentence has a prepositional phrase. First find the preposition; that's the beginning of the prepositional phrase. Then find the object of the preposition; that's the end of the phrase. Put a box around the entire prepositional phrase, and ignore the words inside the box as you find the other parts of the sentence.*

2. *What is the action verb? Write the verb to the right of your center line.*

3. *Find the subject. Ask "who" or "what" before the verb. [Prompt the student with specific questions like "Who started?" or "Who polished?"] Write the subject to the left of the center line on your frame.*

4. *Is there a direct object that receives the action of the verb? I will ask you a question that will help you find the direct object.*

   Sentence 1: Started what?

   Sentence 2: Polished what?

Write the direct object to the right of the verb on your diagram. The direct object is separated from the verb by a short, straight line.

5. *Look at the direct object. Are there any single words that describe the direct object? These adjectives can tell what kind, which one, how many, or whose. Also look for the articles (a, an, the), because they act like adjectives. Write each adjective on a slanted line below the direct object it describes.*

6. *Look again at the prepositional phrase inside the box. This is an adjective phrase that describes the direct object. An adjective phrase can tell what kind, which one, how many, or whose. Write the preposition on the slanted line below the direct object, and write the object of the preposition on the flat line.*

7. *Are there any words in the prepositional phrase that describe the object of the preposition? These adjectives can tell what kind, which one, how many, or whose. Also look for the articles (a, an, the), because they act like adjectives. Write each adjective on a slanted line below the object of the preposition it describes.*

Answer Key: 1. Olive started a collection $\boxed{\text{of pretty rocks.}}$

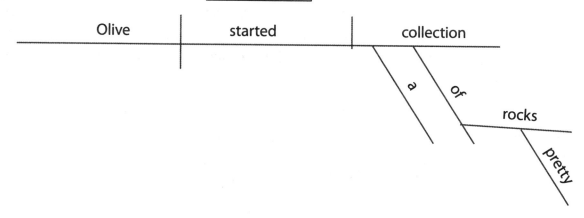

2. She polished the rocks $\boxed{\text{in her collection.}}$

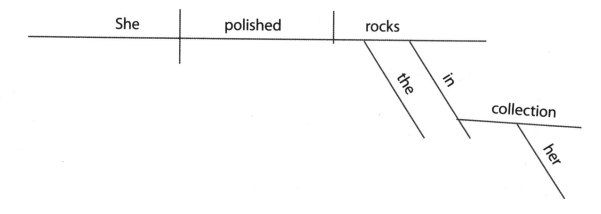

LESSON 46

New: Prepositional Phrases That Describe Indirect Objects

Read "Learning to Read" (Lesson 40) three times to the student. Then ask the student to try to say parts of the first through eighth stanzas along with you (or the tape recorder).

Instructor: A preposition is a word that shows the relationship of a noun or pronoun to another word in the sentence. Let's say that definition together, and then you say it by yourself.

Together, then student alone: A preposition is a word that shows the relationship of a noun or pronoun to another word in the sentence.

If the student knows the list of prepositions in **Exercise 1**, have him review it by saying it once. If he does not yet have the whole list memorized, focus on the last section today (*to* through *without*), and review the previous sections. The student may check off his accomplishments in the workbook.

Workbook: <u>Prepositions</u>

Aboard, about, above, across.
After, against, along, among, around, at.

Before, behind, below, beneath.
Beside, between, beyond, by.

Down, during, except, for, from.
In, inside, into, like.

Near, of, off, on, over.
Past, since, through, throughout.

To, toward, under, underneath.
Until, up, upon.
With, within, without.

Instructor: Read the first sentence in **Exercise 2** to me.

Workbook: 1. The teacher gave the girl with the trumpet a prize.

Instructor: What is the preposition in the sentence?
Student: *with*

Instructor: Circle the preposition *with*. With what? With the trumpet. Underline "with the trumpet." "With the trumpet" is the prepositional phrase. A prepositional phrase begins with a preposition and ends with a noun or pronoun. That noun or pronoun is called the object of the preposition. In the prepositional phrase "with the trumpet," the object of the preposition is the noun *trumpet*. Write "O.P." over the word *trumpet*.

Answer Key:
                                                 O.P.
   1.   The teacher gave the girl (with) the trumpet a prize.

Instructor: Now you will find the preposition, object of the preposition, and prepositional phrase for yourself. I will ask you questions to help you. Read each of the sentences, numbers 2 through 8, in your workbook. Circle the preposition, write "O.P." over the object of the preposition, and underline the whole prepositional phrase.

Answer Key:
                                         O.P.
   2.   Jerry threw a boy (in) left field the ball.

Instructor: What is the preposition?
Student: *In*

Instructor: What is the object of the preposition?
Student: *Field*

Instructor: What is the prepositional phrase?
Student: *In left field*

Answer Key:
                                            O.P.
   3.   Mr. Warren sold the man (across) the street his coin collection.

Instructor: What is the preposition?
Student: *Across*

Instructor: What is the object of the preposition?
Student: *Street*

Instructor: What is the prepositional phrase?

Student: *Across the street*

Answer Key:

O.P.

4. Diana showed the child (at) the flower show a rose.

Instructor: What is the preposition?
Student: *At*

Instructor: What is the object of the preposition?
Student: *Show*

Instructor: What is the prepositional phrase?
Student: *At the flower show*

Answer Key:

O.P.

5.   Katrina brought the lady (inside) the pet shop a new fish.

Instructor: What is the preposition?
Student: *Inside*

Instructor: What is the object of the preposition?
Student: *Shop*

Instructor: What is the prepositional phrase?
Student: *Inside the pet shop*

Answer Key:

O.P.

6.   Aunt Robin mailed her relative (up) the street a gift.

Instructor: What is the preposition?
Student: *Up*

Instructor: What is the object of the preposition?
Student: *Street*

Instructor: What is the prepositional phrase?
Student: *Up the street*

Answer Key:

O.P.

7.   Ryan got the monkey (on) skates ten peanuts.

Instructor: What is the preposition?
Student: *On*

Instructor: What is the object of the preposition?
Student: *Skates*

Instructor: What is the prepositional phrase?
Student: *On skates*

Answer Key: O.P.
8. Pablo cooked the guest ⟨of⟩ honor delicious tortillas.

Instructor: What is the preposition?
Student: *Of*

Instructor: What is the object of the preposition?
Student: *Honor*

Instructor: What is the prepositional phrase?
Student: *Of honor*

Instructor: Let's review the definition of an adjective. An adjective is a word that describes a noun or pronoun. Adjectives tell what kind, which one, how many, and whose. Say that with me.

Together: An adjective is a word that describes a noun or pronoun. Adjectives tell what kind, which one, how many, and whose.

Instructor: Sometimes prepositional phrases act like adjectives. They describe nouns or pronouns. They tell what kind, which one, how many, and whose. When prepositional phrases act like adjectives, they are called adjective phrases. Look at the first sentence in **Exercise 3**.

Instructor: What is the preposition?
Student: *With*

Instructor: What is the object of the preposition?
Student: *Trumpet*

Instructor: What is the prepositional phrase?
Student: *With the trumpet*

Instructor: Put a box around the prepositional phrase "with the trumpet." Now let's find the subject and the verb in the sentence. The subject and the verb are never part of the prepositional phrase, so ignore all the words inside the box. Look for the subject and the verb in the rest of the sentence. What is the action verb?

Student: *Gave*

Instructor: What is the subject? Who gave?

Student: *Teacher*

Instructor: This sentence has a direct object that receives the action of the verb. Gave what?

Student: *Prize*

Instructor: *Prize* is the direct object. (The teacher certainly didn't give the girl!) The sentence also has an indirect object. An indirect object is a noun or pronoun that is **between** the action verb and the direct object of a sentence. It answers the question "to whom" or "for whom" the action is done, but the words *to* or *for* are usually not in the sentence. *To* or *for* are just understood. What is the indirect object of the sentence "The teacher gave the girl with the trumpet a prize"? Gave a prize to whom?

Student: *Girl*

Instructor: Write "I.O." for indirect object over *girl*. Now let's find the adjective phrase. Which girl? Answer me with the prepositional phrase you have already put in the box.

Student: *With the trumpet*

Instructor: "With the trumpet" acts like an adjective because it tells which one. It describes the indirect object *girl*. Which girl? The one with the trumpet. Draw an arrow starting at the adjective phrase "with the trumpet" and pointing back to *girl*, because this is the noun it describes. The adjective phrase follows the noun or pronoun it describes. Let's practice finding the prepositional phrases that act like adjectives in Sentences 2-8 and putting boxes around them. Write "I.O." over the indirect object in each sentence. Then draw an arrow from the adjective phrase back to the indirect object, because this is the noun or pronoun the adjective phrase is describing.

Answer Key:

1. The teacher gave the girl I.O. with the trumpet a prize.

Answer Key:

2. Jerry threw a boy I.O. in left field the ball.

Instructor: What is the prepositional phrase? Put a box around it.
Student: *In left field*

Instructor: What is the verb?
Student: *Threw*

Instructor: What is the direct object? Threw what?
Student: *Ball*

Instructor: What is the indirect object? Threw a ball to whom? Write "I.O." over it.
Student: *Boy*

Instructor: The prepositional phrase is an adjective phrase describing the indirect object. Which boy?
Student: *In left field*

Instructor: Draw an arrow from the adjective phrase back to the indirect object.

Answer Key:

                                                   I.O.

3. Mr. Warren sold the man [across the street] his coin collection.

Instructor: What is the prepositional phrase? Put a box around it.
Student: *Across the street*

Instructor: What is the verb?
Student: *Sold*

Instructor: What is the direct object? Sold what? Answer me with one word.
Student: *Collection*

Instructor: What is the indirect object? Sold his coin collection to whom? Write "I.O." over it.
Student: *Man*

Instructor: The prepositional phrase is an adjective phrase describing the indirect object. Which man?
Student: *Across the street*

Instructor: Draw an arrow from the adjective phrase back to the indirect object.

Answer Key:

                                                 I.O.

4. Diana showed the child [at the flower show] a rose.

Instructor: What is the prepositional phrase? Put a box around it.
Student: *At the flower show*

Instructor: What is the verb?
Student: *Showed*

Instructor: What is the direct object? Showed what?
Student: *Rose*

Instructor: What is the indirect object? Showed the rose to whom? Write "I.O." over it.
Student: *Child*

Instructor: The prepositional phrase is an adjective phrase describing the indirect object. Which child?
Student: *At the flower show*

Instructor: Draw an arrow from the adjective phrase back to the indirect object.

Answer Key:
                     I.O.
5. Katrina brought the lady inside the pet shop a new fish.

Instructor: What is the prepositional phrase? Put a box around it.
Student: *Inside the pet shop*

Instructor: What is the verb?
Student: *Brought*

Instructor: What is the direct object? Brought what?
Student: *Fish*

Instructor: What is the indirect object? Brought a fish for whom? Write "I.O." over it.
Student: *Lady*

Instructor: The prepositional phrase is an adjective phrase describing the indirect object. Which lady?
Student: *Inside the pet shop*

Instructor: Draw an arrow from the adjective phrase back to the indirect object.

Answer Key:
                     I.O.
6. Aunt Robin mailed her relative up the street a gift.

Instructor: What is the prepositional phrase? Put a box around it.
Student: Up the street

Instructor: What is the verb?
Student: Mailed

Instructor: What is the direct object? Mailed what?
Student: Gift

Instructor: What is the indirect object? Mailed the gift to whom? Write "I.O." over it.
Student: Relative

Instructor: The prepositional phrase is an adjective phrase describing the indirect object. Which relative?
Student: Up the street

Instructor: Draw an arrow from the adjective phrase back to the indirect object.

Answer Key:

                      I.O.

7. Ryan got the monkey on skates ten peanuts.

Instructor: What is the prepositional phrase? Put a box around it.
Student: On skates

Instructor: What is the verb?
Student: Got

Instructor: What is the direct object? Got what?
Student: Peanuts

Instructor: What is the indirect object? Got peanuts for whom? Write "I.O." over it.
Student: Monkey

Instructor: The prepositional phrase is an adjective phrase describing the indirect object. Which monkey?
Student: On skates

Instructor: Draw an arrow from the adjective phrase back to the indirect object.

Answer Key:

                  I.O.

8. Pablo cooked the guest of honor delicious tortillas.

Instructor: What is the prepositional phrase? Put a box around it.
Student: *Of honor*

Instructor: What is the verb?
Student: *Cooked*

Instructor: What is the direct object? Cooked what?
Student: *Tortillas*

Instructor: What is the indirect object? Cooked tortillas for whom? Write "I.O." over it.
Student: *Guest*

Instructor: The prepositional phrase is an adjective phrase describing the indirect object. Which guest?
Student: *Of honor*

Instructor: Draw an arrow from the adjective phrase back to the indirect object.

Instructor: Read the sentence in **Exercise 4**, and look at its diagram.

Workbook: Jerry threw a boy in left field the ball.

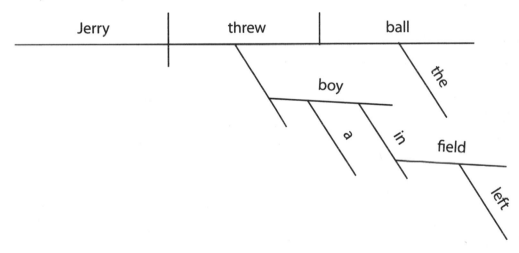

Point to the words on the diagram as you read the explanation below. Pointing to each thing as you explain will make the material easier to understand.

Instructor: *Threw* is the action verb. *Jerry* is the subject. *Ball* is the direct object. *Boy* is the indirect object. There is a prepositional phrase in the sentence: "in left field." The prepositional phrase is an adjective phrase describing the indirect object *boy*. Which boy? A boy in left field. "In left field" is an adjective phrase that describes *boy*. The preposition *in* is written on the slanted line. The object of the preposition, *field*, is written on the flat line. *In* is written on the slanted line that connects *field* to *boy* because the preposition *in* shows the relationship between the noun *field* and the noun *boy*. Which boy? A boy in left field. Look again at the object of the preposition, *field*. There is a word in the prepositional phrase that describes *field*; it is the adjective *left*. What kind of field? Left field. *Left* is written on a slanted line beneath the word it describes.

Instructor: Now you will diagram some sentences with prepositional phrases in **Exercise 5** of your workbook. These prepositional phrases are adjective phrases that describe the indirect object. You read the sentence, and I will help you identify the prepositional phrases. Then I will ask you questions to help you fill in the diagram. For Sentences 1 and 2, fill in the frame. For Sentence 3, trace the dotted frame before you fill it in. Remember to copy the words exactly as they appear in the sentence. If the words begin with a capital letter in the sentence, they should also be capitalized in the diagram.

Use the following dialogue to help the student fill in each diagram.

1. *This sentence has a prepositional phrase. First find the preposition; that's the beginning of the prepositional phrase. Then find the object of the preposition; that's the end of the phrase. Put a box around the entire prepositional phrase, and ignore the words inside the box as you find the other parts of the sentence.*

2. *What is the action verb? Write the verb to the right of your center line.*

3. *Find the subject. Ask "who" or "what" before the verb. [Prompt the student with specific questions like "Who mailed?" or "Who got?"] Write the subject to the left of the center line on your frame.*

4. *Is there a direct object that receives the action of the verb? I will ask you a question that will help you find the direct object.*

   Sentence 1: Mailed what?

   Sentence 2: Got what?

   Sentence 3: Cooked what?

   Write the direct object to the right of the verb on your diagram. The direct object is separated from the verb by a short, straight line.

5. *Is there an indirect object between the verb and the direct object? I will ask you a question that will help you find the indirect object.*

   Sentence 1: Mailed a gift to whom?

   Sentence 2: Got peanuts for whom?

Sentence 3: Cooked tortillas for whom?

6. Look at the direct object. Are there any words that describe the direct object? These adjectives can tell what kind, which one, how many, or whose. Also look for the articles (a, an, the), because they act like adjectives. Write each adjective on a slanted line below the direct object it describes.

7. Look at the indirect object. Are there any single words that describe the indirect object? These adjectives can tell what kind, which one, how many, or whose. Also look for the articles (a, an, the), because they act like adjectives. Write each adjective on a slanted line below the indirect object it describes.

8. Look again at the prepositional phrase inside the box. This is an adjective phrase that describes the indirect object. An adjective phrase can tell what kind, which one, how many, or whose. Write the preposition on the slanted line below the indirect object, and write the object of the preposition on the flat line.

9. Are there any words in the prepositional phrase that describe the object of the preposition? These adjectives can tell what kind, which one, how many, or whose. Also look for the articles (a, an, the), because they act like adjectives. Write each adjective on a slanted line below the object of the preposition it describes. (Omit this question for Sentences 2 and 3.)

Answer Key: 1. Aunt Robin mailed her relative up the street a gift.

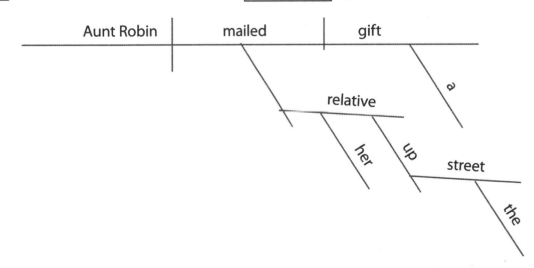

2. Ryan got the monkey on skates ten peanuts.

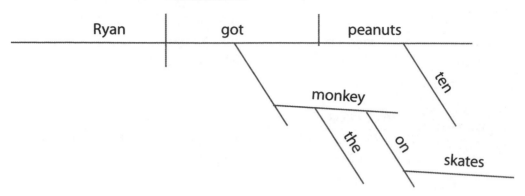

3. Pablo cooked the guest of honor delicious tortillas.

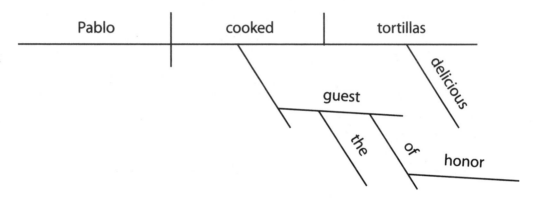

LESSON 47

New: Prepositional Phrases That Describe Predicate Nominatives
Review: Helping Verbs

Read "Learning to Read" (Lesson 40) three times to the student. Then ask the student to try to say parts of the ninth and tenth stanzas along with you (or the tape recorder).

Instructor: Let's begin by reviewing the definition of a verb. A verb is a word that does an action, shows a state of being, links two words together, or helps another verb. Say that with me.

TOGETHER: A verb is a word that does an action, shows a state of being, links two words together, or helps another verb.

Instructor: A helping verb helps another verb. Listen to this sentence: Carolers were singing "Silent Night." What were they doing? Answer me in a complete sentence starting with "They were …"

Student: *They were singing "Silent Night."*

Instructor: But if I just said "They singing 'Silent Night,'" that wouldn't sound right! *Singing* needs **another** verb to help it. The verb *were* is helping the verb *singing*. Working together, the verbs make sense in the sentence. The verb *were* is called a helping verb because it helps the main verb, *singing*. Read the list of helping verbs in **Exercise 1** of your workbook one time. Then we will practice chanting them together without your looking at them.

If the student remembers the chant from the previous levels and can say the helping verbs by himself, move on to **Exercise 2**.

TOGETHER (three times):
Am [clap]
Is [clap]
Are, was, were. [clap]
Be [clap]
Being [clap]
Been. [clap] [clap]
Have, has, had [clap]

Do, does, did [clap]
Shall, will, should, would, may, might, must [clap, clap]
Can, could!

Instructor: Repeat after me: A preposition is a word that shows the relationship of a noun or pronoun to another word in the sentence.

Student: *A preposition is a word that shows the relationship of a noun or pronoun to another word in the sentence.*

If the student knows the list of prepositions in **Exercise 2**, have him review it by saying it once. If the student stumbles, have him say that section three times with you. Then he should say the entire list three times. The student may check off his accomplishments in the workbook.

Workbook: Prepositions

Aboard, about, above, across.
After, against, along, among, around, at.

Before, behind, below, beneath.
Beside, between, beyond, by.

Down, during, except, for, from.
In, inside, into, like.

Near, of, off, on, over.
Past, since, through, throughout.

To, toward, under, underneath.
Until, up, upon.
With, within, without.

Instructor: Read the first sentence in **Exercise 3** to me.

Instructor: What is the preposition in the sentence?
Student: *Of*

Instructor: Circle the preposition *of*. Of what? Of character. Underline "of character." "Of character" is the prepositional phrase. A prepositional phrase begins with a preposition and ends with a noun or pronoun. That noun or pronoun is called the object of the preposition. In the prepositional phrase "of character," the object of the preposition is the noun *character*.

Instructor: Now you will find the preposition, object of the preposition, and prepositional phrase for yourself. I will ask you questions to help you. Read each of the sentences, numbers 2 through 8, in your workbook. Circle the preposition, write "O.P." over the object of the preposition, and underline the whole prepositional phrase.

Answer Key:

O.P.

1.   A teacher should be a person ⟨of⟩ character.

Answer Key:

O.P.

2.   Misty was a wild horse ⟨from⟩ Virginia.

| Instructor: | What is the preposition? |
| Student: | *From* |

| Instructor: | What is the object of the preposition? |
| Student: | *Virginia* |

| Instructor: | What is the prepositional phrase? |
| Student: | *From Virginia* |

Answer Key:

O.P.

3.   A hammer is one tool ⟨for⟩ my toolbox.

| Instructor: | What is the preposition? |
| Student: | *For* |

| Instructor: | What is the object of the preposition? |
| Student: | *Toolbox* |

| Instructor: | What is the prepositional phrase? |
| Student: | *For my toolbox* |

Answer Key:

O.P.

4.   This story could be one tale ⟨about⟩ honesty.

| Instructor: | What is the preposition? |
| Student: | *About* |

| Instructor: | What is the object of the preposition? |
| Student: | *Honesty* |

Instructor: What is the prepositional phrase?
Student: *About honesty*

Answer Key: O.P.

5. Tall Sam will be a player (on) the field.

Instructor: What is the preposition?
Student: *On*

Instructor: What is the object of the preposition?
Student: *Field*

Instructor: What is the prepositional phrase?
Student: *On the field*

Answer Key: O.P.

6. Next Thursday may be our first holiday (in) the fall.

Instructor: What is the preposition?
Student: *In*

Instructor: What is the object of the preposition?
Student: *Fall*

Instructor: What is the prepositional phrase?
Student: *In the fall*

Answer Key: O.P.

7. Sow bugs must have been the insects (under) the rocks.

Instructor: What is the preposition?
Student: *Under*

Instructor: What is the object of the preposition?
Student: *Rocks*

Instructor: What is the prepositional phrase?
Student: *Under the rocks*

Answer Key: O.P.

8. Carolyn had been the gymnast (with) the most points.

Instructor: What is the preposition?
Student: *With*

Instructor: What is the object of the preposition?
Student: *Points*

Instructor: What is the prepositional phrase?
Student: *With the most points*

Instructor: Let's review the definition of an adjective. An adjective is a word that describes a noun or pronoun. Adjectives tell what kind, which one, how many, and whose. Say that with me.

Together: An adjective is a word that describes a noun or pronoun. Adjectives tell what kind, which one, how many, and whose.

Instructor: Sometimes prepositional phrases act like adjectives. They describe nouns or pronouns. They tell what kind, which one, how many, and whose. When prepositional phrases act like adjectives, they are called adjective phrases. Look at the first sentence in **Exercise 4**.

Instructor: What is the preposition?
Student: *Of*

Instructor: What is the object of the preposition?
Student: *Character*

Instructor: What is the prepositional phrase?
Student: *Of character*

Instructor: Put a box around the prepositional phrase "of character." Now let's find the subject and the verb in the sentence. The subject and the verb are never part of the prepositional phrase, so ignore all the words inside the box. Look for the subject and the verb in the rest of the sentence. What are the verbs in the sentence? There is a helping verb and a linking verb.
Student: *Should be*

Instructor: What is the subject? Who should be?
Student: *Teacher*

Instructor: This sentence has a predicate nominative. Remember, a predicate nominative is a noun or pronoun in the complete predicate that *renames* the subject. Who should a teacher be? Answer me with one word.

Student: *Person*

Instructor: *Person* is the predicate nominative. Write "P.N." over *person*. Now let's find the adjective phrase that describes the predicate nominative. What kind of person? Answer me with the prepositional phrase you have already put in the box.

Student: *Of character*

Instructor: "Of character" acts like an adjective because it tells what kind. It describes the predicate nominative *person*. What kind of person? A person of character. Draw an arrow starting at the adjective phrase "of character" and pointing back to *person*, because this is the noun it describes. The adjective phrase follows the noun or pronoun it describes. Let's practice finding the prepositional phrases that act like adjectives in Sentences 2-8 and putting boxes around them. Write "P.N." over the predicate nominative in each sentence. Then draw an arrow from the adjective phrase back to the predicate nominative, because this is the noun or pronoun the adjective phrase is describing.

Answer Key:

P.N.
1. A teacher should be a person of character.

Answer Key:

P.N.
2. Misty was a wild horse from Virginia.

Instructor: What is the prepositional phrase? Put a box around it.
Student: *From Virginia*

Instructor: What is the linking verb?
Student: *Was*

Instructor: What is the subject? Who was?
Student: *Misty*

Instructor: What is the predicate nominative? What was Misty? Write "P.N." over it.
Student: *Horse*

Instructor: The prepositional phrase is an adjective phrase describing the predicate nominative. What kind of horse?
Student: *From Virginia*

Instructor: Draw an arrow from the adjective phrase back to the predicate nominative.

Answer Key:

                       P.N.

3.   A hammer is one tool for my toolbox.

Instructor: What is the prepositional phrase? Put a box around it.
Student: *For my toolbox*

Instructor: What is the linking verb?
Student: *Is*

Instructor: What is the subject? What is?
Student: *Hammer*

Instructor: What is the predicate nominative? What is a hammer? Write "P.N." over it.
Student: *Tool*

Instructor: The prepositional phrase is an adjective phrase describing the predicate nominative. What kind of tool?
Student: *For my toolbox*

Instructor: Draw an arrow from the adjective phrase back to the predicate nominative.

Answer Key:

                       P.N.

4.   This story could be one tale about honesty.

Instructor: What is the prepositional phrase? Put a box around it.
Student: *About honesty*

Instructor: What are the verbs (helping verb plus a linking verb)?
Student: *Could be*

Instructor: What is the subject? What could be?
Student: *Story*

Instructor: What is the predicate nominative? What could this story be? Write "P.N." over it.
Student: *Tale*

Instructor: The prepositional phrase is an adjective phrase describing the predicate nominative. What kind of tale?
Student: *About honesty*

Instructor: Draw an arrow from the adjective phrase back to the predicate nominative.

Answer Key:

P.N.

5. Tall Sam will be a player on the field.

Instructor: What is the prepositional phrase? Put a box around it.
Student: On the field

Instructor: What are the verbs (helping verb plus a linking verb)?
Student: Will be

Instructor: What is the subject? Who will be?
Student: Sam

Instructor: What is the predicate nominative? What will Sam be? Write "P.N." over it.
Student: Player

Instructor: The prepositional phrase is an adjective phrase describing the predicate nominative. What kind of player?
Student: On the field

Instructor: Draw an arrow from the adjective phrase back to the predicate nominative.

Answer Key:

P.N.

6. Next Thursday may be our first holiday in the fall.

Instructor: What is the prepositional phrase? Put a box around it.
Student: In the fall

Instructor: What are the verbs (helping verb plus a linking verb)?
Student: May be

Instructor: What is the subject? What may be?
Student: Thursday

Instructor: What is the predicate nominative? What may Thursday be? Write "P.N." over it.
Student: Holiday

Instructor: The prepositional phrase is an adjective phrase describing the predicate nominative. What kind of holiday?
Student: In the fall

Instructor: Draw an arrow from the adjective phrase back to the predicate nominative.

Answer Key:

P.N.

7.   Sow bugs must have been the insects under the rocks.

Instructor: What is the prepositional phrase? Put a box around it.
Student: *Under the rocks*

Instructor: What are the verbs (two helping verbs plus a linking verb)?
Student: *Must have been*

Instructor: What is the subject? Who must have been?
Student: *Bugs*

Instructor: What is the predicate nominative? What must the bugs have been? Write "P.N." over it.
Student: *Insects*

Instructor: The prepositional phrase is an adjective phrase describing the predicate nominative. Which insects?
Student: *Under the rocks*

Instructor: Draw an arrow from the adjective phrase back to the predicate nominative.

Answer Key:

P.N.

8.   Carolyn had been the gymnast with the most points.

Instructor: What is the prepositional phrase? Put a box around it.
Student: *With the most points*

Instructor: What are the verbs (helping verb plus a linking verb)?
Student: *Had been*

Instructor: What is the subject? Who had been?
Student: *Carolyn*

Instructor: What is the predicate nominative? What had Carolyn been? Write "P.N." over it.
Student: *Gymnast*

Instructor: The prepositional phrase is an adjective phrase describing the predicate nominative. Which gymnast?
Student: *With the most points*

Instructor: Draw an arrow from the adjective phrase back to the predicate nominative.

Instructor: Read the sentence in **Exercise 5**, and look at its diagram.

Workbook: A teacher should be a person of character.

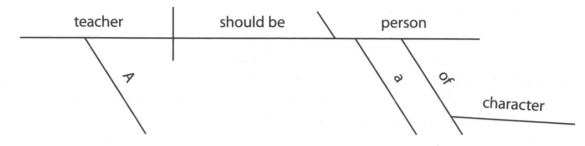

Point to the words on the diagram as you read the explanation below. Pointing to each thing as you explain will make the material easier to understand.

Instructor: *Should be* are the verbs. *Teacher* is the subject. *Person* is the predicate nominative. There is a prepositional phrase in the sentence: "of character." The prepositional phrase is an adjective phrase describing the predicate nominative *person*. What kind of person? A person of character. "Of character" is an adjective phrase that describes *person*. The preposition *of* is written on the slanted line. The object of the preposition, *character*, is written on the flat line. *Of* is written on the slanted line that connects *character* to *person* because the preposition *of* shows the relationship between the noun *character* and the noun *person*. What kind of person? A person of character.

Instructor: Now you will diagram some sentences with prepositional phrases in **Exercise 6** of your workbook. These prepositional phrases are adjective phrases that describe the predicate nominative. You read the sentence, and I will help you identify the prepositional phrases. Then I will ask you questions as you fill in the diagram. For Sentence 1, fill in the frame. For Sentence 2, trace the dotted frame before you fill it in. Remember to copy the words exactly as they appear in the sentence. If the words begin with a capital letter in the sentence, they should also be capitalized in the diagram.

Use the following dialogue to help the student fill in each diagram.

1.   *This sentence has a prepositional phrase. First find the preposition; that's the beginning of the prepositional phrase. Then find the object of the preposition; that's the end of the phrase. Put a box around the entire prepositional phrase, and ignore the words inside the box as you find the other parts of the sentence.*

2.   *What are the verbs? There is a helping verb and a linking verb. Write the verbs to the right of your center line.*

3. *Find the subject. Ask "who" or "what" before the verb. [Prompt the student with specific questions like "What could be?" or "What may be?"] Write the subject to the left of the center line on your frame.*

4. *This sentence contains a predicate nominative. This noun is in the complete predicate of the sentence, but it renames the subject. What is the predicate nominative in this sentence? Because the predicate nominative follows the verb in the sentence, it is written to the right of the verb on the diagram. Write the predicate nominative to the right of the slanted line on your diagram. That slanted line points back toward the subject to remind you that a predicate nominative renames the subject.*

5. *Go back and look again at the simple subject. Are there any words in the complete subject that describe the simple subject? These adjectives can tell what kind, which one, how many, or whose. Also look for the articles (a, an, the), because they act like adjectives. Write each adjective on a slanted line below the subject it describes.*

6. *Look at the predicate nominative. Are there any single words that describe the predicate nominative? These adjectives can tell what kind, which one, how many, or whose. Also look for the articles (a, an, the), because they act like adjectives. Write each adjective on a slanted line below the predicate nominative it describes.*

7. *Look again at the prepositional phrase inside the box. This is an adjective phrase that describes the predicate nominative. An adjective phrase can tell what kind, which one, how many, or whose. Write the preposition on the slanted line below the predicate nominative, and write the object of the preposition on the flat line.*

8. *Are there any words in the prepositional phrase that describe the object of the preposition? These adjectives can tell what kind, which one, how many, or whose. Also look for the articles (a, an, the), because they act like adjectives. Write each adjective on a slanted line below the object of the preposition it describes. (Omit this question for Sentence 1.)*

Answer Key: 1. This story could be one tale about honesty.

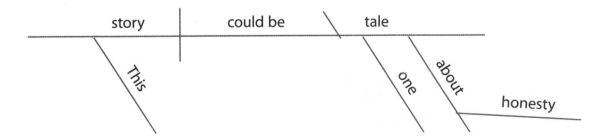

2. Next Thursday may be our first holiday in the fall.

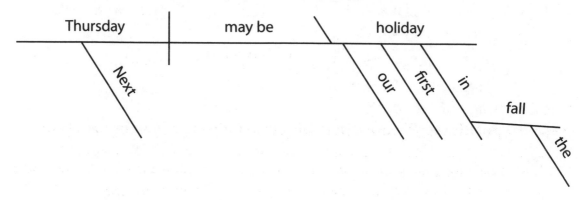

LESSON 48

New: Prepositional Phrases That Describe Objects of the Preposition

---

Read "Learning to Read" (Lesson 40) three times to the student. Then ask the student to try to say parts of the eleventh stanza along with you (or the tape recorder).

Instructor: Say the definition of a preposition with me once, and then say it on your own.

TOGETHER, then student alone: A preposition is a word that shows the relationship of a noun or pronoun to another word in the sentence.

If the student knows the list of prepositions in **Exercise 1**, have him review it by saying it once. The student may check off his accomplishments in the workbook.

Workbook: Prepositions

Aboard, about, above, across.
After, against, along, among, around, at.

Before, behind, below, beneath.
Beside, between, beyond, by.

Down, during, except, for, from.
In, inside, into, like.

Near, of, off, on, over.
Past, since, through, throughout.

To, toward, under, underneath.
Until, up, upon.
With, within, without.

Instructor: Read the first sentence in **Exercise 2** to me.

Instructor: There are two prepositions in this sentence. What are they?
Student: *Near, of*

Instructor: Circle the prepositions *near* and *of.* Near what? Near the center. Underline "near the center." "Near the center" is the prepositional phrase. A prepositional phrase begins with a preposition and ends with a noun or pronoun. That noun or pronoun is called the object of the preposition. In the prepositional phrase "near the center," the object of the preposition is the noun *center*. Write "O.P." over *center*.

Instructor: Look at the second preposition in the sentence, *of*. Of what? Of the ship. Underline "of the ship." "Of the ship" is also a prepositional phrase. The object of the preposition is the noun *ship*. Write "O.P." over *ship*.

Answer Key:

                                         O.P   O.P.

1. A pirate (near) the center (of) the ship raised the flag.

Instructor: Now you will find the prepositions, objects of the preposition, and prepositional phrases for yourself. There are two prepositional phrases in every sentence. I will ask you questions to help you. Read each of the sentences, numbers 2 through 8, in your workbook. Circle the prepositions, write "O.P." over the objects of the preposition, and underline the prepositional phrases.

Answer Key:

                                        O.P.   O.P.

2. The pony (with) white patches (around) his eyes pawed the soft ground.

Instructor: What is the first preposition?
Student: *With*

Instructor: What is the object of that preposition?
Student: *Patches*

Instructor: What is the prepositional phrase?
Student: *With white patches*

Instructor: What is the second preposition?
Student: *Around*

Instructor: What is its object of that preposition?
Student: *Eyes*

Instructor: What is the prepositional phrase?
Student: *Around his eyes*

Answer Key:

                                      O.P.   O.P.

3. Leaves (on) the trees (down) the street are red.

Instructor: What is the first preposition?

Student: *On*

Instructor: What is the object of that preposition?
Student: *Trees*

Instructor: What is the prepositional phrase?
Student: *On the trees*

Instructor: What is the second preposition?
Student: *Down*

Instructor: What is its object of that preposition?
Student: *Street*

Instructor: What is the prepositional phrase?
Student: *Down the street*

Answer Key: O.P.   O.P.
       4.   The statue along the path inside our garden is majestic.

Instructor: What is the first preposition?
Student: *Along*

Instructor: What is the object of that preposition?
Student: *Path*

Instructor: What is the prepositional phrase?
Student: *Along the path*

Instructor: What is the second preposition?
Student: *Inside*

Instructor: What is its object of that preposition?
Student: *Garden*

Instructor: What is the prepositional phrase?
Student: *Inside our garden*

Answer Key: O.P.   O.P.
       5.   The four frogs between the slender reeds near the pond are green.

Instructor: What is the first preposition?
Student: *Between*

Instructor: What is the object of that preposition?
Student: *Reeds*

Instructor: What is the prepositional phrase?
Student: *Between the slender reeds*

Instructor: What is the second preposition?
Student: *Near*

Instructor: What is its object of that preposition?
Student: *Pond*

Instructor: What is the prepositional phrase?
Student: *Near the pond*

Answer Key:

O.P.   O.P.
6. Her clothes(in)the basket(beside)the washer are clean.

Instructor: What is the first preposition?
Student: *In*

Instructor: What is the object of that preposition?
Student: *Basket*

Instructor: What is the prepositional phrase?
Student: *In the basket*

Instructor: What is the second preposition?
Student: *Beside*

Instructor: What is its object of that preposition?
Student: *Washer*

Instructor: What is the prepositional phrase?
Student: *Beside the washer*

Answer Key:

O.P.   O.P.
7. The gifts(on)the bed(in)my room were splendid.

Instructor: What is the first preposition?
Student: *On*

Instructor: What is the object of that preposition?
Student: *Bed*

Instructor: What is the prepositional phrase?
Student: *On the bed*

Instructor: What is the second preposition?
Student: *In*

Instructor: What is the object of that preposition?
Student: *Room*

Instructor: What is the prepositional phrase?
Student: *In my room*

Answer Key:

                                                                  O.P.   O.P.

8.   That instrument (in) the case (upon) the floor is a violin.

Instructor: What is the first preposition?
Student: *In*

Instructor: What is the object of that preposition?
Student: *Case*

Instructor: What is the prepositional phrase?
Student: *In the case*

Instructor: What is the second preposition?
Student: *Upon*

Instructor: What is its object of that preposition?
Student: *Floor*

Instructor: What is the prepositional phrase?
Student: *Upon the floor*

Instructor: Let's review the definition of an adjective. An adjective is a word that describes a noun or pronoun. Adjectives tell what kind, which one, how many, and whose. Say that with me.

TOGETHER: An adjective is a word that describes a noun or pronoun. Adjectives tell what kind, which one, how many, and whose.

Instructor: Sometimes prepositional phrases act like adjectives. They describe nouns or pronouns. They tell what kind, which one, how many, and whose. When prepositional phrases act like adjectives, they are called adjective phrases. Look at the first sentence in **Exercise 3**.

Instructor: What is the first preposition?
Student: *Near*

Instructor: What is the object of that preposition?
Student: *Center*

Instructor: What is the prepositional phrase?
Student: *Near the center*

Instructor: Put a box around the prepositional phrase "near the center."

Instructor: What is the second preposition?
Student: *Of*

Instructor: What is the object of that preposition?
Student: *Ship*

Instructor: What is the prepositional phrase?
Student: *Of the ship*

Instructor: Put a box around the prepositional phrase "of the ship." Now let's find the subject and the verb in the sentence. The subject and the verb are never part of a prepositional phrase, so ignore all the words inside the boxes. Look for the subject and the verb in the rest of the sentence. What is the action verb?
Student: *Raised*

Instructor: What is the subject? Who raised?
Student: *Pirate*

Instructor: Write "S" for subject over *pirate*. Now let's find the adjective phrase that describes the subject. Which pirate? Answer me with the first prepositional phrase you have put in a box.

Student: *Near the center*

Instructor: "Near the center" acts like an adjective because it tells which one. It describes the subject *pirate*. Which pirate? The one near the center. Draw an arrow starting at the adjective phrase "near the center" and pointing back to *pirate*, because this is the noun the adjective phrase describes. The adjective phrase follows the noun or pronoun it describes.

Instructor: There is another prepositional phrase in the sentence. What is it?

Student: *Of the ship*

Instructor: The prepositional phrase "of the ship" acts like an adjective to describe a noun in the sentence. The pirate of the ship? No. The flag of the ship? No. It is the **center** of the ship. The word *center* is a noun. It is the object of the preposition in the phrase "near the center." Write "O.P." over *center*. Which center? The center of the ship. Draw an arrow starting at the adjective phrase "of the ship" and pointing back to *center*, because this is the noun it describes. The adjective phrase follows the noun or pronoun it describes.

Answer Key:

S   O.P.
1. A pirate │near the center│of the ship│raised the flag.

Instructor: Let's practice finding the prepositional phrases that act like adjectives in Sentences 2–8 and putting boxes around them. We will write "S" over the subject and "O.P." over the object of the preposition in the first prepositional phrase in each sentence. Then we will draw one arrow from the first adjective phrase back to the subject it describes, and draw another arrow from the second adjective phrase back to the object of the preposition it describes. I will ask you questions to help you with each sentence.

Answer Key:

S   O.P.
2. The pony │with white patches│around his eyes│pawed the soft ground.

Instructor: What is the first prepositional phrase? Put a box around it.

Student: *With white patches*

Instructor: What is the object of the preposition in that phrase? Write "O.P." over it.

Student: *Patches*

Instructor: What is the second prepositional phrase? Put a box around it.
Student: *Around his eyes*

Instructor: What is the verb?
Student: *Pawed*

Instructor: What is the subject? What pawed?
Student: *Pony*

Instructor: The first prepositional phrase is an adjective phrase describing the subject. Which pony?
Student: *With white patches*

Instructor: Draw an arrow from that adjective phrase pointing back to the subject. The second prepositional phrase is an adjective phrase describing the object of the preposition in the first phrase. Which patches?
Student: *Around his eyes*

Instructor: Draw an arrow from that adjective phrase back to the object of the preposition in the first phrase.

Answer Key:

S   O.P.
3. Leaves on the trees down the street are red.

Instructor: What is the first prepositional phrase? Put a box around it.
Student: *On the trees*

Instructor: What is the object of the preposition in that phrase? Write "O.P." over it.
Student: *Trees*

Instructor: What is the second prepositional phrase? Put a box around it.
Student: *Down the street*

Instructor: What is the linking verb?
Student: *Are*

Instructor: What is the subject? What are?
Student: *Leaves*

Instructor: The first prepositional phrase is an adjective phrase describing the subject. Which leaves?
Student: *On the trees*

Instructor: Draw an arrow from that adjective phrase pointing back to the subject. The second prepositional phrase is an adjective phrase describing the object of the preposition in the first phrase.

Instructor: Which trees?
Student: *Down the street*

Instructor: Draw an arrow from that adjective phrase back to the object of the preposition in the first phrase.

Answer Key:

S   O.P.

4. The gifts on the bed in my room were splendid.

Instructor: What is the first prepositional phrase? Put a box around it.
Student: *On the bed*

Instructor: What is the object of the preposition in that phrase? Write "O.P." over it.
Student: *Bed*

Instructor: What is the second prepositional phrase? Put a box around it.
Student: *In my room*

Instructor: What is the linking verb?
Student: *Were*

Instructor: What is the subject? What were?
Student: *Gifts*

Instructor: The first prepositional phrase is an adjective phrase describing the subject. Which gifts?
Student: *On my bed*

Instructor: Draw an arrow from that adjective phrase pointing back to the subject. The second prepositional phrase is an adjective phrase describing the object of the preposition in the first phrase. Which bed?
Student: *In my room*

Instructor: Draw an arrow from that adjective phrase back to the object of the preposition in the first phrase.

Answer Key:

S   O.P.

5. That instrument in the case upon the floor is a violin.

Instructor: What is the first prepositional phrase? Put a box around it.
Student: *In the case*

Instructor: What is the object of the preposition in that phrase? Write "O.P." over it.
Student: *Case*

Instructor: What is the second prepositional phrase? Put a box around it.
Student: *Upon the floor*

Instructor: What is the linking verb?
Student: *Is*

Instructor: What is the subject? What is?
Student: *Instrument*

Instructor: The first prepositional phrase is an adjective phrase describing the subject. Which instrument?
Student: *In the case*

Instructor: Draw an arrow from that adjective phrase pointing back to the subject. The second prepositional phrase is an adjective phrase describing the object of the preposition in the first phrase. Which case?
Student: *Upon the floor*

Instructor: Draw an arrow from that adjective phrase back to the object of the preposition in the first phrase.

Instructor: Read the sentence in **Exercise 4**, and look at its diagram.

Workbook: Leaves on the trees down the street are red.

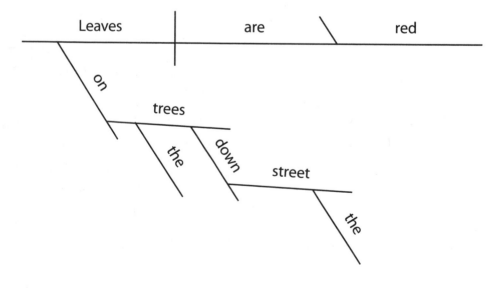

Point to the words on the diagram as you read the explanation below. Pointing to each thing as you explain will make the material easier to understand.

Instructor: *Are* is the linking verb. *Leaves* is the subject. *Red* is the predicate adjective. There are two prepositional phrases in the sentence: "on the trees" and "down the street." The prepositional phrase "on the trees" is an adjective phrase describing the subject *leaves*. Which leaves? The leaves on the trees. "On the trees" is an adjective phrase that describes *leaves*. The preposition *on* is written on the slanted line. The object of the preposition, *trees*, is written on the flat line. *On* is written on the slanted line that connects *trees* to *leaves* because the preposition *on* shows the relationship between the noun *trees* and the noun *leaves*. Which leaves? The leaves on the trees. Look again at the object of the preposition, *trees*. There is a word in the prepositional phrase that describes *trees*; it is the article *the*. *The* is written on a slanted line beneath the word it describes. There is something else describing the object of the preposition, *trees*. The second prepositional phrase, "down the street," is an adjective phrase that tells which trees. The preposition *down* is written on the slanted line connected to *trees*. The object of the preposition, *street*, is written on the flat line. *Down* is written on the slanted line that connects *street* to *trees* because the preposition *down* shows the relationship between the noun *street* and the noun *trees*. Which trees? The trees down the street. Look again at the object of the preposition, *street*. There is a word in the second prepositional phrase that describes *street*; it is the article *the*. *The* is written on a slanted line beneath the word it describes.

Instructor: Now you will diagram some sentences with two prepositional phrases in **Exercise 5** of your workbook. The first prepositional phrase is an adjective phrase that describes the subject; the second prepositional phrase is an adjective phrase that describes the object of the preposition in the first phrase. First, we will put boxes around the prepositional phrases. Then you will read the sentence, and I will ask you questions as you fill in the diagram. For Sentences 1 and 2, fill in the frame. For Sentence 3, trace the dotted frame before you fill it in. Remember to copy the words exactly as they appear in the sentence. If the words begin with a capital letter in the sentence, they should also be capitalized in the diagram.

Use the following dialogue to help the student fill in each diagram.

1. *This sentence has two prepositional phrases. For each phrase, first find the preposition; that's the beginning of the prepositional phrase. Then find the object of the preposition; that's the end of the phrase. Put a box around each prepositional phrase, and ignore the words inside the boxes as you find the other parts of the sentence.*

2. *What is the linking verb? Write the verb to the right of your center line.*

3. *Find the subject. Ask "who" or "what" before the verb. [Prompt the student with a specific question like "What is?" or "What are?"] Write the subject to the left of the center line on your frame.*

4. *This sentence contains a predicate adjective. This adjective is in the complete predicate of the sentence, but it describes the subject. A predicate adjective can tell what kind, which one, how many, or whose. Can you find an adjective in the complete predicate that describes the subject? Because the predicate adjective follows the verb in the sentence, it is written to the right of the verb on the diagram. Write the predicate adjective to the right of the slanted line on your diagram. That slanted line points back toward the subject to remind you that a predicate adjective describes the subject.*

5. *Go back and look again at the simple subject. Are there any single words in the complete subject that describe the simple subject? These adjectives can tell what kind, which one, how many, or whose. Also look for the articles (a, an, the), because they act like adjectives. Write each adjective on a slanted line below the subject it describes.*

6. *Look again at the prepositional phrase inside the first box. This is an adjective phrase that describes the subject. An adjective phrase can tell what kind, which one, how many, or whose. Write the preposition on the slanted line below the subject, and write the object of the preposition on the flat line.*

7. *Are there any words in the first prepositional phrase that describe the object of the preposition in that phrase? These adjectives can tell what kind, which one, how many, or whose. Also look for the articles (a, an, the), because they act like adjectives. Write each adjective on a slanted line below the object of the preposition it describes.*

8. *Look again at the prepositional phrase inside the second box. This is an adjective phrase that describes the object of the preposition in the first phrase. An adjective phrase can tell what kind, which one, how many, or whose. Write the preposition on the slanted line below the object of the preposition in the first phrase. Then write the object of that second prepositional phrase on its own flat line.*

9. *Are there any words in the second prepositional phrase that describe the object of the preposition in that phrase? These adjectives can tell what kind, which one, how many, or whose. Also look for the articles (a, an, the), because they act like adjectives. Write each adjective on a slanted line below the object of the preposition it describes.*

Answer Key: 1. The statue along the path inside our garden is majestic.

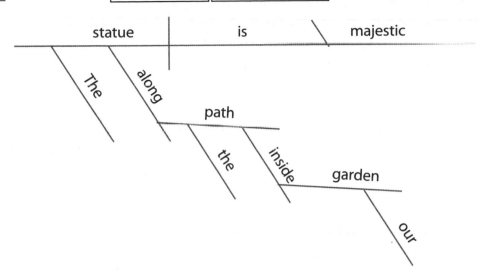

2. The four frogs between the slender reeds near the pond are green.

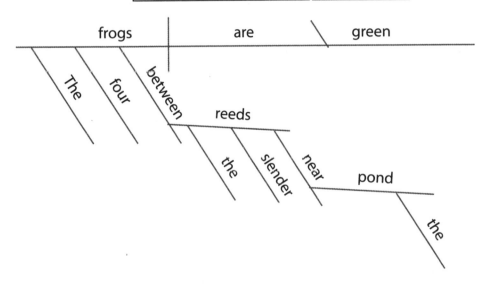

3. Her clothes in the basket beside the washer are clean.

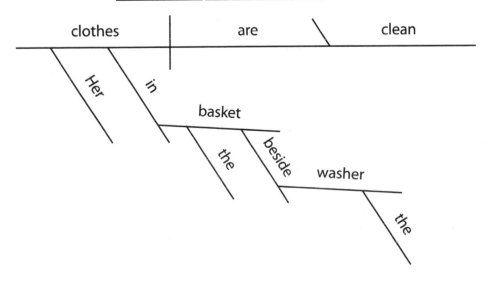

Optional Dictation Exercise

The following selection is slightly adapted from *Alice's Adventures in Wonderland* by Lewis Carroll. Today's dictation is what Alice did when she suddenly saw a white rabbit run by her. The rabbit was dressed in a little waistcoat. It took a watch out of its pocket, glanced at the time, and dashed away. Alice jumped up and followed the rabbit. Tell the student you will pause briefly when you get to a comma. After he has written the sentences, have him circle the prepositions and then underline the prepositional phrases. (The word *to* is part of an infinitive; it is not a preposition. Remind the student that a preposition is always part of a prepositional phrase with an object of the preposition.)

Dictation: She ran (across) the field (after) it, and was just (in) time to see it pop (down) a large rabbit-hole (under) the hedge.

LESSON 49

New: Prepositional Phrases That Describe Verbs

Read "Learning to Read" (Lesson 40) three times to the student. Then ask the student to try to say parts of the whole poem along with you (or the tape recorder).

Instructor: What is the definition of a preposition?

Student: *A preposition is a word that shows the relationship of a noun or pronoun to another word in the sentence.*

If the student knows the list of prepositions in **Exercise 1**, have him review it by saying it once. The student may check off his accomplishments in the workbook.

Workbook: Prepositions

Aboard, about, above, across.
After, against, along, among, around, at.

Before, behind, below, beneath.
Beside, between, beyond, by.

Down, during, except, for, from.
In, inside, into, like.

Near, of, off, on, over.
Past, since, through, throughout.

To, toward, under, underneath.
Until, up, upon.
With, within, without.

Instructor: Read the first sentence in **Exercise 2** to me.

Instructor: What is the preposition in the sentence?

Student: *Beyond*

Instructor: Circle the preposition *beyond*. Beyond what? Beyond the moon. Underline "beyond the moon." "Beyond the moon" is the prepositional phrase. A prepositional phrase begins with a preposition and ends with a noun or pronoun. That noun or pronoun is called the object of the preposition. In the prepositional phrase "beyond the moon," the object of the preposition is the noun *moon*. Write "O.P." over *moon*.

Answer Key:

O.P.
1. I see stars (beyond) the moon.

Instructor: Now you will find the preposition, object of the preposition, and prepositional phrase for yourself. I will ask you questions to help you. Read each of the sentences, numbers 2 through 8, in your workbook. Circle the preposition, write "O.P." over the object of the preposition, and underline the whole prepositional phrase.

Answer Key:

O.P.
2. Water was running (down) the hillside.

Instructor: What is the preposition?
Student: *Down*

Instructor: What is the object of the preposition?
Student: *Hillside*

Instructor: What is the prepositional phrase?
Student: *Down the hillside*

Answer Key:

O.P.
3. Gabrielle worked (past) lunchtime.

Instructor: What is the preposition?
Student: *Past*

Instructor: What is the object of the preposition?
Student: *Lunchtime*

Instructor: What is the prepositional phrase?
Student: *Past lunchtime*

Answer Key:

O.P.
4. Gentle breezes blew (through) open windows.

Instructor: What is the preposition?

Student: *Through*

Instructor: What is the object of the preposition?
Student: *Windows*

Instructor: What is the prepositional phrase?
Student: *Through open windows*

Answer Key:

O.P.

5. Tired Mrs. Ferris rested (in) the afternoon.

Instructor: What is the preposition?
Student: *In*

Instructor: What is the object of the preposition?
Student: *Afternoon*

Instructor: What is the prepositional phrase?
Student: *In the afternoon*

Instructor: Let's review the definition of an adverb. An adverb is a word that describes a verb, an adjective, or another adverb. Say that with me.

TOGETHER: An adverb is a word that describes a verb, an adjective, or another adverb.

Instructor: Adverbs tell how, when, where, how often, and to what extent. Say that with me.

TOGETHER: Adverbs tell how, when, where, how often, and to what extent.

Instructor: Sometimes whole prepositional phrases act like adverbs. They describe verbs. They tell how, when, where, how often, and to what extent. When prepositional phrases act like adverbs, they are called **adverb phrases**. Look at the first sentence in **Exercise 3**.

Instructor: What is the preposition?
Student: *Beyond*

Instructor: What is the object of the preposition?
Student: *Moon*

Instructor: What is the prepositional phrase?
Student: *Beyond the moon*

Instructor: Put a box around the prepositional phrase "beyond the moon." Now let's find the subject and the verb in the sentence. The subject and the verb are never part of the prepositional phrase, so ignore all the words inside the box. What is the action verb?

Student: *See*

Instructor: Write "V" for verb over *see*. What is the subject? Who sees?

Student: *I*

Instructor: This sentence has a direct object that receives the action of the verb. See what?

Student: *Stars*

Instructor: Now let's find the adverb phrase that tells us more about the verb *see*. Where do I see stars? Answer me with the prepositional phrase you have already put in the box.

Student: *Beyond the moon*

Instructor: "Beyond the moon" acts like an adverb because it tells where. It describes the verb *see*. Where do I see stars? Beyond the moon. Draw an arrow starting at the adverb phrase "beyond the moon" and pointing back to *see*, because this is the verb it describes. In this lesson, the adverb phrase will follow the verb it describes.

Answer Key:

V

1. I see stars beyond the moon.

Instructor: Let's practice finding the prepositional phrases that act like adverbs in Sentences 2 and 3 and putting boxes around them. Write "V" over the verb in each sentence. Then draw an arrow from the adverb phrase back to the verb, because this is the word the adverb phrase is describing. I will ask you questions to help you.

Answer Key:

was running

V

2. Water ran down the hillside.

Instructor: What is the prepositional phrase? Put a box around it.

Student: *Down the hillside*

Instructor: What is the verb? Write "V" over it.

Student: *Ran*

Instructor: What is the subject? What ran?

Student: *Water*

Instructor: The prepositional phrase is an adverb phrase describing the verb. Where did the water run?

Student: *Down the hillside*

Instructor: Draw an arrow from the adverb phrase back to the verb.

Answer Key:

3. Gabrielle worked past lunchtime.

Instructor: What is the prepositional phrase? Put a box around it.

Student: *Past lunchtime*

Instructor: What is the verb? Write "V" over it.

Student: *Worked*

Instructor: What is the subject? Who worked?

Student: *Gabrielle*

Instructor: The prepositional phrase is an adverb phrase describing the verb. When did Gabrielle work?

Student: *Past lunchtime*

Instructor: Draw an arrow from the adverb phrase back to the verb.

Instructor: Read the sentence in **Exercise 4**, and look at its diagram.

Point to the words on the diagram as you read the explanation below. Pointing to each thing as you explain will make the material easier to understand.

Workbook: Gentle breezes blew through open windows.

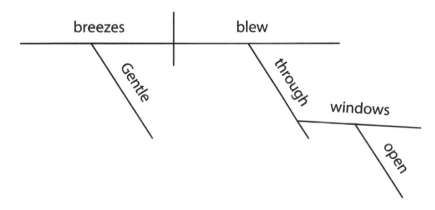

Instructor: *Blew* is the action verb. *Breezes* is the subject. *Gentle* is an adjective that tells what kind of breezes. There is a prepositional phrase in the sentence: "through open windows." The prepositional phrase is an adverb phrase describing the verb *blew*. Where did breezes blow? Through open windows. The preposition *through* is written on the slanted line. The object of the preposition, *windows*, is written on the flat line. *Through* is written on the slanted line that connects *windows* to *blew* because the preposition *through* shows the relationship between the noun *windows* and the verb *blew*. Where did breezes blow? Through open windows. Look again at the object of the preposition, *windows*. There is a word in the prepositional phrase that describes *windows*; it is the adjective *open*. *Open* is written on a slanted line beneath the word it describes.

Instructor: Now you will diagram some sentences with prepositional phrases in **Exercise 5** of your workbook. These prepositional phrases are adverb phrases that describe the verb. First we will locate the prepositional phrases. Then you will read the sentence, and I will ask you questions as you fill in the diagram. For Sentences 1 and 2, fill in the frame. For Sentence 3, trace the dotted frame before you fill it in. Remember to copy the words exactly as they appear in the sentence. If the words begin with a capital letter in the sentence, they should also be capitalized in the diagram.

Use the following dialogue to help the student fill in each diagram.

1. *This sentence has a prepositional phrase. First find the preposition; that's the beginning of the prepositional phrase. Then find the object of the preposition; that's the end of the phrase. Put a box around the entire prepositional phrase, and ignore the words inside the box as you find the other parts of the sentence.*

2. *What is the action verb? Write the verb to the right of your center line.*

3. *Find the subject. Ask "who" or "what" before the verb. [Prompt the student with specific questions like "Who rested?" or "Who fell?" or "Who worked?"] Write the subject to the left of the center line on your frame.*

4. *Go back and look again at the simple subject. Are there any words in the complete subject that describe the simple subject? These adjectives can tell what kind, which one, how many, or whose. Also look for the articles (a, an, the), because they act like adjectives. Write each adjective on a slanted line below the subject it describes.*

5. *Look again at the prepositional phrase inside the box. This is an adverb phrase that describes the verb. An adverb phrase can tell how, when, where, how often, or to what extent. Write the preposition on the slanted line below the verb, and write the object of the preposition on the flat line.*

6. *Are there any words in the prepositional phrase that describe the object of the preposition? These adjectives can tell what kind, which one, how many, or whose. Also look for the articles (a, an, the), because they act like adjectives. Write each adjective on a slanted line below the object of the preposition it describes. (Omit this question for Sentence 3.)*

Answer Key: 1. Tired Mrs. Ferris rested in the afternoon.

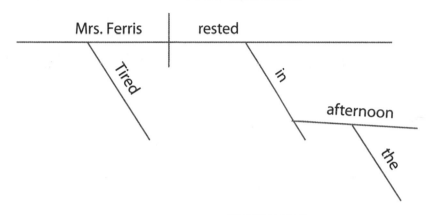

2. Clumsy Humpty Dumpty fell off the wall.

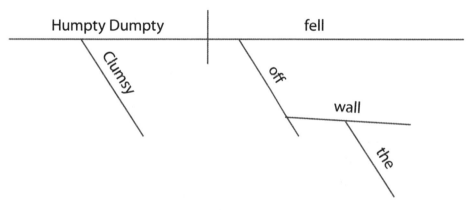

3. The harvesters worked until noon.

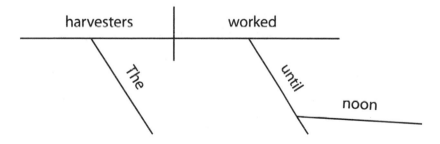

LESSON 50

Summary Exercise: *How Do We Measure Weight?*

Read "Learning to Read" (Lesson 40) three times to the student. Then ask the student to try to say the whole poem with you (or the tape recorder). The student should practice saying the whole poem to himself in a mirror.

Instructor: Today I am going to read a selection aloud to you from the science book *How Do We Measure Weight?* by Chris Woodford. Weight is caused by gravity, a force that pulls things toward Earth. Today's summary exercise is about a balance scale, one of the instruments that measure weight. I will read the selection only once. *(If the student is a fluent reader, you may choose to have* him *read it aloud or silently).* Then I want you to tell me in your own words what you remember.

How Do We Measure Weight?

Children can compare their weights by sitting on a seesaw. Suppose two friends sit on either end of the seesaw at the same distance from the middle, or pivot point. When they lift up their legs, if one end of the seesaw goes down farther than the other, then the child on that end weighs the most.

Lots of weighing machines work like seesaws. These machines are called scales or balances. They have two pans on either side. They also have a set of weights of different sizes. The weights can be lifted on and off the pans. To weigh an object, you put it on one pan. Then you put weights on the other pan. When the scales balance, there is the same weight on each side. If you count the weights, you know how much the object weighs.

You can also put the weights on first. To measure 10 ounces of candies, for example, a shopkeeper puts 10 ounces of weights on one pan. Then she or he pours candies into the other pan until the scales balance.

LESSON 51

Review: Adjectives

Read "Learning to Read" (Lesson 40) three times to the student. Then ask the student to say the poem along with you or the tape recorder. If the student is ready, he should recite the poem to real people today. If he is not, continue practicing daily until he is ready.

Instructor: Let's review the definition of an adjective. An adjective is a word that describes a noun or pronoun. Say that definition with me.

TOGETHER: An adjective is a word that describes a noun or pronoun.

Instructor: Adjectives tell what kind, which one, how many, and whose. Say that with me two times.

TOGETHER (two times): Adjectives tell what kind, which one, how many, and whose.

Instructor: In the sentences of **Exercise 1** in your workbook, underline each adjective that tells what kind and draw an arrow to the noun that it describes.

Answer Key: 1. Black birds soared overhead.

2. Funny jokes caused everyone to laugh.

3. Wild horses ran around everywhere.

4. Bright lights almost blinded us.

Instructor: Remember adjectives don't *always* come *before* the nouns they describe. **Predicate** adjectives are adjectives that describe the subject **but are found in the predicate of the sentence** (Lesson 32). The predicate tells us what is said about the subject (Lesson 28). Remember the word *predicate* comes from the Latin word *praedicare* meaning "to proclaim." The predicate of a sentence is what is said or proclaimed about the subject. Read the first sentence in **Exercise 2** of your workbook.

Instructor: What is the verb?
Student: *Was*

305

Instructor: What is the subject?
Student: *Rose*

Instructor: What is said or proclaimed about the subject *rose* in this sentence?
Student: *It was prickly.*

Instructor: *Prickly* is an adjective in the predicate that tells us something about the subject *rose*. What kind of rose? A prickly rose. Underline *prickly*. To remind yourself that *prickly*, although it is in the predicate, tells us something about the subject *rose*, draw an arrow from *prickly* back to the subject it describes (*rose*). In Sentences 2, 3, and 4, underline the adjective in the predicate and draw an arrow back to the subject it describes. All of these predicate adjectives tell what kind.

Answer Key: 1. The rose was <u>prickly</u>.

2. Cotton is <u>soft</u>.

3. The meat was <u>tough</u>.

4. Lemons are <u>sour</u>.

Instructor: In addition to telling what kind, adjectives also tell which one (Lesson 13). In **Exercise 3** of your workbook, you will see a list of adjectives that tell which one. Each adjective modifies a noun. For each adjective-noun pair, I will ask you a question. You will answer the question with the phrase. This will help you recognize adjectives that tell which one.

Answer Key:

(Q: Which cupcake is it?)	**this** cupcake
(Q: Which cupcake is it?)	**that** cupcake
(Q: Which cupcakes are they?)	**these** cupcakes
(Q: Which cupcakes are they?)	**those** cupcakes
(Q: Which notebook is it?)	**this** notebook
(Q: Which notebook is it?)	**that** notebook
(Q: Which notebooks are they?)	**these** notebooks
(Q: Which notebooks are they?)	**those** notebooks
(Q: Which mouse is it?)	**this** mouse

(Q: Which mouse is it?)	**that** mouse
(Q: Which mice are they?)	**these** mice
(Q: Which mice are they?)	**those** mice
(Q: Which movie is it?)	**this** movie
(Q: Which movie is it?)	**that** movie
(Q: Which movies are they?)	**these** movies
(Q: Which movies are they?)	**those** movies

Instructor: Here are more adjectives that can tell you which one. Read aloud the list in **Exercise 4** of your workbook.

Workbook: first, second, third, fourth, fifth, sixth, seventh, eighth, ninth, tenth

last

next

final

each

other

another

Instructor: In **Exercise 5** of your workbook, underline each adjective that tells which one, then draw an arrow to the noun it describes. You may look at the list in **Exercises 3** and **4** if you need help finding the adjectives that tell which one.

Answer Key:
1. Joe liked art in <u>first</u> grade.

2. <u>Those</u> crayons in the box were new.

3. The <u>next</u> year he was given watercolors.

4. He painted with them <u>each</u> day.

5. <u>Other</u> children preferred to draw with pencils.

Instructor: Adjectives can also tell how many. These adjectives might tell a definite amount like one raisin, two raisins, three raisins, or no raisins, or they might tell an indefinite number like most raisins, many raisins, few raisins, or several raisins. In **Exercise 6** of your workbook, read aloud the list of adjectives that tell how many.

Workbook: one, two, three, four, five, six, seven, eight, nine, ten

no

many

few

most

some

several

another

all

every

more

both

Instructor: In **Exercise 7** of your workbook, underline each adjective that tells how many, then draw an arrow to the noun it describes.

Answer Key: 1. In the tourist area, a <u>few</u> squirrels have become too bold.

2. A lady put <u>some</u> nuts in her little purse to hide them from the squirrels.

3. <u>No</u> nuts were put out on the ground.

4. <u>One</u> squirrel was cuter than the rest.

5. <u>Another</u> squirrel was bolder than the rest.

6. He grabbed her purse containing <u>several</u> nuts and scampered away.

7. <u>Every</u> day after that she made sure not to put nuts in her purse!

Instructor: Now let's review adjectives that tell whose. Often these adjectives have an apostrophe in them. An apostrophe changes the way a word acts in a sentence (Lesson 14). The word *boy* (without the apostrophe and the **s**) is a noun that names a person. But when you add an apostrophe and the letter **s** to *boy*, the new word, *boy's*, tells you whose. The boy's shirt is blue. Whose shirt? The boy's shirt. That apostrophe-**s** turns the noun into an adjective! In your workbook, add an apostrophe-**s** to the nouns in **Exercise 8.** The noun will turn into an adjective that tells whose. Write that adjective in the blank in your workbook.

Answer Key:

Singular Noun	Adjective That Tells Whose
sailor	the **sailor's** uniform
Mrs. Primm	**Mrs. Primm's** family
pin	the **pin's** point
cup	a **cup's** handle
tree	the **tree's** roots

Instructor: Remember that an apostrophe turns a **plural** noun into an adjective, too. If the noun already ends in **s**, you just add an apostrophe. In **Exercise 9**, change the plural noun to an adjective that tells whose by adding an apostrophe.

Answer Key:

Plural Noun	Adjective That Tells Whose
writers	the **writers'** stories
doctors	the **doctors'** offices
shops	the **shops'** displays
trees	the **trees'** leaves
drawers	the **drawers'** handles

Instructor: Some plural nouns do not end in **s**. These are called irregular plurals, because they do not form their plurals the regular way. I am going to say a singular noun, then you say its irregular plural right after me.

Instructor: Child
Student: *Children*

Instructor: Tooth
Student: *Teeth*

Proceed as above with the following words: *man, men; woman, women; mouse, mice; goose, geese; deer, deer; sheep, sheep; fish, fish.*

Instructor: If you want turn these irregular plural nouns that do not end in **s** into adjectives, you add an apostrophe–**s**. In **Exercise 10** write the plural form of each bolded word in the first blank. In the second blank, write the plural **possessive** form of the word.

Answer Key:
1. One **woman** joined the other two **women**.

   The **women's** meeting was at ten o'clock.

2. One **goose** honked at the six young **geese**.

   The **geese's** mother was flying away.

3. One **child** invited three **children**.

   The **children's** party was fun.

4. One **sheep** walked with five other **sheep**.

   The **sheep's** path was across the meadow.

5. One **mouse** gathered food for four **mice**.

   The **mice's** dinner was grains of wheat.

6. One **deer** alerted the ten other **deer**.

   All the **deer's** tails were lifted as they bounded away.

Instructor: In **Exercise 11** read the list of personal pronouns that you have learned.

Workbook: <u>Personal Pronouns</u>

I, me, my, mine

You, your, yours

He, she, him, her, it

His, hers, its

We, us, our, ours

They, them, their, theirs

Instructor: Some of these are possessive pronouns that act like adjectives telling whose. In **Exercise 12**, read the pronouns that tell whose. Then read each sentence and underline the pronoun that acts like an adjective in that sentence. Then draw an arrow to the word it describes. Some of these possessive pronouns are **predicate** adjectives.

Answer Key: My, mine, your, yours, his, her, hers, its, our, ours, their, theirs

1. My eyes are brown.

2. The watch is mine. (Note: *mine* is a predicate adjective)

3. Your jeans are faded.

4. The new socks are yours. (Note: *yours* is a predicate adjective)

5. His boots are muddy.

6. Her pet is a kitten.

7. Its paw is hurt.

8. Our aunts missed the bus.

9. The mistake was ours. (Note: *ours* is a predicate adjective)

10. Their friends were waiting.

11. The shiny new car is theirs. (Note: *theirs* is a predicate adjective)

LESSON 52

Review: Adverbs

Review "Afternoon on a Hill" (Lesson 8), "Ozymandias" (Lesson 16), "How Doth…" (Lesson 27), and "Learning to Read" (Lesson 40) today. If the student has trouble remembering the poems, have him practice them daily until he is confident.

Instructor: An adverb is a word that describes a verb, an adjective, or another adverb. Say that with me two times.

TOGETHER (two times): An adverb is a word that describes a verb, an adjective, or another adverb.

Instructor: Adverbs that describe **verbs** usually tell how, when, where, and how often. Read each column of adverbs in **Exercise 1** of your workbook. Begin by reading the title of the column, for example, "How, carefully, quickly," etc.

Workbook:

How	When	Where	How Often
carefully	tonight	outdoors	usually
quickly	today	here	daily
accurately	now	there	nightly
happily	again	indoors	occasionally
faithfully	immediately	everywhere	sporadically
gladly	promptly	anywhere	often
silently	early	inside	regularly

Instructor: Now read the questions below the columns. Choose two adverbs from each column to tell how, when, where, and how often you study.

This is an oral exercise. The student might say, for example, "I study carefully. I study faithfully."

How do I study?   Possible answers:

           I study _____.   carefully

           I study _____.   faithfully

When do I study?

           I study _____.   today

           I study _____.   now

Where do I study ?

           I study _____.   indoors

           I study _____.   anywhere

How often do I study?

           I study _____.   regularly

           I study _____.   often

Instructor: Look at **Exercise 2**. Let's do a quick review. You read the first sentence, and I will ask you a question to help you find the adverb in that sentence.

Workbook: I answer eagerly.

Instructor: **How** do you answer?
Student: *Eagerly*

Instructor: *Eagerly* is an adverb that tells how you answer. Read the next sentence.

Workbook: I answer now.

Instructor: **When** do you answer?
Student: *Now*

Instructor: *Now* is an adverb that tells when you answer. Read the third sentence.

Workbook: I answer here.

Instructor: **Where** do you answer?
Student: *Here*

Instructor: *Here* is an adverb that tells where you answer. Read the fourth sentence.

Workbook: I answer always.

Instructor: **How often** do you answer?
Student: *Always*

Instructor: *Always* is an adverb that tells how often you answer.

Instructor: So far in this lesson, we have focused on adverbs that describe verbs. These adverbs usually tell how, when, where, and how often. But remember, adverbs can describe more than just verbs: they can describe **adjectives** and **other adverbs**, too. You learned eight of these adverbs. They don't tell how, when, where, or how often. They tell you **to what extent**. Read aloud the list of the eight adverbs in **Exercise 3**.

Workbook: too

very

really

quite

so

extremely

rather

slightly

Instructor: These adverbs can describe adjectives, like the adjective cloudy. Read the list in **Exercise 4**.

Workbook: **too** cloudy

very cloudy

really cloudy

quite cloudy

so cloudy

extremely cloudy

rather cloudy

slightly cloudy

Instructor: All of these adverbs tell **to what extent** it is cloudy. We agree that it is cloudy. To what extent is it cloudy? Is it **too** cloudy? Or is it **very** cloudy, or **really** cloudy, or **quite** cloudy, or **so** cloudy, or **extremely** cloudy, or only **rather** cloudy or **slightly** cloudy?

Instructor: In **Exercise 5** you will diagram two sentences with adverbs that describe adjectives. After you read each sentence, I will ask you questions to help you fill in the diagram. For Sentence 1, trace the dotted frame before you fill it in. In the space provided for Sentence 2, draw your own frame just like the one in Sentence 1. Remember to copy the words exactly as they appear in the sentence. If the word begins with a capital letter in the sentence, it should also be capitalized in the diagram.

Use this dialogue to help the student fill in the diagrams.

1. *Find the verb. Write the verb to the right of your center line.*

2. *Find the subject. Ask "who" or "what" before the verb. [Prompt the student with a specific question like "What rolls?" or "What coasts?"] Write the subject to the left of the center line on your frame.*

3. *Now you have found the two most basic parts of the sentence. Go back and look again at the simple subject. Are there any words that describe the subject that come before the verb? These adjectives can tell what kind, which one, how many, or whose. Also look for the articles (a, an, the), because they act like adjectives. Write each adjective on a slanted line below the subject it describes.*

4. *Look again at the adjective. Is there an adverb such as* too, very, really, quite, so, extremely, rather, *or* slightly? *These adverbs tell to what extent. Write the adverb on the slanted line beneath the adjective it describes.*

Answer Key: 1. Very tiny tricycles roll.

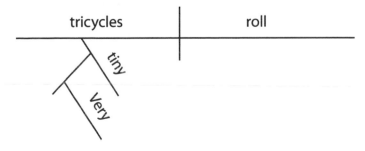

2. Slightly larger bicycles coast.

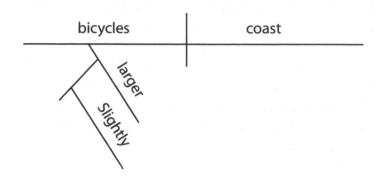

Instructor: In **Exercise 6** read the list of "to what extent" adverbs again.

Workbook: too

very

really

quite

so

extremely

rather

slightly

Instructor: You have seen that these adverbs can describe adjectives. They can also describe other **adverbs**, like the adverb *fast*. Read the list in **Exercise 7** to see what I mean.

Workbook: **too** fast

very fast

really fast

quite fast

so fast

extremely fast

rather fast

slightly fast

Instructor: All these adverbs tell to what extent. He walks fast. To what extent does he walk fast? He walks **too** fast. Or he walks **very** fast, or **really** fast, or **quite** fast, or **so** fast, or **extremely** fast, or only **rather** fast or **slightly** fast.

Instructor: In **Exercise 8**, you will diagram sentences with adverbs that describe other adverbs. You read the sentence, and I will ask you questions to help you fill in the diagram. For Sentences 1 and 2, trace the dotted frame before you fill it in. For Sentences 3 and 4, draw your own frames in the spaces provided.

Use this dialogue to help the student fill in the diagrams.

1. *What is the verb? Write the verb to the right of your center line.*

2. *Find the subject. Ask "who" or "what" before the verb. [Prompt the student with a specific question like "What rolls?" or "What coasts?"] Write the subject to the left of the center line on your frame.*

3. *Now you have found the two most basic parts of the sentence. Go back and look again at the simple subject. Are there any words that describe the subject that come before the verb? These adjectives can tell what kind, which one, how many, or whose. Also look for the articles (a, an, the), because they act like adjectives. Write each adjective on a slanted line below the subject it describes.*

4. *Look again at the adjective in the complete subject. Is there an adverb such as* too, very, really, quite, so, extremely, rather, *or* slightly? *These adverbs tell to what extent. Write the adverb on the slanted line beneath the adjective it describes.*

5. *Go back and look again at the verb. Is there a word that describes the verb? This is an adverb that could tell how, when, where, or how often. Write the adverb on the slanted line below the verb it describes.*

6. *Look again at the adverb that describes the verb. Is there another adverb in the sentence, such as* too, very, really, quite, so, extremely, rather, *or* slightly, *that describes the first adverb? These adverbs tell to what extent. Write one of these adverbs (*too, very, really, quite, so, extremely, rather, *or* slightly*) on the slanted line beneath the adverb it describes.*

Answer Key: 1. Very tiny tricycles roll quite easily.

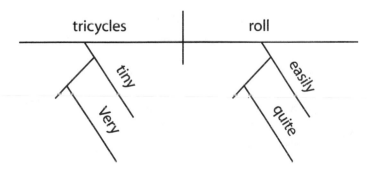

317

2. Slightly larger bicycles coast really smoothly.

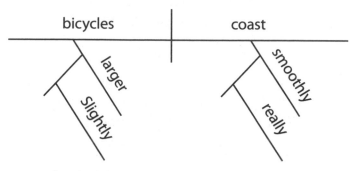

3. Rather bold cyclists race very seriously.

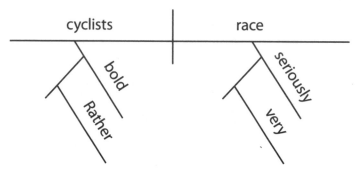

4. Extremely reckless cyclists crash too often.

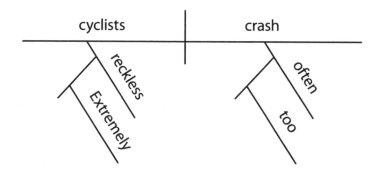

Optional Dictation Exercise

The following dictation is from *The Secret Garden* by Frances Hodgson Burnett. Mary, a disagreeable child orphaned because of a cholera epidemic in India, and Colin, a sickly, neglected, spoiled child, discover the mystery of a secret garden. The dictation for today is what Colin first saw when he ventured outside to see the secret garden Mary had found—he looked up at the sky.

After the student has written the dictation, have him circle the "to what extent" adverb.

Dictation: The arch of it looked (very) high and the small snowy clouds seemed like white birds floating on outspread wings below its crystal blueness.

LESSON 53

Poem Memorization: "The Lake Isle of Innisfree"

Instructor: In Lesson 53 of your workbook, you will find a poem about a man who plans to go to a peaceful island. The poet, William Butler Yeats, spent many holidays in Sligo, a county in western Ireland. The lake isle of Innisfree is there in Sligo. Before I begin reading, you should know that wattles are slender branches or reeds used for building. A linnet is a small bird.

"The Lake Isle of Innisfree"
by William Butler Yeats

I will arise and go now, and go to Innisfree,

And a small cabin build there, of clay and wattles made:

Nine bean rows will I have there, a hive for the honey bee,

And live alone in the bee-loud glade.

And I shall have some peace there, for peace comes dropping slow,

Dropping from the veils of the morning to where the cricket sings;

There midnight's all a glimmer, and noon a purple glow,

And evening full of the linnet's wings.

I will arise and go now, for always night and day

I hear the lake water lapping with the low sounds by the shore;

While I stand on the roadway, or on the pavements gray,

I hear it in the deep heart's core.

Discuss the meaning of the poem with the student. Read the poem to the student three times in a row. Repeat this triple reading twice more during the day. Have the student check the boxes in his workbook when this is done.

LESSON 54

Review: Four Kinds of Verbs
Review: Direct Objects and Indirect Objects
Review: Predicate Nominatives and Predicate Adjectives

Read "The Lake Isle of Innisfree" (Lesson 53) three times to the student. Then ask the student to try to say parts of the first stanza along with you (or the tape recorder).

Instructor: Let's begin by saying the definition of a verb. A verb is a word that does an action, shows a state of being, links two words together, or helps another verb. Say that with me two times.

TOGETHER (two times): A verb is a word that does an action, shows a state of being, links two words together, or helps another verb.

Instructor: Action verbs show action. *Swing, twist,* and *wriggle* are all action verbs. Action verbs are sometimes followed by a direct object that receives the action of the verb. Now you will find the direct objects in a few sentences. To find the direct object, I will ask you "what" or "whom" after the verb. Read each sentence in **Exercise 1**.

Workbook: Whitney cracks walnuts.

Instructor: Cracks **what**?
Student: *Walnuts*

Instructor: *Walnuts* is the direct object. It receives the action of the verb *cracks*. Read the next sentence.

Workbook: Edith eats pecans.

Instructor: Eats **what**?
Student: *Pecans*

Instructor: *Pecans* is the direct object. It receives the action of the verb *eats*. Look at the diagram of the sentence you just read, "Edith eats pecans."

Edith	eats	pecans

Instructor: The direct object *pecans* is written next to the verb *eats*. It is divided from the verb by a short line. Now read the first sentence in **Exercise 2**.

Workbook: Dennis roasted his family some peanuts.

Instructor: Roasted **what**?
Student: *Peanuts*

Instructor: *Peanuts* is the direct object. (Dennis certainly didn't roast his family!) *Peanuts* receives the action of the verb *roasted*. This sentence also has an indirect object. An indirect object is a noun or pronoun that is **between** the action verb and the direct object of a sentence. It answers the question "to whom" or "for whom" the action is done, but the words *to* or *for* are usually not in the sentence. *To* or *for* are just understood. What is the indirect object of the sentence "Dennis roasted his family some peanuts"? Roasted some peanuts for whom?
Student: *Family*

Instructor: *Family* is the indirect object. It tells for whom the peanuts were roasted. Read the next sentence in **Exercise 2** of your workbook. I will ask you questions to help you identify the direct object and the indirect object in each sentence.

Workbook: Dennis gave his father unsalted peanuts.

Instructor: Let's find the direct object. Gave what?
Student: *Peanuts*

Instructor: *Peanuts* is the direct object. Now let's find the indirect object. Gave peanuts to whom?
Student: *Father*

Instructor: *Father* is the indirect object. Read the next sentence.

Workbook: Mother wrote Chris a note.

Instructor: Let's find the direct object. Wrote what?

Student: *Note*

Instructor: *Note* is the direct object. Now let's find the indirect object. Wrote a note to whom?

Student: *Chris*

Instructor: *Chris* is the indirect object. Look at the diagram of the sentence you just read, "Mother wrote Chris a note."

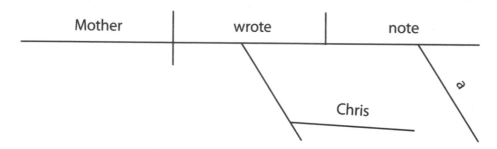

Instructor: *Wrote* is the verb. *Mother* is the subject. The direct object *note* is written next to the verb *wrote*. It is divided from the verb by a short line. Wrote a note to whom? Chris. The indirect object *Chris* is written underneath the verb, on the little horizontal line. When diagramming indirect objects, **nothing is written on the slanted line.** An indirect object is diagrammed on the part of the frame that is usually used for a prepositional phrase. Remember, an indirect object answers the question "to whom" or "for whom." The prepositions *to* or *for* are not written on the diagram; they are just understood.

Instructor: Helping verbs are another kind of verb. They help other verbs. Chant the first part of the list of helping verbs with me.

TOGETHER: Am [clap]
Is [clap]
Are, was, were. [clap]
Be [clap]
Being [clap]
Been. [clap] [clap]

Instructor: Now let's chant the rest of the helping verbs together.

TOGETHER: Have, has, had [clap]
Do, does, did [clap]
Shall, will, should, would, may, might, must [clap, clap]
Can, could!

Instructor: Read the sentences in **Exercise 3**. Circle the helping verbs. There may be more than one helping verb in a sentence. Each helping verb helps the action verb in the sentence make sense by showing time.

Answer Key: Wade (has) hidden.

Marjorie (is) hiding.

They (should be) found.

Instructor: Another type of verb, a state of being verb, just shows that you exist. Let's chant the state of being verbs together. This is the same chant as the first part of the helping verb chant.

TOGETHER: Am [clap]
Is [clap]
Are, was, were. [clap]
Be [clap]
Being [clap]
Been. [clap] [clap]

Instructor: Read the sentences in **Exercise 4** and circle the state of being verb in each one.

Answer Key: They (were) near the farm.

A wagon (was) in the field.

We (are) on the wagon.

Instructor: State of being verbs don't show action or help other verbs—they just show that someone or something exists. There is one more type of verb: linking verbs. Linking verbs link, or join, two words together. These verbs are easy to recognize because they are the same verbs as the state of being verbs: *am, is, are, was, were, be, being, been.* These verbs can do three of the four parts of the verb definition! Read **Exercise 5** to me.

Workbook: The verbs **am, is, are, was, were, be, being, been** can

- help another verb

- show a state of being

- link two words together

Instructor: So if you see the verb *was* in a sentence, you have to read the whole sentence to tell what kind of verb it is. After you read each sentence in **Exercise 6**, I will point out to you how the verb *were* can be used as a helping verb, a state of being verb, or a linking verb.

Answer Key: H.V.
They were walking.

Instructor: *Were* is a helping verb in that sentence. *Were* helps the verb *walking* by showing it was in a past time. Write "H.V." for helping verb over *were*. Read the next sentence.

Answer Key: S.B.V.
They were on a path.

Instructor: *Were* just shows that someone existed on a path. *Were* is a state of being verb in that sentence. Write "S.B.V." for state of being verb over *were*. Read the next sentence.

Answer Key: L.V.
They were tired.

Instructor: *Were* is a linking verb in that sentence. It links the subject *They* with the predicate adjective *tired*. Remember, adjectives tell what kind, which one, how many, or whose. *Tired* describes what kind of people they were. Write "L.V." for linking verb over *were*.

Instructor: Let's use some linking verbs in sentences. In each sentence of **Exercise 7**, I will read you a noun and a linking verb and let you complete the sentence by choosing a predicate adjective that describes the subject. The linking verb in bold print will link, or connect, the subject noun with the adjective you choose. Follow along as I read and point to the parts of the sentences in your workbook. Then you write your chosen answer in the blank.

Workbook: Homemade bread **is** _____.

Instructor: Can you tell me what homemade bread tastes like?
Student: *Homemade bread is [delicious, tasty, chewy].*

Instructor: The linking verb *is* connects the subject *bread* with the adjective *[the word the student chose]*. Can you tell me something about the way chocolate chip cookies look?

Workbook: Chocolate chip cookies **are** _____.

Student: *Chocolate chip cookies are [round, brown, speckled].*

Instructor: The linking verb *are* connects the subject *cookies* with the adjective *[the word student chose]*. How does bread dough feel?

Workbook: The bread dough **was** _____.

Student: *The bread dough was [lumpy, sticky, soft].*

Instructor: The linking verb *was* connects the subject *dough* with the adjective *[the word student chose]*. Let's say the chant of the linking verbs together.

TOGETHER: Am [clap]
Is [clap]
Are, was, were. [clap]
Be [clap]
Being [clap]
Been. [clap] [clap]

Instructor: In **Exercise 8** read the sentence and look its diagram. This sentence contains a linking verb.

Workbook: The oven was hot.

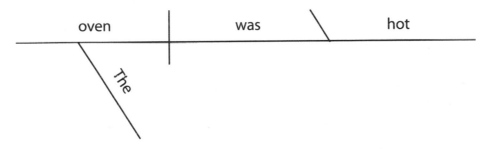

In order to keep the student's eyes focused on what you are explaining, physically point out the words and lines on the student's diagram as they appear in the next two instructor paragraphs.

Instructor: I will point out words as I explain. The linking verb *was* connects the subject of the sentence, *oven*, with the adjective *hot*. Even though *hot* is an adjective that describes the subject *oven*, it is written to the right of the verb on the diagram because it follows the verb in the sentence. Because the adjective is in the complete predicate of the sentence, it is a **predicate** adjective.

Instructor: Remember, the complete predicate is the verb and all the words attached to the verb line on a diagram. These words tell us what is said about the subject. Do you see the slanted line on the diagram above that separates the linking verb *was* from the predicate adjective? That slanted line points toward the subject to remind you that *hot* is an adjective that describes *oven*.

Instructor: In **Exercise 9**, you will see that a linking verb can also link the subject with a noun or pronoun in the complete predicate that renames the subject. Read the three sentences to me. Now answer this question: If you had to choose something for dinner, would you like chicken, pizza, or pie?

Student: *[Chicken, Pizza, or Pie.]*

Instructor: The sentences in **Exercise 9** contain the helping verb *will* and the linking verb *be*. The linking verb connects the subject *dinner* with a noun that renames the subject. What will the dinner be? *[Chicken, Pizza, or Pie]. [Chicken, Pizza, or Pie]* is in the complete predicate of the sentence. A noun or pronoun in the complete predicate that renames the subject is called a **predicate nominative.** Remember *nominate* means "to name." Look again at the three sentences in **Exercise 9**. Write "P.N." over each predicate nominative, and draw an arrow from that word back to the subject it renames.

Answer Key:

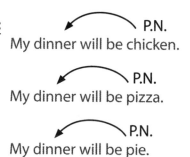

P.N.
My dinner will be chicken.

P.N.
My dinner will be pizza.

P.N.
My dinner will be pie.

Instructor: In **Exercise 10** read the sentence to me and look at its diagram.

Workbook: Our dinner guest will be Dana.

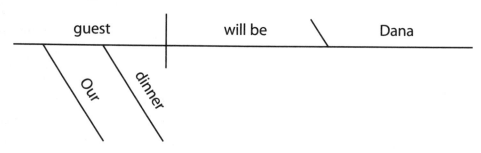

In order to keep the student's eyes focused on what you are explaining, physically point out the words and lines on the student's diagram as they appear in the next two instructor paragraphs.

Instructor: *Will* is a helping verb. *Be* is a linking verb. It connects the subject *guest* with a noun that renames the subject. *Dana* tells who the subject is. Who is the guest? *Dana. Dana* is in the complete predicate of the sentence. A noun or pronoun in the complete predicate that renames the subject is called a **predicate nominative**. Even though *Dana* renames the subject *guest*, it is written to the right of the verb on the diagram because it follows the verb in the sentence.

Instructor: Look again at the diagram. Do you see the slanted line that separates the verbs *will be* from the predicate nominative? That slanted line points back toward the subject to remind you that *Dana* is a predicate nominative that renames the subject *guest*.

Instructor: In **Exercise 11** I will help you diagram two sentences with linking verbs that link the subject to a predicate nominative. You read each sentence, and I will ask you questions as you fill in the diagram. For Sentence 1, trace the dotted frame before you fill it in. For Sentence 2, draw your own frame in the space provided. Remember to copy the words exactly as they appear in the sentence. If the words begin with a capital letter in the sentence, they should also be capitalized in the diagram.

Use the following dialogue to help the student complete the diagrams.

1. *What is the linking verb? This verb links the subject to a word in the complete predicate. Write the verb to the right of your center line.*

2. *Find the subject. Ask "who" or "what" before the verb. [Prompt the student with a specific question like "What are?" or "Who is?"] Write the subject to the left of the center line on your frame.*

3. *This sentence contains a predicate nominative. This noun is in the complete predicate of the sentence, but it renames the subject. What is the predicate nominative in this sentence? Because the predicate nominative follows the verb in the sentence, it is written to the right of the verb on the diagram. Write the predicate nominative to the right of the slanted line on your diagram. That slanted line points back toward the subject to remind you that a predicate nominative renames the subject.*

4. *Go back and look again at the simple subject. Are there any words that describe the subject that come before the verb? These adjectives can tell what kind, which one, how many, or whose. Also look for the articles (a, an, the), because they act like adjectives. Write each adjective on a slanted line below the subject it describes.*

5. *Go back and look again at the verb. Is there a word that describes the verb? This is an adverb that could tell how, when, where, or how often. Write the adverb on the slanted line below the verb it describes.*

6. *Look at the predicate nominative again. Are there any words that describe this noun? These adjectives can tell what kind, which one, how many, or whose. Also look for articles (a, an, the), because they act like an adjective. Write each adjective on a slanted line below the predicate nominative it describes.*

Answer Key: 1. Board games are our evening entertainment.

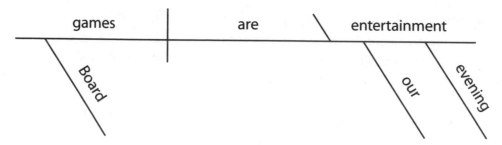

2. Our Dad is usually the first winner.

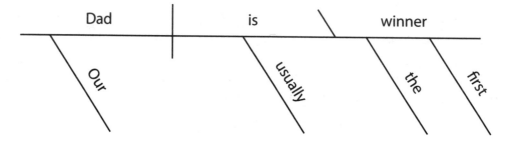

LESSON 55

Review: Simple and Complete Subjects and Predicates

Read "The Lake Isle of Innisfree" (Lesson 53) three times to the student. Then ask the student to try to say parts of the first and second stanzas along with you (or the tape recorder).

Instructor: In **Exercise 1** read the long sentence and look at its diagram.

Workbook: Siberian tigers fiercely attack many deer.

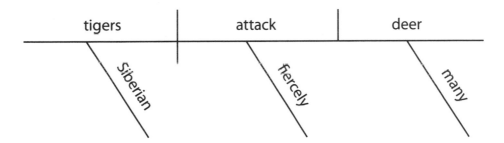

Instructor: Every sentence has a subject and a verb. On a diagram, the subject and the verb are separated by a straight line that runs down through the horizontal line.

Point to each word and line as you explain the diagram in this lesson.

Instructor: To the left of this straight line, you will find all the words that tell you more about the subject, *tigers.* The subject of the sentence is simply the word *tigers,* so it is called the simple subject. But when you add other words that tell you more about tigers, you get a longer, more complete description of the subject. *Siberian* tells us more about *tigers. Siberian tigers* is the complete subject. Look at the diagram in **Exercise 1**. The simple subject is always written on the subject line (*tigers*).

Instructor: The complete subject is the simple subject (*tigers*) and all the words that hang off the simple subject (*Siberian tigers*). The complete subject includes all the words to the left of the straight line that runs down through the horizontal line.

Instructor: Remember that on a diagram, the subject and the verb are separated by a straight line that runs down the center of the frame. Look at the word directly to the right of the center line. This is your verb. What is the verb in the sentence?

Student: *Attack*

Instructor: On a diagram, the complete predicate includes all the words to the right of the straight line that runs down the center of the frame. What is the complete predicate of the sentence?

Student: *Fiercely attack many deer [It's okay if the words are in a different order.]*

Instructor: Now in **Exercise 2**, you will diagram three sentences about tigers. You read each sentence, and I will ask you questions to help you diagram. For Sentence 1, you will fill in the frame. For Sentence 2, you will trace the dotted frame before you fill it in. For Sentence 3, you will draw the frame.

Use the following dialogue to help the student fill in each diagram.

1. *What is the verb? Write the verb to the right of your center line.*

2. *Find the subject. Ask "who" or "what" before the verb. [Prompt the student with a specific question like "What carries?" or "What needs?"] Write the subject to the left of the center line on your frame.*

3. *Is there a direct object that receives the action of the verb? I will ask you a question that will help you find the direct object.*

   Sentence 1: Carry what?

   Sentence 2: Need what?

   Sentence 3: Avoid what?

   Write the direct object to the right of the verb on your diagram. The direct object is separated from the verb by a short, straight line.

4. *Go back and look again at the subject. Are there any words that describe the subject? These adjectives can tell what kind, which one, how many, or whose. Also look for the articles (a, an, the), because they act like adjectives. Write each adjective on a slanted line below the subject it describes.*

5. *Look again at the direct object. Are there any words that describe the direct object? These adjectives can tell what kind, which one, how many, or whose. Also look for the articles (a, an, the), because they act like adjectives. Write each adjective on a slanted line below the direct object it describes.*

6. *Look at the verb. Is there a word that describes the verb? This is an adverb that could tell how, when, where, or how often. Write the adverb on the slanted line below the verb it describes.*

Answer Key: 1. Mother tigers carry baby cubs delicately.

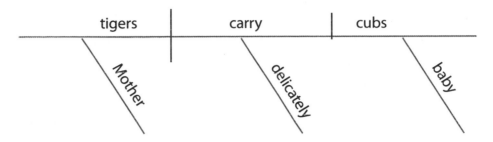

2. Powerful tigers always need vast woodlands.

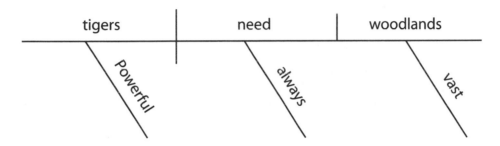

3. Healthy tigers usually avoid most humans.

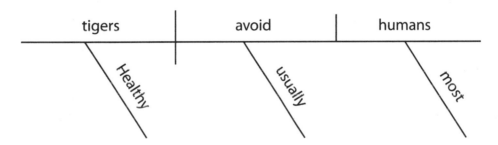

Use the following dialogue to help the student practice identifying the simple subject, complete subject, verb, and complete predicate in the sentences he just diagrammed. You will need to go through the entire dialogue below for each of the three sentences.

Instructor: We will look again at the completed diagrams for **Exercise 2** in your workbook. *[Instructor reads the appropriate sentence.]* On a diagram, the subject and the verb are separated by a straight line that runs down the center of the frame. What is the verb?

Student: *[Carry; Need; Avoid.]*

Instructor: Now look at the word to the left of the center line. What is the simple subject of the sentence? The simple subject is always written on the subject line.

Student: *[Tigers; Tigers; Tigers.]*

Instructor: But when you add other words that tell you more about the subject *tigers*, you get a longer, more complete description of the subject. On a diagram, the complete subject includes all the words to the left of the straight line that runs down the center of the frame. What is the complete subject of the sentence?

Student: *[Mother tigers; Powerful tigers; Healthy tigers.]*

Instructor: Look again at the diagram. The verb and all the words to the right of the center, straight line are in the complete predicate. The verb answers the question "What does the subject do?" But there are other words that tell us more completely what is said about the subject. They answer questions like:

[Sentence 1] "How do tigers carry?" and "What do tigers carry?"
[Sentence 2] "How often do tigers need?" and "What do tigers need?"
[Sentence 3] "When do tigers avoid?" and "What do tigers avoid?"

Together, all of these words that tell us what is said about the subject are called the complete predicate. The complete predicate is written to the right of the straight line that runs down the center of the frame. What is the complete predicate of the sentence?

Student: *[Carry baby cubs delicately; Always need vast woodlands; Usually avoid most humans.]*

Optional Dictation Exercise

The following sentences are adapted from *Gentle Ben* by Walt Morey. A young boy named Mark befriends one of Alaska's fiercest, most unpredictable creatures: a brown bear named Ben.

Once the student has written the dictation, ask him to find the simple subject and the verb in the first sentence.

Dictation: He scratched the base of Ben's tulip ears a last time. The bear rolled his big head so that Mark could scratch first one ear and then the other.

Answer Key: simple subject = He

verb = scratched

LESSON 56

New: Initials
New: Abbreviations for Titles of Respect, Months, and Days of the Week
New: Address Abbreviations
New: Measurement Abbreviations

This is a lengthy lesson. Remember that you can complete lessons over as many days as necessary.

You may need a sheet of paper for the lesson.

Read "The Lake Isle of Innisfree" (Lesson 53) three times to the student. Then ask the student to try to say parts of the first, second, and third stanzas along with you (or the tape recorder).

Instructor: Listen as I say a word: *abbreviation*. Listen to that word again slowly: *abbreviation*. Do you hear the word *brief* in the middle of *abbreviation*? *Brief* means "short." An abbreviation is the shortened form of a word. You will practice some abbreviations in this lesson.

Make sure to check the student's work as he writes the exercises in this lesson. If he misspells an abbreviation or leaves off a period, have him rewrite it.

Instructor: In **Exercise 1** write your full name on line 1. Your full name is your first, middle, and last names. Remember, proper names all begin with capital letters.

Student: [Writes full name, e.g., Robin Lee Finn]

Instructor: On line 2 write your initials. Your initials will be the first letter of each of your names. The word *initial* means "first" or "beginning." When you write initials, each initial is capitalized and followed by a period.

Student: [Writes initials, e.g., R. L. F.]

Instructor: Sometimes initials are used for only the first or middle names, but the last name is written in full. On lines 3 and 5, *I* will write the full names of two people we know. On lines 4 and 6 you write only the initials for the first and middle names of each person, but write the person's last name in full.

Instructor: Titles of respect show that we respect the position of that person. When these titles are written, they are often abbreviated. In **Exercise 2** of your workbook, look at the abbreviated (short) way to write some common titles of respect. I will read aloud the chart to you.

Workbook:

Title of Respect	Abbreviation	Used For
Mister	Mr.	This is the title for a man.
Mistress	Mrs.	This is a title for a married woman.
Doctor	Dr.	This is the title for a physician or for someone with a special degree from a university.
Miss	—	This is not an abbreviation, but a title of courtesy for an unmarried girl or woman.
Mistress or Miss	Ms.	Ms. is an abbreviation for either Mistress or Miss. You should use Ms. when you do not know whether a woman would prefer to be called Mrs. or Miss.
Saint	St.	A title given to one worthy of special religious respect and honor.

Instructor: When you look at a map, you will see the abbreviation for *Saint* in several places. Many cities, rivers, and other geographical features are named after saints. For example, there is St. Louis, Missouri, St. Petersburg, Florida, St. Paul, Minnesota, the St. Lawrence River in Canada, and Mount St. Helens in Washington.

Instructor: I will call out some names, one at a time. Write each one down in **Exercise 3** of your workbook. Be sure to correctly capitalize and punctuate these names. I will help you with spelling if you need it.

Dictate the following names, reminding the student to correctly capitalize and punctuate titles of respect, names, and initials. Help with spelling as necessary. After he has copied the names, he may look at the instructor's book so he can check, erase, and make immediate corrections.

Mr. R. L. Drake

Mrs. Anita Jane Hunter

Miss Jill Ann Black

Dr. Ruth S. Brooks

St. Petersburg

Instructor: There are also abbreviations for the days of the week and months of the year. In **Exercise 4**, write from memory the list of the days of the week. For right now, ignore the blank for the abbreviation. The days of the week are proper nouns; each begins with a capital letter. When you get to *Wednesday,* think **Wed**-nes-day; that will help you spell it correctly. Let's say **Wed**-nes-day together three times.

TOGETHER: **Wed**-nes-day, **Wed**-nes-day, **Wed**-nes-day.

If the student misspells any of the days of the week, have him erase it. Then you write the correctly spelled word (*Sunday, Monday, Tuesday, Wednesday, Thursday, Friday,* or *Saturday*) on a separate sheet of paper. He should then copy the correctly spelled day of the week twice from your model. Then he should write the word from memory on its line in **Exercise 4**. Check it again. Repeat if necessary. Add the word to the student's spelling list for continued review.

Instructor: Now write the abbreviation for each day of the week under the "Abbreviation" column in **Exercise 4**. Each abbreviation begins with a capital letter and ends with a period. The abbreviation is the first syllable for each word. Most of the days have an abbreviation that is the first three letters of the day's name, but for *Tuesday* it is the first four letters and for *Thursday* it is the first five. I will help you spell each abbreviation if you need it.

Answer Key: Day of the Week	Abbreviation
Sunday	Sun.
Monday	Mon.
Tuesday	Tues.
Wednesday	Wed.
Thursday	Thurs.
Friday	Fri.
Saturday	Sat.

Instructor: In **Exercise 5**, from memory, write the list of the months of the year. Ignore the blanks for abbreviations right now. The months of the year are proper nouns; each begins with a capital letter. When you get to *February*, think Feb-**ru**-a-ry; that will help you spell it correctly. Let's say that together three times.

TOGETHER: Feb-**ru**-a-ry, Feb-**ru**-a-ry, Feb-**ru**-a-ry.

If the student misspells any of the months, have him erase it. Then you write the correctly spelled word (*January, February, March, April, May, June, July, August, September, October, November,* or *December*) on a separate sheet of paper. He should then copy the correctly spelled month twice from your model. Then he should write the word from memory on its line in **Exercise 5**. Check it again. Repeat if necessary. Add the word to the student's spelling list for continued review.

Answer Key:

Month of the Year	Abbreviation
1. January	Jan.
2. February	Feb.
3. March	Mar.
4. April	Apr.
5. May	x
6. June	x
7. July	x
8. August	Aug.
9. September	Sept.
10. October	Oct.
11. November	Nov.
12. December	Dec.

Instructor: Now write the abbreviation for each month of the year under the "Abbreviation" column in **Exercise 5**. Each abbreviation begins with a capital letter and ends with a period. There are three months of the year that have such short names that they don't need to be abbreviated! Find the three months with the shortest names and write an X in the abbreviation blank next to that month to show there is no abbreviation for that month (May, June, July). The rest of the months can be abbreviated. Most of the months have an abbreviation that is the first three letters of the day's name, but September's abbreviation is four letters long. I will help you spell each abbreviation if you need it.

Instructor: Do you remember the abbreviation for the word *Saint?* St. The abbreviation for the word *Street* is the same! **Exercise 6** has a list of common abbreviations you see in addresses.

Workbook:

Address	Abbreviation
Street	St.
Road	Rd.
Lane	Ln.
Boulevard	Blvd.
Avenue	Ave.
Drive	Dr.
Court	Ct.
Circle	Cir.
Place	Pl.
Highway	Hwy.
Route	Rt.
Apartment	Apt.

Circle four of the abbreviations that you would like the student to memorize in **Exercise 6** of the student's workbook. Be sure to include the abbreviation(s) in the student's own address. You may also want to include abbreviations found in the addresses of other family members.

Instructor: Now I will dictate four addresses to you. I want you to write the addresses in **Exercise 7** of your workbook, substituting the street abbreviation for the name of the street. You may look at the chart in **Exercise 6** if you need help remembering the correct abbreviation.

First dictate the student's own street address (e.g., "7 Harper Lane"—the student writes "7 Harper Ln."). Then dictate street addresses that use the three other abbreviations you circled in **Exercise 6**. You should preferably dictate the actual street addresses of family members, but it is okay to make up addresses as well.

Instructor: Streets and apartments are not the only words in an address that are abbreviated. States have abbreviations, too. These abbreviations were created by the United States Postal Service to help them sort and deliver mail quickly and accurately. State postal abbreviations are not like regular abbreviations. There are **two** capital letters in the abbreviation and **no** periods! I will dictate the postal abbreviation for our state. Write it down in **Exercise 8** of your workbook. Remember to capitalize both letters and don't put any periods!

Dictate the student's state abbreviation. A full list of all the states' abbreviations can be found on the USPS website at www.usps.com/ncsc/lookups/usps_abbreviations.html.

Instructor: Now I want you to write your own address in **Exercise 9** of your workbook. On the first line you write your street address with abbreviations (just like you did in **Exercise 7**). On the second line write the name of your city or town and place a comma after it. Then write the abbreviation of your state from **Exercise 8**. **There is always a comma between a city and state**. Then write your zip code (five or nine numbers).

If the student does not remember any part of his address (like the zip code), dictate it to him.

Instructor: There are some other common abbreviations you should know. Look at the list of measurement abbreviations in **Exercise 10**. I will read them to you as you follow along.

Workbook:

inch	in.
foot	ft.
yard	yd.
mile	mi.
dozen	doz.
cup	c.
teaspoon	tsp.
tablespoon	Tbsp.

pint	pt.
quart	qt.
gallon	gal.
ounce	oz.
pound	lb.

Instructor: Look at those last two abbreviations. Those are weird, aren't they? *Ounce* is abbreviated "oz." and there isn't a **z** in the word at all! That's because the word *ounce* came to us from the Italian word *onza*, spelled with a **z**. So even though the spelling of the word changed in English, the Italian abbreviation stuck: "oz." *Pound* is abbreviated "lb."—that's even stranger! In Latin, a pound in weight was called "libra pondo." Our word *pound* came from *pondo*, but our abbreviation "lb." came from *libra*.

Instructor: Look at **Exercise 11** in your workbook. Whenever you see a word from **Exercise 10** that can be abbreviated, put a line through it and write the correct abbreviation on top of the word.

Answer Key:

ft.

In 1991, Mike Powell broke the world record for the long jump by jumping 29 ~~feet~~

in.

and 4 1/2 ~~inches~~.

yd.

A football field is 100 ~~yards~~ long.

mi.

The Tour de France is a cycling race that is around 2300 ~~miles~~ long.

Fizzy Fruit Punch *(Note to Instructor: This is a real recipe.)*

gal.

(Makes slightly over 1 ~~gallon~~ of punch before the ice is added)

Ingredients:

qt.

1 ~~quart~~ seltzer water

qt.

1 ~~quart~~ cranberry juice

qt.
1 ~~quart~~ pineapple juice

pt.
1 ½ ~~pints~~ apple juice

c.
½ ~~cup~~ lemon juice (the juice of 3 or 4 lemons)

oz.
8 ~~ounces~~ (1 can) pineapple chunks, undrained

1 lemon, thinly sliced (optional, for garnish)

Directions:

Combine the cranberry juice, pineapple juice, apple juice, lemon juice, and water in a large pitcher. Add lemon slices and pineapple chunks. Chill. When ready to serve, pour the juice mixture into a punch bowl or large container filled with ice. Add the seltzer water just before serving. You can omit the seltzer water and keep the punch in the refrigerator to serve over a number of days.

Instructor: Whew! We have been studying abbreviations for a long time now. What time is it?
Student: *[Time of day]*

Instructor: Is that [time] A.M. or [time] P.M.?
Student: *[A.M. or P.M.]*

Instructor: Did you know that A.M. and P.M. are abbreviations? Look at **Exercise 12**. A.M. stands for *Ante Meridiem*, which is Latin for "before noon." P.M. stands for *Post Meridiem*, which is Latin for "after noon." A.M. and P.M. are abbreviations with all capital letters. Write the time of day in the blank in **Exercise 12**, and be sure to include A.M. or P.M.

Workbook:

Word	Abbreviation	Meaning
Ante Meridiem	A.M.	"before noon"
Post Meridiem	P.M.	"past noon"

Optional Follow-Up

The student can begin to memorize the USPS abbreviations for all fifty states, as this is useful information to know. A full list of all the states' abbreviations can be found on the USPS website at www.usps.com/ncsc/lookups/usps_abbreviations.html. If you collect the state quarters, you can use these as "flashcards." Stick a bit of masking tape on the "Washington side" of each quarter and write the abbreviation. The student can then flip the quarters over to test himself. Explain to the student that most of the state abbreviations consist of the first two letters or the first and last letters of the state's name. But no two states can have the same abbreviation; so some of the abbreviations aren't what you would think (particularly the states beginning with the letter M).

LESSON 57

New: Conjunctions
New: Compound Subjects, Compound Predicates, and Compound Sentences
New: Commas in a Series

Read "The Lake Isle of Innisfree" (Lesson 53) three times to the student. Then ask the student to try to say parts of the poem along with you (or the tape recorder).

Instructor: When you see a highway sign that says "Junction," it means that two roads are joining together. *Junction* means "joining." Words that are used to **join** words or groups of words together are called *conjunctions.* I will say the definition of a conjunction. Then join with me as we say it three times more: A conjunction is a word that joins words or groups of words together.

TOGETHER (three times): A conjunction is a word that joins words or groups of words together.

Instructor: The three most common conjunctions are *and, but, or.* Repeat after me: *and, but, or.*

Student: *And, but, or*

Instructor: In **Exercise 1** read the sentences that use the three most common conjunctions: *and, but, or.* Circle each conjunction. Conjunctions can join simple subjects, simple predicates, or whole sentences. The conjunctions are written in bold print, and the two words or groups of words that are joined are underlined.

Answer Key: Flowers grow (**and**) bloom.

Potatoes (**and**) peas are vegetables.

Plants need sun (**and**) water.

We will eat pancakes (**or**) biscuits.

Will you come Monday (**or**) Tuesday?

You may go, (**but**) come back in an hour.

I will return, (**but**) I would rather stay longer.

Instructor: In **Exercise 2** read the first and second sentences and look at the diagrams.

Workbook: I. Bruce slipped.

2. Bruce slipped **and** fell.

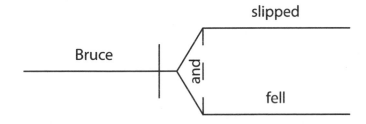

Instructor: Notice that the second sentence has **two** verbs in the predicate. Do you remember that the word *predicate* comes from the Latin word *praedicare* meaning "to proclaim" (Lesson 28)? The predicate of a sentence is what is said or proclaimed about the subject. What is said or proclaimed about Bruce in the second sentence?

Student: *He slipped and fell.*

Instructor: Circle the conjunction in Sentence 2. The conjunction joins the two verbs in the sentence: *slipped* and *fell.* When the predicate of a sentence has two or more verbs joined by a conjunction, we call them **compound predicates.** The word *compound* means "made of two or more parts."

Instructor: Look at the diagram of "Bruce slipped and fell." The verb line splits into two parts. *Slipped* is written on the top line because it comes first in the sentence. *Fell* is written on the bottom line. They are joined by the conjunction *and*, which is written inside the triangle.

The student has diagrammed sentences with two verbs before, but these were verb **phrases**: helping verbs working together with a main verb. Verb phrases function as a unit: they show one action ("He **was running**"), one state of being ("He **has been** here before"), or link the subject to a word in the predicate ("He **may be** tired"). The compound predicates in this lesson show two distinct actions ("He **ran** and **swam**") that are linked by a conjunction.

Instructor: In **Exercise 3**, read the first and second sentences and look at the diagrams.

Workbook: Lisa cooked.

Lisa **and** Ida cooked.

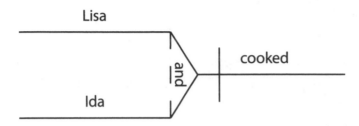

Instructor: Notice that the second sentence has **two** subjects, joined by the conjunction *and*. When a simple sentence has two or more subjects, we call them **compound subjects**. What does the word *compound* mean? Do you remember when we talked about *compound predicates*? The word *compound* means "made of two or more parts." Tell me the two parts of the subject and circle the conjunction that joins them.

Student: *Lisa and Ida*

Instructor: Look at the diagram of "Lisa and Ida cooked." The subject line splits into two parts. *Lisa* is written on the top line because she comes first in the sentence. *Ida* is written on the bottom line. They are joined by the conjunction *and*, which is written inside the triangle.

Instructor: In **Exercise 4**, read the simple sentence, circle the conjunction, and fill in the frame.

Answer Key: Gus(and)Jane ate.

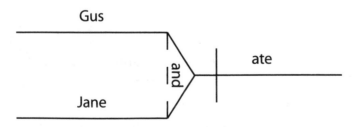

Instructor: In **Exercise 5** you will diagram a simple sentence with **two verbs** in the predicate and **two nouns** in the subject. Read the sentence first.

Workbook: Puppies and kittens lick or sniff.

Instructor: What is the compound subject (the two nouns in the subject)?

Student: *Puppies and kittens*

Instructor: "Puppies and kittens" is the compound subject. What is said about the subject? What is the compound predicate?

Student: *[They] lick or sniff.*

Instructor: "Lick or sniff" is a compound predicate. Circle the conjunction that joins the two nouns and circle the conjunction that joins the two verbs. Now fill in the frame in your workbook. Be sure to write each conjunction on the dotted line that connects the two subjects or the two verbs.

Answer Key: Puppies (and) kittens lick (or) sniff.

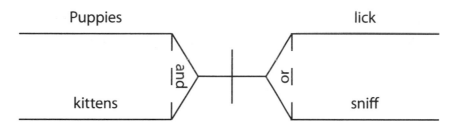

Instructor: Now, in **Exercise 6**, read the sentence aloud and circle the conjunctions in the sentence. Then you draw the frame and fill in the diagram. This sentence is similar to the one in **Exercise 5**. It has a compound subject and a compound predicate.

Answer Key: Brothers (and) sisters giggle (and) laugh.

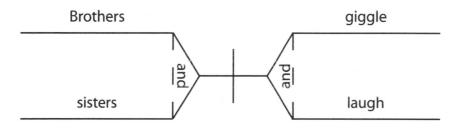

Instructor: You have now learned that a compound subject has two subjects joined by a conjunction. A compound predicate has two verbs joined by a conjunction. A **compound sentence** has two smaller sentences that are joined by a comma and conjunction to make one longer sentence. Look at the sentence and its diagram in **Exercise 7**.

Later in his grammar study, the student will be introduced to the term "clauses." A compound sentence is made up of two independent clauses, each of which could stand alone as an individual sentence because it has a subject, verb, and expresses a complete thought. At this level, we will explain compound sentences as being made up of two smaller sentences, since that is an explanation the student readily understands.

Workbook: Dogs bark, **but** wolves howl.

Dogs	bark	but	wolves	howl

Instructor: "Dogs bark, but wolves howl." This compound sentence has two parts that could each stand alone as its own sentence. "Dogs bark"—that could be a sentence of its own. It has a subject and a verb and expresses a complete thought. "Wolves howl"—that could also be a sentence since it has a subject and a verb and expresses a complete thought. These two parts are joined by a comma and a conjunction. Circle the conjunction in the sentence.

Instructor: Look at the diagram of the sentence in **Exercise 7**. There are two diagrams joined together by a dotted line. The conjunction *but* is written on the dotted line because it joins the two smaller sentences together.

Instructor: In **Exercise 8**, you will fill in the diagram of compound sentences. First, read the sentence aloud and circle the conjunction. Then diagram the verb and the subject for each of the smaller sentences.

Answer Key: 1. Alexa dusted, (and) Terra swept.

Alexa	dusted	and	Terra	swept

2. Ponies trot, (but) horses walk.

Ponies	trot	but	horses	walk

Instructor: We are going to take a little break from diagramming and talk about commas. In your workbook, look back at the sentences in **Exercises 7** and **8**. Did you notice a comma just before the conjunction that joined the two simple sentences? When two sentences are combined by using a conjunction like *and, but,* or *or,* a comma is written before the conjunction. Read that rule in **Exercise 9** of your workbook. Then circle the conjunctions and draw an arrow pointing to the commas in the three example sentences.

Answer Key: 1.   I will get us some water, (and) you stand in line at the airport.

2.   We will not have food on the plane, (but) we will eat supper later.

3.   You can rake the leaves, (or) you can take out the trash.

Instructor: In **Exercise 10** combine the two simple sentences with a comma and the conjunction *and.*

Workbook: The truck will deliver a package.

I will sign for it.

Answer Key: The truck will deliver a package, and I will sign for it.

Instructor: In **Exercise 11** of your workbook, read aloud another rule about using commas. Then copy both of the correctly written sentences onto the lines of your workbook. In sentence one there is a series of nouns. In sentence two there is a series of phrases.

Workbook: Rule: Use commas to separate items in a series.

1.   We packed sandwiches, fruit, chips, and drinks.

2.   Our family loaded the car, drove to the campsite, and ate a picnic lunch.

LESSON 58

New: Commas in Direct Address
New: Commas after Introductory Elements
Review: Commas in a Series
Review: Commas in Compound Sentences
Review: Abbreviations
Learn to Proofread: Insert a Comma

You will need a business-size envelope and first-class stamp for this lesson.

Read "The Lake Isle of Innisfree" (Lesson 53) three times to the student. Then ask the student to try to say parts of the poem along with you (or the tape recorder).

Instructor: Last lesson you practiced diagramming with conjunctions, and you practiced using commas. Before we review these things, I want you to look at two other ways to use commas. When you are talking directly to someone, you often say a person's name to get his attention. This is called **direct address**, because you address someone directly. When you write a sentence that includes a direct address, use a comma to separate the name of the person spoken to (the noun of direct address) from the rest of the sentence. Read the rule in **Exercise 1** of your workbook.

Workbook: Rule: Use a comma to set off a noun of direct address.

Instructor: In **Exercise 1**, read each sentence to me, pausing after the comma. Then copy the sentence onto the line just below it. Pay special attention to where the commas are placed.

Point out the commas in **Exercise 1**, and explain that you use one comma to separate the name if that name is at the beginning or the end of a sentence. Use two commas to separate the name if it is in the middle of a sentence.

Workbook: 1. Mr. Nelson, may I see your new car?

2. Please, Chris, go pick me a tomato.

3. I don't think we can go, Belinda.

Instructor: In **Exercise 2**, read the rule that shows another way to use a comma. Then read the sentences and circle the commas.

These words are called "introductory elements" because they introduce the sentence but have no other function.

Answer Key: 1. Yes, I would like to have lunch now.

2. No, I did not leave my coat outside.

3. Oh, I forgot that I had hung it in the closet.

4. Well, I sometimes have left my coat in the yard.

Instructor: Now let us review from last lesson the ways to use commas correctly. Look at the rule in **Exercise 3** of your workbook: "Use commas to separate items in a series." Items in a series can be nouns like *cement, stone, gravel,* and *dirt.* Or they can be adjectives like *smooth, flat,* and *level.* They can be verbs such as *lift, flatten, dig,* and *dump.* They can be adverbs like *quickly, tirelessly,* and *noisily.* Items in a series can also be phrases, such as "clear the land," "level the roadway," and "pour a smooth surface." Read each sentence, underline the items in the series, and draw arrows pointing to the commas.

Answer Key: 1. Roads may be made of <u>cement</u>, <u>stone</u>, <u>gravel</u>, or <u>dirt</u>.

2. New highway roads should be <u>smooth</u>, <u>flat</u>, and <u>level</u>.

3. Workers use machines that <u>lift</u>, <u>flatten</u>, <u>dig</u>, and <u>dump</u>.

4. They work <u>quickly</u>, <u>tirelessly</u>, and <u>noisily</u>.

5. The huge machines <u>clear the land</u>, <u>level the roadway</u>, and <u>pour a smooth surface</u>.

Instructor: In **Exercise 4** I am going to dictate two sentences to you, one at a time. The first will contain single words in a series and the second will contain phrases in a series. Be sure to add commas where they are needed: I will pause at each comma when I dictate.

Dictation: 1. The tree was tall, leafy, and green.

2. Dan climbed a tree, slipped off a branch, and fell to the ground.

First Language Lessons for the Well-Trained Mind Level 4

Instructor: Read the comma rule in **Exercise 5** of your workbook. Then read the compound sentences that combine two shorter sentences by using a conjunction. Circle the conjunctions, draw an arrow pointing down at the comma, and underline the two shorter sentences.

Student should insert plain commas, not proofreading marks.

Answer Key: 1. Younger brothers copy big brothers, (and) little sisters copy big sisters.

2. Big Brother wanted to play tackle, (but) he knew Little Brother might get hurt.

3. They could build a fort together, (or) they could play hide and seek.

Instructor: In **Exercise 6,** there is a summary of the four comma rules you practiced today. After the rules there are four sentences with no commas! Your job is to place commas correctly in each sentence and then write the number of the rule you used. The sentences are mixed up! For example, Rule 1 does not go with Sentence 1.

Answer Key: 1. Our family went bowling, and then we ate ice cream. Rule **4**

2. Other sports we like are touch football, soccer, badminton, and cycling. Rule **3**

3. No, I do not know how to play hockey. Rule **2**

4. Robert, come here at once! Rule **1**

The following exercise reviews the abbreviations learned in Lesson 56. If the student incorrectly writes an abbreviation, have him erase it immediately. Write the correct abbreviation on a separate piece of paper for him to copy. Then he can write the correct abbreviation in his workbook from memory.

Instructor: Let's review some abbreviations in **Exercise 7**. Read each word and write its abbreviation across from it.

Answer Key:

Word	Abbreviation
Mister	Mr.
Doctor	Dr.
Saint	St.
Sunday	Sun.

Tuesday	Tues.
Thursday	Thurs.
February	Feb.
September	Sept.
mile	mi.
inch	in.
feet	ft.
pound	lb.

The student will mail a family member a note or drawing. Have the address of this family member in front of you for the next exercise if you do not already have it committed to memory.

Instructor: Look at the drawing of an envelope in **Exercise 8**. The upper left-hand corner of the envelope is where you write your return address. This is the address of the person mailing the letter. On the first line of the return address, write the initials of your first and middle names and write your last name in full. On the second and third lines, write your mailing address with your street abbreviation and your state postal abbreviation. Remember to put a comma between your city and state.

Instructor: Now fill in the name and address of a family member to whom you would like to send a note. Write the abbreviation for that person's appropriate title of respect (Mr., Mrs., Miss, etc.) and his or her first and middle initials. Write the person's last name in full. On the second and third lines, write his or her address with its correct abbreviations. I will dictate it to you. Remember to put a comma between the city and state.

Use the envelope template in **Exercise 8** as a model for the student to copy the mailing address and return address onto a real business-size envelope. The student may mail a note, a copied poem, or a drawing. Put a first-class stamp on the letter and mail it.

Learn to Proofread: Insert a Comma ⋏

Instructor: Today you will learn another proofreaders' mark. Look in your workbook at **Exercise 9**. This is the proofreaders' mark you will learn today. It is an arrow with a curved stem that points up. When you see this mark, you should insert a comma. Look at the sample sentence in **Exercise 9**. Read that aloud.

Workbook: Alpacas are soft gentle and affectionate.

Instructor: *Soft, gentle,* and *affectionate* are items in a series and should be separated by a comma. Now, in **Exercise 10**, let's review all the proofreaders' marks you have learned.

Workbook:

Proofreaders' Mark		Meaning
ß	(lc)	make lowercase
b	(caps)	capitalize
⊙		insert period
v̓		insert apostrophe
? ⋏		insert question mark
⋏		insert comma

Instructor: Read the sentence in **Exercise 10**. Use your proofreaders' marks to show the errors in capitalization and punctuation.

Answer Key: have you ever seen an alpaca alpacas are a type of llama from south america caps

their wool is softer and warmer than sheeps wool alpacas can be brown caps

tan or white

LESSON 59

Summary Exercise: *A Little Princess*

Read "The Lake Isle of Innisfree" (Lesson 53) three times to the student. Then ask the student to try to say parts of the poem along with you (or the tape recorder).

Instructor: Today I am going to read a selection aloud to you that is *fiction*. Fiction is a made-up story. I will read it only once. *(If the student is a fluent reader, you may choose to have him read it aloud or silently).* Then I want you to tell me in your own words what you remember. Your summary exercise for today is from *A Little Princess,* by Frances Hodgson Burnett. The story is about Sara Crewe. Her mother had died when she was born. Because the climate in India was bad for her, her loving father sent her to a select boarding school in England. Because her father was wealthy, she was provided with the best of clothes, food, and amusements. When her father unexpectedly died, his money was no longer sent. Then the wicked headmistress, Miss Minchin, took away all of Sara's beautiful clothes, treated her like a slave, and made her stay in a cold, plain attic room. Your summary exercise for today is at a low point in Sara's life just before a mysterious benefactor began a series of events that changed Sara's life and brought a happy ending to the story.

A Little Princess

Sara stood silent for a second.

"I had no dinner," she said next, and her voice was quite low. She made it low because she was afraid it would tremble.

"There's some bread in the pantry," said the cook. "That's all you'll get at this time of day."

Sara went and found the bread. It was old and hard and dry. The cook was in too vicious a humor to give her anything to eat with it. It was always safe and easy to vent her spite on Sara. Really, it was hard for the child to climb the three long flights of stairs leading to her attic. She often found them long and steep when she was tired; but tonight it seemed as if she would never reach the top. Several times she was obliged to stop to rest. When she reached the top landing she was glad to see the glimmer of a light coming from under her door.

LESSON 60

New: Contractions
Review: Personal Pronouns
Review: Adjectives

Read "The Lake Isle of Innisfree" (Lesson 53) three times to the student. Then ask the student to try to say the whole poem with you (or the tape recorder). The student should practice saying the whole poem to himself in a mirror.

Instructor: Today we are going to review adjectives and pronouns. Let's say the definition of an adjective together.

Repeat the definition as many times as necessary for the student to remember it easily.

TOGETHER: An adjective is a word that describes a noun or pronoun. Adjectives tell what kind, which one, how many, and whose.

Instructor: **Adjectives tell what kind**. What kind of day would you say today is? A *clear* day? A *cloudy* day? A *hot* day? These adjectives all tell what kind of day. Do you have another word to tell what kind of day?

Student: *A [adjective] day*

Instructor: **Adjectives tell which one.** *This* foot. *That* window. *These* fingers. *Those* birds. The *next* time. The *final* warning. These adjectives tell which one. Which level is this grammar book? The third level? The fourth level? Answer me with an adjective that tells which one.

Student: *The fourth level*

Instructor: **Adjectives tell how many.** *Five* fingers, *many* grapes, *all* children, *most* cars. Answer me with an adjective that tells how many. How many freckles do you have? Many freckles? Zero freckles? Few freckles? Some freckles?

Student: *I have [adjective] freckles.*

Instructor: **Adjectives tell whose**. Karla's ring, the boys' pets, and the personal pronouns that show possession (we call them the possessive pronouns): *my, mine, your, yours, his, her, hers, its, our, ours, their, theirs*. Answer me with an adjective that tells whose. Whose grammar book is this?

Student: *This is [mine; yours] OR This is [my; your] book.*

Instructor: Before we talk more about personal pronouns, let's review the definition of a pronoun. A pronoun is a word used in the place of a noun. In **Exercise 1** read the list of personal pronouns.

Workbook: Personal Pronouns

I, me, my, mine

You, your, yours

He, she, him, her, it, his, hers, its

We, us, our, ours

They, them, their, theirs

Instructor: Go back and look at the list again and find the pronoun *its*. Circle *its*.

Instructor: Remember, some of the personal pronouns are possessive pronouns that act like adjectives telling **whose**. The pronouns that act like adjectives telling whose are *my, mine, your, yours, his, her, hers, its, our, ours, their, theirs*. Read aloud those pronouns in **Exercise 2** of your workbook.

Workbook: Possessive Pronouns (Adjectives That Tell **Whose**)

My, mine, your, yours, his, her, hers, its, our, ours, their, theirs

Instructor: Some of these possessive pronouns come before the word they describe. The other possessive pronouns can only function as predicate adjectives. Read the two columns in **Exercise 3**.

Workbook:

Adjective+Noun	Predicate Adjective
My pen	The pens are **mine**.
Your shoes	The shoes are **yours**.
His coat	The coat is **his**.
Her book	The book is **hers**.
Its bowl	The bowl is **its**.
Our home	The home is **ours**.
Their car	The car is **theirs**.

Instructor: In **Exercise 4,** read four sentences that use the possessive pronoun *its* to show possession or ownership. This pronoun acts like an adjective telling whose.

Workbook: The cat licked **its** whiskers.

The bird lined **its** nest with grass.

The snake shed **its** skin.

The dog chased **its** tail.

Instructor: Look at **Exercise 5**. There are two little words that are often confused because they are pronounced the same. But these words have two different spellings and two different meanings. The first word is *its*, the possessive pronoun that acts like an adjective that tells whose. The second word is a **contraction**. The word *contract* means "to draw together or shorten." Look at the two words closely. What does the contraction *it's* have that the first word does not?

Workbook: Two little words that are often confused:

its

it's

Student: *It has an apostrophe.*

Instructor: Every contraction has an apostrophe. A contraction occurs when two words are drawn together, or shortened, by dropping some letters. The apostrophe in the contraction tells us where the letters were dropped to form the contraction. In **Exercise 6**, you will see how the contraction *it's* is formed. It can be formed from two sets of words. Look at the first row and read across. When the words *it* and *is* are drawn together, or contracted, the middle letter **i** is dropped and replaced by an apostrophe. The resulting contraction is **i-t**-apostrophe-**s**. When the words *it* and *has* are contracted, the middle letters **h** and **a** are replaced by the apostrophe. The resulting contraction is also **i-t**-apostrophe-**s**. So when you see the contraction *it's*, it is a contracted form of "it is" **or** "it has."

Workbook:

Two Words	Letters That Are Dropped	Contraction
it is	it is	it's
it has	it has	it's

Instructor: When you diagram a sentence with a contraction, you pretend that the contraction is still two words. In **Exercise 7** read the sentence and look at its diagram. This sentence does not have a contraction.

Workbook: It has been a nice day.

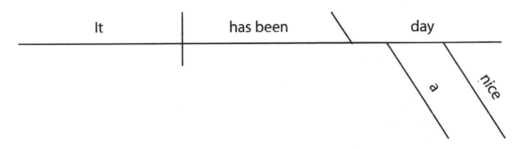

Instructor: In **Exercise 8** read the sentence and look at a diagram of its sentence. This sentence contains the contraction *it's*. Notice on the diagram that the contraction is split apart; we pretend the contraction is still two separate words!

Workbook: It's been a nice day.

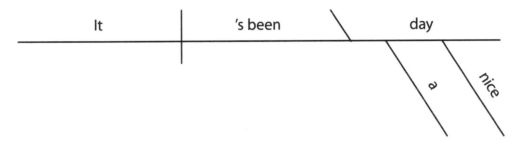

Instructor: Diagram the sentence in **Exercise 9** of your workbook by filling in the frame. *It* is the subject. *Is* is the linking verb. *Turn* is the predicate nominative because it renames the subject *It*. What is *It*? It is my turn. *My* is a possessive pronoun that acts like an adjective telling whose. Whose turn? *My* turn.

Answer Key: It is my turn.

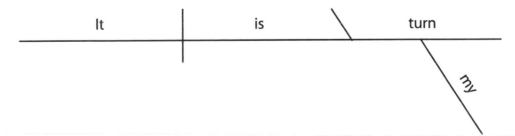

Instructor: Now diagram the sentence in **Exercise 10** of your workbook. This sentence is the same as the one in **Exercise 9**, except this sentence contains the contraction *It's*. Remember to split the contraction apart on the diagram, just like we did in **Exercise 8**, and pretend the contraction is still two separate words!

Answer Key: It's my turn.

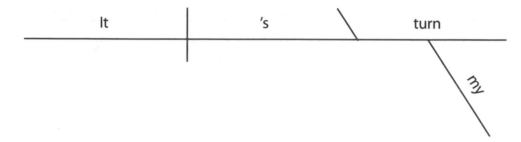

The following exercise is a pretest for contractions. If the student misses any of the contractions, turn to the Optional End Unit on contractions (page 507) and go over the list with the student. He may then take another test. If he misses any answers on that test, review the contractions again tomorrow and take the next test (do not go on to Lesson 61). If necessary, continue to review contractions periodically over the next few weeks until the student is confident.

Instructor: Now I will see how many other contractions you know. Read each pair of words in **Exercise 11** and write the contraction that results when the two words are drawn together.

Answer Key:

Two Words	Contraction
I am	I'm
he is	he's
we are	we're
you have	you've
she has	she's
it had	it'd
they had	they'd
I will	I'll
he will	he'll

you would	you'd
we would	we'd
let us	let's
is not	isn't
were not	weren't
have not	haven't
do not	don't
did not	didn't
can not	can't
will not	won't

LESSON 61

New: The "No" Adverbs and Contractions
Review: Contractions

Read "The Lake Isle of Innisfree" (Lesson 53) three times to the student. Then ask the student to say the poem along with you or the tape recorder. If the student is ready, he should recite the poem to real people today. If he is not, continue practicing daily until he is ready.

Instructor: An adverb is a word that describes a verb, an adjective, or another adverb. Say that definition with me.

TOGETHER: An adverb is a word that describes a verb, an adjective, or another adverb.

Instructor: Most adverbs describe verbs. Adverbs can tell how, when, where, how often, and to what extent. In **Exercise 1** read the sentence to me.

Workbook: The trail led nowhere.

Instructor: *Nowhere* is an adverb that tells **where**. Where did the trail lead? Nowhere! Have you ever been walking on a woodland trail to suddenly find the trail just stops in the middle of the woods? The trail didn't lead to a place; it led nowhere! Look at a diagram of that sentence.

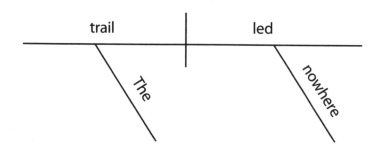

Instructor: The adverb *nowhere* is printed on a slanted line below the verb it describes.

Instructor: In **Exercise 2** read the sentence to me. It contains an adverb that comes before the verb.

Workbook: Garnet never frightens little children.

Instructor: *Never* is an adverb that tells **how often**. How often does Garnet frighten little children? Never! Look at a diagram of that sentence.

Garnet	frightens	children

never *little*

Instructor: The adverb *never* is written on a slanted line below the verb it describes.

Instructor: Now in **Exercise 3** you are going to read a sentence with a new but common adverb. A child might hear this sentence from his or her parent.

Workbook: You should not tease your brother.

Instructor: What is the verb in this sentence? There are two; the helping verb *should* works together with an action verb *tease*. Both verbs—*should* and *tease*—are written together on the verb line of a diagram. There is also an adverb in this sentence, a very common little adverb: *not*. *Not* doesn't tell how, when, where, or how often. It tells "to what extent." You should not tease your brother. **To what extent** should you tease your brother? You should **not** tease him. Look at the diagram of that sentence.

You	should tease	brother

not *your*

Instructor: *Not* is an adverb that describes the verbs *should tease*. It tells to what extent you should tease your brother—you should **not** tease him. Since *not* describes the verbs, it is printed on a slanted adverb line below the verbs.

Instructor: In Lesson 60 you learned about contractions. Remember, a contraction is formed when two words are drawn together and shortened by dropping some letters. In **Exercise 4** read the sentence to me.

Workbook: You shouldn't tease your brother.

Instructor: Even though the adverb *not* is shortened to **n**-apostrophe-**t**, we still place it in the same place on the diagram. Look at the diagram of the sentence you just read.

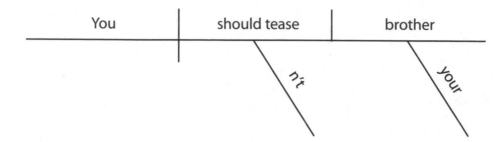

Instructor: Now in **Exercise 5**, it is your turn to diagram some sentences that contain contractions with the word *not*. You read each sentence. I will ask you questions as you fill in the diagram. Remember to copy the words exactly as they appear in the sentence. If the words begin with a capital letter in the sentence, they should also be capitalized in the diagram.

Use the following dialogue to help the student fill in each diagram.

1. *This sentence contains a contraction. Write out the two words that formed the contraction above the contraction itself. [Student writes "has not" and "do not" above the contraction in Sentences 1 and 2.] Remember to think of the contraction as two separate words.*

2. *This sentence has a helping verb and an action verb. The helping verb is part of a contraction. Write only the helping verb [has, do] and the main verb [answered, complain], not the whole contraction, to the right of your center line.*

3. *Find the subject. Ask "who" or "what" before the verb. [Prompt the student with a specific question like "Who has answered?" or "Who does complain?"] Write the subject to the left of the center line on your frame.*

4. *This sentence contains the adverb* not, *although it has been shortened to* **n**-apostrophe-**t**. Not *tells to what extent. Write* **n**-apostrophe-**t** *on the slanted line below the verb it describes.*

Answer Key: 1. Trudy hasn't answered.

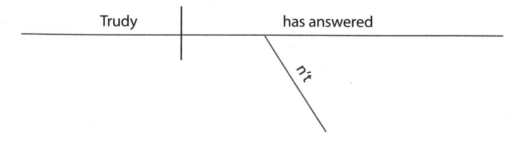

2. We don't complain.

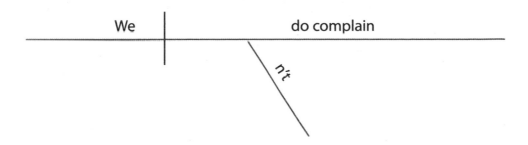

In **Exercise 6**, have the student read each sentence, and then have the student copy each sentence, substituting a contraction for the two words in bold print.

Answer Key:
1. I **was not** lying.   wasn't
2. My little sister **cannot** whistle.   can't
3. **It is** my birthday today.   It's
4. **They would** like to travel.   They'd
5. You **will not** sit still!   won't

Have the student read each sentence in **Exercise 7**. Then have him write the contraction that can be formed from the two words printed in bold.

Answer Key:
1. **He will** manage the field trip.   He'll
2. **I am** cooperative.   I'm
3. **We are** inventing a new game.   We're
4. **Was not** last year's hurricane a disaster?   Wasn't
5. I **do not** know that story.   don't

LESSON 62

Cumulative Poem Review

Instructor: Today you are going to review the poems you have memorized so far. When you recite a poem, you begin with the title and author. I will give you the title and author for each poem. Say the title and the author back to me, and then recite the poem. Remember to stand up straight! Don't fidget while you're reciting! And speak in a nice, loud, slow voice.

You may prompt the student as necessary. If the student repeats the poem accurately, he may check the box in his workbook and move on to the next poem. If he stumbles, ask him to repeat the line he cannot remember three times.

"Afternoon on a Hill"

by Edna St. Vincent Millay

Lesson 8

"Ozymandias"

by Percy Bysse Shelley

Lesson 16

"How Doth…"

by Lewis Carroll

Lesson 27

"Learning to Read"

by Frances Ellen Watkins Harper

Lesson 40

"The Lake Isle of Innisfree"

by William Butler Yeats

Lesson 53

LESSON 63

New: Direct Quotations at the End of Sentences
Review: Four Types of Sentences

The sentence content for the next two lessons is taken from *Why Doesn't the Earth Fall Up? And Other Not Such Dumb Questions about Motion* by Vicki Cobb.

Instructor: In this lesson we are going to review the four different types of sentences: statements, commands, questions, and exclamations. A statement gives information. Statements always end with a period. In **Exercise 1** read the first statement to me.

Workbook: 1. Galileo experimented with how things fall.

Instructor: The second type of sentence is a command. A command gives an order or makes a request. A command sentence ends with either a period or an exclamation point. Read Sentence 2 to me.

Workbook: 2. Drop a heavy object and a light object off a porch or a jungle gym.

Instructor: The third type of sentence is a question. A question asks something. A question always ends with a question mark. Read Sentence 3.

Workbook: 3. Which one reaches the ground first?

Instructor: The fourth type of sentence is an exclamation. An exclamation shows sudden or strong feeling. An exclamation always ends with an exclamation point. Read Sentence 4. Remember to read the exclamation sentence with lots of expression because it shows strong feeling!

Workbook: 4. You get a tie every time!

Instructor: In **Exercise 2**, read the sentences and write either "S" for statement, "C" for command, "Q" for question, or "E" for exclamation after each sentence.

Answer Key: 1.   Galileo performed many experiments about gravity.   **S**

2.   Bring me an egg for an experiment about gravity.   **C**

3.   You cannot make an egg stand on its end!   **E**

4.   Why won't the egg stand on its end?   **Q**

5.   An egg's center of gravity is not at the center of the egg.   **S**

6.   Give me the egg.   **C**

7.   Oh no! I dropped the egg!   **E**

8.   What other interesting facts about gravity can I find?   **Q**

Instructor: People use the four kinds of sentences in conversation every day. In **Exercise 3** follow along while I read the story.

Workbook: 1.   The instructor asked, "**Did Galileo do other experiments**?"

2.   The student replied, "**He did.**"

3.   The instructor ordered, "**Quickly, find out what they were.**"

4.   The student exclaimed, "**I am hurrying**!"

Instructor: Now we are going to read that story together. I will start each sentence, and you will read the words in bold print. These are the exact words the people said. Remember to read with expression.

In **Exercise 4** (below) be sure to point to every punctuation mark as you explain.

Instructor: The sentences you have read are called **direct quotations**. They are the exact words that someone says. There are special punctuation marks placed before and after the exact words a person says. They are called quotation marks. Each of the direct quotations that you read is part of a larger sentence. When a direct quotation is at the end of a sentence, it keeps its own punctuation mark. Look at **Exercise 4** and point to the question mark at the end of Sentence 1. Do you see that it is inside the quotation mark?

Workbook: 1. The instructor asked, **"Did Galileo do other experiments?"**

Instructor: "Did Galileo do other experiments?" is a question. It ends with a question mark. The question mark comes before the last pair of quotation marks. Look at the sentence one more time. Notice that the direct quotation is separated from the rest of the sentence by a comma. And remember, when a direct quotation is at the end of a sentence, it keeps its own punctuation mark. Point to the question mark at the end of the sentence. Do you see that it is inside the quotation mark? Copy Sentence 1 on the lines provided in your workbook.

Instructor: Read Sentence 2.

Workbook: 2. The student replied**, "He did."**

Instructor: "He did" is a statement sentence. It ends with a period. The period comes before the last pair of quotation marks. Look at the sentence one more time. Notice that the direct quotation is separated from the rest of the sentence by a comma. When a direct quotation is at the end of a sentence, it keeps its own punctuation mark. Now copy Sentence 2 on the lines provided in your workbook.

Instructor: Read Sentence 3.

Workbook: 3. The instructor ordered**, "Quickly, find out what they were."**

Instructor: "Quickly, find out what they were" is a command sentence. It ends with a period. The period comes before the last pair of quotation marks. Look at the sentence one more time. Notice that the direct quotation is separated from the rest of the sentence by a comma. I will say this one more time: When a direct quotation is at the end of a sentence, it keeps its own punctuation mark. Point to the period at the end of the sentence. Do you see that it is inside the quotation mark? Now copy Sentence 3 on the lines provided in your workbook.

Instructor: Read Sentence 4.

Workbook: 4. The student exclaimed**, "I am hurrying!"**

Instructor: "I am hurrying!" is an exclamation sentence. It ends with an exclamation point. The exclamation point comes before the last pair of quotation marks. Look at the sentence one more time. Notice that the direct quotation is separated from the rest of the sentence by a comma. Now copy Sentence 4 on the lines provided in your workbook.

Instructor: Have you noticed that the direct quotations you have read all begin with a capital letter? This is the last capitalization rule you will learn in this book. Capitalize the first word in a direct quotation. Say that with me three times.

Together (three times): Capitalize the first word in a direct quotation.

To make sure the student is seeing and paying attention to every punctuation mark and capital letter, have him read the sentences in **Exercise 5**, using the following technique: When he gets to a punctuation mark, he says the name of the punctuation mark. For example, "The student replied [comma] [quotation mark] He did [period] [quotation mark]." Then have him underline each capital letter.

Answer Key:

1. The instructor asked, "Did Galileo do other experiments?"

2. The student replied, "He did."

3. The instructor ordered, "Quickly, find out what they were."

4. The student exclaimed, "I am hurrying!"

Instructor: Now in **Exercise 6** you will copy some famous direct quotations.

Depending on the student's writing ability, choose one to three of the quotations in the workbook for him to copy. If the student copies Sentence 2 ("Away, you scullion!"), tell him that a scullion is a kitchen helper who did the messy work. The word *scullion* comes from the Latin word *scutella*, which means "drinking bowl," because a scullion (or "scullery maid") worked in the area where the dishes were washed and stored. The quotation is from Act 2, scene 1 of Shakespeare's *King Henry IV, Part II*. It is spoken by the character Falstaff.

As he copies, point out the rules below about a direct quotation that comes at the end of a sentence.

Workbook:

a. The exact words a person says are always enclosed by quotation marks.

b. Direct quotations begin with a capital letter.

c. The quotation is separated from the rest of the sentence by a comma.

d. The end punctuation mark always comes inside the quotation marks.

1. Aristotle mused, "Plato is dear to me, but dearer to me is truth."

2. Shakespeare wrote, "Away, you scullion!"

3. William Blake wrote, "Little Lamb, who made thee?"

LESSON 64

New: Direct Quotations at the Beginning of Sentences
Review: Four Types of Sentences

Instructor: Let's review how to diagram the four types of sentences. Let's begin by saying the definition of a sentence. A sentence is a group of words that expresses a complete thought. All sentences begin with a capital letter and end with a punctuation mark. Say that with me.

TOGETHER: A sentence is a group of words that expresses a complete thought. All sentences begin with a capital letter and end with a punctuation mark.

Instructor: There are four different types of sentences: statements, commands, questions, and exclamations. A statement gives information. In **Exercise 1** read the statement sentence.

Workbook: Tim performs experiments regularly.

Instructor: This is a statement: "Tim performs experiments regularly." It gives information. Statements always end with a period. Let's diagram the sentence.

Instructor: What is the verb in this sentence?
Student: *Performs*

Instructor: *Performs* is the verb. Write the verb on the verb line. Now find the subject. Who performs?
Student: *Tim*

Instructor: *Tim* is the subject. Write the subject to the left of the center line on your frame.

Instructor: Look again at the verb *performs*. Is there a direct object that receives the action of the verb? I will ask you a question that will help you find the direct object. Performs what?
Student: *Experiments*

Instructor: *Experiments* is the direct object. Write the direct object to the right of the verb on your diagram. The direct object is separated from the verb by a short, straight line.

Instructor: Look at the verb. Is there a word that describes the verb? This is an adverb that tells how often Tim performs experiments.

Student: *Regularly*

Instructor: Write the adverb *regularly* on the slanted line below the verb it describes. Now your diagram is complete.

Answer Key:

| Tim | performs | experiments |

regularly

Instructor: The second type of sentence is a command. A command gives an order or makes a request. It ends with either a period or an exclamation point. In **Exercise 2** read the command sentence.

Workbook: Observe the surprising results.

Instructor: Now you will diagram this sentence.

Instructor: What is the verb in the sentence?
Student: *Observe*

Instructor: *Observe* is the verb in the sentence. Write the word *Observe* on the verb line. Remember to capitalize *Observe* because it is capitalized in the sentence.

Instructor: Now find the subject. Remember, command sentences do have a subject, but the subject is not written in the sentence. It is understood to be the word *you*. Someone is telling you to observe the surprising results. She does not command you by saying, "**You** observe the surprising results"; she simply says, "Observe the surprising results." So, again, what is the subject of this command sentence? Who should observe the surprising results?

Student: *You*

Instructor: *You* is the subject. Write the word *you* on the subject line. Because the subject *you* is not written in the sentence but is just understood, you should put *you* in parentheses.

Instructor: Look again at the verb *Observe.* Is there a direct object that receives the action of the verb? I will ask you a question that will help you find the direct object. Answer me with one word. Observe what?

Student: *Results*

Instructor: Write the direct object *results* to the right of the verb on your diagram. The direct object is separated from the verb by a short, straight line. Are there any words that describe the direct object *results*? There are two in this sentence. First, find the article (*a, an, the*).

Student: *The*

Instructor: *The* is an article that acts like an adjective that describes *results*. Write the word *the* on the first slanted line beneath *results*.

Instructor: Look again at the direct object *results*. Are there any other words besides the article *the* that describe the direct object? This adjective tells what kind of results they are.

Student: *Surprising*

Instructor: Write the adjective *surprising* on the second slanted line below the direct object *results*. *The* is written on the first adjective line and *surprising* is written on the second adjective line because that is the order they appear in the sentence.

Answer Key:

Instructor: The third type of sentence is a question. A question asks something. A question always ends with a question mark. In **Exercise 3** read the question.

Workbook: Should we record our observations?

Instructor: Diagram this question sentence.

Instructor: In order to find the parts of a question sentence, rearrange the words in the question so that it becomes a statement. Read the question again, and then write it as a statement on the line below.

Answer Key: We should record our observations.

Instructor: There are two verbs in this sentence: a helping and an action verb. What are those verbs?

Student: *Should record*

Instructor: Write both of these verbs on your verb line.

Instructor: What is the subject of the question "Should we record our observations?" Think of the statement "We should record our observations." Who should record our observations?

Student: *We*

Instructor: *We* is the subject of the sentence. Write the word *we* on the subject line. Do not capitalize it, because it is not capitalized in the question sentence.

Instructor: Look again at the verbs: *Should record*. Is there a direct object that receives the action of the verbs? I will ask you a question that will help you find the direct object. Should record what?

Student: *Observations*

Instructor: Write the direct object *observations* to the right of the verb on your diagram. The direct object is separated from the verb by a short, straight line.

Instructor: Are there any words that describe the direct object *observations*? This adjective tells whose observations they are.

Student: *Our*

Instructor: Write the adjective *our* on the slanted line below the direct object it describes. Now your diagram is complete.

Answer Key:

we	Should record	observations

our

Instructor: The fourth type of sentence is an exclamation. An exclamation shows sudden or strong feeling. An exclamation always ends with an exclamation point. In **Exercise 4** read the exclamation sentence. Read it with lots of expression because exclamations show strong feeling!

Workbook: Science days are fun!

Instructor: Diagramming an exclamation sentence is just like diagramming a statement. You will diagram the sentence "Science days are fun!"

Instructor: What is the linking verb in this sentence? This verb links the subject to a word in the complete predicate.

Student: *Are*

Instructor: Write the linking verb *are* to the right of your center line.

Instructor: Now find the subject. Answer me with one word. What are fun?

Student: *Days*

Instructor: Write the word *days* on the subject line.

Instructor: This sentence contains a predicate adjective. This adjective is in the complete predicate of the sentence, but it describes the subject. What kind of days are they?

Student: *Fun*

Instructor: Because the predicate adjective *fun* follows the verb in the sentence, it is written to the right of the verb on the diagram. Write the predicate adjective to the right of the slanted line on your diagram. That slanted line points back toward the subject to remind you that a predicate adjective describes the subject.

Instructor: Go back and look again at the subject. Are there any words in the complete subject that describe the simple subject? This adjective tells what kind of days they are.

Student: *Science*

Instructor: Write the adjective *Science* on a slanted line below the subject it describes. Now your diagram is complete.

Answer Key:

Instructor: People use the four kinds of sentences in conversation every day. Do you remember the sentences we read last lesson about doing an experiment where we drop a heavy object and a light object? In those sentences, each direct quotation, or exact words that a person said, came at the end of the sentence. But in some sentences, the direct quotation comes at the beginning. I am going to read sentences about doing an experiment with a swing. In **Exercise 5** follow along as I read. Notice that this time the direct quotations come at the beginning of the sentences.

Workbook: **"You can experiment to find out if a big swing or a little swing takes longer to go back and forth,"** explained the instructor.

"Stop counting after ten swings," added the instructor.

"What happens when you count ten big swings and ten small ones?" inquired the instructor.

"A big swing takes exactly the same amount of time as a small swing!" declared the student.

Instructor: Now we are going to read those sentences together. You will read the words in bold print. These are direct quotations—the exact words the people said. I will finish reading the words in regular print. Remember to read with expression.

As you go through the sentences in **Exercise 6** (below), be sure to point to every punctuation mark as you explain.

Instructor: Each of the direct quotations that you read is part of a larger sentence. Just like the direct quotations you read last lesson, these direct quotations are enclosed by quotation marks, and they each begin with a capital letter. If the direct quotation is a question or an exclamation, then the quotation itself ends with a question mark or an exclamation point. But if the direct quotation would normally end with a period, then the period is replaced by a comma. Let's look more closely at some of these direct quotations, and I will show you what I mean. Read the first sentence in **Exercise 6**.

Workbook: 1. **"You can experiment to find out if a big swing or a little swing takes longer to go back and forth,"** explained the instructor.

Instructor: "You can experiment to find out if a big swing or a little swing takes longer to go back and forth" is a statement sentence. As you know, statements end with a period. But since the direct quotation statement comes at the beginning of the sentence, the period is replaced by a comma. The comma comes before the last pair of quotation marks. When the quotation comes at the beginning of a sentence, the end of the larger sentence needs its own mark of punctuation. Look at the larger sentence one more time. The sentence ends with a period. Now copy Sentence 1 on the lines provided in your workbook.

Instructor: Read Sentence 2.

Workbook: 2. **"Stop counting after ten swings,"** added the instructor.

Instructor: "Stop counting after ten swings" is a command sentence. Command sentences can end with a period. But since the direct quotation command comes at the beginning of the sentence, the period is replaced by a comma. The comma comes before the last pair of quotation marks. When the quotation comes at the beginning of a sentence, the end of the larger sentence needs its own mark of punctuation. Look at the larger sentence one more time. The sentence ends with a period. Now copy Sentence 2 on the lines provided in your workbook.

Instructor: Read Sentence 3.

Workbook: 3. **"What happens when you count ten big swings and ten small ones?"** inquired the instructor.

Instructor: "What happens when you count ten big swings and ten small ones?" is a question. It ends with a question mark. The question mark comes before the last pair of quotation marks. When the direct quotation question comes at the beginning of a sentence, the end of the larger sentence needs its own mark of punctuation. Look at the larger sentence one more time. The larger sentence ends with a period. Now copy Sentence 3 on the lines provided in your workbook.

Instructor: Read Sentence 4.

Workbook: 4. **"A big swing takes exactly the same amount of time as a small swing!"** declared the student.

Instructor: "A big swing takes exactly the same amount of time as a small swing!" is an exclamation sentence. It ends with an exclamation point. The exclamation point comes before the last pair of quotation marks. When the direct quotation exclamation comes at the beginning of a sentence, the end of the larger sentence needs its own mark of punctuation. Look at the larger sentence one more time. The sentence ends with a period. Now copy Sentence 4 on the lines provided in your workbook.

To make sure the student is seeing and paying attention to every punctuation mark, have him read the sentences in **Exercise 7** and use this technique. When he gets to a punctuation mark, he says the name of the punctuation mark. For example, "[Quotation mark] What happens when you count ten big swings and ten small ones [question mark] [quotation mark] inquired the instructor [period]."

Workbook:

1. "You can experiment to find out if a big swing or a little swing takes longer to go back and forth," explained the instructor.

2. "Stop counting after ten swings," added the instructor.

3. "What happens when you count ten big swings and ten small ones?" inquired the instructor.

4. "A big swing takes exactly the same amount of time as a small swing!" declared the student.

Instructor: In **Exercise 8**, you will see rules about writing direct quotations. Follow along as I read them out loud.

Workbook:

a. The exact words a person says are always enclosed by quotation marks.

b. Direct quotations begin with a capital letter.

c. If the direct quotation would normally end with a period, then the period is changed to a comma. This comma is always inside the quotation mark.

d. If the direct quotation ends with a question mark or exclamation point, that mark is always inside the quotation mark.

e. Since the direct quotation is only a part of the sentence, be sure to complete the sentence with its own end mark.

LESSON 65

New: Indirect Quotations
Review: Direct Quotations
Learn to Proofread: Insert Quotation Marks

Review "The Lake Isle of Innisfree" (Lesson 53) today. If the student has trouble remembering the poem, have him practice it daily until he is confident.

This lesson has sentences about Joan of Arc. Joan of Arc was born in 1412 near the end of the Hundred Years' War, a war between France and England. She was a simple farm girl. When she was thirteen, she said she heard a mysterious, beautiful voice that she believed was the voice of God. The Voice told her that she had been chosen to restore peace to France. The story of Joan of Arc is told in an appropriate manner for the young middle-grade student in the book *Joan of Arc* by Nancy Wilson Ross. The sentences in this lesson are adapted from that book.

Instructor: In **Exercise 1** we are going to read a story together. I will start each sentence, and you will read the words in bold print. These are the exact words the people said. Remember to read with expression.

Workbook: Jean de Metz asked, **"What are you doing here anyway?"**

The captain remarked, **"Go, and let come what may**."

Joan of Arc replied, **"For this deed I was born**."

She said, **"God will grant the victory!"**

As you go through the sentences in **Exercise 2**, be sure to point to every punctuation mark in the student's workbook as you explain.

Instructor: The sentences you have read are called direct quotations. They are the exact words that someone says. Quotation marks are placed before and after the exact words a person says. You also learned a capitalization rule about direct quotations. Repeat after me: Capitalize the first word in a direct quotation.

Student: *Capitalize the first word in a direct quotation.*

Instructor: Each of the direct quotations that we just read is part of a larger sentence. When a direct quotation is at the end of a sentence, it keeps its own punctuation mark. In **Exercise 2**, the sentences have no punctuation. Cover **Exercise 1** so that you cannot see it. Then read each sentence and add in the proper punctuation. I will ask you questions to help you remember the correct form of each sentence.

Instructor: Read Sentence 1. What is the direct quotation in the sentence? What are the exact words the person is saying?

Student: *"What are you doing here anyway?"*

Instructor: Put quotation marks around the direct quotation. The direct quotation "What are you doing here anyway?" is a question. Write a question mark at the end of the quotation. The question mark comes **before** the last pair of **quotation marks**. Remember, when a direct quotation is at the end of a sentence, it keeps its own punctuation mark.

Instructor: Now we need to separate the direct quotation from the rest of the sentence. Insert a comma right after the word *asked* and before the first set of quotation marks.

Answer Key: Jean de Metz asked, "What are you doing here anyway?"

Instructor: Read Sentence 2.

Instructor: What is the direct quotation? What are the exact words the captain says?
Student: *"Go, and let come what may."*

Instructor: Put quotation marks around the direct quotation. "Go, and let come what may" is a command sentence. When a direct quotation is at the end of a sentence, it keeps its own punctuation mark. Put a period **before** the last pair of **quotation marks**.

Instructor: Now we need to separate the direct quotation from the rest of the sentence. Insert a comma right after the word *remarked* and before the first set of quotation marks.

Answer Key: The captain remarked, "Go, and let come what may."

Instructor: Read Sentence 3.

Instructor: What is the direct quotation? What are the exact words Joan of Arc says?
Student: *"For this deed I was born."*

Instructor: Put quotation marks around the direct quotation. The direct quotation "For this deed I was born" is a statement. Statements end with periods. Write a period at the end of the quotation. The period comes **before** the last pair of **quotation marks**. Remember, when a direct quotation is at the end of a sentence, it keeps its own punctuation mark.

Instructor: Now we need to separate the direct quotation from the rest of the sentence. Insert a comma right after the word *replied* and before the first set of quotation marks.

Answer Key: Joan of Arc replied, "For this deed I was born."

Instructor: Read Sentence 4.

Instructor: What is the direct quotation? What are the exact words Joan of Arc says?
Student: *"God will grant the victory!"*

Instructor: Put quotation marks around the direct quotation. The direct quotation "God will grant the victory!" is an exclamation. Write an exclamation point at the end of the quotation. The exclamation point comes **before** the last pair of **quotation marks**. Remember, when a direct quotation is at the end of a sentence, it keeps its own punctuation mark.

Instructor: Now we need to separate the direct quotation from the rest of the sentence. Insert a comma right after the word *said* and before the first set of quotation marks.

Answer Key: She said, "God will grant the victory!"

Instructor: In the sentences you just read, each direct quotation, or exact words that a person said, came at the end of the sentence. But in some sentences, the direct quotation comes at the beginning. In **Exercise 3** we are going to read another story together. You will read the words in bold print. These are direct quotations—the exact words the people said. Notice that this time the direct quotations come at the beginning of the sentences. I will finish reading the words in regular print.

Workbook: **"I am not the King,"** the King declared.

"Please don't play tricks on me," Joan whispered.

"Noble Prince, it is you and none other!" Joan insisted.

"When will you let me go into battle?" Joan asked.

As you go through the sentences in **Exercise 3**, be sure to point to every punctuation mark as you explain.

Instructor: Each of the direct quotations that you read is part of a larger sentence. Just like the direct quotations you read earlier, these direct quotations are enclosed by quotation marks, and they each begin with a capital letter. If the direct quotation is a question or an exclamation, then the quotation itself ends with a question mark or an exclamation point. But if the direct quotation would normally end with a period, then the period is replaced by a comma. In **Exercise 4**, the sentences have no punctuation. Cover **Exercise 3** so that you can't see it, and then read each sentence and add in the proper punctuation. I will ask you questions to help you remember the proper form.

Instructor: Read the first sentence. What is the direct quotation? What are the exact words the King says?

Student: *"I am not the King."*

Instructor: Put quotation marks around the direct quotation. "I am not the King" is a statement sentence. As you know, statements end with a period. But since the direct quotation statement comes at the beginning of a sentence, the period turns into a **comma**. Put a comma after the first *King* and **before** the last pair of **quotation marks**.

Answer Key: 1. "I am not the King," the King declared.

Instructor: Since the quotation comes at the beginning of a sentence, the end of the larger sentence needs its own mark of punctuation. Put in a period at the end of the larger sentence. Read Sentence 2.

Instructor: What is the direct quotation? What are the exact words Joan says?

Student: *"Please don't play tricks on me."*

Instructor: Put quotation marks around the direct quotation. "Please don't play tricks on me" is a command sentence. Command sentences can end with a period. But since the direct quotation command comes at the beginning of a sentence, the period turns into a **comma**. Put a comma after *me* and **before** the last pair of **quotation marks**.

Answer Key: 2. "Please don't play tricks on me," Joan whispered.

Instructor: Since the quotation comes at the beginning of a sentence, the end of the larger sentence needs its own mark of punctuation. Put in a period at the end of the larger sentence. Read Sentence 3.

Instructor: What is the direct quotation? What are the exact words Joan says?

Student: *"Noble Prince, it is you and none other!"*

Instructor: Put quotation marks around the direct quotation. "Noble Prince, it is you and none other!" is an exclamation sentence. It ends with an **exclamation point**. Put an exclamation point after *other* and before the last pair of **quotation marks**.

Answer Key: 3. "Noble Prince, it is you and none other!" Joan insisted.

Instructor: Since the quotation comes at the beginning of a sentence, the end of the larger sentence needs its own mark of punctuation. Put in a period at the end of the larger sentence. Read Sentence 4.

Instructor: Put quotation marks around the direct quotation. "When will you let me go into battle?" is a question. It ends with a **question mark**. Put a question mark after *battle* and **before** the last pair of **quotation marks**.

Instructor: Since the quotation comes at the beginning of a sentence, the end of the larger sentence needs its own mark of punctuation. Put in a period at the end of the larger sentence.

Answer Key: 4. "When will you let me go into battle?" Joan asked.

Instructor: All four of the sentences you have been working with contain direct quotations. You were given the **exact** words the people said. But if I change the words of a direct quotation and give the same information in my own words, it is no longer a direct quotation. It is an **indirect** quotation. An indirect quotation tells you what a person says **without** using his or her exact words. There are no quotation marks in an indirect quotation. In **Exercise 5** read each direct quotation sentence and then read the indirect quotation beneath it.

Workbook: 1. "I am not the King," the King declared.

   The King lied to Joan and said he was not the King.

2. "Please don't play tricks on me," Joan whispered.

   Joan quietly commanded that the King not play tricks.

3. "Noble Prince, it is you and none other!" Joan insisted.

   Joan insisted that she knew he was the King.

4. "When will you let me go into battle?" Joan asked.

   Joan asked the King when she could go into battle.

Learn to Proofread: Insert Quotation Marks

Instructor: Today you will learn a set of proofreaders' marks. Look in your workbook at **Exercise 6**. These are the pair of proofreaders' marks you will learn today. There is a beginning set of quotation marks with an arrowhead below them and an ending set of quotation marks with another arrowhead. When you see the first proofreaders' mark, you should insert beginning quotation marks (or the opening quotation mark). When you see the second proofreaders' mark, insert ending quotation marks (or the closing quotation mark). Read the sentence in **Exercise 6** aloud.

Workbook: All that glistens is not gold, wrote William Shakespeare.

Instructor: "All that glistens is not gold" is a direct quotation and should be enclosed by quotation marks. Now let's review all the proofreaders' marks you have learned. Read the sentences in **Exercise 7**. Use your proofreaders' marks to show the errors in capitalization and punctuation.

Workbook:

Proofreaders' Mark	Meaning
ℓ̸ (lc)	make lowercase
b̲ (caps)	capitalize
⊙	insert period
v̓	insert apostrophe
?	insert question mark
⋀̓	insert comma
v̋	insert beginning quotation mark
v̎	insert ending quotation mark

Answer Key: Did you know that mark Twains name was really samuel Clemens He said If you have nothing to say, say nothing.

Optional Dictation Exercise.

Make sure to use a different voice for the direct quotation; pause significantly at the comma.

Dictation: "There is no substitute for hard work," said Thomas Edison.

LESSON 66

Poem Memorization: "The Height of the Ridiculous"

Instructor: In Lesson 66 of your workbook, you will read about a poet who writes a poem so funny that it's dangerous. Before I begin reading, you should know that *sober* means "serious." The line "There'll be the devil to pay" is a little joke. I'll explain it once we have read through the poem. Listen as I read the poem to you.

"The Height of the Ridiculous"
by Oliver Wendell Holmes

I wrote some lines once in a time

In wondrous merry mood,

And thought, as usual, men would say

They were exceeding good.

They were so queer, so very queer,

I laughed as I would die;

Albeit in a sober way,

A sober man am I.

I called my servant, and he came;

How kind it was of him

To mind a slender man like me,

He of the mighty limb!

"These to the printer," I exclaimed.

And in my humorous way,

I added (as a trifling jest),

"There'll be the devil to pay."

He took the paper, and I watched,

And saw him peep within;

At the first line he read, his face

Was all upon the grin.

He read the next; the grin grew broad,

And shot from ear to ear;

He read the third; a chuckling noise

I now began to hear.

The fourth; he broke into a roar;

The fifth; his waistband split;

The sixth; he burst five buttons off,

And tumbled in a fit.

Ten days and nights, with sleepless eye,

I watched that wretched man,

And since, I never dare to write

As funny as I can.

Instructor: The line "There'll be the devil to pay" is a little joke (a "trifling jest"). There is
an old expression, "There'll be the devil to pay," which means there will be a

problem, but the poet is mostly referring to a printer's devil. A printer's devil was an apprentice in a printing establishment in the 1800s. The poet is going to have to pay the printer's apprentice to print the poem.

Discuss the meaning of the poem with the student. What is the "height of the ridiculous"? After the servant read the ridiculous poem, what happened to him? Read the poem to the student three times in a row. Repeat this triple reading twice more during the day. Have the student check the boxes in his workbook when this is done.

LESSON 67

New: Sentences with More Than One Direct Object, Predicate Nominative, or Predicate Adjective
Review: Commas in Direct Address
Review: Commas in a Series

Read "The Height of the Ridiculous" (Lesson 66) three times to the student. Then ask the student to try to say parts of the first stanza along with you (or the tape recorder).

Instructor: [Student's name], are you listening? I just addressed you by name. When you are talking directly to someone, you often say a person's name to get his attention. This is called **direct address**, because you address someone directly. Remember, when you write a sentence that includes a direct address, use a comma to separate the name of the person spoken to from the rest of the sentence. Read the rule in **Exercise 1** of your workbook.

Workbook: Rule: Use a comma to set off a noun of direct address.

Instructor: In **Exercise 1**, read each sentence to me, pausing after the comma. Then copy the sentence onto the line just below it. Pay special attention to where the commas are placed.

Workbook: 1. Chelsea, may I borrow your calculator?

2. Please, Kyle, do not interrupt me.

3. I can't find my glasses, Mr. Simpson.

Point out the commas in **Exercise 1**, and explain that you use one comma to separate the name if that name is at the beginning or the end of a sentence. Use two commas to separate the name if it is in the middle of a sentence.

Instructor: A noun of direct address does not have a function in a sentence; it is not the subject or an object. When you diagram a sentence with a noun of direct address, that noun is placed on a line that floats above the sentence diagram to show that it does not have a function. It doesn't *do* anything. In **Exercise 2**, you will see diagrams of the sentences you just read. Write each noun of direct address on the floating line above the main diagram.

386

Answer Key: 1. Chelsea, may I borrow your calculator?

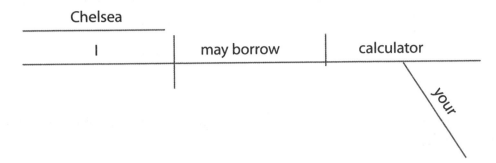

2. Please, Kyle, do not interrupt me.

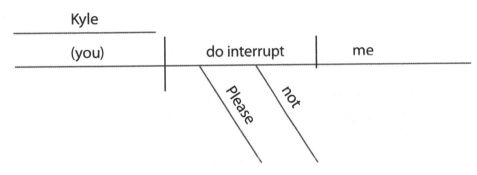

3. I can't find my glasses, Mr. Simpson.

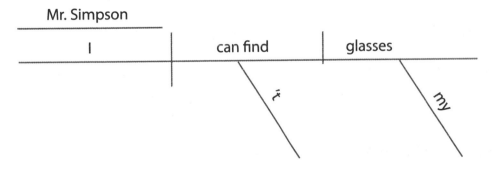

Instructor: When you diagram a sentence with a noun of direct address, the first thing you do is write the noun of direct address on the floating line. Then draw a line through the noun of direct address in your sentence so you can focus on the other functional words: the nouns, pronouns, verbs, adjectives, and adverbs. Diagram the two sentences in **Exercise 3** by filling in the frames. Both of these sentences are commands.

Use the following dialogue to help the student complete the diagrams in **Exercise 3**.

1. *This sentence contains a noun of direct address. Write the name of the person spoken to on the floating line above the diagram. Then draw a line through the name in the sentence, so you can focus on the other words.*

2. *What is the verb? Write the verb to the right of your center line.*

3. *Find the subject. Ask "who" or "what" before the verb. [Prompt the student with a specific question like "Who should pack?" or "Who should dry?"] In a command sentence, the subject is understood to be the word* you. *Write the subject to the left of the center line on your frame. Remember to put* you *in parentheses.*

4. *Is there a direct object that receives the action of the verb? I will ask you a question that will help you find the direct object.*

    Sentence 1: Pack what?

    Sentence 2: Dry what?

    Write the direct object to the right of the verb on your diagram. The direct object is separated from the verb by a short, straight line.

5. *Look again at the direct object. Are there any words that describe the direct object? These adjectives can tell what kind, which one, how many, or whose. Also look for the articles (a, an, the), because they act like adjectives. Write each adjective on a slanted line below the direct object it describes.*

6. *Look again at the verb. Is there a word that describes the verb? This is an adverb that could tell how, when, where, or how often. Write the adverb on the slanted line below the verb it describes.*

Answer Key: 1.   Pack your bags quickly, ~~Aunt Louise~~.

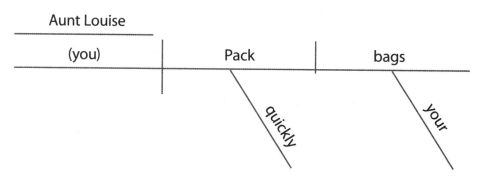

2.   ~~Marty~~, dry the dishes later.

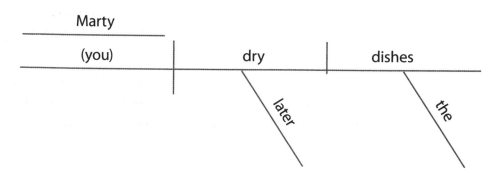

Instructor: Look at the rule in **Exercise 4** of your workbook: "Use commas to separate items in a series." Items in a series can be nouns, pronouns, verbs, adjectives, adverbs, or phrases. Read each sentence, underline the items in the series, and draw arrows pointing to the commas.

Answer Key: 1. We planted <u>tomatoes</u>, <u>peppers</u>, and <u>eggplants</u>.

2. The farmer advised <u>you</u>, <u>him</u>, and <u>me</u>.

3. We <u>tilled</u>, <u>planted</u>, <u>weeded</u>, and <u>watered</u>.

4. The sprouts were <u>small</u>, <u>delicate</u>, and <u>green</u>.

5. They grew <u>quickly</u>, <u>steadily</u>, and <u>healthily</u>.

6. We <u>added fertilizer</u>, <u>removed harmful bugs</u>, and <u>tended the young plants</u>.

Instructor: In Sentences 1 and 2, the nouns in a series were direct objects. Count the underlined words in Sentence 1. How many direct objects does the sentence have? How many nouns receive the action of the verb *planted*?

Student: *Three*

Instructor: In **Exercise 5** of your workbook you will see a diagram of that sentence. Do you see how the direct object line forks into three separate lines? The direct objects are written in order from the top to the bottom line. *Tomatoes* is on the top, *peppers* is in the middle, and *eggplants* is on the bottom, because that is their word order in the sentence. The direct objects are joined by the conjunction *and*, which is written on the dotted line inside the triangle.

Workbook: We planted tomatoes, peppers, and eggplants.

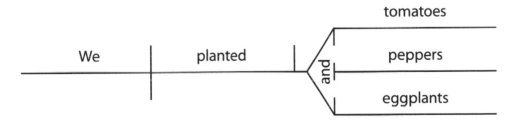

Instructor: Now I want you to diagram the sentence in **Exercise 6** by filling in the frame. This sentence also has three direct objects. Remember to write the direct objects from top to bottom in the order they appear in the sentence.

Answer Key: The farmer advised you, him, and me.

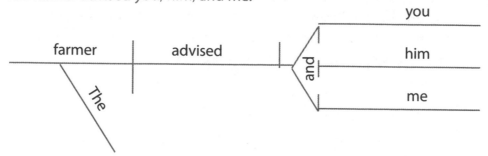

Instructor: Sentences can also have more than one predicate nominative. Read the first sentence in **Exercise 7** and look at its diagram.

Workbook: 1. The tastiest vegetables are peas, carrots, and broccoli.

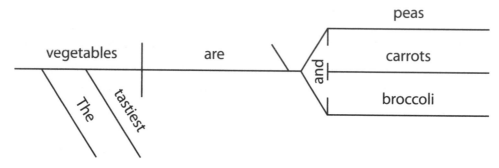

Instructor: This sentence has three predicate nominatives that rename the subject *vegetables*. What are vegetables? *Peas, carrots,* and *broccoli*. In the diagram, the predicate nominative line forks into three separate lines. The predicate nominatives are written in sentence order from the top to the bottom line: *peas, carrots, broccoli*. The predicate nominatives are joined by the conjunction *and*, which is written on the dotted line inside the triangle.

Instructor: Now read the second sentence in **Exercise 7** and fill in its diagram. This sentence has **four** predicate nominatives.

Answer Key: 2. The summer berries are strawberries, blueberries, raspberries, and blackberries.

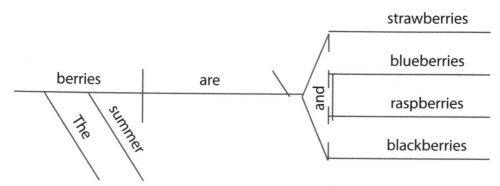

Instructor: Sentences can also have more than one predicate adjective. Read the first sentence in **Exercise 8** and look at its diagram.

Workbook: 1. The sprouts were small, delicate, and green.

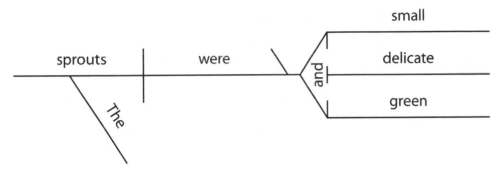

Instructor: This sentence has three predicate adjectives that describe the subject *sprouts*. What kind of sprouts? *Small, delicate,* and *green.* In the diagram, the predicate adjective line forks into three separate lines. The predicate adjectives are written in sentence order from the top to the bottom line: *small, delicate, green.* The predicate adjectives are joined by the conjunction *and*, which is written on the dotted line inside the triangle.

Instructor: Now read the second sentence in **Exercise 8** and fill in its diagram. This sentence has **four** predicate adjectives.

Answer Key: 2. The strawberries were warm, sweet, juicy, and plentiful.

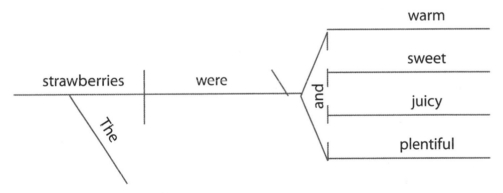

Instructor: In **Exercise 9**, complete the sentences with three direct objects, predicate nominatives, or predicate adjectives of your choice. Separate the items in a series with a comma. The last two items need a comma **and** a conjunction between them.

Instructor: What places would you like to travel to someday?
Student: *1. I will visit [example: Australia, China, and Alaska].*

Instructor: What are the titles of your three favorite books? Remember to capitalize and underline the titles!

Student: 2. *My favorite books are [example: The Hobbit, The Yearling, and Prince Caspian].*

Instructor: What are three **nouns** that describe you: girl, boy, son, daughter, brother, sister, student, athlete, musician, artist, dancer, comedian?

Student: 3. *I am a [example: girl, student, and musician].*

Instructor: Think of your favorite food. What are three adjectives that describe it?

Student: 4. *My favorite food is [example: gooey, warm, and chocolaty].*

Instructor: In **Exercise 10**, diagram the sentences you composed by filling in the rest of the frame. Sentence 1 has three direct objects. Sentences 2 and 3 each have three predicate nominatives. Sentence 4 has three predicate adjectives.

Answer Key (using the sample answers):

1. I will visit Australia, China, and Alaska.

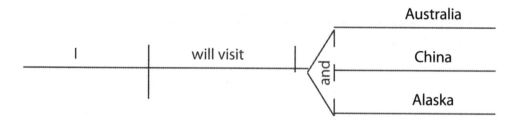

2. My favorite books are <u>The Hobbit</u>, <u>The Yearling</u>, and <u>Prince Caspian</u>.

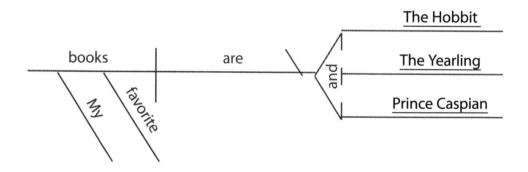

3. I am a girl, a student, and a musician.

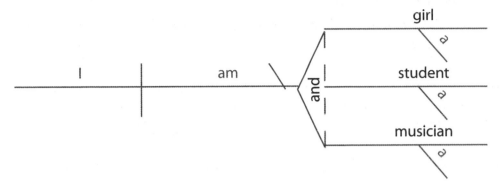

4. My favorite food is gooey, warm, and chocolaty.

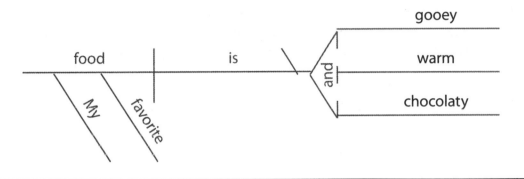

Optional Dictation Exercise

Set a timer for sixty seconds and ask the student to write down on a separate sheet of paper as many flavors of ice cream as he can recall. Then the student will hand you the list, and you dictate a sentence for him. "The ice cream shop had [all the flavors the student lists—don't forget the "and" before the last flavor]."

LESSON 68

Review: Prepositional Phrases

Read "The Height of the Ridiculous" (Lesson 66) three times to the student. Then ask the student to try to say parts of the first and second stanzas along with you (or the tape recorder).

Instructor: Let's begin this lesson by reviewing prepositions. A preposition is a word that shows the relationship of a noun or pronoun to another word in the sentence. Say that definition with me three times.

TOGETHER (three times): A preposition is a word that shows the relationship of a noun or pronoun to another word in the sentence.

Instructor: In your workbook, read the list of prepositions in **Exercise 1**. Then see if you can say all of the prepositions from memory.

If the student has trouble remembering them all, make a note to review this list every day until the student can say it easily.

Workbook: Prepositions

Aboard, about, above, across.
After, against, along, among, around, at.

Before, behind, below, beneath.
Beside, between, beyond, by.

Down, during, except, for, from.
In, inside, into, like.

Near, of, off, on, over.
Past, since, through, throughout.

To, toward, under, underneath.
Until, up, upon.
With, within, without.

Instructor: In Lessons 44–49, you practiced diagramming sentences that contained prepositional phrases. By diagramming the six sentences in this lesson, you will review each of the six ways prepositional phrases can be used in sentences.

Below is a list of the sentences the student will diagram in this lesson. A lesson number is provided for review if you think it is necessary. That lesson number is where the concept was first taught thoroughly.

1. The long canal <u>across Panama</u> was a great achievement.

(from Lesson 44, prepositional phrase describing the subject)

2. The United States built a canal <u>with a lock system</u>.

(from Lesson 45, prepositional phrase describing the direct object)

3. A canal pilot hands the captain <u>of the ship</u> a map.

(from Lesson 46, prepositional phrase describing the indirect object)

4. The Panama Canal is a manmade waterway <u>with a fascinating history</u>.

(from Lesson 47, prepositional phrase describing the predicate nominative)

5. Small electric locomotives with wheels <u>of steel</u> are powerful.

(from Lesson 48, prepositional phrase describing the object of the preposition)

6. Huge supertankers cannot pass <u>through the canal</u>.

(from Lesson 49, prepositional phrase describing the verb)

Instructor: Look at **Exercise 2** in your workbook. Read Sentence 1. This sentence has a prepositional phrase that describes the subject of the sentence. The prepositional phrase is an adjective phrase because it tells which one. I will ask you questions to help you fill in the diagram.

Workbook: 1. The long canal across Panama was a great achievement.

Instructor: What is the prepositional phrase?
Student: *Across Panama*

Instructor: Put a box around "across Panama." Ignore the words inside the box while you find the other parts of the sentence. What is the linking verb?
Student: *Was*

Instructor: Write *was* on the verb line. What is the subject? What was?
Student: *Canal*

Instructor: Write *canal* on the subject line. The linking verb *was* links the subject to a noun in the predicate. What is the predicate nominative? What was the canal? Answer me with one word.

Student: *Achievement*

Instructor: Write *achievement* to the right of the verb. Look again at the simple subject *canal*. Are there any adjectives that describe *canal*? What are they?

Student: *The, long*

Instructor: Write *The* and *long* on the slanted lines beneath *canal*.

Instructor: Look again at the predicate nominative, *achievement*. What are the two adjectives that describe *achievement*?

Student: *A, great*

Instructor: Write these adjectives on the slanted line beneath the noun they describe.

Instructor: The prepositional phrase inside the box is an adjective phrase that describes the subject. Which canal? The one across Panama. Write *across* on the slanted line below the subject. What is the object of the preposition? Across what?

Student: *Panama*

Instructor: Write *Panama* on the flat line. Now your diagram is complete.

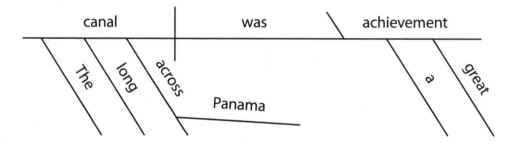

Instructor: Read Sentence 2. This sentence has a prepositional phrase that describes the direct object. The prepositional phrase is an adjective phrase because it tells what kind. I will ask you questions to help you fill in the diagram.

Workbook: 2. The United States built a canal with a lock system.

Ask the following shortened questions to help the student fill in the diagram. The answers are in italics. If the student needs more direction, help him put each word in its proper place on the diagram.

---

1. What is the prepositional phrase? Put a box around it. | With a lock system |

2. What is the verb? *Built*

3. What is the subject? Who built? *United States*

4. What is the direct object? Built what? *Canal*

5. Are there any adjectives that describe the subject? *The*

6. Are there any adjectives that describe the direct object? *A*

7. The prepositional phrase in the box is an adjective phrase that describes the direct object *canal*. Answer with the prepositional phrase. What kind of canal? *With a lock system*

8. What is the preposition? Write it on the slanted line below *canal*. *With*

9. What is the object of the preposition? Write it on the flat line. *System*

10. Are there any adjectives that describe the object of the preposition? *A, lock*

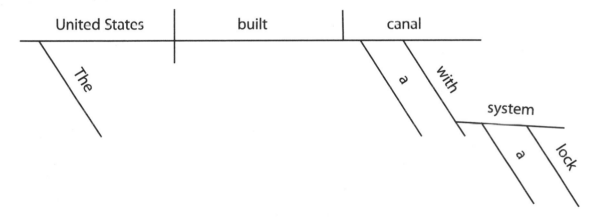

Instructor: Read Sentence 3. This sentence has a prepositional phrase that describes the indirect object. The prepositional phrase is an adjective phrase because it tells which one. I will ask you questions to help you fill in the diagram.

Workbook: 3.   A canal pilot hands the captain of the ship a map.

Ask the following shortened questions to help the student fill in the diagram. The answers are in italics. If the student needs more direction, help him put each word in its proper place on the diagram.

1. What is the prepositional phrase? Put a box around it. $\boxed{\textit{Of the ship}}$

2. What is the verb? *Hands*

3. What is the subject? Who hands? *Pilot*

4. What is the direct object? Hands what? *Map*

5. What is the indirect object? Hands a map to whom? (Note: The indirect object is always written on the flat line beneath the verb.) *Captain*

6. Are there any adjectives that describe the subject? *A, canal*

7. Are there any adjectives that describe the direct object? *A*

8. Are there any adjectives that describe the indirect object? *The*

9. The prepositional phrase in the box is an adjective phrase that describes the indirect object *captain*. Answer with the prepositional phrase. Which captain? *Of the ship*

10. What is the preposition? Write it on the slanted line below *captain*. *Of*

11. What is the object of the preposition? Write it on the flat line. *Ship*

12. Are there any adjectives that describe the object of the preposition? *The*

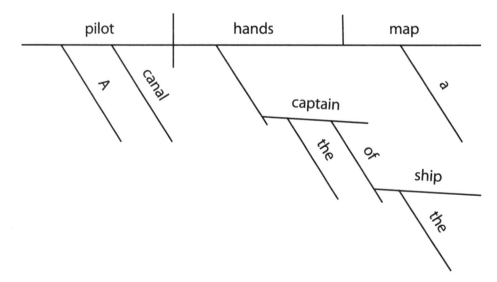

Instructor: Read Sentence 4. This sentence has a prepositional phrase that describes the predicate nominative. The prepositional phrase is an adjective phrase because it tells what kind. I will ask you questions to help you fill in the diagram.

Workbook: 4. The Panama Canal is a manmade waterway with a fascinating history.

Ask the following shortened questions to help the student fill in the diagram. The answers are in italics. If the student needs more direction, help him put each word in its proper place on the diagram.

1. What is the prepositional phrase? Put a box around it. ┌ *With a fascinating history* ┐

2. What is the verb? *Is*

3. What is the subject? What is? *Panama Canal*

4. What is the predicate nominative that renames the subject? The Panama Canal is a what? *Waterway*

5. Are there any adjectives that describe the subject? *The*

6. Are there any adjectives that describe the predicate nominative? *A, manmade*

7. The prepositional phrase in the box is an adjective phrase that describes the predicate nominative *waterway*. Answer with the prepositional phrase. What kind of waterway? *With a fascinating history*

8. What is the preposition? Write it on the slanted line below *waterway*. *With*

9. What is the object of the preposition? Write it on the flat line. *History*

10. Are there any adjectives that describe the object of the preposition? *A, fascinating*

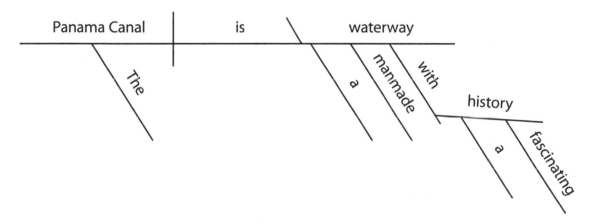

Instructor: Read Sentence 5. This sentence has two prepositional phrases: one describes the subject and the other describes the object of the preposition from the first phrase. The prepositional phrase is an adjective phrase because it tells what kind. I will ask you questions to help you fill in the diagram.

Workbook: 5. Small electric locomotives with wheels of steel are powerful.

Ask the following shortened questions to help the student fill in the diagram. The answers are in italics. If the student needs more direction, help him put each word in its proper place on the diagram.

1. What are the two prepositional phrases? Put a box around each one. $\boxed{\textit{With wheels}}$; $\boxed{\textit{of steel}}$

2. What is the verb? *Are*

3. What is the subject? What are? *Locomotives*

4. What is the predicate adjective that describes the subject? What kind of locomotives? *Powerful*

5. Are there any adjectives in the complete subject that describe the simple subject *locomotives*? *Small, electric*

6. The prepositional phrase in the first box is an adjective phrase that describes the subject *locomotives*. Answer with the first prepositional phrase. Which locomotives? *With wheels*

7. What is the preposition? Write it on the slanted line below *locomotives*. *With*

8. What is the object of the preposition? Write it on the flat line. *Wheels*

9. The prepositional phrase in the second box is an adjective phrase that describes the object of the preposition *wheels* in the first prepositional phrase. Answer with the second prepositional phrase. What kind of wheels? *Of steel*

10. What is the preposition? Write it on the slanted line below *wheels*. *Of*

11. What is the object of the preposition? Write it on the flat line. *Steel*

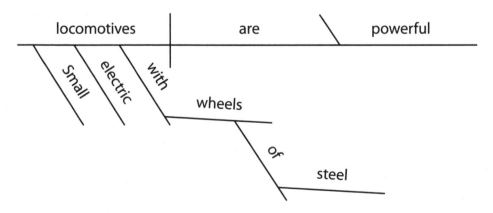

Instructor: Read Sentence 6. This sentence has a prepositional phrase that describes the verb. The prepositional phrase is an adverb phrase because it tells where. I will ask you questions to help you fill in the diagram.

Workbook: 6.   Huge supertankers cannot pass through the narrow canal.

Ask the following shortened questions to help the student fill in the diagram. The answers are in italics. If the student needs more direction, help him put each word in its proper place on the diagram.

---

1.   What is the prepositional phrase? Put a box around it. ⎡*Through the narrow canal*⎤

2.   What is the verb phrase? (Remember, *not* is an adverb, not a verb! You will need to draw a line between "can" and "not" and treat them as two different words.) *Can pass*

3.   What is the subject? What cannot pass? *Supertankers*

4.   Are there any adjectives that describe the subject? *Huge*

5.   Are there any adverbs that describe the verb? There is a special little adverb that tells to what extent the supertankers can pass. Remember: we had to divide it from the word it was attached to. *Not*

6.   The prepositional phrase in the box is an adverb phrase that describes the verbs *can pass*. Answer with the prepositional phrase. Where can the supertankers not pass? *Through the narrow canal*

7.   What is the preposition? *Through*

8.   What is the object of the preposition? *Canal*

9.   Are there any adjectives that describe the object of the preposition? *The, narrow*

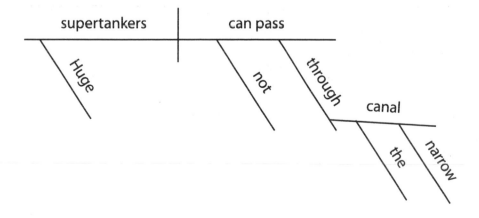

LESSON 69

Review: Adverbs

Read "The Height of the Ridiculous" (Lesson 66) three times to the student. Then ask the student to try to say parts of the first, second, and third stanzas along with you (or the tape recorder).

Instructor: Today we are going to review adverbs. An adverb is a word that describes a verb, an adjective, or another adverb. Adverbs tell how, when, where, how often, and to what extent. Say that definition with me three times.

Together (three times): An adverb is a word that describes a verb, an adjective, or another adverb. Adverbs tell how, when, where, how often, and to what extent.

Instructor: **Adverbs tell how.** Read the sentences in **Exercise 1** of your workbook. After you read each sentence, fill in the blank with an adverb that tells how. Write the adverb in the space. There are options listed for each sentence.

Workbook: Adverbs that tell how.

Pick one adverb from the choices below the sentences. All of the adverbs tell **how**.

1. The doctor examined the anxious patient _____.
   Options: carefully, thoroughly, slowly, calmly

2. The nurse _____ helped the doctor.
   Options: quietly, willingly, gently, swiftly

3. The patient had been _____ hurried to the emergency room.
   Options: abruptly, anxiously, frantically, wisely

4. The doctor _____ took X-rays and ran other tests.
   Options: ably, attentively, skillfully, quickly

5. The patient's family waited _____.
   Options: nervously, fretfully, worriedly, silently

Instructor: **Adverbs tell when.** Look at the paragraph about the family kitchen in **Exercise 2** of your workbook. Cover the answer key under the paragraph. Then underline each adverb that tells when without looking at the answers. When you have found eleven adverbs that tell when, you can check your work.

Answer Key: Our kitchen is a busy place. <u>Early</u> each morning we eat breakfast there <u>before</u> we start the day's activities. <u>After</u> I get up, I dress <u>immediately</u>. <u>Then</u> I hurry to the kitchen to eat. <u>Soon</u> the whole family has eaten and we are ready to finish morning chores. My baby brother spilled his water <u>earlier</u>, and he has <u>already</u> spilled it <u>again</u>! <u>Before</u> I start my regular chores, I <u>first</u> help clean up the spill.

Instructor: **Adverbs tell where.** Look at the paragraph about the city in **Exercise 3** of your workbook. Cover the answer key under the paragraph. Then underline each adverb that tells where without looking at the answers. When you have found nine adverbs that tell where, you can check your work.

Answer Key: When you drive <u>uptown</u> or <u>downtown</u>, there are so many things <u>everywhere</u>, <u>around</u>, and <u>overhead</u> to see. But <u>underneath</u> there are hidden things necessary for city life. Pretend to go <u>down</u> a manhole with me. The tunnel seems very dark <u>inside</u>. I hope there are no spiders or snakes <u>nearby</u>!

Instructor: **Adverbs tell how often.** Look at **Exercise 4** in your workbook. Read aloud the list of "how often" adverbs. Then read the first three sentences and underline any "how often" adverbs you see.

After the student has underlined the adverbs, point out that an adverb describing a verb may come at the beginning, in the middle, or at the end of a sentence.

Workbook: Adverbs that tell how often:

hourly	daily	nightly	monthly	yearly
never	once	twice	rarely	sometimes
often	usually	always	seldom	frequently
weekly	regularly			

Answer Key: 1. Our weather is <u>frequently</u> cold.

2. For that reason, we don't grow poinsettias <u>regularly</u>.

3. <u>Usually</u> the poinsettias will be killed by frost.

Instructor: You are going to diagram Sentences 4 and 5. You will draw the frames. The sentences all have adverbs. On a diagram, an adverb is **always** attached to the verb it describes, even if the adverb is not next to the verb in the sentence.

To start, have the student first draw a basic frame for a sentence with a subject, verb, and direct object. Ask the following shortened questions to help the student fill in each diagram, one at a time. The answers are in italics. If the student needs more direction, help him put each word in its proper place on the diagram.

1. What is the verb? (Sentence 5 has a helping verb and a main verb.)

   Sentence 4: Sends

   Sentence 5: Has forgotten

2. What is the subject? ("Who sends?" or "Who has forgotten?")

   Sentence 4: Grandmother

   Sentence 5: She

3. What is the direct object that receives the action of the verb? ("Sends what?" or "Has forgotten what?")

   Sentence 4: Poinsettia

   Sentence 5: Flower

4. Are there any adverbs that describe the verb? These adverbs tell how often. Draw a slanted line under the verb and write the adverb on that line.

   Sentence 4: Yearly

   Sentence 5: Never

5. Are there any adjectives that describe the direct object? Draw a slanted line for each adjective and write each one under the direct object it describes.

   Sentence 4: A

   Sentence 5: This

Answer Key: 4. Yearly, Grandmother sends a poinsettia.

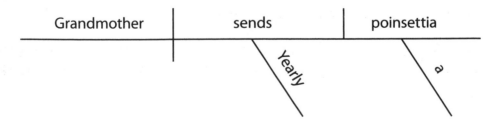

5. She has never forgotten this flower.

She	has forgotten	flower

never *this*

Instructor: Up until this point in the lesson, we have focused on adverbs that describe verbs. These adverbs tell how, when, where, and how often. But there are some adverbs that describe adjectives or other adverbs. These adverbs tell "**to what extent**." Although there are many adverbs like these, we are going to focus on eight extremely common adverbs. In your workbook, read the "to what extent" adverbs at the beginning of **Exercise 5**.

Workbook: Adverbs that tell to what extent:

too   really   quite   so

very   rather   extremely   slightly

Instructor: Now, just below the line of those "to what extent" adverbs, read the sentence and the adverbs that describe to what extent a store can be crowded. These adverbs all describe the predicate adjective.

Workbook: The store was _____ crowded.

To what extent was the store crowded? Was it:

too crowded?

very crowded?

quite crowded?

extremely crowded?

slightly crowded?

Instructor: All these adverbs tell "to what extent" the store was crowded. Choose your favorite adverb and write it in the blank in the sentence.

Instructor: Now fill in the rest of the sentence diagram. Write the "to what extent" adverb you chose on the slanted line beneath the predicate adjective it describes.

Answer Key:

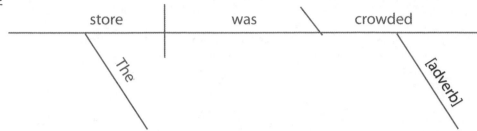

Instructor: In **Exercise 6**, choose another "to what extent" adverb and write it in the sentence "My wool sweater was _____ itchy." Then I will ask you questions to help you diagram that sentence.

Ask the following shortened questions to help the student fill in the diagram. The answers are in italics. If the student needs more direction, help him put each word in its proper place on the diagram.

---

1. What is the verb? *Was*

2. What is the subject? *Sweater*

3. What is the predicate adjective that describes the subject? *Itchy*

4. Are there any adjectives in the complete subject that describe the subject *sweater*? *My, wool*

5. Are there any adverbs that describe the predicate adjective? This adverb tells to what extent the sweater was itchy. *["To what extent" adverb the student chose]*

Answer Key:

LESSON 70

New: Comparing Prepositions and Adverbs

Read "The Height of the Ridiculous" (Lesson 66) three times to the student. Then ask the student to try to say parts of the first through fourth stanzas along with you (or the tape recorder).

Instructor: In this lesson we will talk about adverbs and prepositions. Let's begin by looking at the chart of adverbs in **Exercise 1** of your workbook. You will refer to this chart for **Exercises 2** through **7**.

Workbook:

How	When	Where	How Often	To What Extent
loudly	early	everywhere	sometimes	too
carefully	today	nearby	usually	very
softly	now	uptown	nightly	really
closely	already	indoors	occasionally	quite
anxiously	then	overhead	always	so
gently	yesterday	anywhere	often	extremely
sweetly	tomorrow	inside	rarely	rather
quickly	immediately	around	generally	slightly

Instructor: Read the sentences in **Exercise 2** of your workbook. Write an adverb that tells **how** in the blank. You can think of your own adverb, or you can choose an adverb from the chart.

Possible answers to the sentences in **Exercises 2** through **5** are written in brackets.

Answer Key: 1. The little toddler in pajamas padded [softly] down the stairs.

2. He looked [anxiously] for his mother.

3. Then he began to cry [loudly].

4. His mother came [quickly].

5. She picked him up [gently].

6. His arms hugged her neck [sweetly].

7. He snuggled his head [closely].

8. She [carefully] took him to his bed.

Instructor: Read the sentences in **Exercise 3** of your workbook. Write an adverb that tells **when** in the blank. You can think of your own adverb, or you can choose an adverb from the chart.

Answer Key: 1. Let's plan our afternoon [now].

2. I will want to eat [immediately].

3. We will have a snack [then].

4. If we eat a small snack [early], it won't ruin our appetite for supper.

5. Freda made healthy cookies [yesterday].

6. There are none left [today].

7. [Tomorrow] she will make more.

8. [Already] I am thinking about eating some of those!

Instructor: Read the sentences in **Exercise 4** of your workbook. Write an adverb that tells **where** in the blank. You can think of your own adverb, or you can choose an adverb from the chart.

Answer Key: 1. I love going [uptown] to the sports store.

2. I look [around] when I enter the store.

3. There is interesting equipment [everywhere].

4. I want to stay [inside].

5. I can't find the Ping-Pong balls [anywhere].

6. Then I look [overhead].

7. They are sitting [nearby].

Instructor: Read the sentences in **Exercise 5** of your workbook. Write an adverb that tells **how often** in the blank. You can think of your own adverb, or you can choose an adverb from the chart.

Answer Key: 1. I [generally] eat dinner with the family.

2. [Occasionally] there is a meeting I have to attend.

3. I [rarely] miss dinner more than once a week.

4. We read books together [nightly].

5. [Sometimes] we listen to a book on a CD together.

6. We repeat favorites [often].

7. [Usually] the baby falls asleep while we are listening.

8. Mom [always] puts him in bed without waking him.

Instructor: Do you remember the definition of an adverb? Say it with me.

TOGETHER: An adverb is a word that describes a verb, an adjective, or another adverb. Adverbs tell how, when, where, how often, and to what extent.

Instructor: So far in this lesson we have practiced adverbs describing **verbs**, telling who, when, where, and how often. In the sentences in **Exercise 6**, you will underline eight common "to what extent" adverbs. Look at the "to what extent" column on your chart in **Exercise 1**. Read these adverbs aloud with me.

TOGETHER: Too, very, really, quite, so, extremely, rather, slightly

Instructor: These adverbs typically describe **adjectives** or **other adverbs**. In **Exercise 6**, underline each adverb that tells "to what extent," and draw an arrow to the adjective or other adverb it describes.

The additional information in parentheses is for your benefit only.

Answer Key: 1. Eddie climbed a huge tree so carefully. (describes adverb)

2. He went really high. (describes adverb)

3. He is a very strong boy. (describes predicate adjective)

4. However, sometimes he is too adventurous. (describes predicate adjective)

5. One day, he climbed extremely high up the tree. (describes adverb)

6. I think he was slightly overconfident. (describes predicate adjective)

7. He slipped rather suddenly. (describes adverb)

8. He is okay, but he is so sore. (describes predicate adjective)

Instructor: The sentences in **Exercise 7** contain a mixture of how, when, where, how often, and to what extent adverbs. For each sentence, find the adverb, underline it, and write "how," "when," "where," "how often," or "to what extent" on the blank line after the sentence.

Answer Key:
1. My dog lay <u>nearby</u>. **where**

2. I brush my teeth <u>daily</u>. **how often**

3. The water boiled <u>suddenly</u>. **when**

4. He fell <u>down</u>. **where**

5. I fold my clothes <u>carefully</u>. **how**

6. The policeman stood <u>there</u>. **where**

7. The seagulls were <u>very</u> greedy. **to what extent**

8. The escaping tiger ran <u>far</u>. **where**

Instructor: Remember that **a whole prepositional phrase** can be used as an **adverb** to tell how, when, and where.

Instructor: Look at **Exercise 8.** In each sentence, underline the prepositional phrase that is used as an adverb. Then write "how," "when," or "where" above the phrase.

Answer Key:
1.   when
   All things are difficult <u>in the beginning</u>.

2.   where
   City dwellers often build houses <u>near the street</u>.

3.   where
   The taxi waited <u>outside the restaurant</u>.

4.   when
   People evacuated the island <u>before the storm</u>.

5.   when
   Jared played outside <u>until dark</u>.

6.   how
   I divided the treats <u>with great care</u>.

Instructor: Read the sentences in **Exercise 9**.

Workbook: Adverbs

Pearl climbed **up**.

Jamie walked **along**.

The jogger lagged **behind**.

Instructor: Did you think the words in bold were prepositions? No, they are not! I will tell you the trick to figuring out whether a word is a preposition: A preposition is **always part of a prepositional phrase.** A preposition is **always followed by its object,** the object of the preposition.

Instructor: So what is the function of the words *up, along,* and *behind* in **Exercise 9**? They are adverbs! They tell where. Pearl climbed. Climbed where? Up. Jamie walked. Walked where? Along. The jogger lagged. Lagged where? Behind. Don't be fooled into thinking the words in your preposition list are **always** used as prepositions. They can sometimes be used as adverbs. It all depends on how the word works in the sentence. In **Exercise 10,** you will see these adverbs turn into prepositions when an object is added. Then the words *up, along,* and *behind* will be part of a prepositional phrase.

Workbook: Prepositions

Pearl climbed **up the stairs.**

Jamie walked **along the path.**

The jogger lagged **behind the others.**

Instructor: Remember, a preposition is **always** part of a prepositional phrase. A preposition is **always** followed by its object, the object of the preposition. Read the pairs of sentences in **Exercise 11**. In each pair, you will see a word that is used as an adverb in the first sentence and then as a preposition in the second sentence.

Workbook: Adverbs and Prepositions

Look above.
Look above your head.

Ridgley did without.
Ridgley did without money.

Explore within.
Explore within the sunken ship.

Search outside.
Search outside the neighborhood.

Ernest slid down.
Ernest slid down the waterslide.

Glance around.
Glance around the store.

Stay inside.
Stay inside the car.

Instructor: Now, in **Exercise 12**, you will diagram three of the sentence pairs you just read. Read each sentence. I will help you locate any prepositional phrases, and then I will ask you questions to help you fill in the diagram frame.

Use the following dialogue to help the student complete the diagrams in **Exercise 12**.

1. *This sentence has a prepositional phrase. Put a box around the entire prepositional phrase, and ignore the words inside the box as you find the other parts of the sentence.*

2. *What is the verb? Write the verb to the right of your center line.*

3a. *Find the subject. Ask "who" or "what" before the verb. [Prompt the student with a specific question like "Who slid?" or "Who did?"]*

3b. *Find the subject. Ask "who" or "what" before the verb. [Prompt the student with a specific question like "Who should glance?"] In a command sentence, the subject is understood to be the word* you. *Write the subject to the left of the center line on your frame. Remember to put* you *in parentheses.*

4. *Look again at the verb. Is there a word that describes the verb? This is an adverb that could tell how, when, where, or how often. Write the adverb on the slanted line below the verb it describes.*

5. *Look again at the prepositional phrase inside the box. This is an adverb phrase that describes the verb. An adverb phrase can tell how, when, where, how often, or to what extent. Write the preposition on the slanted line below the verb, and write the object of the preposition on the flat line.*

6. *Are there any words in the prepositional phrase that describe the object of the preposition? These adjectives can tell what kind, which one, how many, or whose. Also look for the articles (a, an, the), because they act like adjectives. Write each adjective on a slanted line below the object of the preposition it describes.*

Answer Key: 1. Ernest slid down.   *(Ask questions 2, 3a, and 4)*

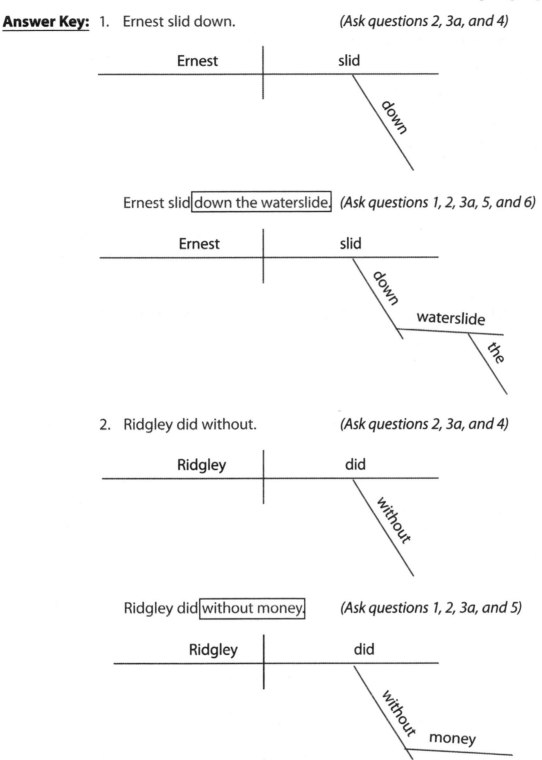

Ernest slid down the waterslide. *(Ask questions 1, 2, 3a, 5, and 6)*

2. Ridgley did without.   *(Ask questions 2, 3a, and 4)*

Ridgley did without money.   *(Ask questions 1, 2, 3a, and 5)*

3. Glance around. *(Ask questions 2 and 3b)*

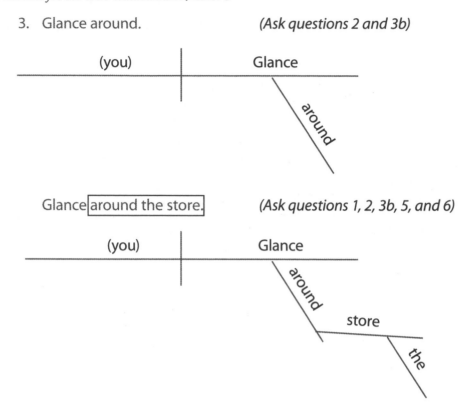

Glance around the store. *(Ask questions 1, 2, 3b, 5, and 6)*

Optional Dictation Exercise

The following sentences are from *The Indian in the Cupboard* by Lynne Reid Banks. Gillon found a small white metal cupboard in the alley and gave it to his brother Omri for a birthday present. Omri put a plastic toy Indian in the cupboard on his bedside table. The next morning he was petrified when he heard something alive in the cupboard. When he opened the cupboard door, he found a small *live* Indian. Today's dictation is from Chapter 4 when the Indian and his horse first stepped out into "The Great Outdoors."

After the student writes the dictation, have him underline two prepositional phrases that tell "where" [along the lawn, beside the path], and an adverb telling to what extent [quite].

Dictation: The horse's speed was remarkable, but Omri found that by running along the lawn beside the path he could keep up quite easily.

LESSON 71

Review: Conjunctions
Review: Compound Subjects and Compound Predicates
Review: Commas in a Series
Review: Commas in Direct Address

Read "The Height of the Ridiculous" (Lesson 66) three times to the student. Then ask the student to try to say parts of the first through fifth stanzas along with you (or the tape recorder).

Instructor: Today we are going to review conjunctions (introduced in Lesson 57). Remember that *junction* means "joining." Highway signs that say "Junction" mean two roads ahead are joining together. In grammar, a *conjunction* is a word that **joins** words or groups of words together. Say the definition of a conjunction with me two times.

TOGETHER (two times): A conjunction is a word that joins words or groups of words together.

Instructor: The three most common conjunctions are *and, but, or.* Say those three conjunctions to me.

Student: *And, but, or*

Instructor: In **Exercise 1** read two sentences that use these conjunctions. Circle each conjunction. The conjunctions are written in bold print, and the two words that are joined are underlined.

There will be practice with conjunctions joining groups of words (whole sentences) when the student reviews compound sentences in the next lesson.

Answer Key: 1. Girls **and** boys are music students.

2. Men **or** women can be their teachers.

415

Instructor: In **Exercise 2** read the two sentences and look at the diagram of the second sentence.

Instructor: Notice that the second sentence has **two** verbs in the predicate. Do you remember that the word *predicate* comes from the Latin word *praedicare* meaning "to proclaim"? The predicate of a sentence is what is said or proclaimed about the subject. What is said or proclaimed about the musicians in the sentence?

Student: *They tuned and practiced.*

Instructor: Circle the conjunction in the second sentence. The conjunction *and* joins the two verbs in the sentence: *tuned* and *practiced*. When the predicate of a sentence has two or more verbs joined by a conjunction, we call it a **compound predicate**. The word *compound* means "made of two or more parts."

Answer Key: Musicians tuned.

Musicians tuned(and)practiced.

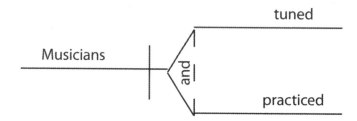

Instructor: Look at the diagram of "Musicians tuned and practiced." The verb line splits into two parts. *Tuned* is written on the top line because it comes first in the sentence. *Practiced* is written on the bottom line. They are joined by the conjunction *and*, which is written inside the triangle.

Many sentences have two or more verbs, but most often these are sentences with verb **phrases**: helping verbs working together with a main verb. Verb phrases function as a unit: they show one action ("They **are playing**"). The compound predicates in this lesson show two distinct actions ("They **tuned** and **practiced**") and are linked by a conjunction.

Instructor: In **Exercise 3**, read the second sentence and look at its diagram.

Instructor: Notice that the second sentence has **two** subjects, joined by the conjunction *and*. When a simple sentence has two or more subjects joined by a conjunction we call it a **compound subject**. What does the word *compound* mean again? (We talked about *compound predicates* in the sentence about musicians.) The word *compound* means "made of two or more parts." What are the two parts of this sentence that are joined by a conjunction? Tell me the two parts and circle the conjunction that joins them.

Student: *Nan and Ray*

Answer Key: Nan sang.

Nan(and)Ray sang.

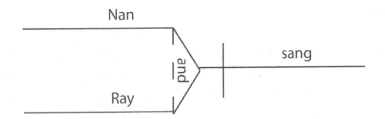

Instructor: Look at the diagram of "Nan and Ray sang." The subject line splits into two parts. *Nan* is written on the top line because she comes first in the sentence. *Ray* is written on the bottom line. The two subjects are joined by the conjunction *and*, which is written inside the triangle.

Instructor: In **Exercise 4**, read the sentence, circle the conjunction, and fill in the frame.

Answer Key: Jane(and)Grace listened.

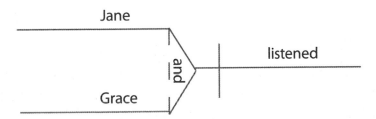

Instructor: In **Exercise 5** you will diagram a simple sentence with **two verbs** in the predicate and **two nouns** in the subject. Read the sentence first.

Workbook: Singers and dancers laugh or talk.

Instructor: What is the compound subject (the two nouns in the subject)?
Student: *Singers and dancers*

Instructor: "Singers and dancers" is the compound subject. What is said about the subject? What is the compound predicate?
Student: *[They] laugh or talk.*

Instructor: "Laugh or talk" is a compound predicate. Circle the conjunction that joins the two nouns, and circle the conjunction that joins the two verbs. Now fill in the frame in your workbook. Be sure to write each conjunction on the dotted line that connects the two subjects or the two verbs.

Answer Key: Singers(and)dancers laugh(or)talk.

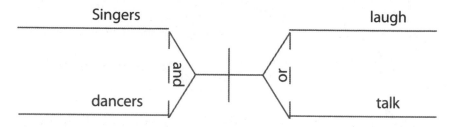

Instructor: Now, in **Exercise 6**, read the sentence aloud and circle the conjunctions in the sentence. Then **you** draw the frame and fill in the diagram. This sentence is similar to the one in **Exercise 5**. It has a compound subject and a compound predicate.

Answer Key: Conductors(and)performers smile(and)bow.

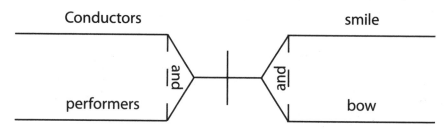

Instructor: In **Exercise 7** of your workbook, read aloud a rule about using commas. Then copy the correctly written sentences onto the lines of your workbook. In Sentence 1 there is a series of nouns in the subject. In Sentence 2 there is a series of nouns in the predicate. In Sentence 3 there is a series of phrases.

Workbook: Rule: Use commas to separate items in a series.

1. Violins, violas, and cellos are musical instruments with strings.

2. Brass instruments are trumpets, trombones, and tubas.

3. We bought tickets, attended the concert, and enjoyed the music.

Instructor: In **Exercise 8** of your workbook read each sentence aloud and add commas to the appropriate places. The first will contain single words in a series in the subject, the second will contain single words in a series in the predicate, and the third will contain phrases in a series.

Answer Key:
1. Strings, woodwinds, brass, and percussion are four families of musical instruments in a symphony orchestra.

2. Some modern flutes are made with gold, silver, or nickel plating.

3. I love the clash of cymbals, the bright ring of the triangle, and the click of the castanets.

Instructor: You also use commas when you talk directly to someone and you mention someone else in the conversation. Listen to this sentence: "You, Sam, and I need to be at the youth orchestra practice early." Not only is it correct grammar, it is good manners. It is polite to open a door for someone else before you walk through it yourself. It is polite for you to say other persons' names before mentioning your own. [In **Exercise 9** of your workbook, read the sentences that show the polite way to talk directly to someone when you mention yourself and another person.] Sentence 1 has commas placed correctly. You will add the proper commas to Sentences 2 and 3.

Answer Key:
1. You, Greg, and I will practice together before Friday's rehearsal.

2. You, Skyler, and I have been chosen for special solo parts.

3. You, Mr. Olson, and I will work on our parts first.

Instructor: Items in a series can be nouns in the subject (a compound subject) or verbs in the predicate (a compound predicate). Items in a series can **also** be direct objects, predicate nominatives, or predicate adjectives (Lesson 67).

Instructor: Now I want you to diagram the sentence in **Exercise 10** by filling in the frame. This sentence has three direct objects. Remember to write the direct objects from top to bottom in the order they appear in the sentence.

Answer Key: Percussionists play xylophones, timpani, and gongs.

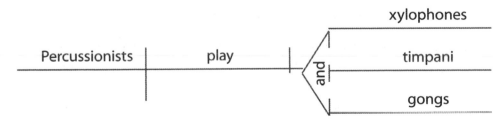

Instructor: Now read the sentence in **Exercise 11** and fill in its diagram. This sentence has three predicate nominatives.

Answer Key: Some woodwinds are flutes, clarinets, and oboes.

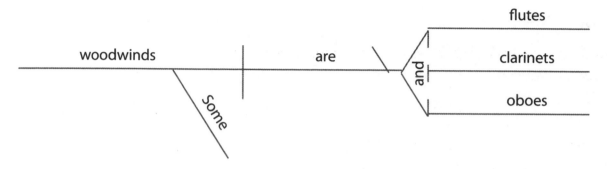

Instructor: Now read the sentence in **Exercise 12** and fill in its diagram. This sentence has three predicate adjectives.

Answer Key: The song was slow, quiet, and stirring.

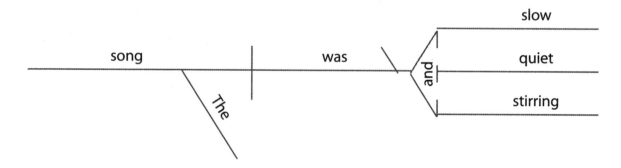

LESSON 72

New: Avoiding Comma Splices and Run-on Sentences
Review: Sentence Fragments
Review: Conjunctions
Review: Compound Sentences
Learn to Proofread: Insert a Semicolon

Read "The Height of the Ridiculous" (Lesson 66) three times to the student. Then ask the student to try to say parts of the first through sixth stanzas along with you (or the tape recorder).

Remember that you can divide long lessons up over several days.

Instructor: Do you remember the definition of a sentence? A sentence is a group of words that expresses a complete thought. Say that to me.

Student: *A sentence is a group of words that expresses a complete thought.*

Instructor: Some groups of words are just pieces of sentences. These pieces of sentences are called fragments. We first learned about fragments in the beginning of this book (Lesson 11). Fragments do not make sense by themselves—you need to add words, like a subject or a verb, to make a sentence that expresses a complete thought. Look at the fragments in **Exercise 1** of your workbook. Tell me what is missing: a subject or a verb. Then add words to make that fragment a complete sentence. Tell me the sentence out loud.

Answer Key: Fragment		Sample Answers
The opossum.	(needs verb)	The opossum **pretended it was dead.**
Soaked the garden.	(needs subject)	**The rain** soaked the garden.
Was tired.	(needs subject)	**Tommy** was tired.
The Giant Squid.	(needs verb)	The Giant Squid **lurks under the sea.**

Instructor: What is the definition of a conjunction?

Student: *A conjunction is a word that joins words or groups of words together.*

Instructor: What are the three most common conjunctions?
Student: *And, but, or*

Instructor: In the last lesson you reviewed that conjunctions can join two subjects to make sentences with compound subjects. Conjunctions can also join two verbs to make sentences with compound predicates or join two sentences to make one longer sentence. A **compound sentence** has two smaller sentences that are joined by a comma and conjunction to make one longer sentence. Read the compound sentences in **Exercise 2**. Circle the comma and the conjunction that joins the two smaller sentences together.

Answer Key: I am an engineer, but I would like to be an astronaut.

I will sing a song, or I will dance.

Terry can hide, and you can find him.

Instructor: Have you ever heard the word *splice*? It means "to join ends together." You can splice two pieces of rope by weaving together the frayed strands at the end of both pieces. You can splice two wooden boards by overlapping the ends and bolting them together. You can splice broken movie film (the kind they use at theaters) or the film of a cassette tape by using special tape. *Splice* means "to join ends together." In compound sentences, like the ones you just read in **Exercise 2**, the two smaller sentences are spliced together with a comma **and** a conjunction. That is a strong splice. If you just used a comma and left out the conjunction, the splice would be too weak to hold the sentences together properly. This weak, improper splice is called a comma splice. Read the sentences with a comma splice in **Exercise 3**. After you read each sentence, draw a line through it to show that it is incorrect.

Answer Key: I am your brother, you are my sister.

We walked to the store, we bought our groceries there.

Beauty is fleeting, wisdom endures.

Instructor: You need a comma **and** a conjunction to hold together two smaller sentences. A comma is not enough. Sometimes a writer forgets to put anything at all between two sentences! This is called a run-on sentence. Two sentences just run together; they aren't properly joined by a comma and a conjunction. Read the run-on sentences in **Exercise 4**. After you read each sentence, draw a line through it to show that it is incorrect.

Answer Key: ~~Edward Lear was a book illustrator he wrote nonsense poetry in his spare time.~~

~~He came from a family with twenty-one children he was the youngest.~~

~~He was very industrious he worked constantly.~~

Instructor: Those run-on sentences needed a comma and a conjunction, or they needed a much stronger punctuation mark: a semicolon. A semicolon can properly join two smaller sentences into a compound sentence without needing any help from a conjunction! Read the compound sentences in **Exercise 5**. Circle each semicolon that joins the two smaller sentences.

Answer Key: I collect shells; you collect sea glass.

Dark clouds gathered; thunder rumbled in the distance.

Herbivores eat plants; carnivores eat meat.

Instructor: Read each sentence in **Exercise 6**. Then decide if it is a fragment, a sentence with a comma splice, a run-on sentence, or a compound sentence. Remember, a compound sentence can be joined by a comma and a conjunction **or** a semicolon alone. Write the correct abbreviation in the blank.

Answer Key:

      F = fragment

      CS = comma splice

      RO = run-on sentence

      C = correct (a compound sentence)

The magma boiled, and pressure was building up below the surface. **C**

Churning and bubbling underground. **F**

The earth shook, steam poured out of the cracks in the ground. **CS**

There was an explosion hot lava and ash catapulted into the air! **RO**

The air, black with dust, ash, and smoke. **F**

Hot lava streams gushed down the sides of the volcano; the lava glowed red, yellow, and orange. **C**

Lava is molten rock it hardens and blackens as it cools. **RO**

Erupting volcanoes disrupt the atmosphere, the dusty and smoky air lingers for a long time. **CS**

Instructor: Look at the first compound sentence and its diagram in **Exercise 7**. There are two smaller diagrams joined together by a dotted line. The conjunction *but* is written on the dotted line because it joins the two smaller sentences together.

Workbook: The bobcat chased the rabbit, but the rabbit escaped into its burrow.

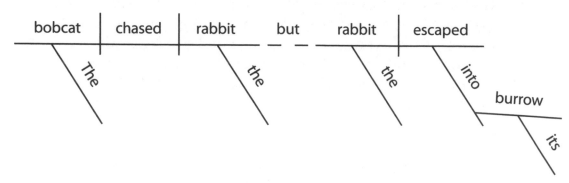

Instructor: Look at the second sentence and its diagram. This sentence is joined by a semicolon. The semicolon is written where the conjunction would normally go, joining the two smaller sentences together.

Workbook: The bobcat slunk away; the rabbit rested comfortably.

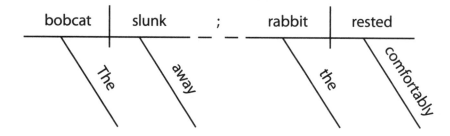

Instructor: Now you will diagram some compound sentences in **Exercise 8** of your workbook. Some of these sentences are joined by a comma and a conjunction; one is joined by a semicolon. You read each sentence, and I will ask you questions as you fill in the diagram. Remember to copy the words exactly as they appear in the sentence. If the words begin with a capital letter in the sentence, they should also be capitalized in the diagram.

Use the following dialogue to help the student complete the diagrams in **Exercise 8**. Because the sentences are made up of two small sentences (independent clauses), you will have to go through the dialogue twice. Follow these instructions closely (for example, "Ask questions 1, 2, 3, etc.") to know which questions to ask.

1. *This is a compound sentence. Ask yourself, "Is it made up of two smaller sentences?" In the written sentence, circle the conjunction (and, but, or) or the semicolon that joins the two sentences. Then write the conjunction or the semicolon on the dotted line that joins*

the two diagrams. Go back to the written sentence and underline the first small sentence. Then underline the second small sentence. First we will complete the diagram for the first small sentence. Then we will complete the diagram of the second small sentence.

2. *What is the verb? Write the verb to the right of your center line.*

3. *Find the subject. Ask "who" or "what" before the verb. [Prompt the student with a specific question like "What have?" or "Who loves?"] Write the subject to the left of the center line on your frame.*

4. *Is there a direct object that receives the action of the verb? I will ask you a question that will help you find the direct object.*

   Sentence 1a: Have what? Sentence 1b: Have what?

   Sentence 2a: Loves what? Sentence 2b: Hates what?

   Write the direct object to the right of the verb on your diagram. The direct object is separated from the verb by a short, straight line.

5. *This sentence contains a predicate adjective. This adjective is in the complete predicate of the sentence, but it describes the subject. A predicate adjective can tell what kind, which one, how many, or whose. Can you find an adjective in the complete predicate that describes the subject? Because the predicate adjective follows the verb in the sentence, it is written to the right of the verb on the diagram. Write the predicate adjective to the right of the slanted line on your diagram. That slanted line points back toward the subject to remind you that a predicate adjective describes the subject.*

6. *Go back and look again at the simple subject. Are there any words that describe the subject that come before the verb? These adjectives can tell what kind, which one, how many, or whose. Also look for the articles (a, an, the), because they act like adjectives. Write each adjective on a slanted line below the subject it describes.*

7. *Look again at the direct object. Are there any words that describe the direct object? These adjectives can tell what kind, which one, how many, or whose. Also look for the articles (a, an, the), because they act like adjectives. Write each adjective on a slanted line below the direct object it describes.*

8. *Look again at the predicate adjective. Is there an adverb in the sentence, such as* too, very, really, quite, so, extremely, rather *or* slightly, *that describes the predicate adjective? These adverbs tell to what extent. Write one of these adverbs (*too, very, really, quite, so, extremely, rather, *or* slightly) *on the slanted line beneath the adjective it describes.*

Answer Key: 1.   Arabian camels have one hump; Bactrian camels have two humps.
(Ask questions 1, 2, 3, 4, 6, 7, then 2, 3, 4, 6, 7)

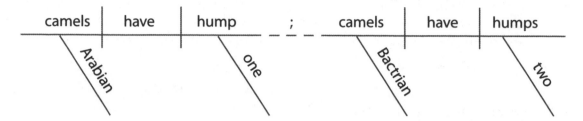

2.   Our baby loves applesauce, but she hates peas.
(Ask questions 1, 2, 3, 4, 6, 7, then 2, 3, 4, 6, 7)

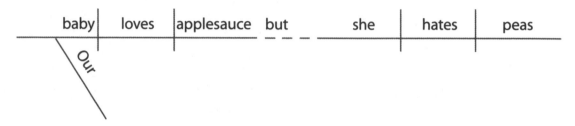

3.   Some peppers are quite mild, but this pepper is extremely hot!
(Ask questions 1, 2, 3, 5, 6, 8, then 2, 3, 5, 6, 8)

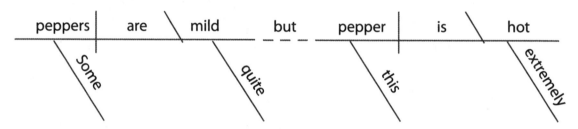

4.   Those mountains are so enormous, and these lakes are really clear.
(Ask questions 1, 2, 3, 5, 6, 8, then 2, 3, 5, 6, 8)

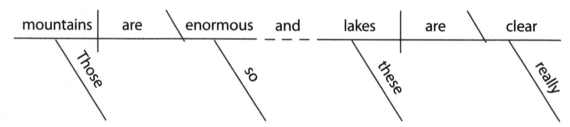

Learn to Proofread: Insert a Semicolon

Instructor: Today you will learn one last proofreaders' mark. Look in your workbook at **Exercise 9**. There is a semicolon with an arrowhead underneath it. When you see that mark, you should insert a semicolon. Look at the sample sentence in **Exercise 9**. Read that aloud.

Workbook: Echidnas have no teeth their sticky tongues lap up ants.

Instructor: "Echidnas have no teeth; their sticky tongues lap up ants" is a compound sentence that needs a semicolon. Now let's review all the proofreaders' marks you have learned. Read the sentences in **Exercise 10**. Use your proofreaders' marks to show the errors in capitalization and punctuation.

Workbook:

Proofreaders' Mark	Meaning
ɓ (lc)	make lowercase
b (caps)	capitalize
⨀	insert period
⌄	insert apostrophe
?	insert question mark
∧	insert comma
⌄	insert beginning quotation mark
⌄	insert ending quotation mark
⌄	insert semicolon

Answer Key: I asked my brother do you know what a monotreme is He didn't know the answer (caps)

I explained that a monotreme is a kind of mammal that lays eggs. An Echidna is a (lc)

monotreme a Platypus is also a monotreme. (lc)

═══════════════════════════════════════

Optional Dictation Exercise

The following sentences are adapted from *The Magician's Nephew* by C. S. Lewis. While exploring passages between attics in a row house, Polly and Digory unexpectedly discovered Digory's mysterious Uncle Andrew. He cunningly offered Polly a yellow ring. I am going to read you a compound sentence that joins two simple sentences with a semicolon. After you write the words, see if you can find where the semicolon should go.

Dictation: Polly had now quite got over her fright and felt sure that the old gentleman was not mad; there was certainly something strangely attractive about those bright rings.

Optional Follow-Up

Draw lines to match any of the following fragments from Column A to the fragments in Column B to make grammatically correct (but possibly silly) sentences.

Column A (Subjects)	Column B (Predicates)
The spunky fox terrier	chewed the man's shoe to shreds.
Last month's bologna sandwich	smelled like a garbage heap.
The rotund pig	grunted, snorted, and squealed.
The prize-winning chili	tasted spicy and delicious.
The wet swimsuits	dripped all over the floor.
The ninja	ducked silently into the shadows.
The fussy baby	needed to drink a bottle and take a nap.
The famous opera singer	dressed as a princess for the final song.

LESSON 73

Summary Exercise: Abraham Lincoln

Read "The Height of the Ridiculous" (Lesson 66) three times to the student. Then ask the student to try to say parts of the first through seventh stanzas along with you (or the tape recorder).

Instructor: Today I am going to read a selection aloud to you from a biography. Do you remember what a biography is? (*Give the student time to tell you if he knows.*) A biography is the true written history of a person's life. I will read you a short portion of a biography of Abraham Lincoln written by a man named Russell Freedman. The selection is about Lincoln's education. He had been able to go to school only "by littles," a few weeks one winter, maybe a month the next. I will read the selection only once. (*If the student is a fluent reader, you may choose to have* him *read it aloud or silently*). Then I want you to tell me in your own words what you remember.

Abraham Lincoln

Mostly, he educated himself by borrowing books and newspapers. There are many stories about Lincoln's efforts to find enough books to satisfy him in that backwoods country. Those he liked he read again and again, losing himself in the adventures of *Robinson Crusoe* or the magical tales of *The Arabian Nights*. He was thrilled by a biography of George Washington, with its stirring account of the Revolutionary War. And he came to love the rhyme and rhythm of poetry, reciting passages from Shakespeare or the Scottish poet Robert Burns at the drop of a hat. He would carry a book out to the field with him, so he could read at the end of each plow furrow, while the horse was getting its breath. When noon came, he would sit under a tree and read while he ate. "I never saw Abe after he was twelve that he didn't have a book in his hand or in his pocket," Dennis Hanks remembered.

LESSON 74

Review: Four Kinds of Verbs
Review: Direct Objects, Indirect Objects, Predicate Nominatives, and Predicate
    Adjectives

Read "The Height of the Ridiculous" (Lesson 66) three times to the student. Then ask the student to try to say parts of the first through eighth stanzas along with you (or the tape recorder).

Instructor: Let's review the definition of a verb. A verb is a word that does an action, shows a state of being, links two words together, or helps another verb. Say that with me two times.

TOGETHER (two times): A verb is a word that does an action, shows a state of being, links two words together, or helps another verb.

Instructor: **Action verbs** show action. *Find, choose,* and *carry* are all action verbs. An action verb is sometimes followed by a direct object that receives the action of the verb. Now you will find the direct objects in a few sentences. To find the direct object, I will ask you "what" or "whom" after the verb. Read the sentence in **Exercise 1** and look at the diagram as I explain it.

Workbook: Mr. Sherman recommended a book.

Instructor: Recommended what?
Student: *Book*

Instructor: Look at the diagram of this sentence. *Mr. Sherman* is the subject, *recommended* is the verb, and *book* is the direct object. It receives the action of the verb *recommended.* It is divided from the verb by a short line.

Instructor: Read the sentence in **Exercise 2** and look at its diagram.

Workbook: Mr. Sherman read Randall a book.

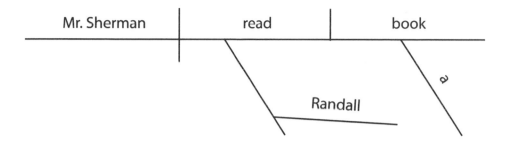

Instructor: What is the verb?
Student: *Read*

Instructor: What is the subject? Who read?
Student: *Mr. Sherman*

Instructor: Read what?
Student: *Book*

Instructor: *Book* is the direct object. (Mr. Sherman certainly didn't read Randall!) *Book* receives the action of the verb *read*. This sentence also has an indirect object. An indirect object is a noun or pronoun that is **between** the action verb and the direct object of a sentence. It answers the question "to whom" or "for whom" the action is done, but the words *to* or *for* are usually not in the sentence. *To* or *for* are just understood. What is the indirect object of the sentence "Mr. Sherman read Randall a book" Read a book to whom?
Student: *Randall*

Instructor: *Randall* is the indirect object. It tells to whom the book was read. The indirect object *Randall* is written underneath the verb, on the little horizontal line. When diagramming indirect objects, **nothing is written on the slanted line.** An indirect object is diagrammed on the part of the frame that is usually used for a prepositional phrase. Remember, an indirect object answers the question "to whom" or "for whom." The prepositions *to* or *for* are not written on the diagram; they are just understood.

Instructor: Look at **Exercise 3**. **Helping verbs** help other verbs. Chant the list of helping verbs with me.

Together: Am [clap]
Is [clap]

Are, was, were. [clap]
Be [clap]
Being [clap]
Been. [clap] [clap]
Have, has, had [clap]
Do, does, did [clap]
Shall, will, should, would, may, might, must [clap, clap]
Can, could!

Instructor: Read the sentences in **Exercise 4**. Circle the helping verbs and underline the action verbs. There may be more than one helping verb in a sentence. Each helping verb helps the action verb in the sentence make sense by showing time. Draw an arrow from each helping verb to the action verb it helps to show time. Then tell me if the time in each sentence is in the past, in the present, or in the future.

Answer Key: 1. I will be memorizing.   (in the future)

        2. A snowstorm is coming.   (in the present)

        3. Woodpeckers have been pecking!   (in the past)

Instructor: Another type of verb, a **state of being verb**, just shows that you exist. Let's chant the state of being verbs together. These are the same as those in the first part of the helping verb chant that is written in **Exercise 3**.

TOGETHER: Am [clap]
Is [clap]
Are, was, were. [clap]
Be [clap]
Being [clap]
Been. [clap] [clap]

Instructor: In **Exercise 5** read the sentences with state of being verbs. Circle the state of being verb in each sentence.

Answer Key: 1. The spacecraft was in outer space.

        2. Three passengers were on board.

        3. They are in the cabin.

Instructor: Look at **Exercise 6**. There is one more type of verb: a **linking verb**. Linking verbs link, or join, two words together. These verbs are easy to recognize because they are the same verbs as the state of being verbs: *am, is, are, was, were, be, being, been*. These verbs can do three of the four parts of the verb definition! Say the definition of a verb once more with me.

Together: A verb is a word that does an action, shows a state of being, links two words together, or helps another verb.

Instructor: Read **Exercise 6** to me.

Workbook: The verbs **am, is, are, was, were, be, being, been** can

- help another verb

- show a state of being

- link two words together

Instructor: So if you see the verb *was* in a sentence, you have to read the whole sentence to tell what kind of verb it is. After you read each sentence in **Exercise 7**, I will point out to you how the verb *are* can be used as a helping verb, a state of being verb, or a linking verb. Read Sentence 1.

Answer Key: H.V.
1.   They are orbiting.

Instructor: *Are* is a helping verb in that sentence. *Are* helps the verb *orbiting* by showing it is in the present time. Write "H.V." for helping verb over *are*. Read Sentence 2.

Answer Key: S.B.V.
2.   They are in space.

Instructor: *Are* just shows that someone exists in space. *Are* is a state of being verb in that sentence. Write "S.B.V." for state of being verb over *are*. Read Sentence 3.

Answer Key: L.V.
3.   They were excited.

Instructor: *Were* is a linking verb in that sentence. It links the subject *They* with the predicate adjective *excited*. Remember, adjectives tell what kind, which one, how many, and whose. *Excited* describes what kind of people they were. Write "L.V." for linking verb over *were*.

Instructor: In **Exercise 8**, read the sentence and look at its diagram.

Workbook: Modern rockets are powerful.

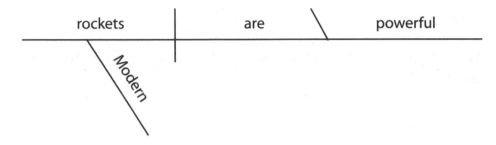

Instructor: What is the linking verb?
Student: *Are*

Instructor: What is the subject? What are?
Student: *Rockets*

Instructor: The linking verb *are* links the subject *rockets* to an adjective in the predicate. Answer me with an adjective from the predicate. Rockets are what?
Student: *Powerful*

Instructor: There is an adjective in the subject that also describes rockets. What kind of rockets?
Student: *Modern*

Instructor: Linking verbs can also link subjects with nouns and pronouns. In **Exercise 9**, read the sentence and look at its diagram. This sentence has a linking verb and a predicate nominative.

Workbook: Neil Armstrong was an astronaut.

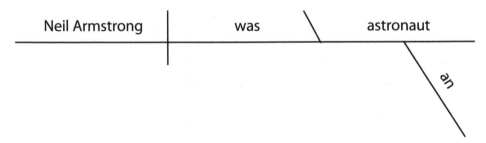

Instructor: What is the linking verb?
Student: *Was*

Instructor: What is the subject? Who was?

Student: *Neil Armstrong*

Instructor: This sentence has a predicate nominative that renames the subject *Neil Armstrong*. Neil Armstrong was what?

Student: *Astronaut*

Instructor: What is the adjective that describes the predicate nominative *astronaut*?

Student: *An*

LESSON 75

New: Comparative and Superlative Adjectives
Review: Adjectives

Read "The Height of the Ridiculous" (Lesson 66) three times to the student. Then ask the student to try to say parts of the poem along with you (or the tape recorder).

Instructor: Let's begin this lesson by saying the definition of an adjective together.

TOGETHER: An adjective is a word that describes a noun or pronoun. Adjectives tell what kind, which one, how many, and whose.

Instructor: **Adjectives tell what kind.** There are many kinds of tomatoes. *Yellow* tomatoes. *Tiny* tomatoes. *Sweet* tomatoes. *Giant* tomatoes. *Juicy* tomatoes. These adjectives all tell what kind of tomatoes. Can you think of another adjective that tells what kind of tomatoes?

Student: *[Red, Cherry, Fat, etc.] tomato*

Instructor: **Adjectives tell which one.** *This* umbrella. *That* elephant. *These* questions. *Those* answers. The *first* frost. The *last* minute. These adjectives tell which one. Which birthday will you celebrate next? Your tenth birthday? Your eleventh birthday? Answer me with an adjective that tells which one.

Student: *My [tenth, eleventh, etc.] birthday*

Instructor: **Adjectives tell how many.** How many toys do you have? *Two* trains, *numerous* marbles, *some* puzzles, *no* model helicopters. Answer me with an adjective that tells how many. How many games do you have? Seven games? Many games? Several games?

Student: *I have [adjective] games.*

Instructor: **Adjectives tell whose.** These include words like *Tan's* rice, *Father's* bowls, and also the personal pronouns that show possession (we call them the possessive pronouns): *my, mine, your, yours, his, her, hers, its, our, ours, their, theirs.* Answer me with an adjective that tells whose. Whose chopsticks are these?

Student: *These are [his, hers, Tan's, etc].*

Instructor: You already know that adjectives can tell what kind. "Bright comets blaze across the sky." What kind of comets? Bright. But imagine you see three comets. They are all bright. How can you tell them apart? Read aloud the list in **Exercise 1**.

Workbook: **bright** comet

brighter comet

brightest comet

Instructor: Look at the adjectives in bold print. These adjectives compare the comets. They are all bright. But the second comet is brighter than the first comet. And the third comet is the brightest of all. Read aloud the three groups of sentences in **Exercise 2**. Pay special attention to the adjectives in bold print. These adjectives compare.

Workbook: The comets we saw had tails.
The tail of the first comet is **long**.
The tail of the second comet is **longer**.
The tail of the third comet is **longest**.

The planets vary in size.
Uranus is a **large** planet.
Saturn is a **larger** planet.
Jupiter is the **largest** planet.

You can tell the relative temperature of a star by its color.
Red stars are **hot**.
White stars are **hotter**.
Blue stars are **hottest**.

Instructor: Adjectives like *longer*, *larger*, and *hotter* are called **comparative**, because they **compare** two things. Comparative adjectives usually end in **er**. Adjectives that end in **est** are called **superlative**. Do you hear the word *super* in *superlative*? A sun-sized star is big. A giant star is bigger. The biggest star of all is a **Super** Giant.

Instructor: Usually comparative adjectives end in **er** and superlative adjectives end in **est**. But there are some comparative and superlative adjectives that don't follow the regular pattern. Read the list of irregular comparative and superlative adjectives in **Exercise 3**.

Workbook: Irregular Comparative and Superlative Adjectives

Adjective	Comparative Form	Superlative Form
good	better	best
bad	worse	worst
little	less	least
much	more	most
many	more	most

Instructor: Read the sentences in **Exercise 4**. For each set of sentences, fill in the correct comparative and superlative adjectives. You can look at the chart in **Exercise 3** if you need help.

Answer Key:
1. A brightly lit city is **bad** for stargazing.

   A cloudy night is <u>worse</u> for stargazing.

   A rainstorm is <u>worst</u> for stargazing.

2. A reflector telescope is **good**.

   A refractor telescope is <u>better</u>.

   A catadioptric telescope is <u>best</u>.

3. **Many** astronauts are space travelers.

   <u>More</u> astronauts plan to travel.

   <u>Most</u> astronauts help do research.

4. New astronauts spend **much** time planning.

   They spend <u>more</u> time studying.

   They spend the <u>most</u> time training.

5. Third graders study a **little** astronomy.

   Second graders study <u>less</u> astronomy.

   First graders study the <u>least</u> amount of astronomy.

Instructor: In **Exercise 5,** I will help you diagram three sentences containing comparative and superlative adjectives. You read the sentence. I will ask you questions as you fill in the diagram. Remember to copy the words exactly as they appear in the sentence. If the word begins with a capital letter in the sentence, it should also be capitalized in the diagram.

Use the following dialogue to help the student fill in each diagram. After the student reads each sentence, you will prompt him with the questions in italics listed across from that sentence.

1a. *What is the linking verb? This verb links the subject to a word in the complete predicate. Write the verb to the right of the center line.*

1b. *What is the verb? Write the verb to the right of your center line.*

2. *Find the subject. Ask "who" or "what" before the verb. [Prompt the student with a specific question like "What is?" or "What glows?"] Write the subject to the left of the center line on your frame.*

3. *Now you have found the two most basic parts of the sentence. Go back and look again at the subject. Are there any words that describe the subject? These adjectives can tell what kind, which one, how many, or whose. Also look for the articles (a, an, the), because they act like adjectives. Write each adjective on a slanted line below the subject it describes.*

4. *This sentence contains a predicate adjective. This adjective is in the complete predicate of the sentence, but it describes the subject. A predicate adjective can tell what kind, which one, how many, or whose. Can you find an adjective that follows the verb that still describes the subject? Because the predicate adjective follows the verb in the sentence, it is written to the right of the verb on the diagram. Write the predicate adjective to the right of the slanted line on your diagram. That slanted line points back toward the subject to remind you that a predicate adjective describes the subject.*

Answer Key: 1.   That supernova is large.   (Ask questions 1a, 2, 3, and 4)

2. A larger supernova glows.   (Ask questions 1b, 2, and 3)

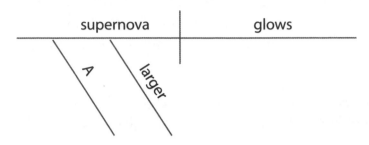

3. The largest supernova dazzles.   (Ask questions 1b, 2, and 3)

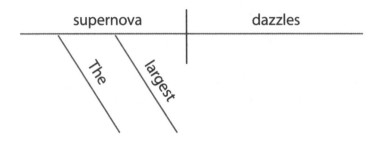

Optional Dictation Exercise

The following sentences are adapted from *Look at the Sky...and Tell the Weather* by Eric Sloane. Tell the student, "Can you predict the weather by looking at the sky? Eric Sloane said that one of life's greatest joys can be simply looking at the sky. He tells how older generations forecast the weather just from observing the sky. And he tells how wet and dry weather affects wood in everything from houses to bridges. Builders did not cover wooden bridges just to keep off snow and rain. Your dictation today will tell you another reason they covered old bridges."

After the student has written the dictation, ask him to find a superlative adjective (*bad, worse,* ***worst***).

Dictation: They cover bridges just as much to keep the sun out. A dry bridge will loosen its joints and sag. That is the worst thing a wooden bridge can do.

LESSON 76

New: Comparative and Superlative Adverbs

Read "The Height of the Ridiculous" (Lesson 66) three times to the student. Then ask the student to try to say parts of the poem along with you (or the tape recorder).

Instructor: Let's begin this lesson by saying the definition of an adverb together.

TOGETHER: An adverb is a word that describes a verb, an adjective, or another adverb. Adverbs tell how, when, where, how often, and to what extent.

Instructor: **Adverbs tell how.** How do trucks transport goods across the country? They transport *steadily*. Can you think of one or more adverbs that tell how trucks transport goods across the country?

Student: *They transport [quickly, noisily, rapidly, etc.].*

Instructor: **Adverbs tell when.** When will the delivery truck arrive at the supermarket? It will arrive *tonight*. Can you think of one or more adverbs that tell when the truck will arrive?

Student: *It will arrive [late, tomorrow, today, etc.].*

Instructor: **Adverbs tell where.** Where will the driver park? He will park *here*. Can you think of one or more adverbs that tell where the driver will park?

Student: *He will park [there, nearby, close, anywhere].*

Instructor: **Adverbs tell how often**. How often does the truck driver deliver goods? He delivers *daily*. Can you think of one or more adverbs that tell how often the driver delivers?

Student: *He delivers [weekly, often, regularly, etc.].*

Instructor: **Adverbs tell to what extent**. You have learned eight of these adverbs: *too, very, really, quite, rather, so, slightly,* and *extremely*. These adverbs typically describe adjectives or other adverbs. After a long cross-country trip, to what extent do you think the driver was tired? He was *very* tired. I will say the list of "to what extent" adverbs again, and you will choose one or more that describe to what extent the driver was tired: *too, really, quite, rather, so, slightly, extremely, very.*

441

Student: *The driver was [too, really, quite, rather, so, slightly, extremely, very] tired.*

Instructor: You already know that adverbs can tell how. "Trains carry goods to their destination fast." How do they carry goods to their destination? *Fast.* But imagine you have three different ways to transport goods. They can all transport goods fast. How can you tell them apart? Read aloud the sentences in **Exercise 1**.

Workbook: Trains carry goods to their destination **fast.**

Delivery trucks carry goods to their destination **faster.**

Airplanes carry goods to their destination **fastest.**

Instructor: Look at the adverbs in bold print. These adjectives compare the three modes of transportation. They all carry goods fast. But delivery trucks carry goods faster than trains. And airplanes carry goods fastest. Read aloud the three groups of sentences in **Exercise 2**. Pay special attention to the adverbs in bold print. These adverbs compare.

Workbook: Helicopters fly **high.**
Cargo planes fly **higher.**
Jetliners fly **highest.**

The horse-drawn cart from Ireland will arrive **late.**
The ox-drawn cart from India will arrive **later.**
The farmer pushing the wheelbarrow from China will arrive the **latest.**

A scuba diver dives **deep.**
A military submarine dives **deeper.**
The small submarine the *Trieste* dives the **deepest.**

Instructor: Adverbs like *higher, later,* and *deeper* are called comparative, because they compare two things. Just like comparative adjectives, comparative adverbs usually end in **er**. Adverbs that end in **est** are called superlative: *highest, latest,* and *deepest.*

Instructor: Usually comparative adverbs end in **er** and superlative adverbs end in **est**. But there are some comparative and superlative adverbs that don't follow the regular pattern. Read the list of irregular comparative and superlative adverbs in **Exercise 3**.

Workbook: Irregular Comparative and Superlative Adverbs

Adverb	Comparative Form	Superlative Form
well	better	best
badly	worse	worst
little	less	least
much	more	most

Instructor: Read the sentences in **Exercise 4**. For each set of sentences, fill in the correct comparative and superlative adjectives. You can look at the chart in **Exercise 3** if you need help.

Answer Key:
1. Private jets cost **much** to build.

   Supersonic airliners cost <u>more</u> to build.

   Spacecraft cost the <u>most</u> to build.

2. Driving a hybrid car pollutes **little**.

   Riding an electric scooter pollutes <u>less</u>.

   Walking pollutes the <u>least</u>.

3. Small cars maneuver **well**.

   Motorcycles maneuver <u>better</u>.

   In-line skates maneuver <u>best</u>.

4. Old freight trains shook you up **badly**.

   Old tractors shook you up <u>worse</u>.

   A covered wagon shook you up the <u>worst</u>.

Instructor: In **Exercise 5** I will help you diagram three sentences containing comparative and superlative adverbs. You read the sentence. I will ask you questions as you fill in the diagram. Remember to copy the words exactly as they appear in the sentence. If the word begins with a capital letter in the sentence, it should also be capitalized in the diagram.

Use the following dialogue to help the student fill in each diagram.

First Language Lessons for the Well-Trained Mind, Level 4

1. What is the verb? Write the verb to the right of your center line.

2. Find the subject. Ask "who" or "what" before the verb. [Prompt the student with a specific question like "What were built?"] Write the subject to the left of the center line on your frame.

3. Now you have found the two most basic parts of the sentence. Go back and look again at the subject. Are there any words that describe the subject? These adjectives can tell what kind, which one, how many, or whose. Also look for the articles (a, an, the), because they act like adjectives. Write each adjective on a slanted line below the subject it describes. (Note: Tell the student that a hyphenated word such as four-lane is considered to be one adjective.)

4. Look again at the verb. Is there a word that describes the verb? This is an adverb that could tell how, when, where, or how often. Write the adverb on the slanted line below the verb it describes.

Answer Key: 1. Some country lanes were built straight.

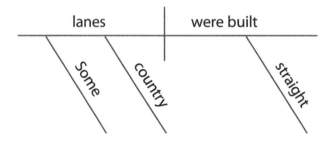

2. Four-lane highways were built straighter.

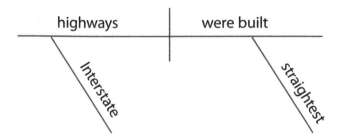

3. Interstate highways were built straightest.

444

LESSON 77

Review: Four Types of Sentences
Review: Pronouns (Personal, Demonstrative, and Interrogative)

Read "The Height of the Ridiculous" (Lesson 66) three times to the student. Then ask the student to try to say the whole poem with you (or the tape recorder). The student should practice saying the whole poem to himself in a mirror.

The sentence content for this lesson is taken from *The Story of Salt* by Mark Kurlansky.

Instructor: Let's review how to diagram commands and questions. In **Exercise 1**, read the command sentence.

Workbook: Gather salt crystals near the ocean.

Instructor: Now I will help you diagram this sentence onto the empty frame in **Exercise 1** of your workbook. This sentence contains a prepositional phrase. What is it?

Student: *Near the ocean*

Instructor: Put a box around "near the ocean" and ignore the words inside that box while you find the main parts of the sentence. What is the verb?

Student: *Gather*

Instructor: *Gather* is the verb. Write the word *Gather* on the verb line. Remember to capitalize *Gather* because it is capitalized in the sentence. Now find the subject. Remember, command sentences do have a subject, but the subject is not written in the sentence. It is understood to be the word *you*. Someone is telling you to gather salt crystals. She does not command you by saying "You gather salt crystals"; she simply says "Gather salt crystals." So, again, what is the subject of this command sentence? Who should gather salt crystals?

Student: *You*

Instructor: *You* is the subject. Write the word *you* on the subject line. Because the subject *you* is not written in the sentence but is just understood, put *you* in parentheses.

Instructor: Look again at the verb *Gather.* Is there a direct object that receives the action of the verb? I will ask you a question that will help you find the direct object. Answer me with one word. Gather what?

Student: *Crystals*

If the student answers "salt," tell him that the word *salt* is being used as an adjective in this sentence (not a noun) to describe what kind of crystals. A direct object must be a noun or pronoun.

Instructor: Write the direct object *crystals* to the right of the verb on your diagram. The direct object is separated from the verb by a short, straight line. Are there any words that describe the direct object *crystals*?

Student: *Salt*

Instructor: *Salt* is an adjective that tells what kind of crystals. Write the word *salt* on the first slanted line beneath *crystals*.

Instructor: Look at the prepositional phrase in the box. "Near the ocean" is an adverb phrase that describes the verb. It tells where. Answer me with the prepositional phrase. Where should you gather?

Student: *Near the ocean*

Instructor: Write the preposition *near* on the slanted line below the verb. What is the object of the preposition? Near what?

Student: *Ocean*

Instructor: Write *ocean* on the flat line. Are there any adjectives that describe *ocean*?

Student: *The*

Instructor: Write this adjective on the slanted line beneath the noun it describes. Now your diagram is complete.

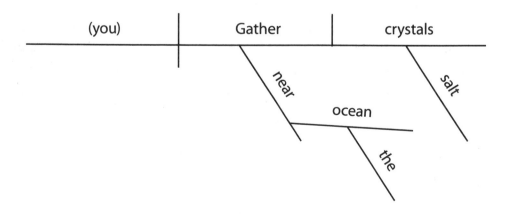

Instructor: In **Exercise 2**, read the question.

Workbook: Can you preserve food with salt?

Instructor: Now I will help you diagram this sentence.

Instructor: In order to find the subject of a question sentence, it is helpful to rearrange the words in the question so that it becomes a statement. Read the question in **Exercise 2** again, and rearrange the words to make a statement. Write the statement on the line below.

Answer Key: You can preserve food with salt.

Instructor: Now diagram this sentence on the empty frame in **Exercise 2** of your workbook. This sentence contains a prepositional phrase. What is it?

Student: *With salt*

Instructor: Put a box around "with salt" and ignore the words inside that box while you find the main parts of the sentence. There are two verbs in this sentence: a helping verb and an action verb. What are those verbs?

Student: *Can preserve*

Instructor: Write both of these verbs on your verb line. Remember to capitalize *Can* on the diagram because it is capitalized in the sentence. What is the subject of the question "Can you preserve food with salt?" Think of the statement "You can preserve food with salt." Who can preserve food?

Student: *You*

Instructor: Look again at *Can preserve*. Is there a direct object that receives the action of the verb? I will ask you a question that will help you find the direct object. Can preserve what?

Student: *Food*

Instructor: Write the direct object *food* to the right of the verb on your diagram. The direct object is separated from the verb by a short, straight line.

Instructor: Look at the prepositional phrase in the box. "With salt" is an adverb phrase that describes the verb. It tells how. Answer me with the prepositional phrase. How do you preserve food?

Student: *With salt*

Instructor: Write the preposition *with* on the slanted line below the verb. What is the object of the preposition? With what?

Student: *Salt*

Instructor: Write *salt* on the flat line. Now your diagram is complete.

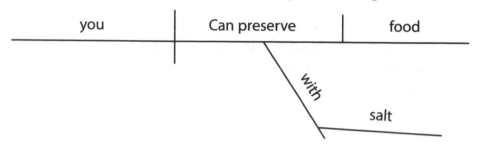

Remind the student that he is not to put punctuation on the diagram. If the student is curious, you **can** preserve food with salt. Salting food removes the moisture and rids fresh food of harmful bacteria. Add salt to milk or cream to make cheese. Add salt to cabbage to make sauerkraut. Add salt to cucumbers to make pickles. Add salt to meat to make ham or bacon. Add salt to fish to make salt fish. Salt was the first preservative, and it allowed people to travel long distances for the first time (they could take food with them).

Instructor: Let's review pronouns. Say the definition of a pronoun with me.

TOGETHER: A pronoun is a word used in the place of a noun.

Instructor: Now we are going to practice the list of personal pronouns.

If the student already knows the list of pronouns, have him say them alone from memory once. If he needs to review, say the list with him three times. Here is the list for your reference.

<u>Pronouns</u>
I, me, my, mine
You, your, yours
He, she, him, her, it
His, hers, its
We, us, our, ours
They, them, their, theirs

Instructor: A pronoun is a word that takes the place of a noun. There is a special name for the noun that is replaced. It is called the antecedent. Read the sentence in **Exercise 3**. The pronoun is in bold. The antecedent is circled. There is an arrow that starts at the pronoun and points back to its antecedent. Remember, the antecedent is the noun the pronoun replaces.

Workbook: When Li Bing drilled a hole in the ground, **he** found an underground spring of very salty water.

Instructor: If a pronoun replaces more than one person, place, thing, or idea, it can have more than one antecedent noun. Read the sentence in **Exercise 4**.

Workbook: Roman fish sauce is made by combining fish intestines and salt in earthen jars until **they** ferment into a smelly liquid.

Instructor: Read the sentences in **Exercise 5**. The pronoun is in bold. Find the antecedent and circle it. Then draw an arrow from the pronoun to its antecedent, the noun the pronoun replaces. The third sentence has two pronouns that each have their own antecedent.

Answer Key: King Louis XIV of France raised taxes on salt for **his** people.

When the Incas, Mayans, and Aztecs lost power, **they** lost control of the local salt trade.

Americans love salty ketchup; **we** put **it** on everything!

Instructor: The personal pronouns can be divided into three groups: subject pronouns, object pronouns, and possessive pronouns. The possessive pronouns act like adjectives that tell whose: *my, mine, your, yours, his, her, hers, its, our, ours, their,* and *theirs.* Read each sentence in **Exercise 6** of your workbook. Circle the possessive pronoun that acts like an adjective that tells whose. Then draw an arrow to the noun it describes. Some of these possessive pronouns are predicate adjectives.

Answer Key: 1. His car shuddered and died.

2. The house down the street is theirs.
   (Note: *theirs* is a predicate adjective)

3. Digging holes makes my back ache.

4. The cake in the middle is (ours).
   (Note: *ours* is a predicate adjective)

5. The best drawing was (hers).
   (Note: *hers* is a predicate adjective)

6. (Her) Spanish accent is beautiful.

7. Mom's rings will be (yours) one day.
   (Note: *yours* is a predicate adjective)

Instructor: The other two groups of personal pronouns are subject pronouns and object pronouns. Let's review the difference between subject pronouns and object pronouns. Subject pronouns are the pronouns that are typically used as subjects of sentences. Object pronouns are the pronouns used as objects in sentences. Read the lists of subject pronouns and object pronouns in **Exercise 7** of your workbook.

Workbook:

Subject Pronouns	Object Pronouns
I	me
he	him
she	her
we	us
they	them

Instructor: Subject pronouns are typically used as subjects. You also use a subject pronoun for a predicate nominative, since it **renames** the subject. Object pronouns are the pronouns used as objects, like direct objects, indirect objects, and objects of the preposition. Read the sentences in **Exercise 8** in your workbook and circle the subject and object pronouns. Write "S" over a pronoun if it is a subject pronoun used as the subject or predicate nominative. If the pronoun is an object pronoun used as the direct or indirect object or an object of the preposition in the sentence, write "O" over it.

Answer Key:

          S   O

1. (He) played (me) a song on the piano.

          S   S

2. (It) is (I).

S   O

3. (They) baked (us) a cake for dessert.

        S   O

4. (We) asked to stay near (her.)

      S   O

5. (I) forgave (him)

Instructor: In addition to personal pronouns, you also learned demonstrative pronouns: *this, that, these,* and *those.* These pronouns demonstrate, or point out, something. Look at **Exercise 9** in your workbook. Read the first sentence.

Workbook: <u>This</u> is my favorite holiday.

Instructor: Now let's think of a noun for which the underlined pronoun could stand. What is your favorite holiday?

Student: *[Christmas, Thanksgiving, Independence Day, etc.]*

Instructor: The pronoun *This* stands for the noun [*holiday student chose*]. [*Holiday student chose*] is your favorite holiday. **This** is your favorite holiday. Now read the rest of the sentences in **Exercise 9**. After you read each sentence, substitute a noun for which the underlined pronoun could stand.

Workbook: <u>That</u> is very noisy.
Student: *[The lawnmower, The parakeet, The videogame, etc.] is very noisy.*

Workbook: <u>These</u> smell terrible!
Student: *[The dogs, The garage cans, The diapers, etc.] smell terrible!*

Workbook: <u>Those</u> are very nutritious.
Student: *[The nuts, The carrots, The granola bars, etc.] are very nutritious.*

Instructor: Now we are going to review pronouns that we use when we ask questions. These question pronouns have a special name. They are called **interrogative pronouns** (Lesson 38). The word *interrogative* means "asking a question." So, interrogative pronouns are pronouns you use when you are asking a question. They come near the beginning of a sentence. Read the list of interrogative pronouns in **Exercise 10** and find and circle the interrogative pronouns in the sentences below.

After the student has completed the exercise, you can have him ask you questions and you can read him the answers in italics.

Answer Key: (Who) first discovered oil in a salt dome?

Answer: Edwin Drake, in 1859

(What) was the first civilization to produce salt on a grand scale?

Answer: The Egyptians

(Which) was the animal used to carry salt across the Sahara Desert?

Answer: The camel

(Who), according to legend, discovered that a shellfish could be used to dye cloth purple?

Answer: The story is that Hercules and his dog were walking on a beach when his dog bit a shellfish called a murex. The dog's mouth turned purple, and Hercules had the brilliant idea that murex could be used to dye cloth. (But you also needed salt, of course!)

With (whom) did England make an alliance for salt?

Answer: Portugal. England had lots of fish; Portugal had lots of salt needed to preserve that fish.

(Which) comes from the Latin word for salt: *salary* or *soldier*?

Answer: Salary! The Latin word for salt is "sal." It is the root of salary, *because Roman soldiers were often paid in salt (that was their salary).*

(What) is a nef?

Answer: A nef is a large and beautiful French salt dispenser. (The word nef *means "ship" in French). It was always set near the king at the dining table.*

(Whom) could you ask for more information about salt?

Answer: Your librarian

LESSON 78

New: Interjections
Review: Direct Address
Review: Introductory Elements

Read "The Height of the Ridiculous" (Lesson 66) three times to the student. Then ask the student to say the poem along with you or the tape recorder. If the student is ready, he should recite the poem to real people today. If he is not, continue practicing daily until he is ready.

Instructor: [Student's name], are you ready to begin today's lesson? I just addressed you by name. When you are talking directly to someone, you often say a person's name to get his attention. This is called **direct address**, because you address someone directly. Remember, when you write a sentence that includes a direct address, you use a comma to separate the name of the person spoken to from the rest of the sentence. You use one comma to separate the name if that name is at the beginning or the end of a sentence. You must use two commas to separate the name if it is in the middle of a sentence. Read the sentences in **Exercise 1** and underline the noun of direct address.

Answer Key: 1. <u>Gordon</u>, you are late.

2. You are the winner, <u>Corrine</u>, and I congratulate you!

3. You are an excellent photographer, <u>Miss Simpkins</u>.

Instructor: A noun of direct address does not have a function in a sentence; it is not the subject or an object. When you diagram a sentence with a noun of direct address, that noun is placed on a line that floats above the sentence diagram to show that it does not have a function. It doesn't *do* anything. In **Exercise 2**, you will see diagrams of the sentences you just read. Write each noun of direct address on the floating line above the main diagram.

First Language Lessons for the Well-Trained Mind, Level 4

Answer Key:

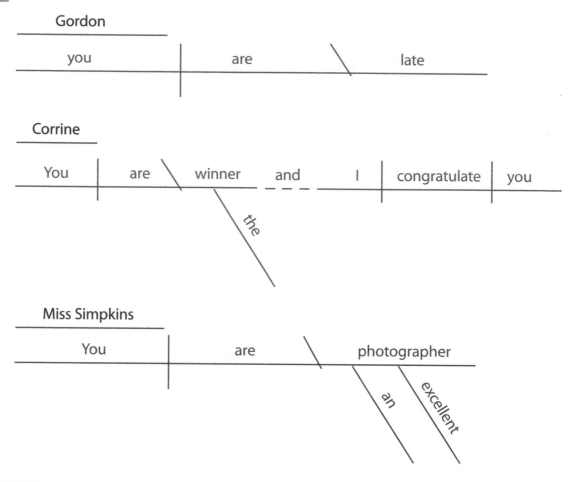

In this lesson the student will learn how to identify, define, and diagram an interjection. Although interjections are rarely used in formal or academic writing, the student will still encounter them in creative writing and dialogue.

Instructor: Today we are going to talk about another part of speech called an **interjection**. When you suddenly say just one or two words with strong feeling, we call that an interjection. Interjections might show excitement ("Hooray!") or surprise ("Yikes!") or concern ("Oh no!"). An interjection is followed by a comma or an exclamation point that separates it from the main sentence. Say the definition of an interjection with me three times: An interjection is a word that expresses sudden or strong feeling.

TOGETHER (three times): An interjection is a word that expresses sudden or strong feeling.

Instructor: Read the sentences in **Exercise 3**, and read the interjection with strong feeling.

Workbook: **Quick!** The green slime is oozing toward us!

Whew, you managed to avoid it.

Outstanding! It evaporates in the sunlight!

Instructor: Notice that in these sentences, each interjection is followed by a comma or an exclamation point that separates it from the main sentence. If the interjection is followed by a comma, the next word is **not** capitalized. If the interjection is followed by an exclamation point, the next word **is** capitalized.

Instructor: Interjections are always separated from the rest of the sentence by a comma or an exclamation point. When you diagram an interjection, you need to separate it from the rest of the sentence diagram. Just like a noun of direct address, an interjection sits on a floating line above the main diagram. In **Exercise 4**, you will see diagrams of two sentences with interjections. Complete each diagram by adding the interjection on the floating line above the main diagram.

Answer Key: 1.   Wow! It's a solar eclipse!

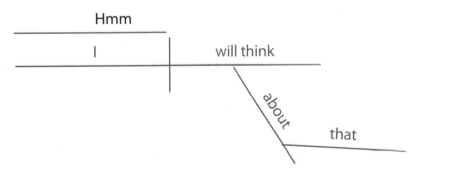

2.   Hmm, I will think about that.

Instructor: You might wonder why some interjections are followed by a comma and others by an exclamation point. Some interjections are strong; they must be said forcefully and with a lot of feeling. "Oh! I am being bitten by fire ants!" These strong interjections need exclamation points. Some other interjections are mild; they can be said casually. "Oh, I forgot to clip my fingernails today." Read aloud the sentences in **Exercise 5**, and see how an interjection can be strong (and need an exclamation point) or mild (and need only a comma).

Workbook: Strong and Mild Interjections

Hey! You just crushed my Venus Fly Trap!
Hey, I'm really sorry.

Whew! We just missed getting hit by an asteroid!
Whew, I'm exhausted.

Ah! An eel is in the tub!
Ah, the bath water feels warm and lovely.

Instructor: Words like *yes* and *no* can be strong interjections. "Yes! My team won the World Series!" or "No! You can't eat those berries because they are poisonous!" *Yes* and *no* can also be answers to questions. Did you remember your pencil? "Yes, I did, "or "No, I forgot it." When used this way, *yes* and *no* are called **response words**, because they are said in response to a question. Read the sentences in **Exercise 6**. The first sentence in each pair has a strong interjection; the second sentence has a response word.

Workbook: **Strong Interjection:** Yes! I just won a gold medal in the Olympics!
Response Word: Yes, I did have to train very hard.

Strong Interjection: No! Don't let the baby topple my Lego tower!
Response Word: No, I didn't put it away when you asked me.

Instructor: Interjections and response words are both called **introductory elements** because they introduce the sentence but have no other function. They are not subjects or verbs or objects. The introductory elements—interjections and response words—and nouns of address are all diagrammed the same way. They are written on a floating line above the main diagram.

Instructor: Now you will diagram four sentences in **Exercise 7** by filling in the frames. When you diagram a sentence with a noun of direct address or introductory element, the first thing you do is write the noun of direct address or the interjection or the response word on the floating line. Then draw a line through that word **in your sentence** so you can focus on the functional words: the nouns, pronouns, verbs, adjectives, adverbs, and prepositions.

Use the following dialogue to help the student complete the diagrams in **Exercise 7**. Follow the instructions closely (for example, "Ask questions 1, 2, 3," etc.) to know which questions to ask.

1.   *Does this sentence have a noun of direct address, interjection, or a response word? Write the word on the floating line above the main diagram and then cross it out in the sentence.*

2. *This sentence has a prepositional phrase. First find the preposition; that's the beginning of the prepositional phrase. Then find the object of the preposition; that's the end of the phrase. Put a box around the entire prepositional phrase, and ignore the words inside the box as you find the other parts of the sentence.*

3. *What is the verb? Write the verb to the right of your center line. [Sentences 3 and 4 have two verbs: a helping verb and a main verb.]*

4. *Find the subject. Ask "who" or "what" before the verb. [Prompt the student with a specific question like "Who has?" or "Who found?"] Write the subject to the left of the center line on your frame.*

5. *Is there a direct object that receives the action of the verb? I will ask you a question that will help you find the direct object.*

   Sentence 1: Have what?

   Sentence 2: Found what?

   Sentence 4: Can borrow what?

   Write the direct object to the right of the verb on your diagram. The direct object is separated from the verb by a short, straight line.

6. *Look again at the direct object. Are there any words that describe the direct object? These adjectives can tell what kind, which one, how many, or whose. Also look for the articles (a, an, the), because they act like adjectives. Write each adjective on a slanted line below the direct object it describes.*

7. *Look again at the verb. Is there a word that describes the verb? This is an adverb that could tell how, when, where, or how often. Write the adverb on the slanted line below the verb it describes.*

8. *Look again at the prepositional phrase inside the box. This is an adverb phrase that describes the verb. An adverb phrase can tell how, when, where, how often, or to what extent. Write the preposition on the slanted line below the verb, and write the object of the preposition on the flat line.*

9. *Are there any words in the prepositional phrase that describe the object of the preposition? These adjectives can tell what kind, which one, how many, or whose. Also look for the articles (a, an, the), because they act like adjectives. Write each adjective on a slanted line below the object of the preposition it describes.*

Answer Key: 1. Clayton, you have overdue library books. (Ask questions 1, 3, 4, 5, and 6)

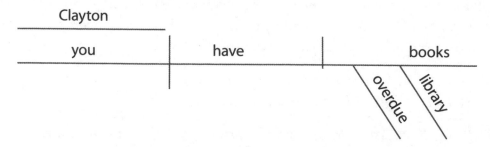

2. Good! You found them under your bed! (Ask questions 1, 2, 3, 4, 5, 8, and 9)

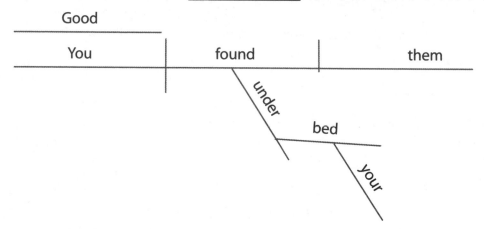

3. Well, we should go to the library now. (Ask questions 1, 2, 3, 4, 7, 8, and 9)

4. Yes, we can borrow more books today. (Ask questions 1, 3, 4, 5, 6, and 7)

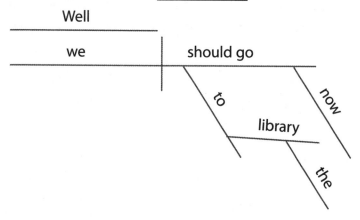

LESSON 79

Review: Abbreviations
Review: Contractions

Review "Afternoon on a Hill" (Lesson 8) today. If the student has trouble remembering the poem, have him practice it daily until he is confident.

This lesson reviews abbreviations learned in Lesson 56. If the student incorrectly writes an abbreviation in an exercise, have him erase it immediately. Write the correct abbreviation on a separate piece of paper and have him copy it *on that same piece of paper.* Then he can write the correct abbreviation in his workbook from memory.

Instructor: In this lesson we are going to review the abbreviations we have learned. Remember, an abbreviation is the shortened form of a word. Your name can be abbreviated. Your initials are the first letters of your first, middle, and last names. Each initial is capitalized and is followed by a period. Write your initials on the line in **Exercise 1** of your workbook.

Instructor: I will call out some titles of respect, and I want you to write the abbreviation for each one in **Exercise 2**.

Doctor	(Dr.)
Mistress	(Mrs.)
Saint	(St.)
Mister	(Mr.)

Instructor: Write your address in **Exercise 3**, using the correct abbreviation for our street, and the state postal abbreviation. Remember to put a comma between the city and state.

Instructor: In **Exercise 4**, you will see a list of the days of the week. Write the abbreviation for the days of the week in the blanks.

Answer Key:

Day of the Week	Abbreviation
Sunday	Sun.
Monday	Mon.
Tuesday	Tues.
Wednesday	Weds.
Thursday	Thurs.
Friday	Fri.
Saturday	Sat.

Instructor: In **Exercise 5**, read each sentence and draw a line through the names of the months that can be abbreviated. Write the correct abbreviation over each month.

Answer Key:

                            Dec.   Jan.   Feb.
The winter months are ~~December~~, ~~January~~, and ~~February~~.

                      Mar.   Apr.
The spring months are ~~March~~, ~~April~~, and May.

                                        Aug.
The summer months are June, July, and ~~August~~.

                    Sept.   Oct.   Nov.
The fall months are ~~September~~, ~~October~~, and ~~November~~.

Instructor: In **Exercise 6**, there is a list of items Selma needs to buy at the home improvement store. Draw a line through each word that can be abbreviated and write its abbreviation above it.

Answer Key:

           in.
120 ~~inches~~ of board

       ft.
8 ~~feet~~ of rope

       yd.
6 ~~yards~~ of chicken wire

       doz.
1 ~~dozen~~ lightbulbs

pt.
1 ~~pint~~ paint thinner

qt.
2 ~~quarts~~ white paint

gal.
1 ~~gallon~~ blue paint

oz.
6 ~~ounces~~ white glue

lb.
25 ~~pounds~~ sand

Instructor: In **Exercise 7**, draw a line through each word that can be abbreviated and write its abbreviation above it.

Answer Key:

oz.
6 ~~ounces~~ chocolate chips

oz.
6 ~~ounces~~ butterscotch chips

tsp.
1 ~~teaspoon~~ vanilla extract

c.
1 ~~cup~~ peanuts

oz.
1 can chow mein noodles, 5½ ~~ounces~~

Optional:

Tbsp.
2 ~~tablespoons~~ coconut flakes OR mini M&Ms

Instructor: In **Exercise 8** we will review contractions. A contraction occurs when two words are drawn together and shortened by omitting some letters. Every contraction has an apostrophe in it. The apostrophe tells us where the letters were omitted to form the contraction. Read each pair of words. Then write the contraction that is formed when these two words are drawn together and shortened.

Answer Key:

they are	they're
he would	he'd
could not	couldn't
I am	I'm
will not	won't
we will	we'll
you have	you've
it is	it's
it has	it's
she had	she'd

LESSON 80

Review: Eight Parts of Speech
Review: Simple and Complete Subjects and Predicates

Review "Ozymandias" (Lesson 16) today. If the student has trouble remembering the poem, have him practice it daily until he is confident.

Instructor: In this lesson, we will review all the eight parts of speech: nouns, pronouns, verbs, adjectives, adverbs, prepositions, conjunctions, and interjections. Let's begin with nouns. What is the definition of a noun?

If the student does not know any of the definitions in this lesson, say the definition with him three times, and then have him say the definition three times alone. If the student does not know a list (such as pronouns, helping verbs, or prepositions), say it with him three times and make a note to review the list every day until he knows it.

Student: *A noun is the name of a person, place, thing, or idea.*

Instructor: A noun can be a name common to many persons, places, or things: *man, park, day, bird.* These are common nouns. A noun can also name one special person, place, or thing: *Mr. Kline, Yellowstone National Park, Monday,* your pet bird *Tweety.* These are proper nouns. Proper nouns always begin with a capital letter.

Instructor: What is the definition of a pronoun?

Student: *A pronoun is a word used in the place of a noun.*

Instructor: A personal pronoun is a word used in the place of a person's name. The personal pronouns include subject pronouns, object pronouns, and possessive pronouns. Say the list of personal pronouns for me.

Personal Pronouns
I, me, my, mine
You, your, yours
He, she, him, her, it
His, hers, its
We, us, our, ours
They, them, their, theirs

Instructor: You also learned about another kind of pronoun: demonstrative pronouns. These pronouns point out, or demonstrate, something. Can you name the four demonstrative pronouns?

Student: *This, that, these, those*

Instructor: There is one more kind of pronoun you learned about in this book: interrogative pronouns. In what kind of sentence can you find an interrogative pronoun?

Student: *In a question sentence*

Instructor: The interrogative pronouns are *who, whom, which,* and *what*. "*Who* are you?" "*Whom* do you see?" "*Which* is your book?" "*What* is your book about?" Interrogative pronouns always come at or near the beginning of a sentence.

Instructor: What is the definition of a verb?

Student: *A verb is a word that does an action, shows a state of being, links two words together, or helps another verb.*

Instructor: Action verbs show action. Can you name three action verbs?

Student: *[Jump, run, yell, whistle, etc.]*

Instructor: State of being verbs show state of being, and linking verbs link the subject to another word in the sentence. Can you say the chant of the state of being verbs and the linking verbs? (They are the same verbs.)

<u>State of Being Verbs and Linking Verbs</u>
Am [clap]
Is [clap]
Are, was, were. [clap]
Be [clap]
Being [clap]
Been. [clap] [clap]

Instructor: State of being verbs just show that someone or something exists. "I *am*." "He *is* in here." "We *are* on top of the Ferris Wheel." Linking verbs link the subject to a predicate nominative (a noun or pronoun in the predicate) or a predicate adjective (an adjective in the predicate that describes the subject. "I *am* a girl." "This *is* she." "They *are* hilarious!" "The eagles *were* breathtaking." Helping verbs help another verb. Can you say the chant of the helping verbs? The first part of the helping verb chant is the same as the state of being verbs and linking verbs chant.

Am [clap]
Is [clap]
Are, was, were. [clap]
Be [clap]
Being [clap]
Been. [clap] [clap]
Have, has, had [clap]
Do, does, did [clap]
Shall, will, should, would, may, might, must [clap, clap]
Can, could!

Instructor: Helping verbs help the main verb by showing time. "I *am* helping." "He *was being* questioned." "I *will* bake a cake for you." "I *could* eat an elephant!"

Instructor: What is the definition of an adjective?
Student: *An adjective is a word that describes a noun or pronoun. Adjectives tell what kind, which one, how many, and whose.*

Instructor: I own a gerbil. What kind of gerbil? I own a *fat* gerbil. Which gerbil? I own *that* gerbil. How many gerbils? I own *one* gerbil. Whose gerbil? I own *my* gerbil. There are also three special, little adjectives that are called articles. Name the three articles.
Student: *A, an, the*

Instructor What is the definition of an adverb?
Student: *An adverb is a word that describes a verb, an adjective, or another adverb. Adverbs tell how, when, where, how often, and to what extent.*

Instructor: I walk. How do I walk? I walk *slowly*. When do I walk? I walk *early*. Where do I walk? I walk *nearby*. How often do I walk? I walk *regularly*. "To what extent" adverbs describe adjectives or other adverbs. To what extent do I walk regularly? I walk *very* regularly. The "to what extent" adverbs you learned are *too, very, really, quite, so, rather, slightly,* and *extremely*.

Instructor: What is the definition of a preposition?
Student: *A preposition is a word that shows the relationship of a noun or pronoun to another word in the sentence.*

Instructor: Say the list of prepositions for me.

Prepositions
Aboard, about, above, across.
After, against, along, among, around, at.

Before, behind, below, beneath.
Beside, between, beyond, by.

Down, during, except, for, from.
In, inside, into, like.

Near, of, off, on, over.
Past, since, through, throughout.

To, toward, under, underneath.
Until, up, upon.
With, within, without.

Instructor: A preposition is always part of a prepositional phrase. A prepositional phrase has a preposition and an object of the preposition. It may also contain adjectives that describe the object of the preposition. Listen to these prepositional phrases: *on the washing machine, around town, behind the two-headed monster, during the Super Bowl, throughout the earth, under the ocean floor.* A prepositional phrase can act as an adjective phrase describing a noun or pronoun or an adverb phrase describing a verb.

Instructor: What is the definition of a conjunction?
Student: *A conjunction is a word that joins words or groups of words together.*

Instructor: What are the three most common conjunctions?
Student: *And, but, or*

Instructor: A conjunction can join two or more words together: "I had oatmeal *and* raisins." A conjunction can join two or more phrases together: "I will ride my bike *or* take the bus." A conjunction can even join two sentences together: "Marie likes to look at snakes, *but* she doesn't like to touch them."

Instructor: What is the definition of an interjection?
Student: *An interjection is a word that expresses sudden or strong feeling.*

Instructor: Listen to these interjections: "*Ow!* I stubbed my toe!" "*Whew,* that was an exhausting hike." "*Eek!* The tarantulas have escaped from their terrarium again!"

Instructor: Now read the sentences in **Exercise 1**. Label each word a noun, pronoun, verb, adjective, adverb, preposition, conjunction, or interjection.

For *our* and *their*, accept either "pronoun" or "adjective."

Answer Key:

        adj   n   prep p/adj   n   v adj   n

1. The name of our galaxy is the Milky Way.

        adj   n   c   n   v   prep p/adj   n

2. Many stars and planets are within our galaxy.

        adj   n   prep p/adj n v   v   prep adj   n

3. The interior of our galaxy is choked with space dust.

        p   v   p/adj   n prep adj   n

4. This clouds our view of distant stars.

        adj   n   v   n prep p/adj n

5. Some galaxies have stars on their edges.

        adj   adj   n v   v   prep adj   n   prep p/adj   n

6. These orphan stars are wandering from the center of their galaxies.

        p   v   adv prep adj n prep n

7. They are drifting slowly into the void of space.

        i   adj   n   prep adj adj   n   v   v   adj

8. Wow! The view from an orphan star would be spectacular!

Instructor: Every sentence has a subject and a verb. On a diagram, the subject and the verb are separated by a straight line that runs down through the horizontal line. Look at the diagram of the first sentence in **Exercise 2**.

Workbook: 1. The name of our galaxy is the Milky Way.

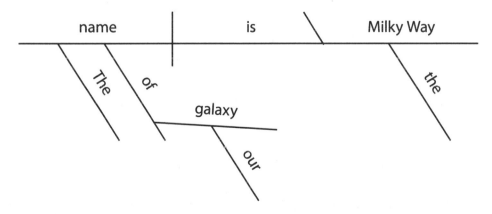

Point to each word and line as you explain the parts of the diagram.

Instructor: The subject of the sentence is simply the word *name*, so it is called the simple subject. The complete subject is the simple subject (*name*) and all the words that hang off the simple subject (*The name of our galaxy*). The complete subject includes all the words to the left of the straight line that runs down through the horizontal line.

Instructor: The complete predicate is the verb (*is*) and all the words attached to the verb line (*is the Milky Way*). The complete predicate includes all the words to the right of the straight line that runs down the center of the frame.

Instructor: Now diagram the rest of the sentences in **Exercise 2** by filling in the frames. After you have filled in the entire frame, write the simple subject, complete subject, verb, and complete predicate on the lines above each diagram.

The purpose of this exercise is for the student to correctly identify the simple and complete subjects and predicates. Therefore, give the student help in filling in the diagram if he needs it.

Answer Key: 2. Many stars and planets are within our galaxy.

Simple subject: **stars, planets**

Complete subject: **Many stars and planets**

Verb: **are**

Complete predicate: **are within our galaxy**

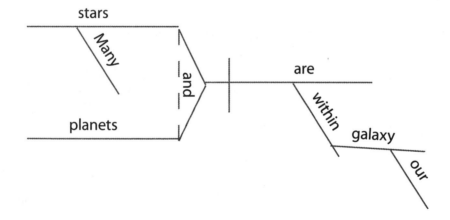

3. The interior of our galaxy is choked with space dust.

    Simple subject: interior

    Complete subject: The interior of our galaxy

    Verb: is choked

    Complete predicate: is choked with space dust

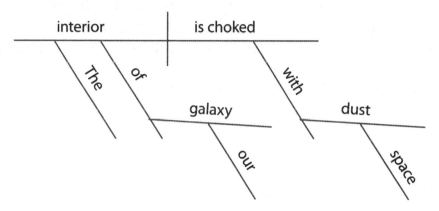

4. This clouds our view of distant stars.

    Simple subject: This

    Complete subject: This

    Verb: clouds

    Complete predicate: clouds our view of distant stars

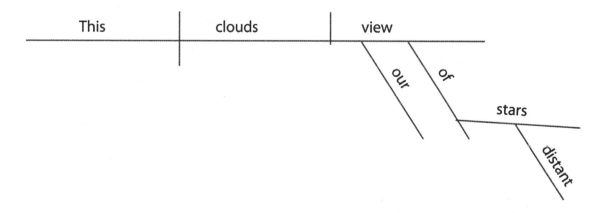

LESSON 81

Review: Prepositional Phrases

Review "How Doth…" (Lesson 27) today. If the student has trouble remembering the poem, have him practice it daily until he is confident.

Instructor: Let's begin this lesson by reviewing prepositions. A preposition is a word that shows the relationship of a noun or pronoun to another word in the sentence. Say that definition for me three times.

Student (three times): A preposition is a word that shows the relationship of a noun or pronoun to another word in the sentence.

Instructor: In your workbook, read the list of prepositions in **Exercise 1**. Then see if you can say all of the prepositions from memory.

List of Prepositions
Aboard, about, above, across.
After, against, along, among, around, at.

Before, behind, below, beneath.
Beside, between, beyond, by.

Down, during, except, for, from.
In, inside, into, like.

Near, of, off, on, over.
Past, since, through, throughout.

To, toward, under, underneath.
Until, up, upon.
With, within, without.

Instructor: Prepositions can be used in either adjective phrases describing nouns or adverb phrases describing verbs. By diagramming the five sentences on the frames in your workbook, you will review each of the five ways prepositional phrases can be used in sentences.

The sentences in this lesson are about ice, the solid form of water. For most substances, the solid form is heavier than the liquid form. But because water molecules form a crystalline structure when they freeze (think about snowflakes and ice crystals in your freezer), ice is **less dense** than water. Ice floats on water. If it didn't, cold air would freeze the water on the top of a lake and that ice would sink. Then more cold air would freeze the newly exposed water and that ice would sink. Eventually, the entire lake would freeze, killing all the fish! As it is, ice floats on the top of a lake, trapping the heat in the water below and preventing its contact with the cold air above.

Instructor: Look at **Exercise 2** in your workbook. Read Sentence 1. This sentence has a prepositional phrase that describes the subject of the sentence. The prepositional phrase is an adjective phrase because it tells what kind. I will ask you questions to help you fill in the diagram.

If the student needs more guidance than this exercise provides, review Lesson 44.

Workbook: 1.   The solid form of water is ice.

Instructor: What is the prepositional phrase?
Student: *Of water*

Instructor: Put a box around "of water." Ignore the words inside the box while you find the other parts of the sentence. What is the linking verb?
Student: *Is*

Instructor: Write *is* on the verb line. What is the subject? What is?
Student: *Form*

Instructor: Write *form* on the subject line. The linking verb *is* links the subject to a noun in the predicate. What is the predicate nominative? What is the form?
Student: *Ice*

Instructor: Write *ice* to the right of the verb. Look again at the simple subject *form*. Are there any adjectives that describe *form*? What are they?
Student: *The, solid*

Instructor: Write *The* and *solid* on the slanted lines beneath *form*. The prepositional phrase inside the box is an adjective phrase that describes the subject. What kind of form? The form of water. Write the preposition *of* on the slanted line below the subject. What is the object of the preposition? Of what?
Student: *Water*

Instructor: Now your diagram is complete.

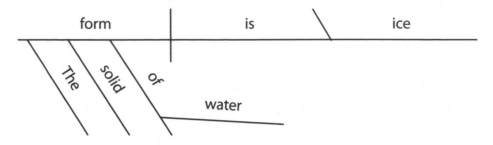

Instructor: Read Sentence 2. This sentence has a prepositional phrase that describes the predicate nominative. The prepositional phrase is an adjective phrase because it tells what kind. I will ask you questions to help you fill in the diagram.

Workbook: 2.   Ice is a crystalline structure of water molecules.

Ask the following shortened questions to help the student fill in the diagram. The answers are in italics. If necessary, help him put each word in its proper place on the diagram. If the student needs more guidance than this exercise provides, review Lesson 47.

---

1.   What is the prepositional phrase? Put a box around it.   *Of water molecules*

2.   What is the verb?   *Is*

3.   What is the subject? What is?   *Ice*

4.   What is the predicate nominative that renames the subject? The ice is a what? Answer me with one word.   *Structure*

5.   Are there any adjectives that describe the predicate nominative?   *A, crystalline*

6.   The prepositional phrase in the box is an adjective phrase that describes the predicate nominative. Answer with the prepositional phrase. What kind of structure?
Of water molecules

7.   What is the preposition?   *Of*

8.   What is the object of the preposition?   *Molecules*

9.   Are there any adjectives that describe the object of the preposition?   *Water*

Answer Key:

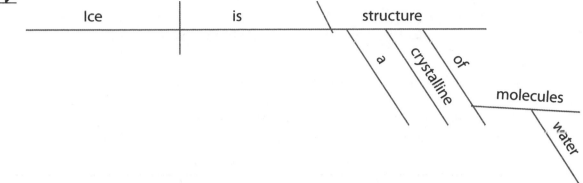

Instructor: Read Sentence 3. This sentence has a prepositional phrase that describes the verb. The prepositional phrase is an adverb phrase because it tells where. I will ask you questions to help you fill in the diagram.

Workbook: 3. Ice floats on water.

Ask the following shortened questions to help the student fill in the diagram. The answers are in italics. If necessary, help him put each word in its proper place on the diagram. If the student needs more guidance than this exercise provides, review Lesson 49.

1. What is the prepositional phrase? Put a box around it. *On water*

2. What is the verb? *Floats*

3. What is the subject? What floats? *Ice*

4. The prepositional phrase in the box is an adverb phrase that describes the verb. Answer with the prepositional phrase. Where can the ice float? *On water*

5. What is the preposition? *On*

6. What is the object of the preposition? *Water*

Answer Key:

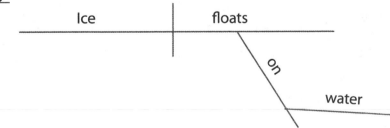

Instructor: Read Sentence 4. This sentence has a prepositional phrase that describes the direct object. The prepositional phrase is an adjective phrase because it tells which one. I will ask you questions to help you fill in the diagram.

Workbook: 4.   Air temperatures freeze the water on a lake's surface.

Ask the following shortened questions to help the student fill in the diagram. The answers are in italics. If necessary, help him put each word in its proper place on the diagram. If the student needs more guidance than this exercise provides, review Lesson 45.

---

1. What is the prepositional phrase? Put a box around it. *On a lake's surface*

2. What is the verb? *Freeze*

3. What is the subject? What freezes? *Temperatures*

4. What is the direct object? Freeze what? *Water*

5. Are there any adjectives that describe the subject? *Air*

6. Are there any adjectives that describe the direct object? *The*

7. The prepositional phrase in the box is an adjective phrase that describes the direct object. Answer with the prepositional phrase. Which water? *On a lake's surface*

8. What is the preposition? *On*

9. What is the object of the preposition? *Surface*

10. Are there any adjectives that describe the object of the preposition? *A, lake's*

Answer Key:

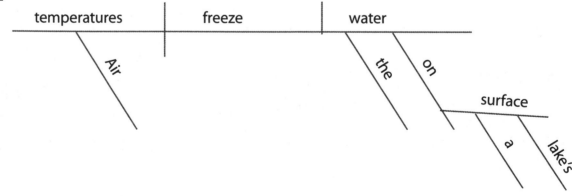

Instructor: Read Sentence 5. This sentence has two prepositional phrases: one describes the subject and the other describes the object of the preposition from the first phrase. The prepositional phrase is an adjective phrase because it tells which one. I will ask you questions to help you fill in the diagram.

Workbook: 5. The ice layer on top of the lake insulates the deep water.

Ask the following shortened questions to help the student fill in the diagram. The answers are in italics. If necessary, help him put each word in its proper place on the diagram. If the student needs more guidance than this exercise provides, review Lesson 48.

---

1. What are the two prepositional phrases? Put a box around each one.
   On top; of the lake

2. What is the verb? *Insulates*

3. What is the subject? What insulates? Answer me with one word. *Layer*

4. What is the direct object that receives the action of the verb? Insulates what? *Water*

5. Are there any adjectives that describe the subject? *The, ice*

6. Are there any adjectives that describe the direct object? *The, deep*

7. The prepositional phrase in the first box is an adjective phrase that describes the subject. Answer with the first prepositional phrase. Which layer? *On top*

8. What is the preposition? *On*

9. What is the object of the preposition? *Top*

10. The prepositional phrase in the second box is an adjective phrase that describes the object of the preposition in the first prepositional phrase. Answer with the second prepositional phrase. Which top? *Of the lake*

11. What is the preposition? *Of*

12. What is the object of the preposition? *Lake*

13. Are there any adjectives that describe the object of the preposition? *The*

Answer Key:

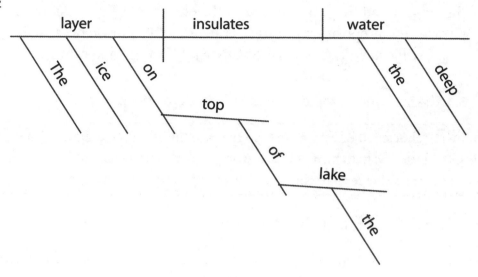

LESSON 82

Review: Capitalization Rules
Review: Proofreaders' Marks

The student will need to consult a calendar for this lesson to determine which day of the week his birthday falls on this year.

Review "Learning to Read" (Lesson 40) today. If the student has trouble remembering the poem, have him practice it daily until he is confident.

Instructor: Say the definition of a noun with me.

TOGETHER: A noun is the name of a person, place, thing, or idea.

Instructor: Nouns can be either common or proper. A common noun is a name common to many persons, places, or things. A proper noun is a special, "proper" name for a person, place, or thing. Proper nouns always begin with a capital letter. The word *student* is a common noun, but *[student's name]* is a proper noun. I am going to say a common noun to you, and I want you answer my question with a proper noun (a special, "proper" name for a common noun).

Instructor: *Child* is a common noun. What is the special, "proper" name of a child that you know?

Student: *[Answers will vary]*

Instructor: *City* and *town* are common nouns. What is the special, "proper" name of the city [or town] in which you live?

Student: *[Name of city or town]*

Instructor: This brings us to the first capitalization rule we learned in this book: Capitalize the proper names of persons, places, things, and animals. Say that for me.

Student: *Capitalize the proper names of persons, places, things, and animals.*

Instructor: The names of holidays are also proper nouns. Repeat the next rule after me: Capitalize holidays.

Student: *Capitalize holidays.*

Instructor: Do you know the name of the next holiday we will celebrate? [Instructor tell student if necessary.] Write the name of that holiday in **Exercise 1** of your workbook. Remember, all proper nouns begin with a capital letter.

Instructor: We also capitalize the names of deities. Read the sentence in **Exercise 2** of your workbook, and circle the name of the deity. This sentence is from a speech by Patrick Henry that you will read more of later in the lesson.

Answer Key: It is only in this way that we can hope to arrive at truth, and fulfill the great responsibility which we hold to ⟨God⟩ and country.

Instructor: You just practiced the third capitalization rule. Repeat after me: Capitalize the names of deities.

Student: *Capitalize the names of deities.*

Instructor: Repeat the fourth capitalization rule after me: Capitalize the days of the week and the months of the year, but not the seasons.

Student: *Capitalize the days of the week and the months of the year, but not the seasons.*

Instructor: The days of the week and the months of the year are proper nouns. They each begin with a capital letter. In what season is your birthday: winter, spring, summer, or fall? Look at a calendar. Turn to your birthday month. Which day of the week does your birthday fall on this year? Write this information in **Exercise 3** of your workbook. Remember to capitalize the day of the week and the month of the year, but not the season.

Workbook: My birthday is in the _____.

My birth month is _____.

My birthday falls on a _____ this year.

Instructor: The first, last, and other important words in the titles of books, magazines, and newspapers are capitalized. In **Exercise 4** there is a list of **un**important words. Read them aloud to me.

Workbook: This is a list of unimportant words:

- Articles (*a, an, the*)

- Conjunctions (*and, but, or*)

- Prepositions that are four letters or less (such as *at, by, for, from, in, into, like, near, of, off, on, over, past, to, up, upon, with*)

Instructor: In **Exercise 5**, notice that none of the words in these titles are capitalized. Rewrite the titles using correct capitalization. Then underline the entire title.

Answer Key: **Book**
cheaper by the dozen   <u>Cheaper by the Dozen</u>

Magazine
ranger rick   <u>Ranger Rick</u>

Newspaper
houston chronicle   <u>Houston Chronicle</u>

Instructor: Titles of stories, poems, and songs are also capitalized. They follow the same rules as books, magazines, and newspapers: capitalize the first, last, and other important words. These titles are put in quotation marks, rather than being italicized or underlined. Read aloud the titles in **Exercise 6**. Rewrite the titles with correct capitalization. Be sure to put these titles of stories, poems, and songs in quotation marks.

Answer Key: **Story**
the emperor's new clothes   "The Emperor's New Clothes"

Poem
song of marion's men   "Song of Marion's Men"

Song
simple gifts   "Simple Gifts"

Instructor: We have just practiced the fifth capitalization rule: Capitalize the first, last, and other important words in titles of books, magazines, newspapers, stories, poems, and songs. Say that with me two times.

TOGETHER (two times): Capitalize the first, last, and other important words in titles of books, magazines, newspapers, stories, poems, and songs.

Instructor: One of the personal pronouns is always capitalized, no matter where it is in the sentence. What pronoun is always capitalized? (Hint: It is the pronoun you most often use to refer to yourself.)

Student: I

Instructor: Repeat the sixth capitalization rule after me: Capitalize the word *I*.
Student: *Capitalize the word I.*

Instructor: Earlier in the lesson you capitalized the title of a poem, "Song of Marion's Men." Read one verse from that poem now in **Exercise 7** of your workbook.

Francis Marion was a general in the Revolutionary War. His men were too few in number to meet the British in open battle, so they would creep out of the woods and swamps and attack a small number of British troops. Then Marion's men would retreat back into the forest. They helped to drive the British General Cornwallis north into Virginia, where he surrendered at Yorktown.

Instructor: Repeat the seventh capitalization rule after me: Capitalize the first word in every line of traditional poetry.

Student: *Capitalize the first word in every line of traditional poetry.*

Instructor: Reread the poem to yourself and circle the capital letter in the first word in every line of the poem.

Answer Key: "Song of Marion's Men"
by William Cullen Bryant

(O)ur band is few, but true and tried,

(O)ur leader frank and bold;

(T)he British soldier trembles

(W)hen Marion's name is told.

(O)ur fortress is the good greenwood,

(O)ur tent the cypress tree;

(W)e know the forest round us,

(A)s seamen know the sea.

Instructor: There is one last capitalization rule that you have learned. Repeat after me: Capitalize the first word in every sentence.

Student: *Capitalize the first word in every sentence.*

Instructor: In **Exercise 8** of your workbook, you will see a portion of the speech that Patrick Henry delivered at the Virginia Convention on March 23, 1775. Read aloud these sentences from Henry's speech, and then circle the capital letter at the beginning of each sentence.

Answer Key: (I)s life so dear, or peace so sweet, as to be purchased at the price of chains and slavery? (F)orbid it, Almighty God! (I) know not what course others may take; but as for me, give me liberty or give me death!

Instructor: The capitalization rules are written in **Exercise 9**. I will read each rule to you, and you will read it back to me. Then you will read the paragraph that follows the rules, and underline each capital letter. Write the number of the capitalization rule that goes along with that capitalized word.

Workbook: Capitalization Rules

1. Capitalize the proper names of persons, places, things, and animals.

2. Capitalize holidays.

3. Capitalize the names of deities.

4. Capitalize the days of the week and the months of the year, but not the seasons.

5. Capitalize the first, last, and other important words in titles of books, magazines, newspapers, stories, poems, and songs.

6. Capitalize the word *I*.

7. Capitalize the first word in every line of traditional poetry.

8. Capitalize the first word of every sentence.

9. Capitalize the first word in a direct quotation.

Answer Key:

5 5
The *Constitution*

8 1   8
The *Constitution* is a famous warship that never lost a battle. It was launched

1   4
at Boston on October 21, 1797.

8 1   8
The *Constitution* weathered forty-two battles. During a particularly fierce

1   1 1   9   1
battle with an English warship near Cape Race, a sailor said, "There were English

1   6 or 8   8
gun shots bouncing off the sides of the *Constitution*! I couldn't believe my eyes! It

8   1.
was as if her sides were made of iron." The ship earned the nickname "Old

1   1 or 8 1   1

Ironsides." Oliver Wendell Holmes wrote a poem for the ship, protesting the order

8

that the ship be destroyed in 1830. Here are a few verses:

7

Her deck, once red with heroes' blood,

7

Where knelt the vanquished foe,

7

Where winds were hurrying o'er the flood,

7

And waves were white below,

7

No more shall feel the victor's tread,

7

Or know the conquered knee;

7

The harpies of the shore shall pluck

7

The eagle of the sea!

There are two words in the poem the student may not know. *Vanquished* means "defeated in battle." A *harpy* is a mythical hideous monster that is half-human, half-bird. The quotation in the story is the imagined words of the sailor.

If you are curious, the *Constitution* was not destroyed in 1830; public outcry was too great. It was rebuilt and restored to service until 1855. Then it was put out of commission and used as a training ship until 1877. In 1897, it was dry-docked and repaired to be used as a memorial. By the 1920s, it had again fallen into disrepair and was slated to be destroyed. American children raised funds to restore the ship, and it spent three years touring the ports of the United States. It now resides in the Boston Naval Shipyard.

Learn to Proofread: Review All Marks

Instructor: Today we will review all the proofreaders' marks you have learned. Read the sentences in **Exercise 10**. Use your proofreaders' marks to show the errors in capitalization and punctuation.

Workbook:

Proofreaders' Mark	Meaning
B̸ (lc)	make lowercase
b̳ (caps)	capitalize
⊙	insert period
’ over ∨	insert apostrophe
? over ∧	insert question mark
∧ over ,	insert comma
“ over ∨	insert beginning quotation mark
” over ∨	insert ending quotation mark
; over ∨	insert semicolon

Answer Key: What happened after patrick henrys speech The delegates voted to put the colony (caps x2)

in a state of Defense. George Washington accepted the position of commander of (lc)

the virginia forces. He said It is my full intention to devote my life and fortune to (caps)

the cause in which we are engaged. The decision was made the colonies would

fight the British.

LESSON 83

Review: Compound Subjects and Verbs
Review: Compound Sentences
Review: Fragments, Comma Splices, and Run-on Sentences

Review "The Lake Isle of Innisfree" (Lesson 53) today. If the student has trouble remembering the poem, have him practice it daily until he is confident.

Instructor: Do you remember the definition of a sentence? A sentence is a group of words that expresses a complete thought. Say that to me.

Student: *A sentence is a group of words that expresses a complete thought.*

Instructor: Some groups of words are just pieces of sentences. These pieces of sentences are called fragments. Fragments do not make sense by themselves—you need to add words, like a subject or a verb, to make a sentence expressing a complete thought. Look at the fragments in **Exercise 1** of your workbook. Tell me what is missing: a subject or a verb. Then add words to make that fragment a complete sentence. Tell me the sentence out loud.

Answer Key:	Fragment	Sample Answers
	Was covered with jelly.	**The toddler's face** was covered with jelly. (needs subject)
	The frisky pony.	The frisky pony **trotted around the ring.** (needs verb)
	A young bald eagle.	A young bald eagle **has a black head.** (needs verb)
	Hummed a cheerful tune.	**The boy** hummed a cheerful tune. (needs subject)

Instructor: What is the definition of a conjunction?

Student:　*A conjunction is a word that joins words or groups of words together.*

Instructor: What are the three most common conjunctions?

Student:　*And, but, or*

Instructor: A conjunction can join two verbs. In **Exercise 2** read the first sentence and look at its diagram.

Workbook:　1.　The bear sniffed and snorted.

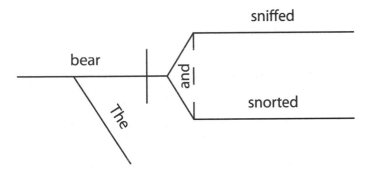

Instructor: Notice that the sentence has **two** verbs in the predicate. Do you remember that the word *predicate* comes from the Latin word *praedicare* meaning "to proclaim"? The predicate of a sentence is what is said or proclaimed about the subject. What is said or proclaimed about the bear in the sentence?

Student:　*It sniffed and snorted.*

Instructor: The conjunction *and* joins the two verbs in the sentence: *sniffed* and *snorted*. When the predicate of a sentence has two or more verbs joined by a conjunction, we call it a **compound predicate.** The word *compound* means "made of two or more parts."

Instructor: Look at the diagram of "The bear sniffed and snorted." The verb line splits into two parts. *Sniffed* is written on the top line because it comes first in the sentence. *Snorted* is written on the bottom line. They are joined by the conjunction *and,* which is written inside the triangle.

Instructor: Now read the second sentence in **Exercise 2** and diagram it in the space below. You draw the frame. This sentence also has a compound predicate, so the diagram will look like the diagram for Sentence 1.

Answer Key: The bear nibbled and swallowed.

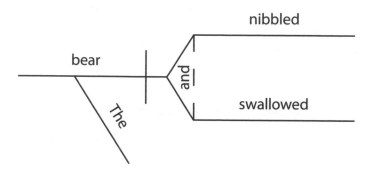

Instructor: A conjunction can also join two subjects. In **Exercise 3**, read the first sentence and look at its diagram.

Workbook: 1. Humans and bears stand on two feet.

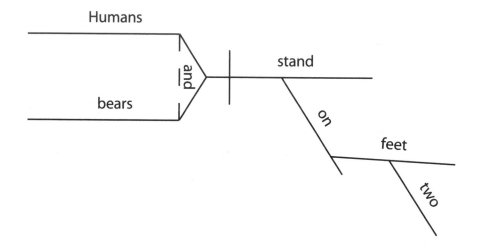

Instructor: Notice that this sentence has **two** subjects, joined by the conjunction *and*. When a simple sentence has two or more subjects joined by a conjunction, we call it a **compound subject**. Remember, the word *compound* means "made of two or more parts." What are the two parts of this sentence that are joined by a conjunction?

Student: *Humans and bears*

Instructor: Look at the diagram of "Humans and bears stand on two feet." The subject line splits into two parts. *Humans* is written on the top line because it comes first in the sentence. *Bears* is written on the bottom line. The two subjects are joined by the conjunction *and*, which is written inside the triangle.

Instructor: Now read the second sentence in **Exercise 3** and diagram it in the space below. You draw the frame. This sentence has a compound subject, so the diagram will look like the diagram for Sentence 1.

Answer Key: 2. Mothers and cubs forage in the wilderness.

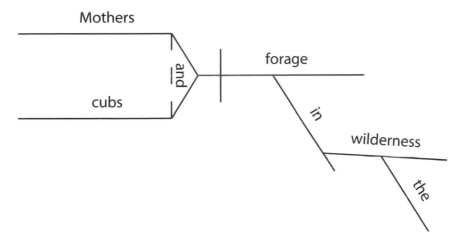

Instructor: In **Exercise 4** you will fill in the frame of a sentence with a compound subject and a compound predicate.

Answer Key:

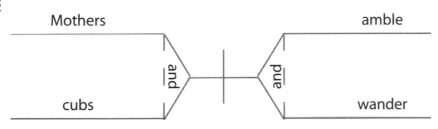

Instructor: Conjunctions can join two subjects to make sentences with compound subjects. Conjunctions can also join two verbs to make sentences with compound predicates. Conjunctions can also join two sentences to make one longer sentence. A **compound sentence** has two smaller sentences that are joined by a comma and conjunction to make one longer sentence. Read the compound sentences in **Exercise 5**, and circle the comma and the conjunction that joins the two smaller sentences together.

Answer Key: Bears are shy of humans, but they will explore their campsites.

You can research black bears, or you can research grizzlies.

Grizzlies are enormous, and they can run with surprising speed.

Instructor: Do you remember the meaning of the word *splice*? It means "to join ends together." In compound sentences, like the ones you just read in **Exercise 5**, the two smaller sentences are spliced together with a comma **and** a conjunction. That is a strong splice. If you just used a comma and left out the conjunction, the splice would be too weak to hold the sentences together properly. This weak, improper splice is called a comma splice. Read the sentences with a comma splice in **Exercise 6**. After you read each sentence, draw a line through it to show that it is incorrect.

Answer Key: ~~Bears gain weight before their long sleep, they lose it during the winter.~~

~~Bears in the Northwest love salmon, it's their favorite food.~~

~~Bears love fish, they eat mice as well.~~

Instructor: You need a comma **and** a conjunction to hold together two smaller sentences. A comma is not enough. Sometimes a writer forgets to put anything at all between two sentences! This is called a run-on sentence. Two sentences just run together; they aren't properly joined by a comma and a conjunction. Read the run-on sentences in **Exercise 7**. After you read each sentence, draw a line through it to show that it is incorrect.

Answer Key: ~~Black bears have smooth and shiny coats grizzlies have coarse fur.~~

~~The black bear can climb trees he is quite agile.~~

~~Be wary of all bears they are wary of you!~~

Instructor: Those run-on sentences needed a comma and a conjunction, or they needed a much stronger punctuation mark: a semicolon. A semicolon can properly join two smaller sentences into a compound sentence without needing any help from a conjunction! Read the compound sentences in **Exercise 8**. Circle each semicolon that joins the two smaller sentences.

Answer Key: Grizzlies have brown fur(;)they can also have grizzled, gray-streaked fur.

Store your food away from your campsite(;)a bear might come for it!

Bears have a keen sense of smell(;)it is much better than yours!

Instructor: Read each sentence in **Exercise 9**. Then decide if it is a fragment, a sentence with a comma splice, a run-on sentence, or a compound sentence. Remember, a compound sentence can be joined by a comma and a conjunction **or** a semicolon alone. Write the correct abbreviation in the blank.

Answer Key: 1. Native to temperate and arctic zones. **F**

2. Bears are omnivores; they eat both plants and animals. **C**

3. The "big bear" constellation Ursa Major. **F**

4. Bears walk flat on the soles of their feet, their footprints look somewhat like a human's. **CS**

5. The word "bear" comes from the Middle English word "bere" it means "brown." **RO**

6. Teddy bears were named for Theodore Roosevelt he was a hunter who would not shoot a bear cub. **RO**

7. Grizzly bears have short tails, but they have long front claws! **C**

8. Black bears eat mostly roots and berries, they are also tempted by human food. **CS**

Instructor: Look at the first compound sentence and its diagram in **Exercise 10**. There are two smaller diagrams joined together by a dotted line. The conjunction *but* is written on the dotted line because it joins the two smaller sentences together.

Workbook: 1. The biologist followed the bear, but the bear clambered down some rocks.

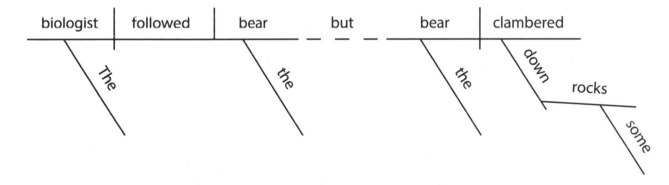

Instructor: Look at the second sentence and its diagram. This sentence is joined by a semicolon. The semicolon is written where the conjunction would normally go, joining the two smaller diagrams together.

Workbook: 2. The biologist sighed; the bear was gone.

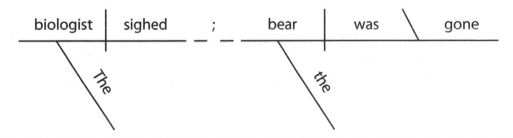

Instructor: Now you will diagram some compound sentences in **Exercise 11** of your workbook. Some of these sentences are joined by a comma and a conjunction; one is joined by a semicolon. You read each sentence, and I will ask you questions as you fill in the diagram. Remember to copy the words exactly as they appear in the sentence. If the words begin with a capital letter in the sentence, they should also be capitalized in the diagram.

Use the following dialogue to help the student complete the diagrams in **Exercise 11**. Because the sentences are made up of two small sentences (independent clauses), you will have to go through the dialogue twice. Follow the instructions below closely (for example, "Ask questions 1, 2, 3," etc.) to know which questions to ask.

1. *This is a compound sentence. Ask yourself, "Is it made up of two smaller sentences?" In the written sentence, circle the conjunction (and, but, or) or the semicolon that joins the two sentences. Then write the conjunction or the semicolon on the dotted line that joins the two diagrams. Go back to the written sentence and underline the first small sentence. Then underline the second small sentence. First we will complete the diagram for the first small sentence. Then we will complete the diagram for the second small sentence.*

2. *What is the verb? Is there a helping verb? Write the verb to the right of your center line.*

3. *Find the subject. Ask "who" or "what" before the verb. [Prompt the student with a specific question like "Who uses?" or "Who will switch?"] Write the subject to the left of the center line on your frame.*

4. *Is there a direct object that receives the action of the verb? I will ask you a question that will help you find the direct object.*

   First half of Sentence 1: Uses what?

   Second half of Sentence 1: Will switch what?

   First half of Sentence 3: Can lift what?

   Second half of Sentence 3: Can flip what?

   Write the direct object to the right of the verb on your diagram. The direct object is separated from the verb by a short, straight line.

5. *This sentence contains a predicate adjective. This adjective is in the complete predicate of the sentence, but it describes the subject. A predicate adjective can tell what kind, which one, how many, or whose. Can you find an adjective in the complete predicate that describes the subject? Because the predicate adjective follows the verb in the sentence, it is written to the right of the verb on the diagram. Write the predicate adjective to*

the right of the slanted line on your diagram. That slanted line points back toward the subject to remind you that a predicate adjective describes the subject.

6. *Go back and look again at the simple subject. Are there any words that describe the subject that come before the verb? These adjectives can tell what kind, which one, how many, or whose. Also look for the articles (a, an, the), because they act like adjectives. Write each adjective on a slanted line below the subject it describes.*

7. *Look again at the direct object. Are there any words that describe the direct object? These adjectives can tell what kind, which one, how many, or whose. Also look for the articles (a, an, the), because they act like adjectives. Write each adjective on a slanted line below the direct object it describes.*

8. *Look again at the verb. Is there a word that describes the verb? This is an adverb that could tell how, when, where, or how often. Write the adverb on the slanted line below the verb it describes.*

Answer Key: 1. A mother usually uses the same den, but she will switch dens occasionally.
(Ask questions 1, 2, 3, 4, 6, 7, and 8; then 2, 3, 4, 6, 7, and 11)

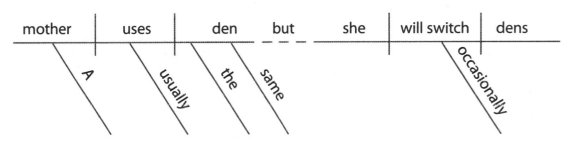

2. Bears are elusive; they are fearful.
(Ask questions 1, 2, 3, and 5; then 2, 3, and 5)

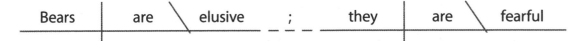

3. Grizzlies can lift heavy rocks, and they can flip stumps.
(Ask questions 1, 2, 3, 4, and 7; then 2, 3, and 4)

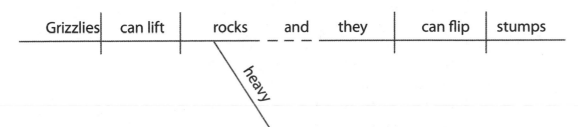

LESSON 84

Review: Punctuation
Review: Direct and Indirect Quotations

You will need a calendar for this lesson.

Review "The Height of the Ridiculous" (Lesson 66) today. If the student has trouble remembering the poem, have him practice it daily until he is confident.

Instructor: In this lesson we will review all the punctuation rules you have learned in this book. Let's start with sentences. All sentences end with a mark of punctuation (Lesson 35). A statement ends with a period. A command ends with a period **or** an exclamation point. A question ends with a question mark. An exclamation ends with an exclamation point. Read the sentences in **Exercise 1** and tell me whether they are a statement, command, question, or exclamation. Then write the correct punctuation mark at the end of the sentence.

Answer Key: Did you know a coral reef is made up of the skeletons of tiny animals? Q

These animals are called polyps. S

Look at the purple, yellow, tan, and green coral formations. (Also accept !) C

Coral polyps can sting! E

Instructor: A period is not just used to end a sentence. Most abbreviations are followed by a period (Lesson 56). Read each of the words in **Exercise 2** and write its abbreviation. If the word is capitalized, you should also capitalize the abbreviation.

Answer Key: Mister   Mr.

Saint   St.

Street   St.

February   Feb.

March   Mar.

Wednesday	Wed.
Thursday	Thurs.
mile	mi.
inch	in.
cup	c.
pound	lb.
Ante Meridiem	A.M.
Post Meridiem	P.M.

Instructor: Initials are abbreviations of a person's name (Lesson 56). Write the initials for your full name in **Exercise 3** of your workbook.

If the student's name were Darren Patrick Wright, his full initials would be D. P. W.

Instructor: Let's move on to a different punctuation mark: the apostrophe. To turn a noun into an adjective that tells whose, add an apostrophe (Lesson 14). If the noun is singular or is an irregular plural, add an apostrophe and the letter **s**. If the noun is plural and already ends in an **s**, simply add the apostrophe. Look at the chart in **Exercise 4**. Read the noun, and then add an apostrophe-**s** or just an apostrophe to turn the word into an adjective that tells whose.

Answer Key: Noun				Adjective That Tells Whose
sun	the	sun's	rays	sun's
corals	the	corals'	skeletons	corals'
men	the	men's	snorkels	men's

Instructor: Apostrophes are also used in contractions. The apostrophe marks the place where one or more letters were omitted when the two words were drawn together (Lesson 60). Read the words in **Exercise 5**. Then write the contraction that is formed when the two words are drawn together.

Answer Key:		
they are	they're
it has	it's
will not	won't

does not	doesn't
let us	let's
I have	I've

Instructor: Now let's review when you use commas. Use commas to separate items in a series (Lesson 57). These items can be individual words like nouns, verbs, or adjectives. The items can also be groups of words, or phrases. Read the sentences in **Exercise 6** and place commas to separate the items in a series.

Answer Key: Coral formations can look like tree branches, animal antlers, or leaves.

Fish, mollusks, sea anemones, and starfish live among coral reefs.

Instructor: You also use commas to set off a noun of direct address (Lesson 58). When you are talking directly to someone, you often say a person's name to get his attention. This is called direct address, because you address someone directly. When you write a sentence that includes a direct address, use a comma to separate the name of the person spoken to from the rest of the sentence. Read the sentences in **Exercise 7** and set off the noun of direct address with a comma or commas.

Answer Key: Edward, coral polyps take calcium out of the water and store it in their bodies.

You may not know, Anne, that when a coral polyp dies it leaves its limestone skeleton behind.

Instructor: You also use commas to separate introductory elements from the rest of a sentence (Lessons 58 and 78). An introductory element can be an interjection like *Hmm, Wow,* or *Oh.* An introductory element can also be a response word like *yes* or *no.* Read the sentences in **Exercise 8**, and draw a comma after the mild interjection or the response word.

Answer Key: Hmm, I think I would like to go snorkeling and see a coral reef.

Wow, I didn't know there was so much marine life near a reef.

Yes, let's make plans to visit there soon.

Instructor: Mild interjections are separated from the rest of a sentence by a comma. Strong interjections are separated from the rest of a sentence by an exclamation point (Lesson 78). Write an exclamation point after each strong interjection in **Exercise 9**.

Answer Key: Incredible! There are tiny, one-celled plants living inside a coral polyp!

Amazing! These plants make food for themselves and the coral!

Instructor: You also use a comma to separate a city and state (Lesson 56). Read the sentence in **Exercise 10** and write commas between the cities and states.

Answer Key: We drove from Madison, Indiana, to Nashville, Tennessee.

Instructor: You also use a comma to separate the day and the year when writing a date (Lesson 5).

Help the student find today's date on a calendar. He should write today's date in **Exercise 11** of his workbook.

Instructor: Use a comma before a conjunction in a compound sentence (Lesson 57). Write commas before the conjunctions in the compound sentences in **Exercise 12** of your workbook.

Answer Key: Coral polyps can get food from the tiny plants inside them, or they can get food by eating tiny animals in the water.

Polyps have stinging tentacles, and they use these tentacles to capture and kill tiny animals.

Instructor: Compound sentences can also be joined by a semicolon (Lesson 72). Read each compound sentence in **Exercise 13** and put in a semicolon to separate the two smaller sentences.

Answer Key: Coral release millions of egg bundles at the same time; it helps them survive.

The number of eggs overwhelms the egg-eating predators; they can only eat so much!

Instructor: Now let's review direct quotations (Lessons 63 and 64). Direct quotations are the exact words that someone says. A direct quotation is always enclosed in quotation marks. Look at **Exercise 14** in your workbook. Each of the direct quotations that you are about to read is part of a larger sentence. A direct quotation at the end of a sentence is separated from the rest of the sentence by a comma. The quotation ends with its own punctuation mark (Lesson 63). Read each sentence, and then write in the correct punctuation: commas, quotation marks, periods, question marks, and exclamation points.

Answer Key: Jason asked, "Did you know that crushed coral is the foundation of some Pacific islands?"

Janice exclaimed, "I would love to visit one!"

Instructor: If a direct quotation comes at the beginning of a sentence, and that direct quotation would normally end with a period, the period is changed to a comma. Question marks and exclamation points remain unchanged. The larger sentence also ends with its own mark of punctuation (Lesson 64). Read each sentence in **Exercise 15**, and then write in the correct punctuation: commas, quotation marks, periods, question marks, and exclamation points.

Answer Key: "Did you know there are three types of coral reefs?" asked Janice.

"There are fringing reefs, barrier reefs, and atolls," answered Martin.

LESSON 85

Cumulative Poem Review

Instructor: In this last lesson, you will review all the poems you have memorized this year. When you recite a poem, you begin with the title and author. I will give you the title and author for each poem. Say the title and the author back to me, and then recite the poem. Remember to stand up straight! Don't fidget while you're reciting! And speak in a nice, loud, slow voice.

You may prompt the student as necessary. If the student repeats the poem accurately, he may check the box in his workbook and move on to the next poem. If he stumbles, ask him to repeat the line he cannot remember three times.

"Afternoon on a Hill" by Edna St. Vincent Millay, Lesson 8

"Ozymandias" by Percy Bysse Shelley, Lesson 16

"How Doth…" by Lewis Carroll, Lesson 27

"Learning to Read" by Frances Ellen Watkins Harper, Lesson 40

"The Lake Isle of Innisfree" by William Butler Yeats, Lesson 53

"The Height of the Ridiculous" by Oliver Wendell Holmes, Lesson 66

OPTIONAL END UNIT

CONTRACTIONS

You will need a rubber band for this lesson.

Instructor: In this lesson we will go over the list of contractions. The word *contract* means "to draw together or shorten."

Pick up the rubber band.

Instructor: I am stretching out this rubber band. Watch as I now let it contract—it is drawing together, or shortening. So a contraction occurs when two words are drawn together and shortened by dropping some letters. Every contraction has an apostrophe in it. The apostrophe tells us where the letters were dropped to form the contraction.

Point out each thing as you explain the list.

Instructor: Look at the list in your workbook. In each group of words you will first see two words in regular black print. Under those two words you will see the same two words, but one or more of the letters will be underlined. Those are the letters that will be left out when the contraction is formed. An apostrophe will take the place of those missing letters. We will alternate reading these groups of words. You will point to each word as you or I read. That will help you keep your place. This is the way we will read these groups of words:

1. Read aloud the two words that are first in each group.

2. Point to the letters that will be left out when the contraction is made.

3. Read aloud the contraction.

it is	it has	I am	I have
it is	it has	I am	I have
it's	it's	I'm	I've
I will	I would	you are	you have
I will	I would	you are	you have
I'll	I'd	you're	you've
you will	you would	he is	he has
you will	you would	he is	he has
you'll	you'd	he's	he's
he will	he would	she is	she has
he will	he would	she is	she has
he'll	he'd	she's	she's
she will	she would	let us	
she will	she would	let us	
she'll	she'd	let's	
we are	we have	we will	we would
we are	we have	we will	we would
we're	we've	we'll	we'd
they are	they have	they will	they would
they are	they have	they will	they would
they're	they've	they'll	they'd
is not	are not	was not	were not
is not	are not	was not	were not
isn't	aren't	wasn't	weren't
has not	have not	cannot	does not
has not	have not	cannot	does not
hasn't	haven't	can't	doesn't
should not	would not	could not	do not
should not	would not	could not	do not
shouldn't	wouldn't	couldn't	don't

Instructor: There is one contraction that does not follow the normal pattern. I will read it to you. Then I want you to read it to me.

will not
won't

Instructor: When "will not" is shortened to *won't,* the **ill** changes to **o**! This is the only contraction that has this strange change.

If this is the first day going through this end unit, the student should take Test 1 in his workbook. He should do this without looking at the list in his workbook. Once he has completed the test, have him check his work by comparing his answers to the chart in the workbook (or the answer key in your instructor book). If any answers were incorrect, have him erase his answer and copy it correctly into his workbook. Repeat this entire lesson tomorrow, except have him take Test 2. He should check and correct his work as he did the day before. If he missed more than four contractions, review the list of contractions with him daily until he is confident.

Test 1 Answer Key:

Two Words	Contraction
I am	I'm
she is	she's
you are	you're
I have	I've
it has	it's
you had	you'd
he had	he'd
she will	she'll
it will	it'll
they would	they'd
he would	he'd
let us	let's
are not	aren't
has not	hasn't
should not	shouldn't
do not	don't
does not	doesn't
can not	can't
will not	won't

Test 2 Answer Key:

Two Words	Contraction
it is	it's
they are	they're
we have	we've
he has	he's
I had	I'd
she had	she'd
you will	you'll
they will	they'll
I would	I'd
it would	it'd
let us	let's
was not	wasn't
had not	hadn't
could not	couldn't
do not	don't
can not	can't
will not	won't

WRITING LETTERS LESSON 1

Writing Dates

Thank-You Letter Rough Draft

Instructor: Now that you are learning all of this grammar, don't forget that grammar is important because it helps us communicate well in words! You're going to use some of this grammar knowledge when you write letters.

Instructor: Every time you write a letter, you should include the date. To write a date, write the full name of the month, and then write the number of the day in that month. Put a comma after the number, and finish by writing the year. I will write some dates for you.

In **Exercise 1**, on the lines labeled "Instructor," write out for the student the date on which he was born and the birth date for another member of the family.

Instructor: Do you know what this first date is? Notice that the name of the month is always capitalized. It is a proper noun.

Instructor: Now I want you to copy your birth date as well as the second birth date I have written for you. Copy each date on the line directly below the date I have written.

Instructor: I am going to give you three important dates. I would like you to write each date on one of the lines in **Exercise 1**. The first date is January 1, 2009 (New Year's Day, 2009). The second date is April 1, 1999 (April Fool's Day, 1999). The third date is December 25, 2006 (Christmas Day, 2006).

Answer Key: 1. January 1, 2009

2. April 1, 1999

3. December 25, 2006

Instructor: In this lesson you are going to write a thank-you letter. You begin the letter by writing today's date. The first copy of any piece of writing is a rough draft. You will compose the letter today, and then copy it over neatly in the next lesson.

Use the following format to help the student write the rough draft of his letter in his workbook. As you see mistakes, point them out and have the student erase and make corrections. He will make a final copy of the letter in the next lesson. If the student is a reluctant writer, he may dictate the rough draft for you to write down.

Date (Today's date, written on the right-hand side of the paper)

Greeting (Dear _____,)

Explain to the student that a comma always comes after the greeting. Remind the student to include the abbreviation for the appropriate title of respect (Lesson 56). The letter may even be written to a member of the immediate family; everyone loves to get mail!

Body of the Letter

This will be the message you are communicating to the receiver. In this letter, you may thank the receiver for:

- a gift
  - Why did you like it?
  - What will you use it for?
- an invitation to an occasion (accepting or declining)
  - Why are you excited about going? (Or why will you hate to miss it?)
- having been entertained or taken somewhere
  - What was your favorite memory from the trip or visit?
- doing something special for you (a kind deed)
  - How did this help you?
  - How did the kind deed make you feel?

Read the above list of composition starters to the student, and have him choose one of the subjects. Ask him the prompting questions about that subject, and have him talk to you about what he would like to write. This is orally composing the body of the letter. This is an all-important step that should precede writing words down on paper.

As he writes down the body of the letter, remind the student of what he has orally composed (e.g., "What happened when you saw the penguins at the zoo?"). Aim for the student to write a paragraph of about four sentences. He should indent the paragraph about the space of two of his fingers.

Closing (You may choose "Love," "Sincerely," or "Yours truly." A comma always follows the closing.)

Writer's Name

WRITING LETTERS LESSON 2

Thank-You Letter Final Copy

Instructor: Today we will make a neat, final copy of the letter you wrote last lesson.

Assist the student as necessary to make a neat final version of the letter on the lined page in his workbook (or you may choose to have him write on his own stationery). Then have him go through the Final Thank-You Letter Checklist on page 352 of his workbook. He will mail this letter.

Instructor: We will address and mail this letter in the next lesson!

WRITING LETTERS LESSON 3

Addressing the Envelope

You will need a business-size envelope and a first-class stamp.

Instructor: Can you tell me your address?

Student: *[Says address, including city and state.]*

Write the student's complete address on the blanks provided in **Exercise 1** of the workbook. Do not include any abbreviations. Make sure you include a comma between your city and state. Include the zip code. Have the student read the address.

Instructor: Now you are going to review how to abbreviate, or shorten, some words in addresses. In **Exercise 2** of your workbook, I will say each street name and point to its abbreviation. Notice that each abbreviation begins with a capital letter and ends with a period.

Workbook:

Name	Abbreviation
Avenue	Ave.
Boulevard	Blvd.
Circle	Cir.
Court	Ct.
Drive	Dr.
Highway	Hwy.
Lane	Ln.
Road	Rd.
Street	St.

Instructor: The post office has special abbreviations for the names of states. They do not have periods like regular abbreviations. Every state abbreviation has two letters, and both letters are capitalized. The abbreviation for our state is _____. Write these two capital letters in the blank in **Exercise 3** of your workbook.

For a complete list of state postal abbreviations, go to the United States Postal Service website: www.usps.com/ncsc/lookups/abbrstate.txt.

Instructor: I already wrote your complete address in **Exercise 1**. Notice that there is a comma between the name of your city [town] and your state. I want you to copy this full address in **Exercise 4**. It does not have any abbreviations.

Instructor: Now in **Exercise 5** of your workbook, I will write your full address in your workbook using abbreviations. You will copy it onto the lines in **Exercise 6**.

Have the student practice writing his address using the correct abbreviations for his street and state until he can do it from memory. (Depending on the student and the length of the address, you may have to practice this over a number of days.)

Instructor: In the last lesson you wrote a thank-you note. You are going to mail it today! In order to mail a letter, you need to put it in an envelope and address it properly. The envelope has to have two names and addresses on it. The most important name and address are those of the person to whom you are sending the letter. But you also need to include your own name and address. This is called the "return address."

Write the address and the return address on the model of an envelope in the student's workbook. The student will copy this model onto the envelope. The addresses should include the appropriate abbreviations. Then help the student fold the letter. First, fold up the bottom third of the paper, and then fold down the top third. Put the folded letter in the stamped envelope. Seal and mail it!

WRITING LETTERS LESSON 4

Friendly Letter Rough Draft

Instructor: In this lesson you are going to write a letter to a member of your family.

The student should choose to send the letter to an adult member of the family who is not aware of what the student has been learning. Use the format below to help the student write the rough draft of his letter in his workbook. As you see mistakes, point them out and have the student erase and make corrections. If the student is a reluctant writer, he may dictate the rough draft for you to write down. The student will make a final copy of the letter in the next lesson.

Date (Today's date, written on
the right-hand side of the paper)

Greeting (Dear _____,)

Explain to the student that a comma always comes after the greeting. Remind the student to include the abbreviation for the appropriate title of respect (Lesson 56).

Body of the Letter

Read the following list of composition starters to the student, and have him choose one of the subjects. Ask him the prompting questions about that subject, and have him talk to you about what he would like to write. This is orally composing the body of the letter. This is an all-important step that should precede writing words down on paper. As he writes down the body of the letter, remind the student of what he has orally composed (e.g., "What did you say about King Tut?"). Aim for the student to write a paragraph of about four sentences. He should indent the paragraph about the space of two of his fingers.

Instructor: This will be the message you are communicating to the receiver. In this letter, you may tell the receiver:
- something interesting you learned this past week
  - Why did you find it interesting?
  - Have you read any books about the topic?
  - Did you learn something new?

- a special errand or outing you took recently
  - Where did you go?
  - What did you do there?
  - What special memory do you have from the trip?
- something funny that happened
  - Who were the people or animals involved?
  - What happened before the funny incident?
  - What did you do when you saw or heard about the funny incident?
- the weather
  - What has the weather been like—hot, cold, stormy, cloudy, etc.?
  - Has this weather been unusual?
  - Did you like this weather? If so, why? If not, why not?
- any news about you or your family
  - Who are the people you are going to tell about?
  - What special things are you going to tell about?

Closing (You may choose "Love,"
"Sincerely," or "Yours truly."
Remember that a comma
always follows the closing.)

Writer's Name (Student writes
his own name that includes
at least one initial.)

WRITING LETTERS LESSON 5

Friendly Letter Final Copy

Instructor: Today we will make a neat, final copy of the letter you wrote last lesson.

Assist the student as necessary to make a neat final version of the letter on the lined page in his workbook (or you may choose to have him write on his own stationery). Then have him go through the checklist on the previous page. He will mail this letter.

Instructor: We will address and mail this letter in the next lesson!

WRITING LETTERS LESSON 6

Addressing the Envelope

Instructor: In the last lesson you wrote a friendly letter. You are going to mail it today! In order to mail a letter, you need to put it in an envelope and address it properly. The envelope has to have two names and addresses on it. The most important name and address are those of the person to whom you are sending the letter. But you also need to include your own name and address.

Write the address and the return address on the model of an envelope in the student's workbook. The student will copy this model onto the envelope. The addresses should include the appropriate abbreviations. Then help the student fold the letter. First, fold up the bottom third of the paper, and then fold down the top third. Put the folded letter in the stamped envelope. Seal and mail it!

 **WRITING LETTERS LESSON 7**

Business Letter Rough Draft

Instructor: In this lesson you are going to write a business letter. We are going to pretend that you bought this book—and that half of its pages were missing! You will need to write a letter to the publisher and complain. You also want a free book to replace this one.

Use the format below to help the student write the rough draft of his letter in his workbook. As you see mistakes, point them out and have the student erase and make corrections. If the student is a reluctant writer, he may dictate the rough draft for you to write down. The student will make a final copy of the letter in the next lesson.

Date (Today's date, written on the right-hand side of the paper)

Greeting (Dear _____:)

Explain to the student that a colon always comes after the greeting of a business letter. If you are writing a company and you don't know the name of the particular person who takes care of customer complaints, you can simply use the company name instead. So this letter should be written to "Dear Peace Hill Press."

Body of the Letter

Explain to the student that a business letter that has a complaint in it should have two paragraphs. The first paragraph should contain the complaint. The second paragraph should contain the customer's demands or requests. Aim for the student to write two paragraphs of about two sentences each. He should indent each paragraph about the space of two of his fingers.

Help the student come up with the sentences. The two sentences in the first paragraph should contain the following information:

- The date that you bought the book
- Where you bought the book
- How much you paid for the book
- Which pages were missing

The two sentences in the second paragraph should contain the following information:

- What you want the company to do about it (perhaps send you a replacement book? Or provide you with your money back?)
- Any information the company will need to fulfill this request (your address, for example)

Closing (Only use "Sincerely" for a business letter.)

Writer's Name (Student writes his own name that includes at least one initial.)

WRITING LETTERS LESSON 8

Business Letter Final Copy

Instructor: Today we will make a neat, final copy of the letter you wrote last lesson.

Assist the student as necessary to make a neat final version of the letter on his own stationery. Then have him go through the checklist on Student Page 365. He will mail this letter.

Instructor: We will address and mail this letter in the next lesson!

WRITING LETTERS LESSON 9

Addressing the Envelope

Instructor: In the last lesson you wrote a business letter. You are going to mail it today! In order to mail a letter, you need to put it in an envelope and address it properly. The envelope has to have two names and addresses on it. The most important name and address are those of the person to whom you are sending the letter. But you also need to include your own name and address.

Write the address and the return address on the model of an envelope in the student's workbook. The student will copy this model onto the envelope. The addresses should include the appropriate abbreviations. Then help the student fold the letter. First, fold up the bottom third of the paper, and then fold down the top third. Put the folded letter in the stamped envelope. Seal and mail it!

Instructor: You can send this letter to Peace Hill Press and we will acknowledge it! Send it to the following address:

Peace Hill Press

18001 The Glebe Lane

Charles City, VA 23030

WRITING LETTERS LESSON 10

Emailing a Business Letter

Instructor: In the last three lessons you wrote a business letter. Sometimes you will need to send a business letter by mail, as we did yesterday. But more often, you will need to email your complaints!

Today we are going to type your business letter into an email. There are a few important differences between written letters and emailed letters. Look at your workbook as I explain them.

Use your email program for the following exercise. You may either type the email as your student watches or allow the student to type it. For the address, you may use letters@ peacehillpress.com. We will acknowledge receipt of the email!

Workbook: **Subject line:**

Greeting:

First line of letter. This is where you explain your problem.

Second line of letter. This is where you tell the company what you need it to do for you.

Closing,

Name
Address
Phone number
Email address

Instructor: In the subject line, we will type the problem. Can you put the problem into one sentence or phrase?

Use something brief and straightforward such as "Missing pages in FLL4."

Instructor: The greeting is the same in an email as in a business letter. However, notice that you don't need to put any address information above it. Then you will double-space and begin with the first paragraph of your letter. You don't use indents to show paragraphs in an email. Instead, each paragraph begins at the left-hand margin and is single spaced. You double-space between them to show where a new paragraph starts.

Instructor: Your closing, name, and contact information should all be lined up with the left-hand margin as well. Double-space between the letter and the closing, and between the closing and your name. Provide your full contact information after your name—your "snail mail" address, your phone number, and your email address. Even though the company can probably see your email address in the email itself, it is always best to be safe and type it out for them!

Instructor: Now that we have looked at the proper form of a business email message, we will type it into an email form and send it!

DICTIONARY SKILLS LESSON 1

Alphabetizing by First, Second, Third, or Fourth Letter

Before doing the dictionary skills lessons, the student needs to know the definitions of the eight parts of speech.

The exercises in this lesson may be done orally if you wish.

Instructor: In this lesson you will practice putting words in alphabetical, or **A-B-C**, order. In your mind, you need to be able to say the alphabet in order or sing the alphabet song. If you can do that, you can put the words *chimney*, *brave*, and *artist* in alphabetical order. Read the list in **Exercise 1**. The words are in alphabetical order.

Workbook: artist

brave

chimney

Instructor: The word *artist* comes first in the list because it begins with the first letter of the alphabet, **a**. The word *brave* comes after the word *artist* because *brave* begins with the letter **b**. A comes before **b** in the alphabet. The word *chimney* is last in the list because it begins with the letter **c**. The letter **c** comes after the letters **a** and **b** in the alphabet. When you are alphabetizing, which means putting words in alphabetical order, just think of the alphabet in your mind, **a**, **b**, **c**, **d**, **e**, **f**, **g**, and so on. In **Exercise 2**, I will show you how to alphabetize some more words: *train*, *dark*, and *zero*. The first thing you do is look at the first letter of each word.

Workbook: train

dark

zero

Instructor: The word *train* begins with **t**, *dark* begins with **d**, and *zero* begins with **z**. If you say the alphabet in order, which letter do you say first: **t**, **d**, or **z**? Think **a**, **b**, **c**, **d**, **e**, **f**, **g** .... The letter **d** comes first. That means the word *dark* comes before *train* or *zero*. Say the alphabet again. Now, what word comes after *dark*: *train* or *zero*? Does **t** or does **z** come first?

Student: **t**

Instructor: **T** comes before the letter **z**, so the word train comes next in alphabetical order. Zero is last. The three words are written in alphabetical order in **Exercise 3**.

Workbook: dark

train

zero

Instructor: There are three groups of words in **Exercise 4**. Rewrite each group in its own alphabetical order. Remember to think or sing the alphabet while you are doing this exercise.

Answer Key: 1. chin

escape

grouch

2. horn

icicle

porpoise

3. rice

three

umbrella

Instructor: You now know how to put words that begin with different letters in alphabetical order. But what do you do if you have words that all begin with the same letter? Then you need to look at the second letter of each word. Again, think to yourself **a**, **b**, **c**, **d**, **e**, **f**, **g**, and so forth. In **Exercise 5**, I will show you how to alphabetize some words that all begin with the same letter: vanilla, verse, and voyage. Look at the second letter in each word.

Workbook: **va**nilla

verse

voyage

Instructor: Each word begins with the letter **v**, but the second letter in each word is different. The word *vanilla* has **a** as the second letter, *verse* has **e** as the second letter, and *voyage* has **o** as the second letter. If you say the alphabet in order, which letter do you say first **a**, **e**, or **o**? Think **a**, **b**, **c**, **d**, **e**, **f**, **g** . . . . The letter **a** comes first. That means the word *vanilla* comes before *verse* or *voyage*. Say the alphabet again. Now, what word comes after *vanilla*: *verse* or *voyage*? Does **e** or does **o** come first?

Student: **e**

Instructor: **E** comes before the letter **o**, so the word *verse* comes next in alphabetical order. *Voyage* is last. Go back and look at the second letter of each word in **Exercise 5**. The three words are written in alphabetical order.

Instructor: In **Exercise 6**, look at the *third* letter in each word and rewrite the list in alphabetical order on the lines provided.

Answer Key: 1. ve**g**etable

2. ve**h**icle

3. ve**l**vet

Instructor: Your list should read *vegetable, vehicle, velvet*, because the alphabetical order of the words' third letters is **g, h, l**. In **Exercise 7** rewrite each group of words in alphabetical order, looking at the *fourth* letter of each word.

Answer Key: 1. van**d**al

van**e**

van**i**sh

2. squ**a**sh

squ**e**al

squ**i**rrel

DICTIONARY SKILLS LESSON 2

Looking Up Words in the Dictionary

Use your own student's dictionary for **Exercises 1, 2, 3,** and **4**.

Instructor: When you are reading and you encounter a word you are not familiar with, you can look it up in the dictionary to find out its pronunciation, its part of speech, and its meaning. When you are writing, if you are not sure of the spelling or the meaning of a word, you should look it up in the dictionary.

Instructor: You should practice finding words quickly in the dictionary. Words are organized in the dictionary by alphabetical, or **A-B-C**, order. In **Exercise 1** look at these lines of the alphabet.

Demonstrate for the student that the line breaks in the alphabet occur where you pause when you sing the alphabet song (the **ABC** song).

Workbook: A B C D E F G

H I J K L M N O P

Q R S T U V W X Y Z

Instructor: If the word you are looking up begins with one of the letters in the first line (**A**, **B**, **C**, **D**, **E**, **F**, **G**), open the dictionary near the front. Then flip the pages forward or backward to find the word. There are special words written at the top of each page in the dictionary that will help speed up your search. These pairs of words are called guide words.

On the left, find the first guide word at the top of a dictionary page. That word will be the first word listed alphabetically on that page. On the right, find the second guide word at the top of the page. It will be the last word that is defined on this page. Alphabetically, all the words on this page will come *after* the first guide word and *before* the last guide word.

Now let's practice finding some guide words in your dictionary. Look at the guide words to see if the word you are looking for is on that page.

Instructor: In **Exercise 2** find these words in your dictionary. Remember to open the dictionary near the front. Use the guide words to help you quickly find the exact page.

Workbook: fox

box

Instructor: If the word you are looking up begins with one of the letters in the middle of the alphabet (**H, I, J, K, L, M, N, O, P**), open your dictionary near the middle. Then flip the pages forward or backward to find the word. In **Exercise 3** find these words in your dictionary. Remember to open the dictionary near the middle.

Workbook: keep

oil

Instructor: If the word you are looking up begins with one of the letters near the end of the alphabet (**Q, R, S, T, U, V, W, X, Y, Z**), open the dictionary near the end. Then flip the pages forward or backward to find the word. In **Exercise 4** find these words in your dictionary. Remember to open the dictionary near the end.

Workbook: ten

van

Instructor: In **Exercise 5**, look at the copy of a dictionary page. What are the two guide words? (*Say* and *scare*.)

Find the word *scale*.

In this lesson you will begin learning some skills that will help you use your own dictionary easily. The word *scale* is called an *entry* word. It is written in bold print. Look closely at the word. In the second and third entries you will notice a black dot in the center of *scal•ing, scale•less, and scale•like*. This dot divides the words into syllables. When you are writing a paragraph, sometimes you do not have enough space to write an entire word at the end of the line. You have two options. You can write the word on the next line like in the first sentence of **Exercise 6**. Read that sentence.

437   say • scare

¹say \'sā\ *vb* **said** \'sed\; **say•ing** \'sā-ing\   **1** : to express in words   **2** : to give as one's opinion or decision   : DECLARE ⟨I *say* you are wrong⟩   **3** : ¹REPEAT 2, RECITE ⟨*say* one's prayers⟩

²say *n*   **1** : an expression of opinion ⟨everybody had a *say* at the meeting⟩   **2** : the power to decide or help decide

say•ing \'sā-ing\ *n*   : PROVERB

scab \'skab\ *n*   **1** : a crust that forms over and protects a sore or wound   **2** : a plant disease in which crusted spots form on stems or leaves

scab•bard \'skab-ərd\ *n*   : a protective case or sheath for the blade of a sword or dagger

scab•by \'skab-ē\ *adj* **scab•bi•er; scab•bi•est**   **1** : having scabs   **2** : diseased with scab

sca•bies \'skā-bēz\ *n, pl* **scabies**   : an itch or mange caused by mites living as parasites in the skin

scaf•fold \'skaf-əld\ *n*   **1** : a raised platform built as a support for workers and their tools and materials   **2** : a platform on which a criminal is executed

¹scald \'skȯld\ *vb*   **1** : to burn with or as if with hot liquid or steam   **2** : to pour very hot water over   **3** : to bring to a heat just below the boiling point

²scald *n*   : an injury caused by scalding

¹scale \'skāl\ *n*   **1** : either pan of a balance or the balance itself   **2** : an instrument or machine for weighing

²scale *vb* **scaled; scal•ing**   **1** : to weigh on scales   **2** : to have a weight of

³scale *n*   **1** : one of the small stiff plates that cover much of the body of some animals (as fish and snakes)   **2** : a thin layer or part (as a special leaf that protects a plant bud) suggesting a fish scale — **scaled** \'skāld\ *adj* — **scale•less** \'skāl-ləs\ *adj* — **scale•like** \-ˌlīk\ *adj*

⁴scale *vb* **scaled; scal•ing**   **1** : to remove the scales of   **2** : ²FLAKE

⁵scale *vb* **scaled; scal•ing**   **1** : to climb by or as if by a ladder   **2** : to regulate or set according to a standard — often used with *down* or *up* ⟨had to *scale* down the budget⟩

⁶scale *n*   **1** : a series of tones going up or down in pitch in fixed steps   **2** : a series of spaces marked off by lines and used for measuring distances or amounts   **3** : a number of like things arranged in order from the highest to the lowest   **4** : the size of a picture, plan, or model of a thing compared to the size of the thing itself   **5** : a standard for measuring or judging

scale insect *n*   : any of a group of insects that are related to the plant lice, suck the juices of plants, and have winged males and wingless females which look like scales attached to the plant

¹scal•lop \'skäl-əp, 'skal-\ *n*   **1** : an edible shellfish that is a mollusk with a ribbed shell in two parts   **2** : any of a series of rounded half-circles that form a border on an edge (as of lace)

²scallop *vb*   **1** : to bake with crumbs, butter, and milk   **2** : to embroider, cut, or edge with scallops

¹scalp \'skalp\ *n*   : the part of the skin and flesh of the head usually covered with hair

²scalp *vb*   : to remove the scalp from

scaly \'skā-lē\ *adj* **scal•i•er; scal•i•est**   : covered with or like scales ⟨a *scaly* skin⟩

scamp \'skamp\ *n*   : RASCAL

¹scam•per \'skam-pər\ *vb*   : to run or move lightly

²scamper *n*   : a playful scampering or scurrying

scan \'skan\ *vb* **scanned; scan•ning**   **1** : to read or mark verses so as to show stress and rhythm   **2** : to examine or look over ⟨*scanning* the field with binoculars⟩ ⟨*scanned* the headlines⟩   **3** : to examine with a sensing device (as a scanner) especially to obtain information

scan•dal \'skan-dəl\ *n*   **1** : something that causes a general feeling of shame   : DISGRACE   **2** : talk that injures a person's good name

scan•dal•ous \'skan-də-ləs\ *adj*   **1** : being or containing scandal   **2** : very bad or objectionable ⟨*scandalous* behavior⟩

Scan•di•na•vian \ˌskan-də-'nā-vē-ən, -vyən\ *n*   : a person born or living in Scandinavia

scan•ner \'skan-ər\ *n*   : a device that converts a printed image (as text or a photograph) into a form a computer can use (as for displaying on the screen)

¹scant \'skant\ *adj*   **1** : barely enough ⟨a *scant* lunch⟩   **2** : not quite full ⟨a *scant* quart of milk⟩   **3** : having only a small supply ⟨*scant* of money⟩

²scant *vb*   : to give or use less than needed   : be stingy with

scanty \'skant-ē\ *adj* **scant•i•er; scant•i•est**   : barely enough

¹scar \'skär\ *n*   **1** : a mark left after injured tissue has healed   **2** : an ugly mark (as on furniture)   **3** : the lasting effect of some unhappy experience

²scar *vb* **scarred; scar•ring**   : to mark or become marked with a scar

scar•ab \'skar-əb\ *n*   : a large dark beetle used in ancient Egypt as a symbol of eternal life

scarce \'skeərs, 'skaərs\ *adj* **scarc•er; scarc•est**   **1** : not plentiful   **2** : hard to find   : RARE **synonyms** see RARE — **scarce•ness** *n*

scarce•ly \'skeər-slē, 'skaər-\ *adv*   **1** : only just ⟨*scarcely* enough to eat⟩   **2** : certainly not

scar•ci•ty \'sker-sət-ē, 'skar-\ *n, pl* **scar•ci•ties**   : the condition of being scarce

¹scare \'skeər, 'skaər\ *vb* **scared; scar•ing**   : to be or become frightened suddenly

²scare *n*   **1** : a sudden fright   **2** : a widespread state of alarm

¹scallop 1

\ə\ abut	\au̇\ out	\i\ tip	\ȯ\ saw	\u̇\ foot
\ər\ further	\ch\ chin	\ī\ life	\ȯi\ coin	\y\ yet
\a\ mat	\e\ pet	\j\ job	\th\ thin	\yü\ few
\ā\ take	\ē\ easy	\ng\ sing	\th\ this	\yu̇\ cure
\ä\ cot, cart	\g\ go	\ō\ bone	\ü\ food	\zh\ vision

Workbook: 1. The ferocious reptile I saw was angry, and it had gray and green

scalelike skin.

Instructor: Or, you can divide the word *scalelike* into two parts, like in the second sentence of **Exercise 6**. Read that sentence.

Workbook: 2. The ferious reptile I saw was angry, and it had gray and green *scale-*

like skin.

Instructor: The dot in the middle of the entry word tells you where you can divide a word if you need to. There is a different dictionary mark for syllable divisions.

Instructor: A syllable is a part of a word containing one vowel sound. If a word has two syllables, it has two vowel sounds. Syllable divisions are printed within slash marks (\…\). On your dictionary page, find the word **scam•per** *scam-pər*\. It has two syllables. Let's clap as we pronounce the word in two syllables: *scam-per*. Find the word **scar•ci•ty** *sker-sət-ē ˈskar-*\. Let's clap as we pronounce the three syllables.

Find the word **Scan•di•na•vian** \\,*skan-də-ˈnā-vē-ən, -vyən*\. The *-vyen* is showing you that the last two syllables could be correctly pronounced as one syllable. So the word could be pronounced as a five-syllable word, *Scan-di-na-vi-an*, or as a four-syllable word, *Scan-di-na-vian*.

Instructor: Look again at the word **Scan•di•na•vi•an**. When you pronounce a word, some of those syllables are accented and others are not.

I am going to point to the tiny mark (′) just before the letters **na.** It is called an accent mark. This accent mark is printed just before that syllable to show you that this is the syllable that you should say the loudest. *Scan-di-NA-vi-an*.

Instructor: Look at the tiny mark (,) just before the letters **skan**. This is also an accent mark. This accent mark is printed just before and below the first syllable to show you that this syllable is not as loud as the other syllable. Some syllables are not accented at all—they are said quietly.

Some dictionaries will use a bold tilted mark (′) to indicate strong stress and a plain tilted mark (′) to indicate medium stress. In that case both marks appear at the top of the word.

Instructor: Often the unaccented syllable barely makes a sound. Notice the schwa (ə) in *Scandinavian*. The schwa is the same sound that you hear in the beginning and end of the word <u>America</u>. It is similar to a very quiet short-**u** vowel sound.

Look at the pronunciation key at the bottom of the dictionary page in your workbook. This key tells you that the schwa sound is in the word *abut* [the word *abut* means "to touch along a border," as in "America *abuts* Mexico along the river called the Rio Grande"].

Any of the vowels in an unaccented syllable may be pronounced with this sound. In *Scandinavian,* both an **i** and an **a** are pronounced like a schwa.

Instructor: Now, put your finger on the first bolded entry for *scallop*. Move your finger a little to the right of the entry word and you will see the phonetic spelling: *ˈskäl-əp*\\ or \\ˈskal-\\.

Instructor: This phonetic spelling shows you how to pronounce the word. Do you see the two dots? This is a pronunciation symbol. This symbol represents a sound. At the bottom right-hand corner of the dictionary page there is a key that tells you the sound that each letter and symbol represents. Find this letter and symbol in the pronunciation key: *ä*\\. Different regions pronounce the words slightly differently. Some people pronounce the vowel **a** like the vowel in *cot* and others pronounce the vowel **a** like the vowel sound in *cart*. Either pronunciation is considered acceptable.

 **DICTIONARY SKILLS LESSON 3**

Pronunciation Letters and Symbols

Instructor: On page 372 of your workbook, look again at the first dictionary entry for *scale*. Now move your finger to the right. There you will see the letters and symbols that give the phonetic spelling of the word. These tell you how to pronounce the word. You saw letters and symbols for phonetic spelling in the last lesson when you worked with the words *Scandinavia* and *scallop*. For now, move your finger a little more to the right. You will see an abbreviation next to the phonetic spelling of the word *scale*. This abbreviation is written in a different kind of print called italics. The *n* is an abbreviation for a part of speech. It tells you that the first definition of the word *scale* is a noun. Point to each abbreviation in **Exercise 1** and read aloud the part of speech for which it stands.

Workbook: *adj* adjective

adv adverb

conj conjunction

interj interjection

n noun

prep preposition

pron pronoun

vb verb

Instructor: Look again back at the dictionary entries. For the words given in **Exercise 2** of your workbook, write the abbreviation for the part of speech for that entry in the blank at the end of the line.

Before the student writes the abbreviation for the part of speech for each entry, have him read aloud to you the definitions. (Definition 2 is not a modern usage.)

Answer Key: 1. ¹scale ___*n*___

2. ²scale ___*vb*___

3. ³scale ___*n*___

4. ⁴scale ___*vb*___

5. ⁵scale ___*vb*___

6. ⁶scale ___*n*___

Instructor: In **Exercise 3**, the word *scale* is used in sentences. On the blank at the end of each sentence write the number of the definition that makes sense in that sentence. (The sentence numbers will not match the numbered entries!)

Answer Key: 1. My music teacher wants me to learn the G scale. ___6___

2. The scale said I gained five pounds last year. ___1___

3. Please scale that fish before cooking it. ___4___

4. The dragon lost a large scale where he rubbed the jagged rock. ___3___

5. Be careful when you scale the cave wall! ___5___

Instructor: In **Exercise 4** there are phonetic spellings for five words. Using the pronunciation guide at the bottom of the dictionary page printed in **Dictionary Skills Lesson 2**, see if you can pronounce each of the words.

Answer Key: 1. scanner

2. scald

3. scallop

4. scarcely

5. scaly

Optional Follow-Up

Using your own dictionary, have the student browse and practice using the pronunciation letters and symbols for words he knows. This will make him familiar with the notations. Then find some words that may be new to him and see if he can decipher the word.

DICTIONARY SKILLS LESSON 4

Words with More Than One Meaning and/or Pronunciation

The student will need his dictionary for this lesson. We used *Merriam-Webster's Elementary Dictionary* (Merriam-Webster, 2000). If the student is using a different dictionary and the phonetic symbols are different, you can look up the words and copy the phonetic spelling that the dictionary uses. A different dictionary may put the pronunciation key in a different place on the page. It may also have additional definitions or present the definitions in a different order.

Instructor: Look up the word *beaver* in the dictionary. Look at the abbreviation to the right of the phonetic spelling. What part of speech is the word *beaver*?

Student: *Noun*

Instructor: After the part of speech, you will see the definition. Read the definition of the word *beaver* to me.

Student: *[Reads definition]*

Instructor: *Beaver* has only one definition. The word always means the same thing. But some words have more than one definition. In **Exercise 1** read these two sentences in which the word *bark* has two different meanings!

Workbook: The **bark** on the north side of the tree is covered with moss.

The watchdog will **bark** if he hears an intruder.

Instructor: Words that are spelled alike and pronounced alike but have different meanings are called **homonyms**. The origin of this word is from the Greek language. In Greek, *homo* means "same" and *nym* is a shortened form of the word for "name." *Homonym* means "same name." In these sentences, the word *bark* has the "same name" but different meanings. In the first sentence, the word *bark* means "the covering on the outside of a tree." In the second sentence, the word *bark* means "to make a sharp cry."

Instructor: Look up the word *bark* in your dictionary. There are five different entries for the word *bark*. I will read them for you as you follow along with your eyes. Each time I get to an abbreviation (**n** or **vb**), I want you to tell me what that abbreviation means.

Instructor: Next, I want you to find the word *fair* in your dictionary. It has many definitions. Read the definitions to me that show how *fair* is used as an adjective.

Student: *[Reads definition]*

Instructor: In the left column of **Exercise 2** in your workbook, read each sentence about a fairy-tale princess in the left column. Then draw a line to the words in the right column that tell the meaning of *fair* in that sentence.

Answer Key:

The **fair** maiden had long braids.   Not dark; blond

In **fair** weather she sat in the sun.   Beautiful

She was **fair** with her servants.   Within the foul lines

The umpire called, "**Fair** ball."   Observing the rules

When she played games she was **fair**. Neither good nor bad

Her **fair** hair was admired by all.   Not cloudy

Though not strong, she was a **fair** hitter. Not showing favorites

Instructor: Now, in the dictionary, read me the definition that shows how *fair* is used as an adverb. (*In a fair manner.*) Then, look at Sentence 1 in **Exercise 3**. In this sentence, *fair* is an adverb describing how she will play. Now look at Sentence 2. In Sentence 2, *fair* is an adjective describing the kind of play the princess enjoys. In each sentence, draw an arrow from the word *fair* to the word it describes. Then write *adv* above *fair* used as an adverb and write *adj* above *fair* used as an adjective.

Answer Key:

      adv
1. She will play **fair.**

    adj
2. She enjoys **fair** play.

Instructor: Now, in the dictionary, read me the definition that shows how *fair* is used as a noun. Then read the sentences in **Exercise 4**. Write **n** for noun above each word *fair* in these three sentences.

Answer Key:

        n
1 The antique **fair** was full of interesting old dishes and tools.

n

2. There were many different breeds of chickens at the state **fair.**

n

3. I bought a special art book at the library's book **fair.**

Instructor: There are some other kinds of words that are **spelled alike**, but they have different meanings or different pronunciations. Read the two sentences in **Exercise 5** out loud. Notice that although each word in bold print is spelled **L-E-A-D**, the words have different meanings and different pronunciations. These are called homographs. *Homograph* means "same writing."

Workbook: 1. The sinker on the fishing line was made of **lead.**

2. Our trail guide will **lead** the way on the trail to the top of the mountain.

Instructor: In the first sentence, *lead* is the kind of metal heavy enough to make a fishing line sink. In the second sentence, the trail guide will go before the hikers—he will *lead* them.

Instructor: The words *lead* and *lead* are spelled alike but have different meanings and different pronunciations. Often words in the dictionary will have more than one meaning and more than one phonetic spelling.

Instructor: There is another group of words called *homophones*. Homophones are pronounced alike but are different in meaning or spelling. In **Exercise 6** read the pairs of sentences that contain homophones. Remember, **homophones** are **pronounced alike** but are different in meaning or spelling.

Workbook: 1. Jason was **billed** for the computer he ordered.

He wanted to **build** a computer but did not know how.

2. The baby has **grown** so much that she cannot even fit into her pajamas.

Her mother will **groan** about the expense of all new clothes!

Instructor: Knowing the Greek origins of the following words may help you remember which words are homonyms, or homographs, or homophones. The more you know about where words come from, the more you can enjoy word study. Look at **Exercise 7** in your workbook. I will read the Greek words and their meanings. Then you read the definitions that are numbered below.

Workbook: **Homo** – Greek, meaning same; similar; alike.

Nym – Greek, meaning name

Graph – Greek, meaning write or draw

Phone – Greek, meaning sound or voice

1. Words that are spelled alike and **pronounced alike** but have different meanings are called **homonyms (same name)**.

2. Words that are **spelled alike** but have different pronunciations and different meanings are called **homographs (same writing)**.

3. Words that are pronounced alike but have different meanings or spellings are **homophones (same sound)**.

Optional Follow-Up

   If the student needs extra practice with dictionary skills, or just enjoys word origins, you may use these words as a starting resource.

Homonyms (same name)

Spelled alike and pronounced alike but have different meanings:

present (a gift) / present (time not past or future)

pen (an enclosure for animals) / pen (a writing instrument)

muffler (part of car) / muffler (article of clothing to keep one warm)

right (correct) / right (opposite of left)

rose (flower) / rose (past tense of "to rise")

Homographs (same writing)

Spelled alike but have different pronunciations and different meanings:

bass (fish), bass (musical stringed instrument)

close (shut the door), close (That was too close for comfort!)

does (She does play well), does (female deer)

dove (bird), dove (She dove into the pool)

refuse (I refuse to do that), refuse (trash)

Homophones (same sound)

Pronounced alike but have different meanings or spellings:

ate (past tense of "to eat") / eight (a number)

clothes (articles to wear) / close (shut)

flower (the bloom of a plant) / flour (finely ground grain)

hare (animal related to a rabbit) / hair (threadlike growth on skin)

thrown (past tense of sending through the air) / throne (chair of royal person)

DICTIONARY SKILLS LESSON 5

Synonyms and Antonyms

The student will need his thesaurus for this lesson. The following exercises are keyed to *Roget's Children's Thesaurus* (ISBN 0-673-65137-1). If the student is using a different children's thesaurus, be sure to read through the lesson ahead of time and make any adjustments necessary.

Instructor: Today we are going to learn about synonyms. Read the three sentences in **Exercise 1**.

Workbook: The sun at the beach was **bright.**

The sun at the beach was **glaring.**

The sun at the beach was **brilliant.**

Instructor: The three words in bold print, *bright, glaring*, and *brilliant*, all mean the same thing. They are synonyms. **Synonyms** are words that have the **same** meaning. Say that definition with me three times.

Together (three times): **Synonyms are words that have the same meaning.**

Instructor: You can remember that synonyms have the same meaning by thinking to yourself, "SSSSynonyms have the ssssame meaning." A thesaurus is a book that contains lists of synonyms. It can be helpful to have a thesaurus on hand when you are writing. For example, if you write the sentence "Joe likes to *eat* cookies," you could make it more descriptive by substituting a synonym for *eat*.

Help the student look up the word *eat*. Explain that you must first look up the word in the Synonym Index in the back of the thesaurus, and then turn to the page number printed next to the index entry for *eat*. Read through the page for the entry word *eat* while the student follows along.

Instructor: You are looking at the entry for the word *eat*. The entry contains a list of synonyms. Remember the sentence "Joe likes to *eat* cookies"? Now you can replace *eat* with a more descriptive word. "Joe likes to *nibble* cookies." *Nibble* means to eat in small bites. What if you used the synonym *snack* instead? "Joe likes to *snack* on cookies." When you use the word *snack,* you are indicating that Joe eats cookies between meals. *Snack* does not tell how many or in what manner he eats them. Let's try the word *gobble.* "Joe likes to *gobble* cookies." That really changes the description of how Joe is eating cookies! If you choose that word for the sentence, you are describing Joe's eating cookies quickly in large bites or gulps. Using synonyms for ordinary words can make your sentences more lively and imaginative.

Instructor: Read aloud the story in **Exercise 2**. It contains the words *fill* and *full* over and over again.

Workbook: The Jamison family took the whole morning to **fill** their van to go camping. First the huge tent almost **filled** the space. Then Sherry brought out the sports equipment. Now the car was also **full** of fishing gear. Charles **filled** the back with sleeping bags. Last of all, the car was **full** of people who fastened their seat belts. They were off at last.

Instructor: This paragraph would be much more interesting if the words *fill* and *full* were not used so much! Look up the word *full* in the thesaurus.

Help the student look up the word *full.* Remember to first look up the word in the Synonym Index. Turn to the page listed in the index. Read through the entire thesaurus entry for *full* while the student follows along.

Instructor: You will see *full* and its list of synonyms in **Exercise 3** of your workbook. Read this list to me.

Workbook: full

crowded

packed

stuffed

jammed

crammed

Instructor: Now I am going to read the paragraph in **Exercise 4**. This paragraph is so much better because the words *full* and *fill* are not used so many times. It's okay to have them in a paragraph once, but not five times!

Workbook: The Jamison family took the whole morning to **pack** their van to go camping. First the huge tent was **crammed** in. Then Sherry brought out the sports equipment. In addition, the car was **jammed** with fishing gear. Charles **stuffed** the sleeping bags in the back. Last of all, the whole family **crowded** in and fastened their seat belts. They were off at last.

Instructor: *Crowded, packed, stuffed, jammed,* and *crammed* are all synonyms—they have the same meaning. Look again at the thesaurus entry for the word *full.* Look at the middle of the page. You will see the same words that are in **Exercise 5** of your workbook.

Workbook: ANTONYM: empty

Instructor: *Empty* is the opposite of *full.* These two words are antonyms. Antonyms are opposites. Say that with me three times.

Together (three times): **Antonyms are opposites.**

If your student has a lot of other writing to do for school today, you may do the following exercise orally instead.

Instructor: A thesaurus often includes antonyms at the bottom of the synonym entry. Read each of the sentences in **Exercise 6**. Look up each word in bold in the thesaurus, and find its antonym. Then write the antonym over the word in bold, and read the sentence out loud again—this time using the antonym! The sentence now has the opposite meaning .

Answer Key:

1. I must remind myself to be sure and **remember** my dentist appointment!

forget

2. We will be just in time to catch the first act of the play if we **hurry.**

dawdle, slow down

3. I am going to **mix** water and clay powder to make models.

separate

4. The thing she loves about a restful Sunday morning is the **silence.**

noise

5. Mona thought riding over the **rough** road would shake her teeth out.

smooth

6. Chuck is going to **show** his award so everyone can see it.

hide

Optional Follow-Up

Find the word *look* in your thesaurus, and read how many different ways there are to look at something! Make up sentences using some of these synonyms for *look,* and make faces to illustrate the word. (For example, *glance, gaze, stare, peek, squint.*) If this exercise makes the student laugh, find the words *laugh* and *funny* in your thesaurus. Just reading so many ways to say something is funny and may cause the student to laugh some more.

DEFINITIONS, RULES, AND LISTS

DEFINITIONS TO BE MEMORIZED

A **noun** is the name of a person, place, thing, or idea.

A **pronoun** is a word used in the place of a noun.

A **verb** is a word that does an action, shows a state of being, links two words together, or helps another verb.

An **adjective** is a word that describes a noun or pronoun. Adjectives tell what kind, which one, how many, and whose.

An **adverb** is a word that describes a verb, an adjective, or another adverb. Adverbs tell how, when, where, how often, and to what extent.

A **preposition** is a word that shows the relationship of a noun or pronoun to another word in the sentence.

A **conjunction** is a word that joins words or groups of words together.

An **interjection** is a word that expresses sudden or strong feeling.

A **sentence** is a group of words that expresses a complete thought. All sentences begin with a capital letter and end with a punctuation mark.

GLOSSARY OF ADDITIONAL TERMS TO KNOW

command – a sentence that gives an order or makes a request. A command sentence ends with either a period or an exclamation point.

complete predicate – the verb and other words that tell us what is said about the subject. It is the part of the sentence in which the verb is found.

complete subject – the simple subject and other words that tell us who or what the sentence is about. It is the part of the sentence in which the simple subject is found.

compound predicate – two or more verbs that are joined by a conjunction and that have the same subject.

compound subject – a subject with two or more parts that are joined by a conjunction.

contraction – two words drawn together and shortened by dropping some letters. Every contraction has an apostrophe in it. The apostrophe tells us where the letters were dropped to form the contraction.

direct object – the noun or pronoun in the complete predicate that receives the action of the verb.

direct quotation – the exact words that someone says. Direct quotations are always enclosed by quotation marks.

exclamation – a sentence that shows sudden or strong feeling. An exclamation always ends with an exclamation point.

homonym – words that are spelled alike and pronounced alike but have different meanings.

indirect object – the noun or pronoun that is **between** the action verb and the direct object of a sentence. It answers the question "to whom" or "for whom" the action is done.

indirect quotation – the content of what a person says without using his or her exact words. There are no quotation marks surrounding an indirect quotation.

predicate adjective – an adjective in the complete predicate that describes the subject.

predicate nominative – a noun or pronoun in the complete predicate that renames the subject.

question – a sentence that asks something. A question always ends with a question mark.

simple predicate – the main verb plus any helping verbs.

simple subject – the main word or term that tells us who or what the sentence is about.

statement – a sentence that gives information. Statements always end with a period.

types of sentences – The four different types of sentences are statements, commands, questions, and exclamations.

SUMMARY OF RULES

Forming Plurals

Usually, add **s** to a noun to form the plural.

Add **es** to nouns ending in **s**, **sh**, **ch**, **x**, or **z**.

If a noun ends in **y** after a consonant, change the **y** to **i** and add **es**.

If a noun ends in **y** after a vowel, just add **s**.

Apostrophes

To turn a noun into an adjective that tells whose, add an apostrophe.

If the noun is singular or an irregular plural, add an apostrophe and the letter **s**.

If the noun is plural and already ends in an **s**, simply add the apostrophe.

Use an apostrophe to show where letters have been omitted in a contraction.

Commas in a Series

Put a comma after every item except the last one in the series.

Commas in Dates and Addresses

Use a comma to separate a city and state.

Use a comma to separate the day and year.

Compound Sentences

Use a comma before a conjunction in a compound sentence.

OR Join the two elements of a compound sentence with a semicolon and no conjunction.

Direct Address

Use commas to set off a noun of direct address.

Direct Quotation That Comes at the End of a Sentence

The exact words a person says are always enclosed by quotation marks.

Direct quotations begin with a capital letter.

The quotation is separated from the rest of the sentence by a comma.

The end punctuation mark always comes inside the closing quotation mark.

Direct Quotation That Comes at the Beginning of a Sentence

The exact words a person says are always enclosed by quotation marks.

Direct quotations begin with a capital letter.

If the direct quotation would normally end with a period, then the period is changed to a comma. This comma is always inside the closing quotation mark.

If the direct quotation ends with a question mark or exclamation point, that mark is always inside the closing quotation mark.

Since the direct quotation is only a part of the sentence, the larger sentence must have its own end mark.

Introductory Elements

Use a comma to separate an introductory element from the rest of a sentence.

Use an exclamation point to separate a strong interjection from the rest of a sentence.

LISTS TO BE MEMORIZED

Pronouns

> I, me, my, mine
> You, your, yours
> He, she, him, her, it
> His, hers, its
> We, us, our, ours
> They, them, their, theirs

Helping Verbs

> Am
> Is
> Are, was, were
> Be
> Being
> Been
>
> Have, has, had
> Do, does, did
>
> Shall, will, should, would, may, might, must
> Can, could

State of Being Verbs

> Am
> Is
> Are, was, were
> Be
> Being
> Been

Linking Verbs

> Am
> Is
> Are, was, were
> Be
> Being
> Been

Prepositions

Aboard, about, above, across
After, against, along, among, around, at

Before, behind, below, beneath
Beside, between, beyond, by

Down, during, except, for, from
In, inside, into, like

Near, of, off, on, over
Past, since, through, throughout

To, toward, under, underneath
Until, up, upon
With, within, without

Articles

A, an, the

Common Conjunctions

And, but, or

SAMPLE SCHEDULES

There are 180 days (36 weeks) in a typical school year. This book contains 85 lessons in the main part of the book. These lessons are mandatory. Additionally, there are three optional units at the end of the book: 1 lesson on contractions, 10 lessons on writing letters, and 5 lessons on dictionary skills.

Here are three suggested options:

A. You can do only the 85 lessons in the main part of the book.

B. You can do the entire book and finish with the optional end units.

C. You can do the entire book, interspersing the optional end units among the lessons.

The chart on the next page shows these three options and how they would work over the course of a 36-week school year.

Week	Option A Lessons	Option B Lessons	Option C Lessons
1	1, 2	1, 2	1, 2, 3
2	3, 4	3, 4, 5	4, 5, 6
3	5, 6, 7	6, 7, 8	7, 8, 9
4	8, 9	9, 10, 11	10, 11, 12
5	10, 11	12, 13, 14	DS 1, DS 2
6	12, 13, 14	15, 16, 17	13, 14, 15
7	15, 16	18, 19, 20	16, 17, 18
8	17, 18, 19	21, 22, 23	19, 20, 21
9	20, 21	24, 25, 26	22, 23, 24
10	22, 23, 24	27, 28, 29	25, 26, 27
11	25, 26	30, 31, 32	28, 29, 30
12	27, 28, 29	33, 34, 35	WL 1, WL 2, WL 3
13	30, 31	36, 37, 38	31, 32, 33
14	32, 33, 34	39, 40, 41	34, 35, 36
15	35, 36	42, 43, 44	37, 38, 39
16	37, 38, 39	45, 46, 47	40, 41, 42
17	40, 41	48, 49, 50	43, 44, 45
18	42, 43, 44	51, 52, 53	46, 47, 48
19	45, 46	54, 55, 56	49, 50, 51
20	47, 48, 49	57, 58, 59	52, 53, 54
21	50, 51	60, 61, 62	DS 3, DS 4
22	52, 53, 54	63, 64, 65	55, 56, 57
23	55, 56	66, 67, 68	58, 59, DS 5
24	57, 58, 59	69, 70, 71	60, 61, 62
25	60, 61	72, 73, 74	63, 64, 65
26	62, 63, 64	75, 76, 77	66, 67, 68
27	65, 66	78, 79, 80	69, 70, 71
28	67, 68, 69	81, 82, 83	WL 4, WL 5, WL 6
29	70, 71	84, 85	72, 73, 74
30	72, 73, 74	WL 1, WL 2	75, 76, 77
31	75, 76	WL 3, WL 4	78, 79
32	77, 78	WL 5, WL 6	80, 81
33	79, 80	WL 7, WL 8	WL 7, WL 8
34	81, 82	WL 9, WL 10, DS 1	WL 9, 10
35	83, 84	DS 2, DS 3	82, 83, 84, 85
36	85	DS 4, DS 5	Contractions

BIBLIOGRAPHY

✓ Atwater, Richard and Florence. *Mr. Popper's Penguins.* Boston: Little, Brown & Company, 1938.

✓ Banks, Lynn Reid. *The Indian in the Cupboard.* New York: Avon Books, 1980.

Baum, Frank L. *The Wizard of Oz.* New York: Tor Books, 1993.

Bright, Michael. *Bears and Pandas.* New York: Lorenz Books, 2000.

Brink, Carol Ryrie. *Caddie Woodlawn.* New York: Aladdin Books, 2006.

Bryan, T. Scott. *Geysers: What They Are and How They Work* 2d edition. Missoula, Montana: Mountain Press Publishing Company, 2005.

Burnett, Frances Hodgson. *A Little Princess.* New York: Harper Collins Children's Books, 1985.

✓ ———. *The Secret Garden.* Boston: David R. Godine, Publisher, 1987.

✓ Burton, Virginia Lee. *Mike Mulligan and His Steam Shovel.* Boston: Houghton Mifflin Company, 1939.

✓ Carroll, Lewis. *Alice's Adventures in Wonderland.* New York: Penguin Books, 1960.

✓ Clark, Ann Nolan. *Secret of the Andes.* New York: Viking Press, 1952.

Cobb, Vicki. *Why Doesn't the Earth Fall Up? And Other Not Such Dumb Questions about Motion.* New York: Dutton Juvenile, 1989.

Crewe, Sabrina. *Los Angeles.* Milwaukee, Wisconsin: World Almanac Library, 2004.

Croce, Nicholas. *Newton and the Three Laws of Motion.* New York: The Rosen Group, Inc., 2005.

✓ Dahl, Roald. *Charlie and the Chocolate Factory.* New York: Knopf, 2005.

Dodge, Mary Mapes. *Hans Brinker, or The Silver Skates.* Chicago: Children's Press, 1967. (This edition is preferred for its illustrations, but it is difficult to find.)

———. *Hans Brinker, or The Silver Skates.* New York: Aladdin Classics, 2002.

Doris, Ellen. *Spineless Animals.* Kids and Science. Danbury, Connecticut: Grolier Educational, 1996.

Dyer, Alan. *Space.* Reader's Digest Pathfinders. Pleasantville, New York: Reader's Digest Children's Publishing, Inc., 1999.

Edom, Helen. *Science with Water.* Usborne Science Activities. London: Usborne Publishing Ltd., 1990.

✓ Enright, Elizabeth. *Thimble Summer.* New York: Holt, Rinehart and Winston, 1996.

Freedman, Russell. *Lincoln: A Photobiography.* New York: Ticknor & Fields, 1987.

Freeman, Don. *A Pocket for Corduroy.* New York: Viking Press, 1978.

✓ Grahame, Kenneth. Abridged and illustrated by Inga Moore. *The Wind and the Willows.* Cambridge, Massachusetts: Candlewick Press, 2003.

Harness, Cheryl. *Mark Twain and the Queens of the Mississippi.* New York: Simon and Schuster Books for Young Readers, 1998.

Johnson, Rebecca L. *The Great Barrier Reef: A Living Laboratory.* Minneapolis: Lerner Publications Company, 1991.

Kipling, Rudyard. *Just So Stories.* New York: Viking Press, 1993.

Kurlansky, Mark. *The Story of Salt.* New York: G. P. Putnam and Sons, 2006.

Lang, Andrew. "Joan the Maid." *The Junior Classics.* Ed. Mabel Williams and Marcia Dalphin. New York: P. F. Collier & Son, 1957.

Lawson, Robert. *Rabbit Hill.* New York: Puffin Books, 2007.

Lewis, C. S. *The Last Battle.* New York: Collier Books, 1978.

———.*The Lion, the Witch, and the Wardrobe.* New York: Collier Books, 1978.

———. *The Magician's Nephew.* New York: Collier Books, 1978.

Lewis, Elizabeth Foreman. *Young Fu of the Upper Yangtze.* New York: Henry Holt and Company, 1932.

Lobel, Arnold. *Mouse Soup.* New York: Harper Collins, 1977.

Macaulay, David. *Cathedral.* New York: Houghton Mifflin Company, 1973.

MacGill-Callahan, Sheila. *The Last Snake in Ireland.* New York: Holiday House, Inc., 1999.

Milton, Joyce. *The Story of Paul Revere: Messenger of Liberty.* New York: Parachute Press, Inc., 1990.

Morey, Walt. *Gentle Ben.* New York: Puffin Books, 1992.

Murdoch, David H. *Cowboys.* New York: Alfred A. Knopf, 1993.

Nesbit, E. *The Railway Children.* New York: Puffin Books, 2005.

Phillips, Bob. *The World's Most Crazy, Wacky, and Goofy Good Clean Jokes for Kids.* New York: Galahad Books, 1999.

Pyle, Howard. *Otto of the Silver Hand.* New York: Dover Publications, Inc., 1967.

Rawlings, Marjorie Kinnan. *The Yearling.* New York: Scribner Books, 2002.

Robbin, Irving. *The How and Why Wonder Book of Basic Inventions.* New York: Wonder Books, 1965.

Ross, Nancy Wilson. *Joan of Arc.* New York: Random House, 1953.

Sloan, Eric. *Look at the Sky…and Tell the Weather.* Dover Publications, Inc., 2004.

Spyri, Johanna. *Heidi.* Trans. Helen B. Dole. New York: Grossett and Dunlap, Inc., 1945.

Stille, Darlene R. *Electricity.* Chanhassen, Minnesota: The Child's World, 2005.

Tarkington, Booth. *Penrod.* Northridge, California: Aegypan Press, 2007.

Trumbauer, Lisa. *What is Gravity?* New York: Children's Press, 2004.

Truss, Lynne. *Eats, Shoots & Leaves: Why, Commas Really Do Make a Difference.* New York: G. P. Putnam's Sons, 2006.

Turner, Barrie Carson. *The Living Violin.* New York: Alfred A. Knopf, 1996.

Van Loon, Hendrik Willem, "Napoleon," *The Junior Classics*. Ed. Mabel Williams and Marcia Dalphin. New York: P. F. Collier & Son, 1957.

White, E. B. *The Trumpet of the Swan*. New York: Harper & Row, 1970.

Winter, Jean. *Follow the Drinking Gourd*. New York: Dragonfly Books, 1992.

Woodford, Chris. *How Do We Measure Weight?* Farmington Hills, Minnesota: Blackbirch Press, 2005.

Wyss, Johann; adapted by Eliza Gatewood Warren. *The Swiss Family Robinson*, Great Illustrated Classics edition. Hackensack, New Jersey: Playmore, Inc., 1987.

INDEX